on the
noodle
road

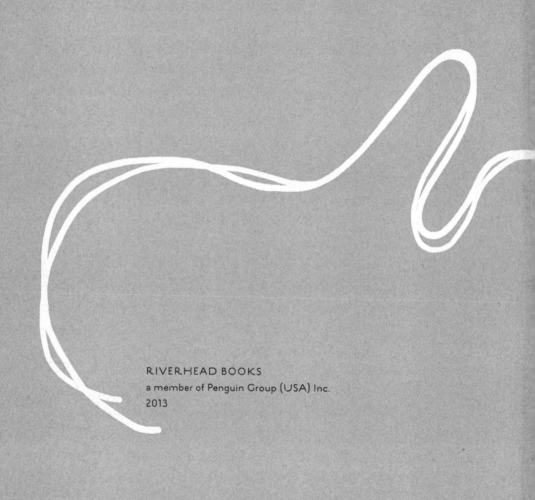

RIVERHEAD BOOKS
a member of Penguin Group (USA) Inc.
2013

on the noodle road

FROM BEIJING TO ROME, WITH LOVE AND PASTA

Jen Lin-Liu

RIVERHEAD BOOKS
Published by the Penguin Group
Penguin Group (USA) Inc., 375 Hudson Street,
New York, New York 10014, USA

USA · Canada · UK · Ireland · Australia
New Zealand · India · South Africa · China

Penguin Books Ltd, Registered Offices: 80 Strand, London WC2R 0RL, England
For more information about the Penguin Group visit penguin.com

Library of Congress Cataloging-in-Publication Data
Lin-Liu, Jen.
On the noodle road : from Beijing to Rome, with love and pasta / Jen Lin-Liu.
pages   cm.
Includes bibliographical references.
ISBN 978-1-59448-726-2
1. Cooking (Pasta)   2. Cooking—Silk Road.   3. Food—Social aspects—
Silk Road.   4. Food habits—Silk Road.   5. Lin-Liu, Jen—Travel—Silk
Road.   6. Silk Road—Social life and customs.   7. Silk Road—Description
and travel.   I. Title.
TX809.M17L58   2013   2013016643
641.82'2—dc23

Printed in the United States of America
1   3   5   7   9   10   8   6   4   2

Book design by Meighan Cavanaugh

Maps by Jeffrey L. Ward

While the author has made every effort to provide accurate telephone numbers, Internet
addresses, and other contact information at the time of publication, neither the publisher
nor the author assumes any responsibility for errors, or for changes that occur after
publication. Further, the publisher does not have any control over and does not
assume any responsibility for author or third-party websites or their content.

Penguin is committed to publishing works of quality and integrity.
In that spirit, we are proud to offer this book to our readers;
however, the story, the experiences, and the words
are the author's alone.

Some names and identifying characteristics have been changed
to protect the privacy of the individuals involved.

For Craig

contents

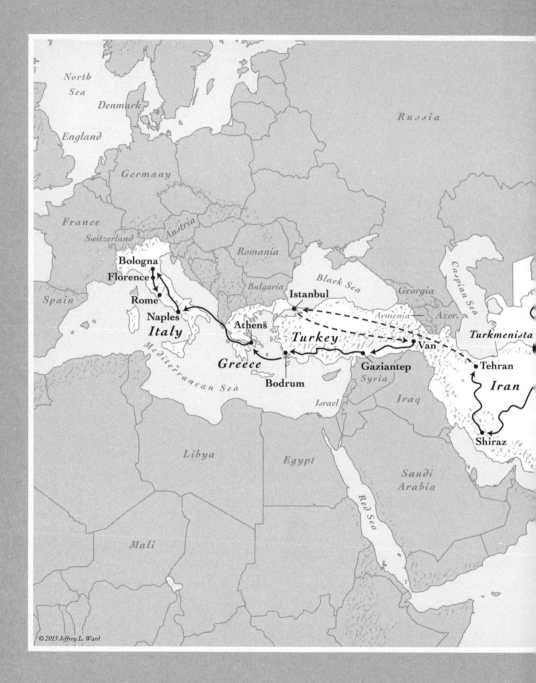

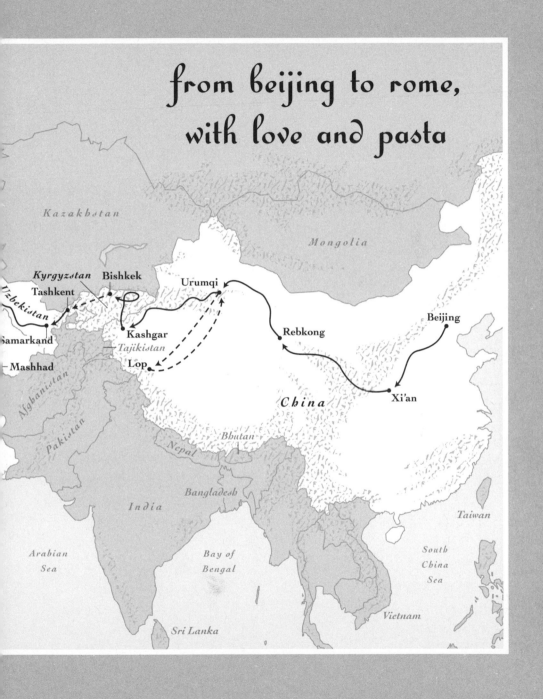

from beijing to rome, with love and pasta

prologue

The year after we married, Craig and I went to Italy for Christmas. It was our first time in Europe together, a break from years of living and traveling in Asia. After a week of hiking along precipitous cliffs on the Amalfi coast that dropped into the sparkling blue Mediterranean, we drove to Rome. In a neighborhood called Trastevere, full of winding alleys and couples in embrace, my husband led me to a restaurant called Le Fate and surprised me with a belated holiday gift: a pasta-making class. In the cluttered kitchen, we stood before the chef and proprietor, a man named Andrea. With dark espresso eyes and curly brown hair, the chef happily played the part of the handsome Italian guy female tourists swoon over. He flirted, chatted, and joked with guests as they arrived. But once class began, he cleared his throat and surveyed the room with narrowed eyes. The room fell as silent as a church before mass.

"Americans," Andrea declared, "think that Italians use a lot of garlic." He placed a single garlic clove on the stainless-steel counter, whacked it with the back of a cast-iron frying pan, and held up the flattened result. "We do *not* use a lot of garlic. *Delete* this information from your brain!"

At the counter, Andrea began breaking eggs with bright yellow yolks into a crater he'd made in a mound of finely ground, refined flour. After working the eggs into the flour, he vigorously kneaded and flattened the dough with a rolling pin, gradually stretching the pliable putty into long sheets almost as thin as newsprint. He wound a sheet tightly around the pin, then swung it to and fro, releasing the dough so that it folded over itself in neat S-shaped layers. After cutting them into slivers, he shook the pieces in the air like a magician, unfurling long, wide strands of pasta.

Over my years of learning how to cook in China, I'd come across many pasta shapes that echoed ones in Italy. Chinese "cat's ear" noodles resembled Italian orecchiette. Hand-pulled noodles, a specialty of China's northwest, were stretched as thin as angel hair. Dumplings and wontons were folded in ways similar to ravioli and tortellini. Even the more obscure shapes of Italian pasta—handkerchief-like squares called *quadrellini*, for example—had their Chinese counterparts. Each time I'd come across a new shape, it seemed coincidental.

But at Andrea's that morning, as I watched and mimicked the pasta-making, it all seemed to add up to something more. Andrea's movements followed the textbook method for making Chinese hand-rolled noodles, a dish I'd practiced countless times in Beijing. It was a revelation. With eggs rather than water, a few extra-clumsy movements, and flour inadvertently winding up all over my hands and face, I, like Andrea, could make fettuccine!

Though the trip was meant to be a break from the Far East, my mind couldn't help drifting back to China as I tasted the food across Italy. In Venice, the seafood risottos reminded me of my grandmother's congee. I learned that the Venetians had a history of sweet-and-sour dishes, thanks to the city's spice trade with the Orient, though many had faded with time. On the Amalfi coast, as we sipped *limoncello* after dinner, a chef told us that Italians, like Chinese, drank liquor infused with other ingredients in order to relieve everyday ailments.

After that trip, I began to cook more Italian food. In an *arrabbiata* sauce, I discovered that the balance of acidic tomatoes, hot chilies, and sugar seemed to echo the flavor of spicy noodle dishes in western China. When I drizzled olive oil and vinegar over my salads, I noticed the effect was similar to the sesame oil and black vinegar in the cold salads of China's north. In the mushrooms, aged meats, and prodigious Parmigiano-Reggiano cheese grated over pastas, I saw the Italian affinity for a flavor called umami that the Chinese highly prize. As I ate the dishes, I realized that the two cuisines also had common philosophies: they were both essentially humble and rustic, elevating the essence of ingredients over fancy preparations. And both were best home-cooked.

With all the parallels and similarities lingering in my head, I found myself thinking about the familiar story of how Marco Polo brought noodles from China to Italy. Even the Chinese knew the tale, but they liked to tell it with embellishment: Marco Polo also tried meat-filled buns in China, which he attempted to re-create when he returned home. But he couldn't remember how to fold the dough, and Italy ended up with a second-rate mess-of-a-bun called pizza.

Both stories are myths—overwhelming evidence shows that Italians were eating pasta before the birth of the Venetian explorer. Most experts trace the Marco Polo story back to a 1929 issue of *The Macaroni Journal*, a now-defunct publication of a pasta trade association. The anonymously written article appeared in between advertisements for industrial pasta-making equipment, and it reads like fiction: Marco Polo arrives by boat to a place that sounds more South Pacific than Chinese and comes across natives drying long strands of pasta. (In reality, Chinese wheat noodles are a tradition of the northern hinterlands and are rarely dried before cooking.) The story was intended to spur the consumption of pasta, back then a novelty to most Americans.

Food historians have since produced an array of conflicting theories about the provenance of noodles. Some credit the ancient Etruscans, suggesting that pictures in caves depict pasta-making. Others attribute the invention to the successors of the Etruscans: Romans flattened sheets of dough called *lagana*, suggesting an early version of lasagna. Or perhaps the first incarnation of noodles appeared with Arab caravan traders, who developed dried ones that were light and easy to transport, predecessors of the instant kind. But then maybe the staple originated in the birth-place of wheat, in the Middle East, and traveled by divergent paths to Italy and China, claims another camp. Still others credit the Uighurs, a Turkic-speaking minority who straddle Central Asia and China.

The more research I did, the more confused I became; it seemed like there were limitless theories about the origin of noodles and how they'd spread. The topic was the subject of endless fascination. "Yes, you *must* find out who invented noodles!" friends told me as I related my research—as if it were as easy as establishing who'd invented the telephone. Then I came across a report that seemed to debunk all the theories: scientists had found a four-thousand-year-old noodle in northwestern China, confirming the conventional wisdom that the Chinese had invented the staple, adding to an impressive list of Chinese inventions that included gunpowder, paper, the printing press, and the compass. But even that news didn't explain how the dish had traveled so many thousands of miles to Italy.

The theories were also intriguing for the wide swath of territory they covered, a region bounded by the seven-thousand-mile-long network of trade routes that connected Europe and Asia known as the Silk Road. It was as much a concept as it was a physical entity. The "Silk Road" was a term coined in 1877, long after the demise of the route itself, by a German explorer and geographer named Baron Ferdinand von Richthofen. Like Marco Polo, the mythical path came with a story. Around the birth of Christ, the Romans were first introduced to an ethereal fabric called silk, which they learned came from a mysterious place called China. The desire for the textile set off one of the first major waves of globalization: caravans of traders and camels traversed barren deserts, grasslands, and mountains to satisfy the demands of emperors. No single route existed; the Silk Road described a tangle of overland paths that undulated through Central Asia and the Middle East before reaching Italy via the Mediterranean Sea. Marco Polo was just one of many adventurers who traveled along them. But the glory of the Silk Road faded with the rise of maritime trade in the fif-teenth century. Territories once widely traversed fell into isolation. Yet the romance of the fabled path persisted through the handful of explorers who made the arduous overland journey and wrote of their experiences.

While conducting my noodle research, I also looked into the movement of ingredients along the Silk Road. Precious flavorings like saffron, which originated in Persia, were traded like diamonds. Pomegranates, which hailed from the Middle East and may have been the real forbidden fruit mentioned in the Bible, found their way into Renaissance kitchens and Chinese gardens alike. The names of certain ingredients hinted at their faraway origins: *xigua*, the Chinese name for watermelon, means "western melon." Conversely, German-speaking Europeans refer to an orange as *applesin*, or "Chinese apple."

I was also surprised to learn that rhubarb had originated in China. The country didn't have a tradition of rhubarb pies or jam, nor did the plant ever make it to the table; it was confined to the drawers of Chinese medicine doctors, who dried and boiled it in potions to loosen their patients' bowels. As rhubarb went west, Central Asians began chewing it raw and Persians folded it into savory stews. Italians made bitter aperitifs with rhubarb, and Marco Polo valued the plant enough to list it in his will. Only after it was introduced to the English did it meet up with sugar and wend its way into sweets. The plant was in such high demand in nineteenth-century England that a powerful Qing Dynasty official proposed a rhubarb embargo against Queen Victoria, hoping to bring a constipated nation to the bargaining table during the Opium War; little did he know that English bowels no longer depended on China's rhubarb—the British had already cultivated it in their own backyards.

Reading the travelogues of past explorers, I discovered that few, if any, of the adventurers had made a trip to document food. The Chinese monk Xuanzang traveled west in the seventh century in pursuit of Buddhist enlightenment. The late nineteenth-century Swedish geographer Sven Hedin mapped out previously uncharted parts of Central Asia. Not long after, British archaeologist Aurel Stein discovered ancient Buddhist scriptures in northwestern Chinese caves and took them home to London. Marco Polo, who looked for new trade routes, did mention food in his diaries: he noted a meal of macaroni but spent more time detailing how his Mongolian companions dined on prairie dogs and camels and pricked the veins of their horses to drink their blood.

It wasn't the most enticing description of a meal, but I was already sold.

I decided that I would travel the Silk Road. I'd go to Rome again, but journeying overland this time, starting from my longtime residence of Beijing. In contrast to previous explorers, I would pursue a culinary mission: I'd investigate how noodles had made their way along the Silk Road; document and savor the changes in food and people as I moved from east to west; learn what remained constant, what tied together the disparate cultures of the Silk Road, and what links made up the chain connecting two of the world's greatest cuisines. I would seek out home cooks, young and old, to see how recipes had been passed down and learn not only their culinary secrets but their stories as well.

I thought I knew what I was getting into—after all, I'd traveled the Chinese portion of the Silk Road before. Though I'd traveled for only a few weeks, my trip had acquainted me with the culinary delights of western China, unknown to much of the world; the country's most celebrated regional cuisines were in the east. But as I'd moved into the Chinese hinterlands, I discovered that the noodles improved, becoming heartier, chewier, and more various. The fruits grew more delicious, too—in the sun-soaked western provinces of China, I tasted the sweetest melons and apricots of my life. The people were equally fascinating. I ate noodles made by a woman with piercing blue irises, striking in a face that otherwise looked Chinese. Pushing into the far northwest region called Xinjiang, I became immersed in a land of Middle Eastern– and Mediterranean-looking people. As I wandered through a bazaar in the ancient trading town of Kashgar—full of mosques, women in burqas, and donkey carts—I had to continually remind myself I was still in China.

It hadn't occurred to me on that maiden journey to venture farther than China's border. But now, with the noodle mystery gnawing at me, along with so many other culinary questions, it became my obsession to travel the

Silk Road from start to finish. I knew what lay at the end of the fabled path, having just vacationed in Italy. But I had no idea what lay in between. There would be many challenges, I knew. Past explorers had written about the physical demands of the journey, across windswept deserts and isolated pastures and over high passes. Even in modern times, with cars and trains, the journey, with its stops, would take me more than six months. I would travel through a string of countries governed by despotic rulers. Much of this terrain was Muslim, a faith I knew little about. Also I wondered about how I'd be treated as a woman, moving across so many male-dominated societies.

And beyond all that, I had recently become a wife. Though, as I fantasized about my journey and began planning my route, that was the furthest thing from my mind. After all, I'd traveled plenty before marriage—why did it have to be any different now? I'd never had to take into account the impact of an extended journey on my partner or my relationship. It was something I didn't think—or want—to figure into my trip. But the nagging question was there: Just how would I manage it—alone, together? That dilemma only grew sharper as my journey began.

china

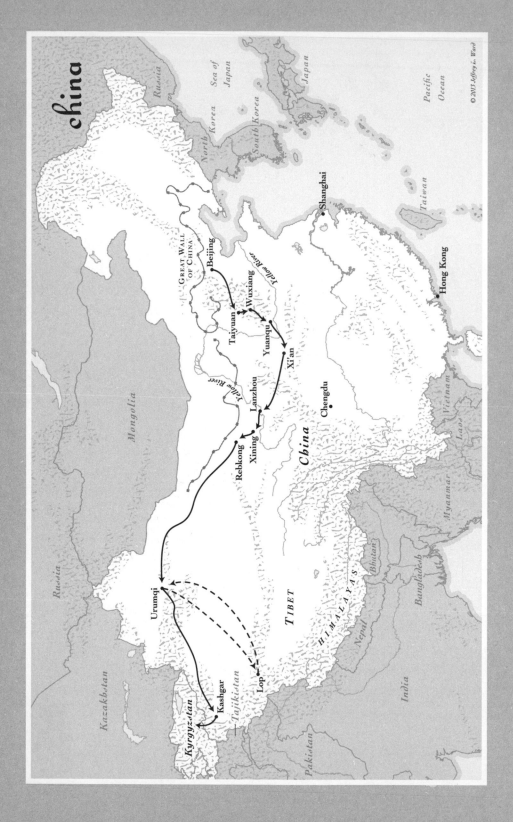

1.

The noodle had disintegrated.

That much I'd heard by the time we met on a Beijing street corner that was coincidentally occupied by a hand-pulled noodle shop. I proposed that we talk about the noodle in question over noodles, my mouth watering at the thought of strands stretched magically thin by hand and bathed in a spicy beef broth. My companion declined, saying he'd already eaten. "But next time, I'll treat *you* to a bowl!" he said, expressing courtesy typical of Chinese.

In his tinted eyeglasses, worn sweater, and slacks, geologist Lu Houyan was an ordinary-looking man. The Chinese Academy of Sciences campus where he led me was equally characterless. But he was the guardian of something intriguing: a four-thousand-year-old noodle, proof that China was the rightful inventor of the widespread staple. As soon as we settled into his third-floor office, he went straight to his computer and booted up a PowerPoint presentation.

"The noodle is real," he said, clicking open a photograph of a tangled yellow mass embedded in dirt. He traced the loops and curlicues with his finger. "Isn't it beautiful? See? It's one piece—you can see the head and the tail."

The site where the noodle was discovered, called Lajia, had been home to an ethnic minority community that had thrived near the Yellow River four thousand years before, until a catastrophic earthquake and flood. As at Pompeii, the tragedy decimated the population but preserved some artifacts, including a number of eating vessels. During excavation, the archaeology team came across an inverted clay bowl and, uncupping it, discovered the single long yellow strand. The noodle had survived because of a vacuum between the sediment cone and the bowl's bottom, Lu explained.

The discovery garnered the attention of *Nature* magazine and major newspapers. Lu seemed tickled by all the interview requests he'd received from foreign journalists, who'd come from as far as America to speak with him. But one troubling detail hadn't made it into any of the publications. I'd learned of it when I first checked the Wikipedia entry for noodles:

> In 2005, Chinese archaeologists claimed to have found the oldest noodles yet discovered [*sic*] in Qinghai. This find, however, is disputed by many experts who suspect its authenticity. Chinese archaeologists claim the evidence disintegrated shortly after discovery, making the claim unverifiable.

Sometime after I first checked Wikipedia and before meeting Lu, someone changed the entry, deleting the entire paragraph and replacing it with the following:

> In 2002, archaeologists found an earthenware bowl containing the world's oldest known noodles, measured to roughly 4000 years BP through radiocarbon dating, at the Lajia archaeological site along the Yellow River in China. The noodles were found well-preserved.

I was curious to find out what had really happened. Had the noodle dissolved? I asked Lu.

"Yes, that's right. *Zao jiu meiyou le!* Early on, the noodle was no more!" he admitted, in a tone no less jovial than the one he'd used to describe the noodle's beauty.

Lu hadn't been at the archaeological site, nor had he seen the noodle intact, he admitted. And he didn't know anything about the altered entry. "That's very strange. I don't know what happened," he said earnestly. I presumed his innocence, given how readily he'd owned up to the noodle's demise, but the additional details he provided only made the noodle more suspect: the excavation team consisted only of a graduate student and a farmer. After discovering the noodle, they placed the bowl back over it and shipped it to Beijing by train. Upon the noodle's arrival at the university, the staff arranged a meeting with one of the academy's leaders and—with great fanfare—lifted the bowl to reveal its contents: tiny yellow shards embedded in dirt.

Lu said the weight of the bowl had crushed the noodle. "This often happens with food we find at archaeological sites. Sometimes we find a bottle of wine and uncork it and the vapors disappear, the liquid dries up," he said.

The professor was part of the forensics team that had studied the noodle's crumbled remains. He tested the noodle dust and established it was made of millet, a substance more brittle than wheat. He spent months trying to plausibly justify how the noodle was made and how it had held up for thousands of years. (That accounted for the discrepancy in the date of discovery in the Wikipedia entry—though the noodle had been found in 2002, it took until 2005, after testing, theorizing, and publicizing the results, before the news reached the pages of *Nature*.)

The region where the noodle was found was famous for hand-pulled noodles, like the ones advertised at the corner shop. But that variety—long, thin, and chewy (again, my mouth watered at the thought of those strands)—required a gluten-based substance like wheat, which did not undergo mass cultivation until later in China's history. Lu's best guess was that this noodle had been pushed through a press. Yet there was no evidence of a press, and I still remained doubtful that any noodle—made of millet, wheat, or anything else—could survive for so long.

Lu agreed to show me what was left. We took an elevator to another floor and entered a small laboratory that held a safe. The safe contained a plastic bag. The bag contained a test tube. The tube contained a fleck of yellow.

"You see, this is all we have," he said regretfully. "It's a very tiny thing. I can't say for sure that the Chinese were responsible for bringing noodles to the West, but I can be very sure that no one will find a noodle that is older than this."

From Lu Houyan's office in northern Beijing, I took a taxi to the city's heart, where my husband and I kept an apartment. It was early in the summer of 2010, and Craig and I had just arrived back in the capital, the eastern terminus of the Silk Road. Northern Beijing—and the city as a whole—was not particularly pleasant. Gray smog often shrouded the sky, so opaque that you could only make out the faint outlines of buildings just blocks away. Cars clogged the wide, impersonal streets and the highways ringing the city, with gridlock increasing by the day as thousands more vehicles were added to the roads. Hundreds of characterless clusters of towers and weirdly shaped, twisting skyscrapers had sprouted up across the city. Construction cranes rose over the rare vacant patches of land, reserving space for the frivolous pet projects of famous architects.

Yet Craig and I had carved out a niche away from the development. We lived in the *hutong*, a small, human-scale patch that urban planners had managed—so far, at least—to save from the bulldozers. The word *hutong* referred to the alleys that ran through the oldest neighborhoods of the capital, so narrow that cars moving toward each other, in slow games of chicken, often got stuck. The alleys ran past gray-brick, single-story residences called *siheyuan*, or courtyards, referring to the gardens enclosed by crumbling residences, once grand and occupied by imperial officials and the wealthy. The neighborhoods were the oldest in Beijing, dating back seven hundred years to the Yuan Dynasty, when the Mongolian conqueror Genghis Khan had built a capital out of a desert basin and expanded his territory all the way to Eastern Europe. Craig and I took sunset walks around Houhai Lake, created several hundred years before for royalty. We often looped past the fifteenth-century Drum and Bell Towers, used as guard and signaling stations when important guests entered the gated city.

We loved the intimacy of the *hutong*. Familiar faces greeted us everywhere: nosy Lady Wang loitered in our apartment complex courtyard, bouncing a feathered ball on a badminton racket and pestering us about when we would have a baby. We exchanged hellos with the local cobbler, a middle-aged woman with rosy cheeks who sat in the alley with her old sewing machine. We stopped for the latest gossip from the stocky, ageless Manchurian who stood outside his small teahouse.

I could chart my whole history in Beijing through these lanes. After living in Shanghai for several years, I'd moved to Beijing's *hutong* in 2004. The cooking school where I'd learned the basics of Chinese cooking was on an alley that jutted north from Peace Boulevard, a large avenue that bisected the district. One of my cooking mentors, Chairman Wang, lived a short bicycle ride north, on Flower Garden Hutong. After I'd fallen in love with Craig, we'd moved to nearby Little Chrysanthemum Hutong, into a rare apartment building with several floors. In our home, I fell into my routines as a writer, working at a desk on the second-floor loft and taking breaks on our rooftop balcony that looked out on the neighborhood's trees, birds, and the sloping gray-tiled courtyard roofs that repeated themselves like waves of an ocean. Just one lane south, in a courtyard home on Black Sesame Hutong, I founded a cooking school of my own.

But Beijing was no longer home. Since 2008, Craig and I had been spending more time in the United States, for our wedding and honeymoon, and then for a fellowship he had been awarded at the Massachusetts Institute of Technology. Before he left, we downsized from our duplex apartment to a tiny one around the corner. While Craig was in Boston, I'd spent the academic year bouncing between China and America, trying to figure out where I belonged.

Not for the first time, I felt caught between East and West. The struggle had begun when I was a child growing up in a 1980s Chinese household in a not-so-diverse part of Southern California. I'd wanted blond hair and didn't understand why we didn't go to church. Food-wise, my tastes were Western. My favorite dish—maybe not coincidentally, it seemed now—was spaghetti with meat sauce. It was one of the few Western meals my mother could make; growing up, I didn't like Chinese noodles, or any Chinese food for that matter. Later, when I attended Columbia University, I tried to embrace my heritage by studying Mandarin and spending a summer abroad in Beijing, even as the undergraduate curriculum emphasized the Western canon. And only after a number of years in China, writing about the country and learning how to cook its food, did I think I'd reached some kind of equilibrium.

But while I'd built a life in China and felt more comfortable with my heritage, as time went on, it became clearer that I'd never blend in seamlessly. Sure, I could pass as a local, with my Asian appearance and the fluency I'd gained in Mandarin. But I remained firmly American, and with my American husband I settled into the lifestyle of many foreigners living overseas. After a period of being enamored with all things local, we'd begun living as if we were back home. We formed friendships with many compatriots, most of them journalists, like us. We passed over Chinese newspapers (which censorship made rote and boring anyway) for *The New York Times* and other American publications. We went to the movies for the latest Hollywood blockbusters. And when it came to food, I was no longer content to eat just Chinese, a cuisine I'd immersed myself in for years. We shopped at a foreign market called Jenny Lou's and dined at new restaurants that served everything from Vietnamese to Spanish to South American, a reflection of how international Beijing had become.

But whenever Craig and I were back in America, I found that I didn't quite fit in there, either. I missed the commotion of Beijing, what Chinese call *renao*: the loud restaurants, the feeling that things were fluid and always changing, the feisty exchanges between locals on the street. In America, the choices at the supermarket—the vast aisles of processed foods, the multitude of shampoos, the freezer section of microwaveable dinners—frankly bewildered me. I preferred the Chinese supermarket and filled our kitchen with soy sauce, tofu, and chili oil. Turning on the television and seeing shows glamorizing the Jersey shore and Manhattan housewives was truly alienating. ("Who's Snooki?" I asked my friends, to their immense amusement.)

Sure, there were things I loved about America. I relished being close to family and friends. I could breathe crisp, unpolluted air. I enjoyed the endless discussions about politics, a topic that Chinese tried to ignore. America had grown more multicultural—we had a biracial president, even. But still, every so often, someone posed the question that had irked me since childhood, an inquiry that seemed more legitimate after I'd been away for so long: "Where are you from?" When Craig and I explained that we'd lived in China for almost a decade, we might as well have said we'd been living on the moon.

So as much as this was a sensory journey from East to West, I wanted also to explore what it meant to be "Eastern" or "Western" in a more conceptual way—I wanted to discover where the ideas converged and conflicted. Traveling through cultures that straddled the East and West, I figured, might reconcile what I'd felt were opposing forces in my life; maybe I would find others who could relate to my struggles.

While Craig had never had to wrestle much over his identity, he knew I did, and he was sympathetic. And he'd felt physically caught between East and West, too; neither of us was ready to commit more years to China, but we weren't ready to move back to America, either. But that didn't mean he was ready to take off with me for more than half a year. What, he asked, would the journey mean for us? Had I thought about how it might impact our relationship, or his life in general? He reminded me of what I'd made a point of writing into our wedding vows, just the year before: we would put our relationship before our careers.

But the meaning of what I'd written was now muddled. Did it mean we had to be together? In which case, he would have to put our relationship before his career but I would not? Or I should give up my fantasy journey to stay at his side? Did my vow rule out going it alone? I felt guilty, but why? Wasn't I justified in wanting to do something for myself, even if I'd taken the vows of marriage?

And it wasn't just my husband who brought up these questions. What did Craig think of the trip? my girlfriends asked. Was he going to come along with me? asked one. I was indignant—would they have posed the same questions had I been a man? When I read travelogues by V. S. Naipaul, Paul Theroux, and Bill Bryson, their partners rarely came up; it was a given that they would play the role of the supportive, if somewhat impatient, wife at home.

But I didn't necessarily want my husband waiting at home. Craig's fellowship was about to end. Having embarked on a transient life already and still free of children, office jobs, and mortgages, we had freedom. I wanted his company, particularly given the length of the trip. I wanted to share the experience of seeing a region we knew next to nothing about. I wanted him along for all the memories I would accumulate, to view the desert sunsets and the ancient architecture of legendary trading posts, to sit down and taste the dishes laden with history, to converse with the cooks I'd meet.

But it was complicated. Craig had just signed a contract to write a book about China and the environment; he wasn't sure how much time he could spare. The longest we'd traveled together was a few weeks at a time, and although we got along on those trips, we had different priorities. Craig was a hiker who would happily trek through jungles or forests, pitching a tent and bathing in lakes and rivers; even the Amalfi coast hadn't been arduous enough for him. My idea of vacation, on the other hand, involved good food, culture, and cities. Food—my passion, my livelihood—was a major sticking point. Although my husband gamely helped me seek out that off-the-map eatery that served the best local dishes or accompanied me to the trendy restaurant of the moment, he didn't make food a priority. The first time he'd cooked for me, he proudly made me something I dubbed "one-pot pasta"—boiled broccoli tossed with penne and sprinkled with Parmesan cheese from a shaker can. Sure, in Italy he'd surprised me with the gift of a pasta class—and willingly taken it with me. But that was a rare instance of enthusiasm he'd shown for cooking, and I knew he'd done it solely for my benefit. Half a year of eating and cooking along the Silk Road was as enticing to him as six months of climbing snowcapped mountains would have been to me. And if I was immersed in cooking, eating, and research for months, I wondered, what would he do? He didn't like to idle. Would he tolerate the endless meals? How would his being there color the reactions of people I met? How professional would it be to show up for meetings with my husband in tow?

When I turned to my girlfriends, I got contradictory advice. One warned that it would be bad to spend so much time apart, especially so early in our marriage. Our relationship would only be able to grow if we were together, she said. Another was just as adamant that I go it alone, an assertion of my independence and autonomy as a writer. Both arguments resonated.

But one thing I knew for certain was that I was committed to the trip, whether or not Craig came along. And I knew, in the back of my head, that it wasn't just my interest in food or even my identity issues that motivated me. It also had to do with the issue I'd been trying to ignore all along: my husband, or, more broadly, marriage. Craig and I had recently broached the subject of having children. They were something we both wanted, in theory. I was in my early thirties and, yes, that biological clock was ticking. But I was hesitant. I still hadn't figured out what my role was as a wife; was I ready to become a mother? I'd heard the tinge of resentment in the voices of girlfriends who'd quickly moved on from marriage to motherhood. Before I considered having children I wanted—I needed—to do this for myself. I insisted to Craig that, odd as it sounded, the trip was my way of showing that I was serious about our future.

In Beijing, the sounds of the *hutong* greeted me. Saws whirred loudly and hammers banged as, in a sign of Beijing's new wealth, workers renovated dilapidated courtyard homes to their previous splendor. The alley echoed with kids squealing and the shuffle of mahjong tiles. Vendors bicycled through, calling out their wares. *"Mai-cai-yah!* Buy your vegetables!" a woman shouted with the pipes of a Mongolian throat singer, pulling a wagon of produce behind her bicycle. *"Da mi! Da mi! Bai mian fen!"* another vendor called, hauling a load of rice and white flour. Every so often, a knife sharpener rode through, rattling metal against a board to create a rhythmic clanging as he belted, *"Mo dao! Mo dao!"*

One vendor's call—a deep, muffled murmur—had befuddled me for years. Finally one day, I stopped him and peered into a crate he'd strapped to the back of his bicycle. Tucked inside a white sheet were sheep's heads, a specialty of the Hui, an ethnic minority. The vendor looked no different from the average Beijinger, aside from his white Muslim cap, called a *doppi*. Islam had arrived in China along the Silk Road more than a thousand years before, converting many Chinese in its path. The Hui were common in Beijing, and, in fact, they and other Muslim minorities had profoundly influenced the capital's cuisine. The Muslim dishes I tasted in Beijing foreshadowed those I'd come across farther along the route. Heads aside, lamb and mutton were everywhere: diners ate thinly sliced tenderloin of sheep simmered in cauldrons, in a dish called hot pot that some believed had Mongolian origins; street vendors roasted skewers of lamb flecked with cumin and chili powder until even the bits of fat were crisp and tasty; dumplings were stuffed with lamb just as often as pork. At the corner shops, smooth, creamy yogurt came in ceramic jars etched with Arabic lettering, defying the stereotype that Chinese disliked dairy. Our neighborhood even boasted a shop that sold "imperial cheese." The snack, more like a dessert custard than an American or European cheese, had been introduced during the Mongolian reign of Genghis Khan, it was rumored. The so-called cheese was so popular that a line stretched out the shop's door and far into the alley every day. I'd noticed all of these details earlier in my time in China, struck by how un-Chinese they seemed. But I'd filed them away, along with those various noodle shapes, and only now that I'd returned to Beijing did I begin to think about how they were linked.

In Beijing, I also began planning my route. The tangle of paths that made up the Silk Road offered endless permutations. I pored over maps for days. Some paths had obvious hazards. I knew, for example, that I wanted to steer clear of Afghanistan, where the American-led war raged on, and Pakistan, which seemed to have little grip on terrorism (during my journey, U.S. forces would covertly enter Pakistan and kill Osama bin Laden). On the other hand, safe Azerbaijan seemed lackluster in comparison to its neighbor Iran, with its intriguing history—culinary and otherwise.

After much deliberation, carefully weighing my culinary aims against the potential dangers, I decided I would move west through China's minority-filled regions before crossing into Central Asia via a trio of "stans": Kyrgyzstan, Uzbekistan, and Turkmenistan. Provided I could get a visa, I would then push on through the deserts of Iran before traveling through Turkey's diverse landscape. Once I reached the Mediterranean, I would take a boat to Italy. Since the entire journey would require more than six months, I had to budget carefully. Thankfully, the Silk Road offered few expensive hotels, but I also knew I couldn't go back to the days of sleeping in communal barracks in youth hostels. I would mostly ride buses and trains, reserving hired cars for the most treacherous parts of my trip.

The path I'd chosen had some risks. Over the previous couple of years, Tibetans and Uighurs in western China, discontent with the government, had launched a string of riots, some deadly. Uzbekistan and Turkmenistan were two of the world's most despotic states. Iran, controlled by a strict ayatollah and an ultraconservative president, Mahmoud Ahmadinejad, was notoriously hostile to America and Americans. Although Turkey was tourist-friendly, conservative Islamists were gaining power and its Kurdish population was growing restive. Few of the countries I would visit were friendly to journalists; Turkey imprisoned more reporters every year than did any other country in the world, Iran was the runner-up, and China came in third place. I had to remind myself that even though I'd navigated the People's Republic as a writer for years, the government still ruled with a heavy hand—especially in the country's west.

The trip would be daunting in other ways. All the expertise I'd acquired in China would be of little use in Central Asia and the Middle East. I'd assumed at first that the Silk Road would take me through the Arab world, but it turned out that it ran mostly through places inhabited by Turkic people and Persians, who, while largely Muslim, didn't consider themselves Arab. And I'd never spent much time in Muslim areas, aside from jaunts to China's western hinterlands and a couple of Southeast Asian islands. I also worried about my identity, which caused me enough headaches in China and America. In the Muslim world, how would they receive a Chinese-

American? Perhaps it would be wise to say I was something other than American, but would it be prudent to lie? And anyway, I didn't wish to be anything else. As for being a woman, I knew in certain places like Iran, I would have to cover myself from head to toe.

While I contemplated all of this, Craig proposed a plan that would involve him in some of the journey: He'd stay in Beijing while I traveled through China but would join me before I crossed its western border. We would travel through Central Asia and Iran together—places that were less familiar and potentially more dangerous. He wasn't sure about Turkey and definitely didn't want to go back to Italy—he'd had enough four-hour-long meals to last him a lifetime.

My husband was the only person I knew who could make going to Italy sound like torture, I thought with a grumble. Plenty of partners would have jumped at the opportunity to take such a trip! Couldn't he just come along and be grateful for the experience? But another part of me understood he wasn't so keen on more China travel, having spent so many years there, and beyond that, he just wasn't excited about tagging along. It was generous of him to want to come on parts of the trip for my benefit. And the prospect of having some time together was enticing. But then again, what if he was only coming for my safety? Wasn't that patronizing? Did he believe I lacked common sense, that I couldn't hack it without him?

I pushed the questions to the back of my head as I went on with my preparations, visiting embassies in Beijing for my visas. I read up on the countries I'd visit. I browsed cookbooks, my mouth watering in anticipation of *ashlyanfu* noodles in Central Asia and *fesenjun* stew in Iran. One afternoon, I stopped by the cooking school I'd founded to chat with the chefs. A couple of years before, when I had little idea that our transient, bi-continental lives were about to begin, I'd founded this little venture as a hobby. To my surprise, it had grown into a full-fledged business. With so much time away from Beijing, I'd shifted responsibilities to the kitchen's manager, a peppy recent college graduate from Boston named Candice. When I was in Beijing, though, I checked in regularly.

As I walked through the alleys, past the busy imperial cheese shop, and through the gate of the courtyard where the cooking school was located, an idea came to me. Why not invite the chefs, my two closest Chinese friends, along for the first bit of my journey? Chef Zhang was from Shanxi, a province west of Beijing famous for noodles, and Chairman Wang had lived there in her youth.

"You want us to come with you?" asked Chef Zhang when I proposed the idea. He and Chairman Wang were prepping in the small but airy open kitchen that looked out on two large tables for communal dining. They were opposites, both physically and personality-wise, but nevertheless got along well. Chef Zhang was short and stocky, a migrant from the hardscrabble countryside. What he lacked in physical stature, he compensated for with a can-do attitude that made him seem both manly and younger than his years. Chairman Wang was a tall, big-boned Beijinger with a grandmotherly disposition. Different as they were, they agreed on one thing: my overland journey seemed unwise. If I wanted to travel, couldn't I afford a plane ticket? In fact, most Chinese had that reaction when I told them about my plans. *Duo lei*, they clucked. How tiring.

I hoped to have Chef Zhang along in his home province, given that he was a noodle maker, I told him. And it would be good for him to see his wife and children, who still lived there. And wasn't Chairman Wang curious about the village where she'd been sent during the Cultural Revolution? She'd labored in the fields and worked in a coal mine for years before returning to Beijing, her hometown.

"What about the kitchen?" Chef Zhang asked.

I hadn't thought that far. "We can close it for a few days," I said. "You guys need a break."

Chef Zhang agreed quickly; heck, for him, it was a free vacation. (I'd offered to pay for their transportation.) But the contemplative Chairman Wang was uncertain. She had a husband at home whom she needed to take care of. Only after he gave the trip his blessing did she agree.

And so, with almost everything finally in order, I packed. I limited myself to the essentials, which I stuffed into a large green backpack. I whittled my wardrobe to eight items, plus a lightweight scarf I could drape over my head and two pairs of shoes. I brought a few toiletries, minimal makeup, and extra contact lenses. The heaviest items were electronics: a Kindle, a mini-laptop, a camera, an iPod, and a phone. I brought Chinese tea and spices as gifts. Optimistically, I packed a bathing suit, forgetting momentarily that I would be traveling through some of the world's most landlocked regions (and most conservative, when it came to women's dress). I contemplated bringing my cleaver, but thought better of it.

In my last week in Beijing, Craig took me out to my favorite restaurants. We had our favorite spicy stir-fries at a neighborhood Sichuan hole-in-the-wall and ate Chairman Wang's juicy pan-fried dumplings at the cooking school. My father flew in from Taiwan, where he lived, and joined us for drinks on the top floor of the Park Hyatt and Peking duck at Duck de Chine. After he left, Craig and I went to our favorite Italian restaurant for a taste of what I'd encounter months later, at the end of my journey. In a stylish dining room, we chowed down on Neapolitan-style pizza, risotto balls, and Italian-style charcuterie. "I'm going to bet this is the best meal you'll have in weeks. I bet you'll even miss my one-pot pasta," he joked.

We stopped at the grand opening of a ceviche eatery nearby and ran into a new intern from my cooking school. With a good number of drinks in her already, the Brit wrapped Craig and me in a bear hug. "I thought you'd already left for the Silk Road!" she exclaimed, adding that she'd just finished reading my first book, a memoir about learning how to cook in China. Turning to my husband, she asked, "Is it true what your wife wrote about you? That you could eat a pill every day in place of food?" And then to me: Wasn't that a deal breaker? How had we managed to stay together? "I had a relationship that broke up over that very issue. I took my African boyfriend back to Europe and all he wanted to eat was shrimp and rice!"

Craig gave her a wry smile and patted me on the shoulder. I made a mental note to tell my cooking school manager to vet our interns more carefully, and shortly thereafter we left and went home—or at least, what counted as home for the time being.

2.

On an August evening cooler than most, I set off from the cooking school with Chef Zhang and Chairman Wang. We wound through the tight, labyrinth-like maze of the courtyard and out through the large wooden door and grand entryway, into the darkness. "You're leaving?" a neighbor called out. *"Yilu shun feng."* The phrase is usually rendered as "Have a good journey," but the literal translation is more poetic: "Let the wind move you on the road."

As we walked through the *hutong*, Chef Zhang gazed with amusement at the bloated backpack on my shoulders. An impish grin spread over his face. Only soldiers donned such things, he said, or foreign tourists who stayed at nearby hostels. He carried a small knapsack, while Chairman Wang pulled a compact valise on wheels behind her. Chef Zhang was dressed casually in a pair of slacks and a polo shirt, while Chairman Wang wore an elegant dress called a *qipao* she'd sewn herself. Her poofy gray hair was in tighter curls than usual, an effect of the dollar-kit perm her husband had given her just before the trip.

Craig accompanied us to the street, where we flagged down a taxi for the train station. My husband and I had stood on this corner many times to hail cabs at the start of numerous trips. Often we'd left together—for work, for vacations, for our wedding. In the last year, with Craig on his fellowship, we'd spent more time apart, and it seemed that with this journey the trend was continuing. I gave my husband a hug and a kiss, hoping that he indeed would join me in a month, as promised. I felt torn between apprehension at leaving my responsibilities and exhilaration at the prospect of a new adventure. Also, I was hungry—hungry for the spicy, hearty flavors that I remembered from my previous journey west across China. Already I was dreaming of bowls of super-thin, chewy noodles pulled by hand, and stir-fried noodle squares in a sauce that reminded me of an *arrabbiata*. Would they be as good as I remembered? And what about beyond, how would those noodles evolve? And what other delicious dishes would I discover?

I wasn't going to taste any of his food, Chef Zhang told me after we boarded the train to his home province and slipped into our compartment. Sipping a warm bottle of Yanjing beer and munching on peanuts, he warned me that he wasn't going to cook on this trip. This was, after all, a vacation.

"You mean you never cook at home?" I asked.

"Nope. The women do all the cooking," he said, taking a swig. The train gathered speed, gently rocking the cabin. "Unless it's an extenuating circumstance." Even in Beijing, he didn't cook for himself, he said. He could whip up dinner from the ingredients in the cooking school fridge. But after a long day of work, he usually went out for noodles or a grilled flatbread called *bing*.

Chairman Wang's cooking duties extended beyond the business. Her husband was a terrible cook, she said, so she usually made him a meal in the morning before she left for work. She told us how once, when she was away, he'd bought noodles at a market and tried to make a sauce. To thicken it, he threw in a white powder that he thought was cornstarch but was actually baking soda. "He kept on adding more, and didn't understand why it didn't thicken, until the sauce erupted like a volcano!" She howled with laughter, then sighed. This time, she'd spent hours making everything he'd eat while she was away.

I hadn't prepared anything for Craig. Preoccupied with the packing and last-minute details, I hadn't even thought about it. What was in our fridge? I wondered. Maybe a tub of yogurt and some eggs. But he would be fine, I assured myself. There were plenty of cheap, tasty restaurants nearby, and friends happy to meet for an impromptu night out. And, who knows, maybe my absence would even motivate him to cook.

While I was excited about sampling the food on the road, Chairman Wang feared the poor hygiene of many restaurants and rarely ate outside her home and the cooking school. On the journey to Shanxi—which began in the evening and lasted until the next afternoon—not a bite of food passed her lips. When I suggested a snack of steamed buns at one point, she made a face. "Don't you know better than to eat steamed buns from random stalls?" In a recent scandal, Chinese journalists had found steamed buns adulterated with ground cardboard. So maybe it wasn't the safest snack. But still, I was curious how she was going to survive the week.

Once we arrived in Shanxi, I tried to drum up excitement about going to a local market. Both chefs looked at me unenthusiastically. "It's the same as the market in Beijing—what's so interesting about that?" they said, nearly in unison.

The chefs saw cooking as a livelihood, not a passion. While Chairman Wang occasionally liked trying new foods (she particularly enjoyed a blue cheese I'd once given her), neither was adventurous. Like most Chinese, they stuck almost entirely to their own cuisine. Once, when I'd asked Chairman Wang if she thought of cooking as a talent, she shrugged. "Being a cook is like being a car mechanic," she said.

The chefs and I had an unusual relationship, to say the least. Our friendships crossed boundaries of generation, nationality, and circumstance. Chairman Wang was in her mid-sixties, just a few years older than my mother, but the history she'd lived through seemed to add to her years. Her title came with her from the vocational cooking school where she'd taught for years—she had been the school's *zhuren*, the chairman or director. It was a fitting name, given the authority she exuded.

At the vocational school, cooking was taught to young working-class men at desks, through rote memorization. Chairman Wang was the only teacher who obliged my request for practical, hands-on instruction. She taught me privately, beginning with the basics: how to mince ginger, garlic, and leeks, the three essential seasonings of northern Chinese cooking, before moving on to more advanced cleaver skills. At the markets, she explained how to select the best cuts of meat and how not to get cheated by vendors (bring your own scale, she said). We stir-fried traditional *jiachang cai*, home-style dishes like lamb with leeks, and she let me in on the secret ingredient in her sweet-and-sour shrimp: ketchup. She coached me through the arduous national cooking exam and celebrated with me when I passed.

Most important, Chairman Wang had taught me how to make dumplings, a dish popular throughout China but best in Beijing. After kneading flour and water together, she rocked a thin rolling pin back and forth over silver dollar–sized disks of dough, flattening them into ultra-thin wrappers as soft as fine leather. In went the carefully calibrated filling, around which she pinched and sealed the dough. My favorites were lamb with pumpkin, and pork with fennel—combinations that seemed somehow Western, though in fact they were both common in Beijing. Boiled or pan-fried, her dumplings were the best I'd ever tasted.

Chef Zhang was in his mid-forties and had come to Beijing fifteen years before to find work. He'd ended up in kitchens not because he liked cooking but because that's where he had an in. In the cutthroat Chinese restaurant world, Chef Zhang was one of the few chefs who'd allowed me into his kitchen. As an intern at his noodle stall on the city's outskirts, I'd learned to make the hand-rolled noodles that were kindred spirits to Andrea's fettuccine in Rome. But his specialty, knife-grated noodles, was unique to China: ribbons of dough flew off his pastry knife into a wok of boiling water. After a boil and a bath in cold water, the noodles were topped with a delicious pork belly sauce that the chef caramelized and braised until it glistened.

I'd written about the chefs in my first book. By the time I'd finished it, however, they'd become much more than sources and subjects; they'd become intimate friends. When Chef Zhang's noodle shop went out of business, he stayed with me while he looked for work; when I was bedridden, Chairman Wang brought me home-cooked meals.

I'd been inspired to open the cooking school after fellow expatriates told me that they, too, wanted to master Chinese dishes. Beijing then had few, if any, recreational cooking schools for foreigners. So the chefs and I began teaching friends in their kitchens, bringing along pork belly, soy sauce, and my collection of woks and cleavers. As the demand for classes rose, I rented two rooms in a courtyard mansion subdivided among many tenants, just a block away from where Craig and I lived. With Chairman Wang's help, I renovated the space into an open kitchen.

It so happened that around this time, the professional cooking school where Chairman Wang had long worked closed and Chef Zhang was unhappy in the job he'd found after his noodle shop folded. So I hired them, not only to teach classes but to cook the nightly dinners, modeled on parties I threw at home. We attracted a steady stream of expatriates and tourists, and over two years received several honors—far exceeding not just my expectations but those of the chefs, who still couldn't quite believe that foreigners were willing to pay good money to learn what was seen in China as a lowly trade.

As the business was growing, I decided on the Silk Road journey, which posed a dilemma: Could I spend six months away from the cooking school without it falling apart? Leaving the kitchen, though, would give me a way to regain some balance in my professional life. I'd always seen myself as a writer, not a cook or an entrepreneur. I decided to trust that the kitchen— like my marriage—would adapt.

It also gave me a way to regain some balance in my relationships with Chef Zhang and Chairman Wang. Mixing friendship with business was more common in China than anywhere else, but still, I was uncomfortable when Chef Zhang persisted in calling me "boss" even though he knew it irked me—I suspect *because* it irked me.

As the train hummed west, we climbed into our respective bunks. Before drifting off to sleep, I wondered what Chef Zhang's *laojia*, his ancestral village, would look like. The concept of *laojia* had endured in China, and perhaps had become more important in the last few decades, as Chinese left their countryside homes en masse for the cities. When Chinese asked where my *laojia* was, I always paused. Though I was born in Chicago, my family had moved to California. But neither was the right answer. They wanted to know where I'd come from, from time immemorial before the migration of my ancestors had begun. And even that was complicated. My mother was born in southern China, just months before the Communist Revolution, and her family fled to Taiwan. My father was born in Taiwan but considered Fujian Province, across the strait in mainland China, his *laojia*, because his ancestors from eight generations before had come from there. By contrast, Chef Zhang didn't have this *laojia* issue; he knew exactly where he was from. Before his generation, the people of his village had stayed put, farming the same land for centuries. But the move to Beijing attenuated Chef Zhang's ties to his home.

In the morning, we arrived in Taiyuan, the capital of Shanxi Province, where we changed trains. While Chairman Wang and I went to buy tickets for a local train, Chef Zhang waited just outside the station with our luggage. There he stood with arms crossed, donning dark sunglasses and a tough-guy smirk, but he was as jittery as a tourist in Tijuana. "There are all kinds of bad guys around here," he muttered when we returned. "People will bump into you and blame you for it to start a fight. People like to take advantage of me because I'm small."

Chef Zhang remained tense until we'd jostled our way back into the station and found seats in the waiting room. "The one thing Shanxi people are, though, is resilient," he said proudly. "In the winter, we eat nothing fresh for months. We have to dry our green beans, pumpkins, and eggplants. But make no mistake, in Shanxi, everyone can eat, especially these days. There aren't any beggars."

Just moments later, a middle-aged woman wearing a ratty plaid shirt knelt in front of him, clasping her hands and lowering her head. He looked at her from head to toe.

"You're normal!" he said, his brows furrowed. "Go home and farm your land." She slunk off. Chef Zhang huffed. "It's not like she was missing an arm or a leg. I'll give money to those people any day."

Chef Zhang's lack of sentimentality was the legacy of a difficult childhood. His parents, impoverished and with too many mouths to feed, gave away Chef Zhang and an older sister. A girl would eventually be given to another family, anyway, when she married, the thinking went. And though Chef Zhang was lucky enough to be born a boy, he was son number four— an unlucky number. A childless uncle and his wife adopted Chef Zhang and his sister, but life in the new household wasn't much easier. Their adoptive mother died when the chef was six, and he barely remembered her; his uncle, a shepherd, was kind but poor, old, and infirm. After the sister left home, Chef Zhang became the caretaker, raising pigs, tending his uncle's flock of sheep, and gathering wild plants from the mountains. After learning how to make noodles from his neighbors when he was eight, he often made the dish for his father and himself.

As we neared his hometown, Chairman Wang asked how he felt about coming home.

"I don't feel much," he said.

She persisted. "Surely you must feel something?"

He shrugged. "I haven't lived here for so long. I'm a vagabond. I experienced too much bitterness when I was young. I associate this place with sadness. I don't have feelings for this place."

Sentiment or no sentiment, I'd assumed we'd see Chef Zhang's family before we did anything else.

"Nah," he said. "My wife is at work and my children are in school. Let's go for some noodles."

The train had dropped us in Wuxiang, a new township near Chef Zhang's village. He had moved to Wuxiang in his teens to work in a coking factory and stayed there through his twenties, marrying and starting a family. In his early thirties, he set off for Beijing on his own to make more money. Each time he returned, he found the place so changed that he could barely recognize it. Since his last trip, Wuxiang had a new square and many more apartment towers. And none of the restaurants looked familiar anymore. A stranger in his own town, he didn't know where to eat.

Bounding down the street, with Chairman Wang and me trailing behind, he accosted a pair of construction workers squatting on the sidewalk, hunched over bowls of noodles.

"Where'd you get those?" he asked eagerly. They pointed to an alley in the distance full of noodle shops.

Chairman Wang rejected the first two eateries that Chef Zhang suggested because they looked dirty. We settled on a third that to me looked no cleaner. I poked my head into the kitchen. The chef, with lean, muscular arms, used a flat iron with a handle to push gobs of dough through a large grater suspended over a wok. (Thousands of miles later, I would learn that Italians and Germans used a similar method to make a pasta called *spatzli* or spaetzle.) After draining the noodles, the chef divided them into bowls and topped them with a sauce of stir-fried tomatoes and scrambled eggs. We garnished them with chili sauce and black vinegar, another wheat-based specialty of Shanxi. Slightly sweet and fragrant, the vinegar reminded me of a light balsamic, and I'd often seasoned salads with it in Beijing.

Chef Zhang looked as ravenous as a child before an ice cream sundae. He slurped the strands with delight. "I love the way they slip down my throat!" he said. Chairman Wang broke her fast tentatively, then picked up speed. The noodles, made of ground wheat, sorghum, and soybeans, had a slightly thicker texture than pure wheat noodles and were immensely satisfying after our long journey. Chef Zhang demolished his bowl in a matter of minutes. Though he wasn't passionate about most food, he truly loved noodles, like no one else I'd ever met. He never tired of showing guests at the cooking school how to make them, and whenever we went out for a meal, they were the first thing he looked for on the menu.

In the evening, we met up with Chef Zhang's wife, Yao, and their three children. A skinny woman who spoke Mandarin with a thick country accent, Yao shyly linked arms with Chairman Wang and me as we walked through town, the teenagers at our sides. When I'd first talked to Chef Zhang about his family, he'd owned up to having two children, the government-permitted number in rural areas. Later, when it came out that he had a third, he explained simply that he had no choice but to break the law because the first two were girls. It wasn't that he didn't like girls, but they would run off and get married; who was going to take care of him when he was old? So he and his wife had tried again and gotten lucky. They'd avoided a fine by registering the boy with another family. Now about to enter high school, he was the spitting image of his father, with the same pumpkin-shaped head, large round eyes, and quick, easy smile. The elder daughter, just about to finish high school, was pretty and playful, while the younger had strands of gray in her hair already, perhaps from a lifetime of worry that she'd be given away like Chef Zhang. She was the most industrious of the three and had won a considerable scholarship with her good grades, which pleased her father immensely.

We went to a restaurant that would have looked ordinary in Beijing but was the town's most luxurious. We sat in a smoky private room where a handful of waitresses attended to us. The two noodle dishes stood out in an otherwise lackluster meal. The first one was a large bowl of cold buckwheat noodles that reminded me of Japanese soba, flecked with sesame seeds and cucumber slivers and doused with the province's trademark vinegar. And after a number of stir-fries, we ended the meal with thick bands of oat noodles clustered like a beehive and steamed in a bamboo basket. We separated them with chopsticks and dipped them into black vinegar and minced garlic. Their appealing nutty flavor and chewiness made me reach for more.

The next morning, a minivan took the chefs, Chef Zhang's younger daughter, and me up the winding road to his village. Pushang straddled a ridge of beautiful red canyons, with terraced emerald fields and trees that were green and leafy from summer rains.

The van dropped us off at the muddy path to Chef Zhang's cousin's house. The cousin was away but had arranged for his wife to host us. Chef Zhang's cousin-in-law, whom he called Saozi (the title for the wife of an elder male relative), was making noodles in the kitchen. She had the standard short coif and red cheeks of many peasants. Dusting off her hands, she said hello before resuming her rolling, pressing out a gigantic sheet of dough made of wheat flour with a pin as long as a baseball bat. She stretched her arms in a V and pushed the weight of her petite frame onto the counter as she rolled. Once the dough was thin enough, she folded it into S-shaped layers the same way I'd seen Andrea do in Rome and used a knife to cut long strands, sprinkling the noodles with cornmeal to keep them from sticking. She served the boiled noodles with a hearty stew of eggplant, to-matoes, and green beans cooked over a wooden fire.

None of the noodles we had in Shanxi came with meat, an expensive luxury. Chef Zhang explained that the area was so poor that few homes had refrigerators, including his cousin's. Perhaps the poverty and the pau-city of the ingredients explained the local ingenuity with dough: the noo-dles themselves had to supply the variety.

The poverty was even more apparent in the dwellings—which were, in essence, caves. They were built into the sides of the village's steep hills, like the homes on Greece's Santorini, if you swapped the Aegean coast for the red loess plateau of northern China. The inclines were so sharp that occa-sionally I found myself walking atop the roofs of homes below. Chef Zhang's childhood dwelling was abandoned—one of millions of homes across China left empty as people sought their fortunes in the cities. Fewer than half of the caves were still occupied, though the ones that were had certain modern comforts. The home of Chef Zhang's cousin, for example, had a facade of white bathroom tiles, a common sight across China. Inside, a row of rooms had windows onto a yard where chickens clucked. Only after examining the home carefully did I notice the telltale signs. Drop ceilings hid the curvature and the kitchen in the back was dark, windowless, and cold—the perfect place for storing food. Caves had other benefits, Chef Zhang said. Construction and materials were cheap. In the winter, the homes stayed warm, and in the summer they stayed pleasantly cool. It was good that the dwellings didn't depend on air-conditioning—cost aside, the electricity was down the day we visited, which often happened in the area. Nobody knew when it would come back on.

So we took a walk to the center of the village, where there were a few general stores and, to my surprise, a large Catholic church, not unlike the ones that dotted Italy. Noodles, it turned out, weren't all China had in common with Italy. Catholicism had a long history in the Middle Kingdom, stretching back to the 1500s when Italian Jesuits like Matteo Ricci traveled overland to China. Chef Zhang told me that before he was born, an Italian priest had lived in the village, but nowadays locals ran the church. His guardian uncle had visited the church often as a young adult, for meals that the nuns handed out to the poor. At dinner the night before, I'd noticed the bracelet of an elderly family friend who'd dined with us. Etched into a tile on the bracelet was an icon of the Virgin Mary. For some reason, the religion seemed to have stuck more in Shanxi than elsewhere in China.

Chef Zhang, though, was a Buddhist. On a visit to the local graveyard, I saw his spiritual side. As we walked along a narrow path that cut through a slope of soybean plots, Chef Zhang explained that this visit was the most important part of his trip. At the top of the hill overlooking the valley, Chef Zhang stopped before a dirt mound; it lacked a tombstone and was covered with overgrown brush. Beneath were the remains of the uncle he considered his father. He laid a stack of bread rolls before the mound and lit sticks of incense. He kneeled and kowtowed three times as cicadas chirped. I'd never seen the chef so solemn and serene. He pulled a thermos from a bag and tossed its contents on the grave: more noodles, this time the instant variety, a staple for even the departed in this region.

Noodles are the mainstay of the cuisine of China's north—a region stretching from Beijing in the east, through Shanxi, and beyond Lajia in the west, where the alleged four-thousand-year-old noodle was found. A culinary Mason-Dixon Line runs across China; north of it, abundant wheat fields feed the population. Home cooks and professional chefs alike are skilled at making handmade noodles, dumplings, and flatbreads, and freshly made noodles can be found everywhere, from humble stalls in the back alleys to fancy restaurants in five-star hotels.

Below the line is rice country. Noodles are common in the south, too, and are eaten on birthdays to symbolize a long life, as they are in the north. But rarely do southern cooks make them from scratch. When southerners make dumplings, they usually purchase premade wrappers. On one visit to southern China, I was forced to make dumplings with a soy sauce bottle because I couldn't find a rolling pin. And wheat flour was such a novelty that the sack I purchased there, with an excessively high gluten ratio, produced rubbery, inedible wrappers.

The wheat-rice line also creates different flavors in the cuisines. Shanxi vinegar, made of wheat, has a unique sweet-sour balance quite different from the lighter southern vinegars, which are usually made of rice. Chinese are so rooted in their diets that when southerners visit the north, they often have trouble eating the rustic, hearty cuisine, with its strong flavor of leeks and garlic and its heavier sauces; the reverse is often true as well. Beijingers complain they can't get full on rice—only noodles will do. Chairman Wang and Chef Zhang, for example, had no interest in eating dim sum, even though it was now readily available in Beijing; to them it was as foreign as Western food. Yet it is southern Chinese food, with its light, delicate flavors and reliance on steaming, braising, and roasting, that has made its way more widely around the world, via strong immigrant networks.

My parents, of southern Chinese heritage, raised me on rice. My father distinctly remembers eating fresh northern noodles for the first time as a teenager. They were so heavy that he found them indigestible. That was pretty much the same reaction I had when I moved to Beijing. Each time I ate noodles, I felt as if I'd been presented with a bottomless bowl of endless strands. No matter how much I slurped and chewed, I could only get halfway through. But after many years in Beijing, I'd come around to the northern way of eating. Going gluten-free would have been sheer torture.

My upbringing in the West had shaped my understanding of noodles, a word that Alan Davidson in *The Oxford Companion to Food* sums up as "a difficult term." I thought of noodles as stringy, starchy things covered in sauce or floating in soup. In the West, noodles couldn't be classified as a dish, but they weren't just an ingredient, either. Chinese, by contrast, defined noodles, *mian*, as part of a broader food category called *mian shi*, or flour-based foods, that had evolved over many centuries and included bread. A defining characteristic is not their shape but that they are made primarily of wheat flour. Some edibles I'd previously thought of as noodles are in fact considered something else: glass noodles, usually made of pulverized mung beans, are called *fensi* (powdered slivers), while rice noodles are called *mi xian* (rice strings). Neither is *mian*. But *mian* could be almost any shape, like flat disks in the case of dumpling wrappers, or wide rings, as I'd seen in Shanxi.

The more I studied the history of noodles, the more I realized how linked they were to wheat. Wheat originated farther west on the Silk Road, in the Middle East, and arrived overland as early as four thousand years before. But it seems from historical texts that Chinese only began eating noodles around the third century AD, making it a relatively new staple, compared to rice, which Chinese have consumed since at least 2500 BC. In their earliest recorded mention, noodles are described in a third-century dictionary as being made of wheat flour. They came in a variety of shapes, including tortoise shells and scorpions, and were cooked in broth. Soon, poets began to wax lyrical about the pleasures of eating noodles. The third-century poet Fu Xuan describes noodles as "lighter than a feather in the wind . . . fine as the threads of cocoons of Shu [a reference to Sichuan Province] . . . as brilliant as the threads of raw silk." Another poet, named Hong Junju, details the noodle-making process:

He kneaded the dough to the right consistency.
Then he would drop it into the water
In long strings
White like autumn silk.
In half a bowl of soup,
We would gulp them down all at once.

After ten bowls in a row,
A smile would come to the lips . . .

Around the sixth century, Chinese began to cultivate wheat widely in the north and invented a specific word for noodles, *mian*. Officials wrote of how noodles in broth were eaten during summer festivals and were thought to ward off evil spells. Dumplings dating back to this period were uncovered in a tomb and are displayed at a museum in Xinjiang (I saw the dumplings later in my trip). Noodles became a part of everyday and ceremonial life. Poems from the Tang Dynasty describe "noodle broth banquets" to celebrate the births of sons. Guests were welcomed into homes with fresh noodles.

During the period of Mongol rule, noodles spread southward, as some Chinese fled south. Noodles began to appear on restaurant menus in central China, and preparations became more complex. Chefs folded radish juice into dough, turning noodles light pink; added ground dried lily bulbs to dough for a sweet, nutty flavor; and began tossing noodles with sesame paste. Doughy strands were often served with Chinese chives, vinegar, sugar, and pickles. A recipe for a Muslim noodle dish called *tutumashi* was important enough to be mentioned in the Mongol court's encyclopedia of food, called *A Soup for the Qan* and written by a doctor of Uighur descent. In the recipe, pellets of dough were soaked in water, molded into thin disks, and boiled, then flavored with fermented milk and basil—ingredients that were rarely found anymore in modern China.

After the Mongol era in the Ming Dynasty, noodle products became increasingly popular and spread over China. Enduring types of fresh noodles—like hand-rolled ones that resemble fettuccine and spaghetti—were invented. Innovations over the next few centuries included sauces with tomatoes, which originated in the New World, as also occurred in Italy. Chinese began drying noodles later than the Italians, and it was only in the early twentieth century that instant noodles, like the ones Chef Zhang served his uncle posthumously, became popular in China. Although instant noodles originated in Japan, the Chinese are now the world's leading consumers of them. While all types of dried noodles can be found in China nowadays, fresh noodles remain a strong tradition in the north—and in the west, as I discovered on my journey.

Chef Zhang had displayed a tinge of sentimentality at his uncle's grave that he hid when it came to his more immediate family. When we'd dined with them the night before going to his village, he and his wife had barely spoken in our presence, although she'd doted over Chairman Wang and me. With Chef Zhang in Beijing, the couple had spent much of their marriage apart. The wife had spent one summer in the capital, when Chef Zhang had his own noodle shop, but otherwise, they saw each other for only a week or two each year. Around the time Craig and I began dating, Chef Zhang had offered his opinion on marriage. "Don't do it," he said. "It's too much trouble."

The arrangement between Chef Zhang and his wife was typical in China—to make a decent living, families often split up. Chef Zhang's situation was better than most. His wife took care of the children, unlike in many families, where the husband and wife both migrated for work, sometimes to separate places, leaving their children with grandparents. In those marriages, the union was often just practical: the goal was to produce children who would eventually care for their parents, in line with Confucian ideals. Sometimes rural parents still arranged marriages. Feelings might grow along the way, but not necessarily. Work often took precedence over family cohesion.

My parents' marriage was an amalgam of East and West. They'd met and fallen in love in college in Taiwan, where they'd grown up, and went to the United States together to pursue PhDs. My father made an early compromise, giving up an opportunity to study at the University of Pennsylvania to attend Northwestern near Chicago with my mother. They'd married in graduate school but in the typically unsentimental Chinese way. My father hadn't proposed—a visit to America by my maternal grandfather had instigated the wedding. Given how rare such occasions were, my mother's sister suggested that this would be a good time for my parents to marry, if they were thinking of tying the knot at all. My mother—in a touch of Western romanticism—donned a hastily procured white wedding dress for the visit to city hall.

A few years later, as they were finishing their PhDs, they gave birth to me, their first child, and we moved to California. Thereafter, my parents made their careers their priority. My father, a physicist, changed jobs numerous times, moving to universities in Los Angeles, Santa Barbara, and Cleveland, while my mother and I lived in San Bernardino County, east of Los Angeles, where my mother worked as a neurobiologist. When I turned seven, we reunited under one roof in San Diego, where my father had found a new job and my mother took time off after my brother's birth and later restarted her career.

Around the time I graduated from college, Confucian traditions called my father back to Taiwan. Ever since he'd left for America, his parents had hoped he would return to live with them, a duty often expected of eldest sons. (He was the eldest of five children.) As his parents got older, that responsibility weighed more on him, and he went to work in Taiwan. My mother stayed behind in California to continue her career. This arrangement produced tension sometimes, I knew, but they were still a couple, and still saw each other regularly. They'd somehow made it work.

Early on in my marriage, however, my father had warned me not to follow his and my mother's example. He worried about the time I would spend apart from Craig on the Silk Road.

"Are you sure you want to do this? It's not good for either of you," he said when he visited Craig and me in Beijing before I left for my journey.

"Why not?" I said lightly. "You and Mom are always apart."

"That's different," he said, clearing his throat. And then, abruptly, he blurted out, "When are you going to have a baby?"

"Oh, Dad!" I said, evading the question. Neither of us was good at sharing personal matters. It was the first and last time he asked. Even though I knew he wasn't pleased with the idea of my embarking on a journey for months (as he hadn't been pleased, at least initially, with my previous adventures in cooking), he grudgingly accepted the idea and wished me well.

The morning Chairman Wang and I left the village of Pushang, Chef Zhang and his younger daughter accompanied us. As we bumped along in the van that snaked down the rolling red hills to Wuxiang Township, he pointed out all the caves embedded in the canyons. When we reached town, Chef Zhang revised what he'd said on the train. It was true that he didn't miss his home when he was away. But it wasn't that he didn't feel anything. "I miss the people," he said. "When I retire, I'll go home and live on the farm. I have two acres of land—that's plenty to grow all I'll need. I'll buy an electric three-wheel cart and take my wife to town to go shopping every once in a while."

While Chef Zhang thought about retiring with his wife, Chairman Wang relived her past as she and I visited Yuanqu, the village where she'd been sent to do manual labor during the Cultural Revolution. Yuanqu lay only a hundred miles to the southwest of Chef Zhang's village as the crow flies, but the area was so mountainous and the roads so bad that we had to take a bus, a train, and a private taxi to get there.

Chairman Wang had been one of millions of students whose lives had been upended by Chairman Mao Zedong's campaign to reverse the country's social order. She'd planned to study medicine but had missed out on college because Mao had closed all universities and sent students to the fields. But despite the hardships, Chairman Wang had fond memories of tilling the land; when she spoke of it, her tone reminded me of how Craig reminisced about his time in the Peace Corps. "We ate idle meals," she'd once told me wistfully, an idiom that means something like "Those were the days."

Since the time Chairman Wang had left, Yuanqu had grown considerably wealthier, more so than Chef Zhang's village. The flatness of the land allowed farmers to grow more crops and to use machines for harvest. And the villagers had found a new source of income from an ancient product, the very thing that had inspired trading between China and Europe centuries before: silk. Barns were filled with endless shelves of silkworms, collectively creating a loud crackle as they munched the mulberry leaves that fueled their production of the threads.

The renewed demand for silk—which China exported to the world—changed not just the farmers' routines but also their eating habits. When Chairman Wang had worked in the village, it was so poor that even wheat was a luxury. The students had mainly farmed sturdier millet and corn to make noodles, porridge, and buns. Despite her fond memories, the mere thought of millet still made Chairman Wang want to retch—she'd eaten so much of it in those years. Now the wealth produced by the silkworms meant that the villagers could afford to buy, rather than grow, their staples. And so we were greeted with rice, not noodles, in each home we visited.

Instead of learning more about noodles, I was treated to a history lesson. During the night we spent in the village, Chairman Wang was lost in a reverie of memories, repeating many of the stories about the Cultural Revolution that I'd heard while cooking with her. Even after seeing the place, I still found it hard to believe that she'd been sent to this village and had been forced to stay in the area for eight years before returning to the capital. A Communist official had simply dropped the students in the village and left them to fend for themselves, I learned. The farmers had treated Chairman Wang well (she'd been the hardest worker among her peers), and officials had rewarded her by allowing her to leave first. Other students had languished in the village longer and one young woman had been involved in a torrid affair with one of the married men we'd come across, my cooking mentor told me.

The next day, I said farewell to Chairman Wang at the train station. Our good-bye was short—my matronly friend was anxious to get back to her husband. "I'll see you in a few months!" she said as she wheeled her bag away. I, in contrast, felt a little more sentimental: my two cooking mentors had been central to my life in China and to my culinary path, and I was glad to have had them with me for the first leg of this new adventure. But after I saw Chairman Wang off, I wondered if I'd also invited the chefs along for the company: I realized I was now continuing west, into the unknown, completely on my own.

3.

After saying good-bye to Chairman Wang, I boarded a bus to Xi'an, the ancient capital that had spurred the silk trade with Europe. I was looking forward to the ride because it would give me my first glimpse of the Yellow River. Though I'd traversed it on my earlier travels, I had no memory of it. The waterway has great symbolic value to the Chinese, however. It's the second-longest river in China, after the Yangtze, and locals consider it the cradle of their civilization, with evidence of human activity dating back thousands of years. In fact, many Chinese believed that noodles had emerged from this river region as well. For my chef friends, the waterway had other culinary significance. After I crossed it and continued west, Chef Zhang had told me, "The noodles will be totally different." Chairman Wang made a connection of a different sort. "It's so polluted, it's like a stew," she said flatly. "Actually, no, it's thicker. It's like sesame paste!"

The bus was so uncomfortably hot and crowded that I dozed off, a skill I'd acquired to adapt to moments of unpleasant travel. I only woke a few hours later, when the bus arrived in Xi'an. Darn, I thought, as the passengers and I pushed and shoved our way off the bus. I'd missed seeing the Yellow River once again. But, as Chef Zhang claimed, the noodles were totally different as I followed the river west. In Xi'an I would taste an appetizer called *ganmianpi*, thick slices of wheat noodles steamed and plunged into cold water to remove the starch, then tossed with bean sprouts and chili oil. In the Hexi Corridor, a narrow passage of desert between two mountain ranges where Marco Polo had noted an abundance of wheat, I'd sample spaghetti-like strands made with egg yolks, like Italian pasta, and topped with thin slices of donkey meat that tasted like corned beef. Further west, in the region of Xinjiang, I'd enjoy *dapanji*, or big plate chicken, a dish of spicy chicken stew flavored with green peppers, chilies, and star anise. After much of the poultry was eaten, the waiters slipped long, thick, tagliatelle-like noodles into the stew to soak up the gravy, giving the dish a second incarnation.

Between Xi'an and Xinjiang, though, there was the city of Lanzhou. The town had the distinction of being one of the world's most polluted metropolises, and the river was indeed the thick brown pool Chairman Wang had described. Even so, I was enthralled. Lanzhou was the home of hand-pulled noodles, the dish I'd wanted to treat Lu the geologist to at the outset of my journey in Beijing. (Coincidentally, Lanzhou was near Lajia, the place where researchers found the supposed four-thousand-year-old noodle.) The artistry involved in making hand-pulled noodles was stunning. I arrived in Lanzhou by train early one morning and made a beeline for the kitchen of a Muslim eatery called Mazilu. A dozen men pounded, kneaded, and pulled gobs of dough, each thumping their respective mounds against the counter. They stretched the dough and folded it in half before twirling it around itself like a dance partner, spinning it into the shape of a super-long French cruller. They wrapped the increasingly stringy dough around their hands to make a loop and stretched the dough as far apart as their arms would go. Through a set of motions that looked like a child's game of cat's cradle, they effortlessly spun a pile of strands as thin as angel hair and snapped them into a vat of boiling water. After the chefs cooked and drained the noodles, they added them to bowls of long-simmered beef broth, topping the bowls with a dash of chili sauce and crumbles of beef.

Locals ate the dish for breakfast. And even though it seemed like an odd way to start one's day, I was eager. It was infinitely better than the lukewarm

plain rice porridge or leftovers that most Chinese had for breakfast. I lifted
a tangle of strands with my chopsticks, carefully pausing for a moment to
inhale the rich broth, scented with ginger, cardamom, and cinnamon. (On
my previous trip through the region, I'd burned my tongue on these noodles in my impatience to try them.) Doing my best slurp through puckered
lips (a Chinese skill I'd never quite nailed), I was rewarded with the fine,
slippery texture of the wispy strands. I'd tried hand-pulled noodles elsewhere in China, but none had come close to the refinement of the dish in
its place of origin. It was a result, some chefs said, of the local water, echoing what New Yorkers said about bagels. Even if noodles hadn't been invented nearby, they had surely reached their highest refinement in this arid
inland region.

As I moved westward, I would discover that China's ethnic minorities
claimed many noodle dishes as their own and may have helped transmit
them farther afield. If the four-thousand-year-old noodle hadn't dissolved,
in fact, the discovery would have confirmed not the Chinese as the inventor
of noodles, but rather a small minority called the Tu, who inhabited the
area four thousand years before through the present. (When I'd asked Lu
the geologist about the possibility of attributing the invention of noodles to
a minority group, he laughed nervously. "That's very sensitive," he said.)

Though it was too early in my trip to say who invented noodles, it was
fairly safe to attribute the hand-pulled variety to the Hui, a claim most Chinese corroborated. The Hui also made various other noodles that I would
discover as I went west, and I'd learn how they and their culinary influence
had migrated to Central Asia. Nearly every minority community I passed
through had its own noodle dishes—from tiny, obscure groups like the Tu
to the Tibetans (who live in western China and Tibet).

Though I was only halfway through China, the western part of the
country seemed like a foreign land. Most people, myself included, don't
readily think of the region at all when they think of the country. In the
densely populated eastern half of the nation, it's easy to think that China is
monolithic, made up of a single ethnicity. More than ninety percent of the

Middle Kingdom is Han, the ethnic group that is practically synonymous with being Chinese.

I am Han. And yet before I arrived in the East, I'd never heard of the term. In America, I'd thought of myself as simply Chinese. But not long after I moved to China, I asked a stranger on the street for directions. My Han face, contrasted with my fumbling Mandarin and foreign mannerisms, confused her. "*Ni shi hanzu, ma?* Are you Han?" she asked, perplexed.

As my Mandarin improved and I picked up on how to interact with locals, indeed I became more "Han." But the designation still felt uncomfortable. Growing up in the white suburbs of America, I'd always felt like a minority. I carried that sensibility with me across the Pacific, only to discover that I was now part of the majority. On top of that, the term "Han" was often used with overtones of dominance and pride. China, just emerging from a dark economic and political period of the twentieth century and with a small population of minorities, hadn't started grappling with issues of race and ethnicity the way America had. The political correctness that had consumed America wasn't evident in the least. More than once, I heard Han Chinese referring to Tibetans as "wild and uneducated." Restaurants specializing in Uighur cuisine often featured dancing, an attribute Hans associated with the minority. For a while, the minority theme park in Beijing, a bad idea to begin with, bore an unfortunate translation: "Racist Park." For all these reasons, I couldn't quite get used to being considered Han. Even in a place where I looked like everyone else, I was a misfit still.

But that discomfort took on a new dimension as I headed west, where most of the non-Han population lives. Aside from China's best-known and most vocal minority, the Tibetans, many other groups are scattered across the largely rural region. Chinese officials have categorized more than fifty other "official" ethnic groups within its borders. Some minorities are more familiar, claiming the ancestry of neighboring countries, like Mongolia, Korea, and Kazakhstan. Others are minuscule in population and have never actively sought to form their own nation, while still others, like the Tibetans and Uighurs, have fought for independence.

Having been a minority in the United States, I found the cultures existing on China's fringes fascinating. As I went west, I passed through Tibetan towns with names like Zag Zag, full of mud-brick homes decorated with colorful prayer flags and surrounded by deserts and canyons that reminded me of Arizona. One restaurateur in a town known as "Little Mecca" told me he was Dongxiang, a minority that traced its lineage back to Genghis Khan's conquests. When I reached China's border with Afghanistan and Pakistan, the dusty streets were full of European-looking boys with light hair and eyes of hazel, green, and even occasionally blue, part of the Uighur minority.

But given my Han appearance, I approached western China cautiously. I worried about being lumped into a dominant group that had sometimes trampled over the rights of minorities and taken over their territories. On previous travels in Tibet, my protestations that I was a minority, too—just not in China—had been met with laughter. Uighurs were less welcoming to me than to obvious foreigners, even after I told them that I was American.

It didn't help that ethnic tensions had recently intensified. Violent riots had broken out in Tibetan regions not long before, followed by deadly demonstrations in Xinjiang, an area where I planned to spend several weeks. But it was the only overland route into Central Asia, and I could not pass up the chance to sample the unique culinary traditions, some rugged and rustic, others refined and artisanal, that lay ahead.

I learned about the Hui minority in Xi'an. The City of Eternal Peace, as it is sometimes called, is one of the few in China where the original city walls still stand. History looms large in Xi'an, which is famous for the Terracotta Warriors, sculptures dating from the third century BC that depict the armies of Qin Shi Huang, the first emperor of a unified China. One resident told me that the construction of the subway was going slowly because every few yards of digging yielded a new archaeological find. Because ancient emperors in Xi'an instigated the silk trade with Europe, some historians say that it, rather than Beijing, should be considered the eastern terminus of the Silk Road.

The Muslim quarter is the city's oldest district. The local government had turned the area's main thoroughfare into a pedestrian walkway lined with historic residences painted ruby red and jade green, giving the area the generic look of many newly renovated tourist traps across China. But behind the facade, the quarter lived up to its name. Nestled in a maze of alleys was a mosque that dated back to the eighth century AD. Inside, students in white skullcaps recited Arabic prayers in unison. Women with the occasional European feature—freckles, hazel eyes, or long noses—bicycled past, their colorful head scarves fluttering in the wind. The Muslim quarter had been the center of Xi'an since the eighth century, when the city was the largest in the world. Back then, as many as a third of its residents had been foreigners.

The Muslim quarter was also the spiritual capital of the Hui, one of the largest minorities in China, with a population of almost ten million. Some academics argued that the Hui shouldn't be considered a separate minority, but rather Han Chinese who'd converted to Islam generations before. But the Hui I met were insistent that their identity was distinct, like that of Jews; it was not mere religious adherence that set them apart from the Han. They were often biracial, the descendants of Hans who'd intermarried with Arabs, Persians, or Turkic people many generations before. I also learned that the Hui were further split into two camps: the "land" Hui who lived in or around Xi'an, where contact with Islam had come overland via the Silk Road, and the "sea" Hui in coastal China, where the religion had spread via maritime routes.

Aside from hand-pulled noodles, the Hui had other distinctive dishes. Ground lamb replaced ground pork in steamed soup dumplings, and sweet rice porridge was flavored with rosewater. But most intriguing was what they did with round bread disks made of wheat flour and baked in coal-heated tin drums. The bread, which nowadays was called *mo*, had gone by the name *tu-tur-mu*.

In my research, I'd learned that bread was the predecessor of noodles. It made intuitive sense, though I'd never quite linked the two in my mind. Historical documents show that China's tradition of noodles grew out of bread. Archaeologists have found evidence in ancient cake-like breads that the Chinese have been baking for more than two thousand years. (It seemed a historical accident that bread was associated with the West while noodles were associated with the East.) And, unlike the four-thousand-year-old noodle, there were documents to back up this find: Chinese breads began to appear in records between the fourth and second centuries BC. The word *bing* surfaces in a fable of Mohist philosophy, a rival of the Confucian school. The story tells of a wealthy landlord who steals the *bing* made in a neighbor's kitchen, despite his fortune. Descriptions of noodles began appearing alongside mentions of bread in the third century AD; the first noodles were called *tang bing*, or "soup bread," and until the sixth century, the word *bing* was used interchangeably to describe both bread and noodles.

As with Chinese noodles, it took me a while to understand the allure of *bing*. *Bing* was a more encompassing concept than what we thought of as bread in the West; it wasn't just something you used to make a sandwich or slathered with butter at the start of a meal. At first, I didn't quite understand the enormous queue that formed every morning in my Beijing neighborhood for *mantou*, steamed buns made of refined white flour. But the longer I lived in the *hutong*, the more I craved starchy bread snacks like *mantou* and *jian bing*, a grilled savory crepe-like pancake cooked on a griddle, brushed with egg, chili oil, and barbecue sauce, sprinkled with coriander and leeks, and folded into a multilayer gluten feast. The longer I lived in China, the more I debated whether I should spend my calories at the wet market on *shou zhua bing*, a flaky, shallow-fried disk that reminded me of Indian roti, or at a stand around the corner that sold piping-hot *zhima bing*, little baked rolls made with a tahini-like sesame paste and sugar.

Xi'an was known for a couple of dishes that employed the bread disks called *mo* in novel ways. The Han Chinese population used them to make *roujia mo*, toasting the bread before halving it and stuffing it with stewed and shredded pork belly, spicy green peppers, and cilantro. It was the best sandwich I'd ever tried. But that dish was off-limits to the Hui, who obeyed the Muslim prohibition on pork. Instead, they used the bread to make a lamb soup called *yangrou paomo*.

A local food writer named Bai Jianbo offered to take me out for the Muslim dish. He was a modest man in his fifties, with a bald, shiny head and a Buddha-like smile. When I met food writers like Bai, I was reminded that the profession in China didn't command the respect and excitement it did in America. In China, food writing was still a fledgling, unglamorous field struggling to free itself from the practice of touting restaurants for pay. Bai had worked as a chef for a dozen years before he'd turned to writing, a shift motivated by a practical reason. On a long trip he'd taken across the country, he discovered how difficult it was for an observant Muslim to eat in China, a country obsessed with pork. He encountered pork stir-fries, pork dumplings, and pork-flavored instant noodles everywhere. "I couldn't even go to KFC because while they don't serve pork, their chickens aren't halal," he said. That inspired him to write a countrywide guide to Muslim restaurants. After it was published, he moved on to writing a Muslim street snack cookbook and a guide to eating in Xi'an. His latest project was an encyclopedia of Hui cuisine, which he was writing in the spirit of the exhaustive imperial encyclopedias that detailed the intricacies of every dish. He estimated it would take him another six years to finish, and he had no idea who would publish it.

We arrived at the warehouse-like canteen around noon, just as diners were lining up to fork over a dollar apiece for the dish. The cashier gave us each a large bowl and a disk of bread. Bai and I settled at a table and broke the bread into crumbs in our bowls, a task he took on as seriously as he did his encyclopedia. After a good five minutes, he glanced over. "You haven't broken them down enough," he said. I ran the crumbs through my fingers yet again. Though the task was painfully repetitive, I appreciated it more after I learned that Chinese historians theorized that the very motion I was engaged in—the pinching of bread, either cooked or raw—was how Chinese first formed noodles.

At last we took our bowls to the open kitchen, which looked out onto a bustling alley near the mosque. The chef carved a few pieces of lamb and placed them into each crumb-filled bowl, along with chopped leeks and a ladleful of rich lamb stock. Glass noodles went in, too—I still thought of them as noodles even now that I knew they weren't considered *mian*. One at a time, each bowl's contents were poured into a wok, stir-fried over a roaring fire for two minutes to seal in the flavors, and returned to the bowl. We carried our meal back to the table and garnished the soup with pickled garlic cloves, chili sauce, and coriander. I held the bowl to my face, breathing in the vapors. My initial bite was instantly gratifying, the disparate flavors of the savory broth, the sweetness of the garlic, and the heat of the chili sauce melding together in the bread bits. The bread's heartiness, in fact, reminded me of that first taste of stuffing on Thanksgiving Day. As I devoured the bowl amid a chorus of slurps echoing in the hall, I broke into a sweat. I recalled how the first noodles had been called "soup bread"—could they have come in this form?

Bai didn't know, but he was certain that "the bread is the key to this dish." As we got up for a stroll through the Muslim quarter, I thought about the name of the bread. *Tu-tur-mu*. Why did that sound familiar? I wondered. It was only later that I pieced it together: the name was a derivative of *tutumashi*, a dish I'd come across in my research—the noodle preparation involving milk and basil that had been mentioned in the food encyclopedia of the Mongol court. Later, I would discover in Turkey that locals ate a noodle dish called *tutmaç*.

From Xi'an, I traveled west to the Tibetan areas of Gansu and Qinghai Provinces. I'd traveled this area alone before on my first western China trip, in 2005, the year before Craig and I had started dating. I'd lived in China for five years by that point and wondered if I'd ever meet a life partner. The pool of men in China was limited, even if half the 1.3 billion people in China were men; actually more than half, due to the effects of traditional gender preference. But I couldn't imagine dating someone with whom I couldn't speak my native language. I suppose I was picky as well. I'd never been the kind of person who "settled," in any sense of the word. I preferred being alone to being with someone with whom I didn't think I had a future.

Being in China also jaded me. In Shanghai, I saw men behaving badly. I met women who'd moved to China with their partners and seen their relationships crumble, as their boyfriends or husbands had affairs, usually with local women. And I thought it was unfair that in foreign journalism, the rigors of the job meant that many of my older female colleagues had gotten used to being alone—getting married or having children would make it difficult to go off and cover breaking news; giving up on marriage and children was the price they had to pay for sticking wholeheartedly to their profession. Meanwhile, most of the male journalists of a certain age married and had children, remaining free to come and go at will.

In any case, as I approached thirty, I started thinking I might be destined to be alone. Though I'd always wanted children, it wasn't a pressing concern. I actually enjoyed being single. I liked being able to work, socialize, and travel when I pleased. And I sometimes wondered if I'd ever feel completely comfortable in a relationship. Maybe I just wasn't cut out for settling down.

On my previous trip, I'd paused in this Tibetan region to visit an elderly single woman named Isabel. She lived in a small dusty town called Rebkong, famous for its *thangka*s, intricate paintings of Buddhist scenes outlined in gold paint. Isabel was in her late seventies, with an elegant British-tinged accent from her years growing up in Hong Kong, and long dark hair touched lightly with gray. She wore draping skirts, hand-me-down shoes, and fleece pullovers.

I'd first met Isabel the year before, halfway around the world in the fancy Long Island enclave called the Hamptons. I'd gone there to visit a friend at her mother's home, and Isabel—whom my friend called "my crazy aunt"—also happened to be passing through. The aunt was drinking a glass of red wine and watching the French Open. A tennis fan myself, I looked on (Sharapova was pummeling a much weaker opponent), and we struck up an instant rapport.

As we talked, I learned that Isabel had gone to Columbia University. After graduating, she'd worked for *Time* magazine as a researcher. She told her bosses she was interested in working as a foreign correspondent but kept getting passed over for reporting jobs, reserved mostly for men in those days. "I kept on watching young men who'd just come out of schools like Amherst get sent into the field," she said. "It was frustrating. So one day, I just quit and bought a ticket to Asia." She worked as a freelance correspondent at a time when few women went overseas as reporters. She covered the conflict in Vietnam, at one point working in Saigon alongside a journalist who later became my adviser at the Columbia School of Journalism.

Though we were decades apart in age, our paths had striking similarities. While at Columbia, I'd worked as an assistant at *Newsweek* and *The New Yorker*. I'd also decided not to work my way up stateside, and had gone to Asia to become a freelance journalist. We were both single. We were both of Chinese descent, which motivated us both to spend time in China.

Isabel asked me how I enjoyed living there. Though she'd lived in New York for the past two decades, she was planning to move to western China in the next few months, she told me. She was tired of America and decided that China was where she'd retire; she'd made a few good Tibetan friends on her frequent visits to the country, and they'd encouraged her to settle in their small town of Rebkong, near the Tibetan Plateau. She invited me to visit once she'd settled.

I took Isabel up on her offer the following year, while I was in northwestern China on assignment. Again I noticed that she had the energy of someone five decades younger. She introduced me to many of her friends, including a monk who'd recently "defrocked" himself, as she put it, and, free of religious constraints, had become a drinking buddy. We stayed out late at nightclubs with the defrocked monk and his friends, and Isabel slung back bottles of beer—a beverage she ingested the way most people drank water—and shots of scotch. We got back to her apartment so late that the gates of her building had closed (a common practice in China), and I had to scale the high fence to gain entrée for my host.

Before I left the next morning, Isabel, in her pajamas, gave me a hug and

wished me well. She'd added, with a look of fondness, that I reminded her
of her younger self.

When I passed through again, Isabel was still living in this remote Tibetan
area. I was excited to catch up with her, even more so after she told me that
she'd helped open a Tibetan restaurant near where she lived. We arranged
to meet in Xining, the capital of Qinghai Province, a two-hour drive from
her home in Rebkong. Arriving by train in Xining (pronounced *shee-ning*),
I glanced out the window and was surprised to find that the sleepy town
had developed considerably in the last five years. Like cities in eastern
China, it had been consumed by spiraling apartment towers. Shiny new
cars clogged the roads. The Communist Party's plans to "develop the
west"—one of its big slogans of the early twenty-first century—were beginning to bear fruit, but the success looked ominous. Thankfully, tucked
away in alleys was some semblance of the city's old self: storefronts sold
huge blocks of yak butter, resembling wheels of cheddar cheese, and butchered meats, both mutton and yak, hung from hooks in the open air. Bill-
boards and signs bore Tibetan Sanskrit alongside Chinese characters.

I'd booked a private room in a youth hostel that turned out to be in a
new apartment tower. When I arrived, I found Isabel at the bar, drinking a
Yellow River beer. She chuckled when she saw me and rose for a hug. She
looked as healthy as the last time I'd seen her, though more wrinkles lined
her face and a few more strands of gray streaked her long hair, which hung
in a low ponytail.

That evening, she took me to a restaurant that served southern Chinese
food—the food of her heritage, and mine. We had egg rolls and shrimp
pastries along with several light stir-fries. The delicate flavors seemed out
of place in this region of spicy, hearty food. While I was disappointed not
to be eating local specialties, particularly because no noodles were served,
Isabel was happy; she disliked the heavy flavors that were typical of the
region.

Several foreign friends who ran philanthropic organizations or were volunteering in the region joined us for dinner, along with a Tibetan man named Karma. He was in his late twenties, had a light goatee, and, like Isabel, wore his long hair in a ponytail. Isabel called him "my son." I was confused, because on my previous journey, she'd introduced me to another Tibetan man who'd also been her "son." Isabel explained that since we'd last met, she'd adopted Karma. The two men, she noted, were more like godsons than sons, though, given that both still had living parents. After dinner, Karma, driving a car that Isabel had bought him, dropped Isabel and me at the hostel and disappeared into the night.

The next day, Karma picked us up and offered to take Isabel and me to his favorite noodle restaurant before we headed to Rebkong. When we pulled up at the eatery, it looked faintly familiar—I wondered if it was the one I'd frequented on my last trip. I'd come down with a terrible flu that kept me confined for days to a small room in a smoky, government-run hotel. When I'd mustered enough strength to leave my room, I found a noodle shop across the street and settled in for my first real meal in days. On the table appeared a large bowl of noodle squares stir-fried in a spicy tomato stew. The flat squares, called *mian pian* in Mandarin, had just the right springiness, and the chili-infused stew, with bits of beef and fresh vegetables, reminded me of an Italian *arrabbiata* sauce, a hint of sugar balancing the heat and acidity. Though I'm usually a slow eater, I finished the bowl in minutes and ordered a second, which I demolished just as quickly. It wasn't only my returning appetite that made the *mian pian* so delicious, I discovered as I regained my health. The noodle squares were simply addictive. Over my weeklong stay, the restaurant became my canteen; I ate there at least once a day, sometimes twice.

Though the surroundings looked familiar, the restaurant's interior looked different. In place of the utilitarian wooden tables and flimsy stools I remembered, velvet covered the dining chairs and birdcage lanterns decorated the ceiling. But when I tasted the noodles, déjà vu struck definitively. Like many places in China, this restaurant had gone upscale.

Though a Hui owned the restaurant and Hui frequented the place, Tibetans also ate here in equal numbers. Tibetans liked noodle squares and considered it their dish, too, Karma told me.

"Yes, that's true," Isabel said, passing up the noodles for a plate of stir-fried green beans. "*Mian pian, mian pian*! That's all they eat in this area." We capped off the meal with bowls of creamy local yogurt sprinkled with sugar, the texture and topping resembling crème brûlée.

With at least Karma's and my hunger sated, we piled into the car and drove to Rebkong. I sat in front with Karma while Isabel lounged in the backseat, drinking a plastic cup filled with vodka, which she'd bought at a grocery on the way. We followed the Yellow River, which ran strikingly clean and glistening blue in this rural area. The river rushed through a winding narrow valley, framed by dry mountains with sharp ridges that splintered and separated like fingers. We passed through villages where new low-rise cement buildings were painted pink and where all the men wore *doppi*, Muslim skullcaps. In the center of each village was a green-domed mosque decorated with a crescent moon like a weather vane. Karma explained that Tibetans and Huis lived in separate villages, just as they sat at separate tables in the restaurant. The farther we drove, the greater the proportion of Tibetan villages.

Halfway to Rebkong, Karma wanted to stretch his legs. "Do you want to eat more noodle squares?" he asked, pulling over at a small line of shops by the road.

Sure, I said. Isabel groaned from the backseat.

In the restaurant's kitchen, a trio of Hui women wearing lacy black head scarves stood around a large wok, holding long, flat strands of dough in their hands and ripping them in a quick, rhythmic fashion into boiling water. As the noodle squares were brought to our table in a light mutton broth, Karma extolled their benefits. "Other noodles are heavy and sit in your stomach for too long. But because these are softer and ripped by hand, when you eat them, they feel like feathers in your stomach."

"Is that so? After I eat just two pieces, they feel like they're congealing in my stomach!" Isabel said skeptically, with a chuckle. She picked her way through a piece of boiled mutton sprinkled with coriander and chili sauce as spicy as if it had been made with habaneros.

We got back in the car and drove farther into the hinterlands as dusk fell, the first stars appearing in the sky. The villages became increasingly Tibetan, with white stupas and colorful banners replacing mosques. We whizzed past a sculpture of the Buddha carved into the side of a hill, signaling our impending arrival in Rebkong. Karma turned into a narrow alley that led to a village and pulled up at a brick compound to drop us off. Isabel, half-drunk, fumbled in the dark for her keys, unlocked the door, and invited me into the wooden bungalow she called home.

Since the last time I visited, Isabel had moved from her apartment in town to a three-room cabin she'd designed herself in a village nearby. When I woke the next morning, she was padding around the main room, drinking coffee and making breakfast. She used *mo*, the round bread disks I knew from Xi'an, as English muffins, halving and toasting them. We ate them with fried eggs and tomato slices while sitting on her wooden patio, looking out onto a pear orchard in her large sloping yard. The "hut," as she called it, had broadband Internet, on which she could watch live tennis and listen to the BBC news, but no running water. She went to a friend's home in town once a week to shower. She'd had her contractor build a seat lined with orange felt in her outhouse, so she didn't have to squat.

Even with few modern amenities, the hut was pleasant, and with the sun shining on the patio, I could see how Isabel could feel at home there. "Every morning, I look out, eat my to-*mah*-toes, and watch my fruit trees grow," she said as she sipped her coffee and let out a trademark chuckle. "You could say I'm pretty contented." She kept busy. In addition to tending to her two "sons," she worked on philanthropic projects. She'd helped set up a community center in Rebkong and raised money for the education of Tibetan girls.

After breakfast, we decided to go into town. We locked the bungalow and walked to the main road, atop of which the farmers had laid the wheat they'd just harvested, taking advantage of cars that whizzed by to thresh the grain. It occurred to me that the wheat that went into the noodles and bread I'd been eating all across China had been run over by car tires. But before I could think much about it, a crackling sound like a gunshot went off. We both jumped. "Was that a gun?" I said. Isabel nodded. Tibetans still kept arms, even though China didn't officially allow its citizens to own them. "Don't worry," she said, trying not to sound too nervous. "They usually just shoot them up in the air."

On the street, we boarded a beat-up minivan that operated like a bus. Dangling from the rearview mirror was a picture of the Dalai Lama. The Chinese government had deemed the Tibetan leader an evil demagogue intent on splitting Tibet from China and banned his image. But even so, Tibetans adored him and still hung his picture everywhere. On the way to town, we passed a large monastery called Longwu Temple, the entrance of which was decorated with enormous prayer wheels that pilgrims spun as they circumambulated the compound. Later, when I went inside the gates, I saw more illicit photos of the Dalai Lama displayed within the temple's dark rooms.

We hopped off the bus in the center of Rebkong, where I was struck by the colors. Monks on motorbikes drove around town clad in deep red loose-flowing gowns, the extra fabric thrown over one shoulder. Tibetan men on the street wore purple, green, or other bright colors, in contrast to the drab gray and black that Chinese men favored in the east. Shops sold shiny, flowery cloth for women's gowns. Even the mops in the hardware shops were colorful, made from pieces of bright blue and leopard-print material. The sun's rays, intensified by the altitude, seemed to make everything even brighter.

Next to a shop selling colorful sportswear was the restaurant that Isabel had bankrolled for her first "son." Wanma was sitting at a table by the window, smoking and chewing on stir-fried yak with bell peppers when we arrived. He had a reddish complexion, small eyes, and rumpled hair. He barely stirred as we sat down, not bothering with the usual greetings of the region. "He's not complicated like Karma," Isabel had said of him. "I worry about him less."

As Isabel and I sipped tea, Wanma told me how he'd come to open the restaurant. He wanted to open an Internet café initially but learned that China's censorship laws made it too risky, so instead decided on selling Han Chinese stir-fries, the kind that Isabel liked. It was moderately successful, but one day the Han chef up and left, and a replacement proved difficult to find. So Wanma put the women in his family in charge of the kitchen, and they began serving what they ate at home, with a few tweaks. (Tibetan men didn't cook much, he admitted.)

Though I didn't know much about Tibetan food, I knew it wasn't like the light vegetarian fare served in overseas Tibetan restaurants in cosmopolitan cities like New York. Few Tibetans, at least here, were vegetarian. Even monks, who were supposed to adhere to a no-meat diet, were often omnivores, going to little cafés near temples to indulge in yak-filled dumplings.

Wanma's wife taught me a few dishes. A pretty woman with a porcelain doll's round face and eyes, she described the food she cooked as *yuanshi*, which means "sticking to the original" or, less flatteringly, "primitive." We began with a common Tibetan dish called *momo*. The yak-filled dumplings, eaten as snacks during and between meals, seemed to riff off of several Chinese dishes made of dough. The name suggested a link with *mo*, the bread disks of Xi'an. She used the same dough as is used for Chinese dumplings and rolled it into the same thin circles. She placed a dollop of ground yak meat, minced onions, salt, and pepper in the center of the circle and wrapped the dough around the filling, pinching the edges together while slowly spinning the dumpling to form a navel-like indent atop it, like a Chinese steamed bun. That likeness continued as she placed the dumplings in a steamer to cook them. Hot out of the steamer, the dumplings were pretty good. The thinness of the skins reminded me of Shanghai soup dumplings, a refined coastal dish, but—perhaps this was the Han imperialist in me—I couldn't help wishing that the filling was pork rather than yak.

But this was yak country. The livestock was native to this high-altitude region, where pigs and vegetables were scarce. Wanma had the kitchen make a new plate of the stir-fried yak with green peppers that he was eating when we arrived, and I was pleased to find that it tasted like steak fajitas. The chefs also sliced yak thinly and grilled it in an iron pot over hot rocks, before dipping it in salt, cumin, and chili oil—seasonings that weren't traditionally used in Tibetan food but were becoming more common as Tibetans began to mix more with Hui and Han Chinese.

I found it harder to get used to the more traditional staples of Tibetan cuisine. Creamy yellow yak butter was ubiquitous, used not just for eating but for candles and sculptures in monasteries. It was even added to tea. But to me it tasted like gamy butter from cows, aged in a cave for months, and dissolving it in tea didn't help. Yak butter tea was often mixed with ground barley, a grain that grew well on the Tibetan Plateau, to make a dish called *tsampa* that was light and portable, perfect for nomadic life. But I was certain its portability rather than its taste made it popular—when I gave it a try, my mouth was coated with a sticky substance that tasted like a dry, unsweetened energy bar.

I really wanted to like Tibetan food. But sympathetic as I was to the Tibetan cause, I couldn't get behind the cuisine.

I told Isabel as much, and she laughed. "I'd give it two stars, at best."

On this second trip to Isabel's, we didn't have any late nights like the last time. I certainly wasn't up for it, given all the travel I'd done. And in any case, since Craig and I had become a couple, staying out late had lost its allure. Rather than battling crowds at a bar or nightclub, I much preferred to cozy up on the sofa at home with my husband and a movie.

Craig and I had met a couple of years before we'd started dating. Mutual friends introduced us when we happened to be having breakfast at the same restaurant. Not long after, we became colleagues when he joined the Beijing bureau of *Newsweek*, which I wrote for from Shanghai. After I quit the magazine and moved to Beijing, we'd unknowingly competed for a spot as Asia bureau chief of Cox Newspapers, which we'd only discovered after I lost the job to him. Even so, we began socializing more. In fact, I'd always felt a spark with Craig, but given our busy travel schedules, we only managed to meet up once in a while, usually with other friends. Over time, I learned that our paths were similar. We'd both grown up in the American suburbs (though he'd grown up on the opposite coast, in Massachusetts), and after college, we'd both come to China as American ambassadors of a sort; Craig had volunteered in the Peace Corps while I'd been on a Fulbright. Both of us wanted to pursue journalism after we finished our programs, and we'd opted to freelance rather than work our way up through steady journalism jobs. Eventually we'd both landed jobs as part-time correspondents for *Newsweek*. He tackled serious topics like the environment, while I mostly wrote features. As a colleague, he was industrious and generous with contacts. As I got to know him personally, I discovered that while he was idealistic and contemplative, he also had a private, mischievous sense of humor.

I was in the midst of my Chinese cooking adventures as we were becoming better friends, and on the day I passed the national cooking exam, he brought over a bottle of wine to celebrate. That evening, on my apartment balcony, in a gentlemanly, old-fashioned way that was becoming more rare among my peers, he asked me out on a date.

Given how jaded I'd become, I was surprised that I fell for Craig as quickly as I did. I'd been immersed in writing a book, content with singledom, and not expecting to settle down anytime soon. But for whatever reason—maybe it was that initial spark, maybe it was the trust we'd built over a couple of years of friendship, maybe it was something more instinctual, a faith that he inspired—I dove in headfirst, without a bit of hesitation.

Once we started dating, we traveled together on impulse. We marked our first month by climbing Mount Fuji. Weeks later, he flew down to meet me in Shanghai, where I'd been interning at a restaurant. Within our first year together, we'd traversed a good amount of Asia and discovered how well we traveled together. He accompanied me on assignment to Bali, where I was charmed to discover he was incapable of lounging by a swimming pool; he'd rather be canoeing in bays or hiking up volcanoes. At one resort, he convinced the hotel staff that he knew how to sail a catamaran, only to admit after we'd pushed out that he'd done it just once before. When the wind picked up, he promptly capsized us, sending me into gales of soaking-wet laughter. Appropriately, it was in transit—on the Star Ferry in Hong Kong Harbor—that I told him I'd marry him. He hadn't even asked, he'd only inquired, in general, whether I was interested in having children some day. But already I'd fallen deeply in love and wanted to spend my life with Craig.

At Isabel's, I recalled something she had said to me on my last visit: "You remind me of a younger version of myself." Now, in my newly married state, she reappeared as a vision of how my life might have turned out. Though Isabel had remained steadfastly independent, a trait I admired, I was starting to see the consequences of her inability to settle down.

One afternoon we met her defrocked monk friend for *tsampa* at his restaurant, a copy of Wanma's nearby. Though the ex-monk had gotten married and had a baby since I'd last seen him, he acted like a carefree bachelor. He drove Isabel and me up a mountain where he and his friends put away dozens of bottles of Yellow River beer and loudly sang Tibetan folk songs. I found myself feeling sorry for Isabel, who was growing old alone and spending her day with an ex-monk who should have been with his wife and children.

The day before I left, Isabel and I stayed in and made ratatouille. She brought out an electric hot plate designed for Chinese cooking and set it on her patio. She heated a pan and added olive oil she'd brought from overseas, then had me throw in diced tomatoes, eggplants, green squash, and onions. The hot plate had a number of settings that described Chinese cooking methods—I toggled between the "hot pot" and "heat milk" settings, neither quite right for the sauté. She added a dash of red wine, made from local Chinese grapes. She poured sake into shot glasses and sliced up a halal sausage I'd brought along as a gift, squeezing wasabi (another overseas item) over it. She boiled spiral Italian pasta, bought in the same store where she'd procured her vodka, and served it with the stew I'd made. The meal, like the house, was a confusion of many cultures, but somehow it felt comforting.

As we ate, we talked about the paths we'd chosen. Though mine had diverged from Isabel's, we still had things in common. After all, I was still traveling alone, asserting my independence, not ready to have children. Isabel told me she'd never wanted children—she couldn't imagine dealing with a baby.

But perhaps she had? That would explain her "sons." Yet what did that mean, when both were grown men with parents of their own, still alive and well? Isabel didn't get along with Karma's parents, who lived in the same village. In fact, she had barely spoken a word to them for months, after a disagreement about the house she'd built, on land they'd leased to her. And Wanma and Karma disliked each other so much that they'd once nearly come to blows. The fight was over her, Isabel told me, but I suspected it was also over the money she showered on them.

We talked about how we were both a mishmash of East and West and how, because of it, we were "screwed up," as she put it. Like me, she was too Eastern to fit in with the West—but to an extreme. She had never gotten an American passport, she told me, because she was a Communist at heart. She was unusually nationalistic about China, saying that she agreed with Mao's proletarian policies and didn't support Tibetan independence, positions that put her at odds with her "sons" and many friends. Yet she was too Western for China. I could see it in her taste in food, her predilection for wine and whiskey, the books that lined her shelves (biographies of human rights leaders like Nelson Mandela), and the sports and news she watched and listened to through her Internet connection. Like me, she couldn't identify with the average local and never felt entirely at home in China, even though being Chinese was part of her identity. Maybe that was why she'd ended up on the Tibetan Plateau, where she didn't have to confront that every day. And maybe that was what had brought me to these parts of China and beyond—like Isabel, I was still trying to find out where I fit in.

4.

On my way to Xinjiang (pronounced *shin-jong*) by train, my friend Nur called me. I was planning to visit him in a couple of weeks in his hometown of Lop, on the very western frontier of China, where he'd been summering. He wondered if I could come immediately. He'd forgotten that I was planning on visiting him, and he'd inadvertently made plans to return to Beijing for school in just over a week.

Given how far he was, the only way I'd make it in time was to fly. I was faced with a logistical dilemma: Should I break a rule I'd set, to only travel by land (and sea)? Or should I pass up the opportunity to stay in a traditional Uighur village?

I decided to scrap the rule. As soon as my train arrived in Urumqi, the capital of Xinjiang, I boarded a plane to Lop, a trip that took two hours but would have taken thirty hours by bus. That was far better than the month the journey took during Marco Polo's time. From the air, I looked down at the Taklamakan, a melon-shaped desert that took up a large swath of Xinjiang. Millions of years before, the desert had been a large sea. Polo had visited Lop and noted that it was only wise to travel across the desert's width—"to travel it in the direction of its length would prove a vain attempt, as little less than a year must be consumed." A string of small towns, including Lop, lined its southern perimeter, but all I could see from my window seat was sand. Nur had told me that on breaks in the arduous bus journey, when travelers stepped off to pray, they washed their hands and faces with the fine sand.

I'd met Nur, an anthropology graduate student at the Central Minorities University in Beijing, through a friend early on in my trip planning. Nur was Uighur, one of China's largest ethnic minorities, who inhabited Xinjiang, a large corner of China's northwest, where the contradictions of Chinese rule were most apparent and bewildering. Uighurs spoke a dialect of Turkish, practiced Islam, and looked Middle Eastern or sometimes downright European. They seemed to belong farther west, but they had coexisted with Han Chinese for more than a millennium, as evidenced by European-looking mummies that had been on display at museums around the world.

Han Chinese, Uighurs, and other minorities (some of whom eventually died out) had tussled over the area since the time of Christ. Early in the twentieth century, the Uighurs, with help from the Soviets, had established an independent nation for several years, but that was crushed by the Communist Red Army in 1949. For decades since, pockets of the population had agitated for independence from China, in a movement akin to Free Tibet. The East Turkestan Islamic Movement, as it was called, was not well known in the West, because the Uighurs lacked a charismatic leader like the Dalai Lama, and Islam didn't appeal to Western sensibilities like Buddhism. In recent years, tensions between Hans and Uighurs had exploded. Deadly riots in Xinjiang broke out the year before I visited, and additional unrest followed my departure.

So even more than other ethnic minorities, many Uighurs saw the Han Chinese as occupiers, colonialists. Though Xinjiang was officially called an "autonomous zone," not a province, the Uighurs had the least freedom of any of China's minorities. While the Hui were allowed to practice Islam with relative freedom, and the Tibetans were unofficially permitted guns, when it came to Uighurs, the authoritarian government exerted a heavy hand, carefully monitoring their religious and educational institutions. So paranoid had the Chinese government become that they'd cut off Internet access for the entire region for nearly a year. While it had been restored shortly before I arrived, it was painfully slow, and, as in the rest of China, many sites were blocked. In recent years, the government had created incentives for Han Chinese to migrate to Xinjiang, as they'd done in Tibet, to overwhelm and dilute the local population.

Aware of the tensions, I'd spent considerable time preparing for Xinjiang. I'd hired Nur as my Uighur tutor, figuring the language would be helpful from China's western border to Turkey, an area that was linguistically and culturally related. Having taught Uighur to other Americans, he'd become acquainted with expressions like "'Sup, dog?"—a greeting he liked to use on me. Nur's hobby was linguistics, and his hero was Noam Chomsky. His glasses often drooped low on his thin nose, and he tied a belt around his skinny waist to hold up his pants. His complexion seemed to indicate he spent too much time in the library. In all those ways, he defied the stereotype Han Chinese held of Uighurs, whom the Hans saw as uneducated and menacing, even potentially terrorists.

When I was in Beijing, we met at my apartment for lessons, and when I was in America, we conversed over Skype. Nur began by teaching me the Uighur alphabet, the loops and scrawls of which were Arabic, and he coached me in basic Uighur pronunciation. It was more similar to English than Chinese but still difficult. We moved on to grammar and vocabulary, concentrating on food terms, and within a few months I could say some important things: *I am a chef and food writer. I like noodles very much. I may look Han but I'm also American.*

During our lessons, Nur would occasionally say something intriguing about how he ate back home. He told me about noodle soups that resembled Chinese ones. It was a rite of passage for boys to learn to slaughter sheep, he mentioned. He described the *tonur* ovens in every yard as being large enough to roast a whole sheep. And during one lesson, he'd invited me to visit him in Lop that summer.

Shortly after my flight touched down, Nur arrived at the airport, disheveled as usual. After saying hello, he surveyed the one large backpack next to me and asked, "Where is your husband?"

When we'd made arrangements, Craig hadn't come up. I later realized that Nur, like most people in the region, simply assumed that because I was a married woman, I would be traveling with my husband. Nur had taught me that the Uighur word for husband, *yoldishim*, also means "walking the same road." But I didn't realize that it was an expression taken literally. And in fact, my traveling alone posed an inconvenience. Locals would automatically assume that he and I were involved, even if I was Han Chinese and ten years older, not to mention a couple of inches taller and probably heavier. Thankfully, though, the locals were polite and hospitable and not overly intrusive (not that I would have known otherwise, given my limited Uighur).

We climbed into the backseat of a small car. Nur's brother-in-law was at the wheel and his five-year-old stood on the passenger side, unconstrained by a seat belt and poking his head out the window. Before we went home, Nur said, we had to register my arrival at the police station. It was a regulation that applied to all foreigners in China, but in practice I'd rarely followed it, having learned that it often invited more hassles than it was worth. Halfway to the police station, Nur came to the same conclusion. "I forgot that you look Chinese! Everyone will think you are Chinese," he said with a chuckle. "The police will never find you here." That was not reassuring, though; Han Chinese was exactly what I didn't want to be in these parts, and while Nur saw beyond my exterior, I wondered if others would.

After we made a U-turn, Nur asked if I was hungry. The question surprised me. Aware that Muslims had just begun celebrating Ramadan, the holy month when observers fasted from sunrise to sundown each day, I'd eaten the lackluster meal on the airplane. Wasn't everyone fasting? I asked.

Nur didn't answer, but a few minutes later his brother-in-law pulled up at a small eatery. I was really okay, I protested, assuming that they'd stopped for my benefit. I tried to halt everyone. The son promptly burst into tears.

"Well, I am a little hungry," I said hastily, and with that blessing the son sped into the restaurant, pushing aside the doorway's beaded curtain.

Nor was the restaurant empty. At the back of the shop, a Hui noodle maker pulled a hunk of dough. One table was occupied by a mother who sat with two boys, while another was occupied by a lone elderly man with a scraggly beard.

"That man must be sick and maybe that woman is pregnant," Nur whispered, explaining that certain people were excused from fasting, including children, the infirm, and women who were either pregnant or breast-feeding.

Bowls filled with the same hand-pulled noodles I'd eaten farther east appeared at our table, the super-thin, chewy strands bathed in a spicy red broth flavored with turnips and garnished with beef slices. They were almost as good as the ones I'd had in Lanzhou. Grateful for the midday meal, I joined the others in quickly polishing it off.

The feast continued at Nur's home. He introduced me to his sister Malika, a pretty woman around my age with a narrow nose, freckles, and light brown hair. He and Malika ushered me to the grandest room of the house, which featured high-domed ceilings and wooden pillars engraved with repeating geometric patterns. It was reserved for entertaining and for putting up guests. Once, when relatives held a wedding nearby, thirty family members and friends had slept in the room. Since I was the only guest at the moment, I had the space to myself.

Nur invited me to sit on a raised platform that ringed the room and poured me a cup of tea infused with rose, cumin, pomegranate seeds, and weeds from the Taklamakan Desert, giving it an earthy quality unlike any other tea I'd tried; I would drink cups of it every day during my visit. Malika came in and out of the room silently, setting out plates heaped with food on a woven red-and-gold blanket called a *meze*.

Meze is also the Turkish word for "appetizers," which Malika began bringing: grapes and pears plucked from the family orchard, followed by platters of dried fruits and nuts, the almonds as intensely flavored as their extract. A few minutes later she returned with a platter of mutton, barbecued so expertly that the fat had melted away and the skin crackled as I sank my teeth into it. Then a plateful of fried fish appeared, a dish I didn't expect given we were so far away from the ocean. They were river fish, Nur explained, a sought-after delicacy in this land-locked region.

It turned out that no one in Nur's family was fasting. It wasn't just because they were only moderately observant Muslims. The siblings, all of whom attended or worked for Chinese institutions, were forbidden to fast. At the start of the holiday at the school where Malika taught, the Han Chinese principal had gone around the classrooms to offer popcorn to everyone. It was the only time of the year that the administration doled out snacks. "Everyone was forced to eat. Otherwise, they were afraid they'd get in trouble," Nur said. It was an example of how in such a politically charged place even an innocuous subject like food was sensitive.

Nevertheless, the assumption was that everyone was fasting, and those who weren't, like Nur's family, generally ate in the privacy of their homes during the day. And it was impolite to point out that someone wasn't fasting—something I did repeatedly the first few days, before I worked out the etiquette of Ramadan.

Nur's home, behind a gate, was a sprawling series of rooms arranged around a courtyard. The large property also contained a barn and an orchard where pears ripened and walnuts plumped, and beyond that, corn shot toward the sky. Near the barn, the family had improvised an open-air kitchen. Next to the *tonur*, the beehive-shaped oven that Nur had told me about, a stove sat on a brick platform; the family had turned an old bed frame into a counter.

Malika generously offered to teach me her favorite Uighur dishes. We began with *polo*, the Uighur word for Indian *pilau*, Persian *polow*, and Turkish pilaf. In most of China, rice was considered filler, not suitable for guests; indeed, guests who only went to banquets could easily get the impression that Chinese didn't eat rice at all. But rice pilaf was the dish that traditionally welcomed guests into Uighur homes. It was also served at weddings and when dignitaries passed through town. It was an honor to be shown such hospitality.

Malika sliced several carrots into matchsticks and diced a few onions. She heated up the *kazan*, a heavier version of a wok, added a generous amount of soybean oil (the same cooking oil Han Chinese used), and dropped in hunks of mutton. After the meat browned, she added carrots and onions. Then she rinsed several pounds of local rice—a grain that was popping up more frequently in the west. She added it to the *kazan*, the sweet scent of onions and frying meat perfuming the air as the pilaf simmered.

While Malika cooked, the men of the household—Nur, his father, and his two brothers—watched while keeping an eye on Malika's two children, a baby daughter and the son I'd met the day before when Malika's husband had picked me up at the airport. (Ethnic minorities were allowed to have two children in China.) Nur's mother had passed away years before, so the burden fell on Malika, the only woman left in the household. She took care of her daughter's meal first, by reaching into the *kazan* for a piece of sheep's liver, now fully cooked. Holding her daughter in her lap, she chewed the liver into bits before transferring them to the baby's mouth. Then she went back to the *kazan*.

"Cooking is a lot of work," Nur observed.

"Especially if the men don't help," I added. Everyone laughed, with varying degrees of comfort.

I asked Malika if she cooked every night.

"I cook every night *and* morning," she said. "In Xinjiang, men don't do anything."

Her father, a Mediterranean-looking man with a light olive complexion, agreed. "We men are very lazy! Malika works, making the same salary as her husband, but she also has to work at home. But we very much respect my daughter's hard work."

Nur nodded. "In Xinjiang, it's a man's world."

But at least one of his brothers brought a ladle of broth from the *kazan* for Malika to taste. And another made tea. We moved to the guest room. This time it was Nur and his brothers who spread out the *meze*.

When the rice was cooked to plump perfection, Malika divided the *polo* among several plates. I got a plate to myself, while the others were shared between pairs of family members. "We eat this with our hands," Nur told me. "That's why the Chinese called it *shouzhua fan*," which means "hand-grabbed rice." He offered me a spoon, but I declined, wanting to eat it the local way. They pushed the rice toward the center of the plate with their fingertips and scooped it into their mouths. The rice packed together more firmly in the center of the plate with every bite, like a giant mound of sushi rice. I marveled at how satisfying the meal was, and how little need there was for such supposed conveniences as a fancy kitchen, baby food, or even tableware.

In our Beijing neighborhood, Craig and I had frequented a couple of Uighur restaurants, arguing over which was better and compromising by going to each other's favorite. But now in Xinjiang, I realized that neither was authentic. Uighur restaurants were to China what Chinese restaurants were to America: cheap, convenient establishments that reliably offered about a dozen of the same dishes. In nearly every city across China, you could find at least one restaurant where a chef in a Muslim skullcap stood out front, grilling lamb skewers, while chefs inside made noodle dishes. It was Hui, or other Muslim minorities, though, that ran many of these establishments across the nation. I discovered that two noodle dishes I associated with the eateries weren't Uighur at all. A hand-pulled noodle dish called *laghman* was probably an offshoot of Hui hand-pulled noodles, *la mian*, given the dish's likeness in name and content, Uighurs admitted. And they disavowed another mainstay, big plate chicken (*dapanji*)—the spicy chicken stew with chewy tagliatelle-like noodles, which they said was also Hui. "We do not traditionally eat spicy food," explained a Uighur anthropologist I met in Urumqi. Nur's family and other Uighurs confirmed this. Finding out that big plate chicken was a fraud was like discovering that fortune cookies were not Chinese.

Uighurs did eat noodles, but bread—its predecessor—was popping up more frequently. It was baked most often in the beehive-shaped *tonur*s (a cousin of the Indian oven known as the tandoor) that were widespread across northwestern China. Bread, in fact, was so important that communities in Xinjiang were often dotted with small, noncommercial bakeries, usually family-run, their sole purpose to bake *nang* and deliver it to nearby homes. I also came across sesame rings called *gerde* that resembled bagels, hole and all. Some enterprising hoteliers catering to foreign tourists even paired the rings with little packets of cream cheese. (It was utterly surreal to be in China, eating a New York breakfast, watching locals who looked European ambling their way to mosque.)

To the Uighurs, bread was sacred. "We cannot live without bread," a Uighur I later met told me. "When we get married, we eat *nang* with salt water as a tradition. We are not allowed to throw *nang* away, however old it might be." I got a sense of how important bread was at Nur's home. In the mornings, we started the day with pieces of hardened *nang*, dipped in the earthy Taklamakan Desert tea or milk to soften it, a way of eating it that allowed the bread to sit on the shelf as long as breakfast cereal. One afternoon, Nur, his father, and I went on an outing and his father brought several rounds of *nang* with him. Any length of travel, even if it was just a few hours, required bread.

I'd finally left behind the vegetable and meat stir-fries that were common across China. In their place was a bounty of the region's nuts and fruits, famous throughout the country; in nearly every large city, Uighur vendors on bicycles pulled wagons behind them filled with walnuts, almonds, and pistachios, along with dried apricots, melons, and grapes. The almonds all had that extract-like intensity. Raisins, both the black and golden variety, were so plump and sweet that even a trick-or-treater wouldn't object to them. Sometimes the fruits and nuts were pressed together with grape molasses called *pekmez* (an ingredient I would see later in my journey) and eaten as a candy called *matang*. And the fresh fruit was even better than the dried, particularly the melons. I fell head over heels for the *hami* melon, a ten-pound football-shaped cousin of the cantaloupe. It had the same ridged exterior and orange-hued flesh, but it was far juicier and sweeter, and crisp like a watermelon. More than once in Xinjiang, I bought a gigantic *hami* melon just for myself and came shockingly close to finishing it.

. . .

The next time Malika and I cooked together, she showed me how to make *poshkal*, Uighur crepes with Chinese chives. Now that I'd spent a few days in the village, the cooking was less of an event and the men left us alone. And once I'd gotten over my hesitation to use Mandarin, I'd discovered that Malika spoke it well, allowing us to communicate freely.

It was around seven in the evening, well before sundown, and the outdoor speakers in the neighborhood were blasting the government-approved news in Uighur. I helped Malika mince a bunch of Chinese chives. Han Chinese often stuffed the long green shoots and scrambled eggs into their dumplings, but I'd always found the vegetable overpowering. They kept popping up along my journey, though, and each time I found them in a new dish, I appreciated them more. Before long, I began to crave them.

The knife I used was long and thin, perfect for slicing enormous melons but not so convenient for mincing, a less important skill in Uighur cuisine than in Han Chinese. While I minced, Malika made the batter. She wiggled her fingers through the stream of flour she poured, to sift it. She mixed in eggs, water, and salt before folding in the chives. She placed a wok over the fire, opting for the Chinese pan because it was smoother and wider than a *kazan*. To make each crepe, she added a healthy ladleful of oil, then poured some batter along the inside edges of the wok, tilting the pan to allow the batter to coat it evenly. When it had firmed into a thin sheet, she removed it and started another. Watching the pancakes come off the wok, I noticed they were reminiscent of one of my favorite Beijing snacks, *jian bing*—wheat-flour crepes cooked on a griddle and served with a sprinkle of coriander and leeks.

As we cooked, Malika opened up. Ever since her mother had died the decade before, she had taken on the household duties, she said. "I was nineteen. My youngest brother was five. It was very difficult for all of us, but my father found another wife two years later." I'd met the stepmother, but she didn't seem close to the children, nor did she live with the family. Nur had told me that she was in the care of other relatives because she was suffering from a heart condition. She'd come to the house once, dressed in a thick smock and counting a string of beads she held in her hand, a tradition shared by Muslims, Buddhists, and Catholics. "Look at how religious she is," Nur had said with scorn.

I asked Malika if she liked to cook. She laughed. "Even if I didn't like it, what could I do about it?"

She told me her job was extra busy around this time of year because the new school year had just begun. I asked if many women in Xinjiang worked, given that many Uighurs continued to be devoutly Muslim. Malika said her situation wasn't unique; although Uighur women traditionally hadn't worked outside their homes, nowadays most were employed, like most women in China. The majority of Uighur women I met, though, stuck to a traditionally female profession like nursing or teaching. "The local imam declared a while ago that it was okay for women to work," Malika said. But women still faced certain restrictions, like a socially enforced dress code that pressured them to wear head scarves, shirts with sleeves that at least covered their elbows, and skirts that hit below the knee. Pants were frowned upon.

"What do you think of those rules?" I asked.

"Islam is loosening up. It's much less strict than it used to be. The imam declaring that women can work was a big step. Anyways," she added, "if my husband made enough money, I wouldn't have a problem not working!"

But that wasn't the case, so every morning Malika dropped off her children with her retired father, fixed their lunch, and dashed off to work. After finishing the school day around six in the evening, she and her husband met at her father's home, and she started the evening chores while the men watched television. Only after dinner did she bundle up her children so that she and her husband could drive them back to their apartment a few miles away. As she spoke about her daily routine, I was struck that it didn't sound so different from the lives of American friends who'd recently become parents.

Malika asked about my journey. How long was I traveling for? Where was I going? And when would my husband join me?

As I explained where I'd been and where I was going, she suddenly interrupted: "You know, I really admire you. You're so free and independent!"

As I'd traveled west from Beijing, it felt as if I was drifting farther from the familiar. After Xi'an, I'd met a Han noodle maker who'd furtively told me her marriage was arranged. In the Tibetan region, Isabel and I had mostly socialized with her male friends. In Xinjiang, more women covered their hair with head scarves, sometimes even their entire faces with burqas. My conversations with women became briefer. I often felt more comfortable with their husbands or brothers or fathers. Now, in this small Uighur village, having found a woman who was instantly at ease with me, spoke so directly, and admired what I was doing, I could not think how to respond.

So instead of saying anything, I stood closer to her, and she to me. Elbow to elbow, we finished cooking. Her son flung a pile of flour into the air, which landed on him like a cloud of desert dust. Occasionally, she shooed her daughter away from the fire. Inside, she had several hungry men waiting for dinner.

The truth was, I was afraid of becoming Malika, a wife burdened with household duties while also juggling a job. But that was the farthest thing from my mind when Craig formally proposed, six months after I'd impulsively blathered that I would marry him. We were at a restaurant set in a fruit orchard on the outskirts of Beijing. We'd just finished a weekend of hiking along the Great Wall, and as we strolled among the trees after a hearty dinner, he unexpectedly paused, pulled out a box with a ring, and asked me to marry him. Through my sobs, I blubbered, "Yes."

We married in San Diego, in a small park overlooking the Pacific, before our closest family and friends, and I wept just as I had when he'd proposed. We said our vows, including the one I'd suggested, to put our relationship before our careers. And after a honeymoon on idyllic Kauai, we settled into our new life as a married couple in Beijing.

Where, after finishing my first book, opening a cooking school, and planning a wedding, I suddenly felt empty. Let down. I had nothing monumental on the horizon. And the realization hit me: almost overnight, it seemed, I'd gone from being a single, independent woman to a wife.

Yikes, a wife. After the wedding, the word sounded so patriarchal, so foreign, so *not me*. I felt guilty. This was what I'd wanted, wasn't it? I was married to the man of my dreams. How could I be unhappy? But *wife* conjured the image of the dissatisfied woman that Betty Friedan had described in *The Feminine Mystique*, who, in my version, wore hair curlers and a robe and yelled at neighborhood cats from a second-floor window of a sprawling, lonely suburban home.

One day, after I'd heard Craig say "wife" on the phone, I asked him if he could call me something else. "Um, okay," he said, not sure whether to laugh or be alarmed. Could I suggest an alternative? But I wasn't anything else—I was a wife, even if he called me partner or spouse or even *airen*, the nice-sounding Chinese word that literally means "lover" but refers to spouses. I couldn't go back to the carefree days of being a girlfriend or a fiancée, with the optimism, the unburdened promise that those words carried.

And then other things I'd thought I wanted before the wedding, like changing my name, began to seem more complicated. I'd figured that I'd change my last name legally but continue using my maiden one professionally. I'd gone through the legal process once before; as a child I'd changed my given name from Ching-Yee to Jennifer—an indication of my identity struggle. But officially going from Lin-Liu to Simons would be entirely different in China, a country where married women keep their maiden name and where the process would take months and involve bureaucratic nightmares. Then I realized changing my name would also mean changing my signature, which seemed bizarre. All the credit card slips, the checks, the books I'd signed as an author would be forever different. And finally I had to admit to myself the biggest reason of all: having no part of my name be Chinese, as conflicted as I was about my identity, seemed just too strange.

These struggles were exacerbated by the turmoil of trying to figure out our lives. Just months after we married, Cox Newspapers folded its foreign bureaus, ending Craig's job. He went back to freelance writing, and soon after he was awarded the yearlong science writing fellowship at MIT, in Cambridge, Massachusetts. It was a path I'd supported, and I'd offered to come along for most of the year. But when it actually came time for his fellowship to begin, I panicked. I was not just a wife; now I was also becoming a *trailing spouse*. What would I do about the cooking school? What about my writing career in China?

Craig had hoped I'd spend most of my time in Cambridge and thought that we could use the year to plot a new course. After spending almost a decade in China, he wanted a new challenge. But, for plenty of reasons, I still wasn't quite ready to leave China. So I spent the year bouncing between opposite sides of the world. In Beijing, I worked at the cooking school and wrote freelance articles. In Cambridge, I took classes at Harvard and read in the libraries. And in my spare time, I cooked.

Though I was a food writer and a trained chef, I didn't cook at home often when we lived in Beijing. China's cheap and delicious selection of restaurants made going out too easy. But in the States, restaurants were expensive, so cooking was the default. Plus, in my image of an idyllic American marriage, eating a home-cooked dinner was a nightly ritual that families were supposed to engage in. It seemed the very foundation of domestic life.

Aside from occasional trips to the Chinese supermarket across the Charles River, I discovered to my delight that there was a Whole Foods nearby, chock-full of organic produce, glistening herbs, and fresh seafood. Craig and I made weekend trips there on our bicycles, filling our knapsacks with groceries whose price tags outraged Craig. ("Whole paycheck," he would mutter as we pedaled away.) During the week, I spent my late afternoons and early evenings in our little apartment kitchen, cooking. But instead of enjoying the ritual, I began to resent it. Craig occasionally would pad in to help wash vegetables or do a little chopping, but then he would just as easily slip out into another room. And there I was, feeling like I was chained to the kitchen, monitoring several bubbling pots and staring at a cutting board heaped with half-minced vegetables.

One evening, as Craig was fixing himself a drink and settling into a plate of cheese and crackers and I was at the stove, I dissolved into a flood of tears. I didn't like doing all of the cooking by myself, I sobbed.

Craig pointed out that I always wanted to decide the menu. I was tyrannical about making everything from scratch. I considered the kitchen my domain. And I refused to order in cheap takeout, insisting that we live up to some Norman Rockwell ideal of domestic life.

But in my revised version of it, the husband contributed equally to the cooking. It wasn't that I wanted Craig to slave away at the stove alone, either; I envisioned cooking as something *fun* we could do together.

"You know me well enough," Craig said. Cooking wasn't something he considered fun, he reminded me. But seeing me in such a state, he gave me a hug and relented: if home-cooked meals were what I wanted, he would try to be supportive and contribute more.

Craig made an effort, but I could tell that he would rather be doing something else, and often I would just shoo him out and relieve him of the tasks he reluctantly undertook. Much of the time, I still found myself alone in the kitchen, sometimes grumbling to myself. I was beginning to realize that I was conflicted by what had become my livelihood. Now that cooking had become a monotonous domestic chore, a duty that had been imposed on me, I wasn't loving it so much. I was confused, though, as to who was doing the imposing—was it Craig, was it society, or was it simply me?

I'd truly enjoyed my stay in Nur's home. Each morning, I conversed with Nur and his father in my feeble Uighur while eating a breakfast of *nang* and tea with them. I took walks in the surrounding countryside, flat farmland where houses sat on roomy, irrigated plots and young children played in the sand. When Malika returned from work, we cooked, chatting as we chopped and stirred. But there was one thing that bothered me.

"I don't think they bathe here," I whispered to Craig on the phone one night.

"Why don't you ask about it?" he suggested.

"Don't be silly!" I said. I didn't want to ask about bathing, lest I embarrass my hosts. As in many homes I'd visited, I didn't see any running water. In the mornings and evenings, I brushed my teeth and washed my face in the courtyard, beneath a low spigot. Calls of nature were answered in the outhouse. Malika washed dishes with water that came from a metal drum. So I made do with a wet towel wipe-down every evening. My hair felt a little greasy by the third day, but I discovered no difference between three-day and five-day unwashed hair. Bizarrely, everyone around me seemed to remain fairly fresh. Maybe the arid climate helped?

Finally, on the day I was to leave, I asked Nur, "Can I, uh, wash my hair?"

"You mean, you want to shower?" Nur said. "I'll prepare some hot water for you." As I conjured an image of my scrawny host engaging in some backbreaking task of heating and hauling buckets of water, he walked down the hall, pushed open a door, and flipped a switch. Behind the door was a white-tiled room with a perfectly modern shower. It was, in fact, the most luxurious shower I'd seen in weeks.

"So sorry!" Nur said after I emerged. An impish smile spread over his face. "I forgot to tell you about the shower. Why didn't you ask?"

Nur's absentmindedness also created plenty of drama around my departure. I'd decided to fly back to Urumqi and from there continue my journey west. Nur had arranged for Malika's husband to take us to the airport. (Nur would fly to Urumqi with me and then continue on to Beijing.) When the appointed time came and went, he called his brother-in-law. He was still more than an hour's drive away, he told Nur. They finally worked out that Nur had stated our departure in Beijing time, the official time that all of China ran on, while Nur's brother-in-law thought he'd meant the unofficial local time, three hours behind, on which most Uighurs ran their lives.

With just an hour before our flight was supposed to leave, we had no time to wait for Malika's husband. So we ran. We ran through the sandy streets of Nur's village, my backpack strapped to me and a knapsack slung over Nur's back, while an uncle, carrying a suitcase on his head, and Nur's father trailed behind us. Once we turned out of the village, we ran some more, on a side street that led to a highway. On the side of the highway, we tried to hail a taxi. But none were free. One occupied taxi slowed down, seeing the frantic expression on our faces. After Nur explained the situation, the passengers—a woman and two children—generously climbed out and Nur, his father, and I hopped in, waving good-bye to the uncle and profusely offering our thanks to the strangers as we puttered off. The driver, though, went at a leisurely pace—"I think this driver is a little chicken," Nur said—and twice we were stopped, by roadblocks the police had set up to monitor locals. We got to the airport twenty-five minutes before our departure time.

At the security gate, we slowed down for a moment and said good-bye to Nur's father. "I'm sorry Nur didn't take care of you better. But you're like a daughter to us and please come back and visit again," he said. Before we boarded our flight that would take Nur far away from his family for months, possibly even more than a year, Nur's father embraced him tenderly and handed him his knapsack. Inside were a dozen rounds of *nang*.

After Nur and I parted ways, Craig joined me in Urumqi, the capital of Xinjiang. Over his three-hour flight from Beijing, he covered as much distance as I had in a month. It was around midnight when he arrived at the guesthouse I'd booked. We were used to traveling apart for long periods and reuniting in random cities. But given the distance I'd traveled and all the things I'd seen and eaten, it seemed much longer than a month since we'd seen each other. It felt a little unreal to see my six-foot-tall husband emerging from the taxi to join me in a grungy hostel in this far-flung desert province. But after we embraced, and I felt his sandy brown hair underneath his baseball cap and looked into his bright blue eyes, it felt like he was coming home.

The next morning, I was excited to have Craig taste some authentic Uighur dishes. But as we left the motel, around nine o'clock Beijing time, we discovered that Urumqi, like the rest of Xinjiang, was still in slumber, with their clocks set three hours behind. The only storefront with its lights on was a Kentucky Fried Chicken.

"I'm not so sure I want to go in there," Craig said warily. I was surprised. He was usually okay with KFC, particularly in transit. "You want to portray me as a food neophyte."

It wasn't a baseless accusation. In my first book, along with describing him as the handsome, intelligent man he is, I'd exaggerated Craig's disinterest in food. He claimed I'd maligned him, and we'd laughed about it. But one day he'd read selected passages out loud, and I had to admit, my words did sound a little unfair.

But KFC was the only restaurant open at that hour. "Where else are we going to go?" I asked. I promised I would not use his compliance against him. So we pushed open the door to the last corporate fast food we would see for thousands of miles.

I had mixed feelings about fast food, especially overseas. I disliked the cultural homogenization it represented and the fact that it gave travelers an easy way to avoid local food. But I didn't object to it for health reasons—how many restaurant meals were actually good for you, after all? And in China, KFC was pretty good. Their fried chicken aside, they'd localized the food. They spiked their chicken burger with spices and served one of the better Chinese breakfasts: egg tarts and soy milk with savory crullers called *you-tiao*. I'd always enjoyed the egg tarts—the crisp and light pastry and the sweet and smooth eggy filling made them as good as ones at fancy dim sum restaurants. But as I sank my teeth into the sweet that morning, I remembered what Bai, the Hui food writer, had said about KFC. They hadn't taken any steps to localize their menu for Muslim minorities—they catered only to Han Chinese.

Craig and I spent a couple days poking around Urumqi and its surrounding areas. We visited the museum with the fourteen-hundred-year-old dumpling—though small and shriveled, it was more intact than the four-thousand-year-old noodle. We visited the *karez*, underground canals that had irrigated desert farmland for centuries. But in general, the area felt little different from eastern China, so we cut our time short and went on to Kashgar, the ancient Silk Road trading post. On the twenty-four-hour train ride, I got a much better feel for the expansiveness of Xinjiang's deserts than I had on the plane. I said as much to Craig when we were playing cards in the dining car in the afternoon.

"These are not deserts," declared one of the Han train conductors, who'd heard me use the Chinese word *sha mo*.

"What are they?" I asked.

She used a word I didn't recognize.

"Maybe it's similar to how Eskimos have lots of words for snow," Craig said.

The next day, we arrived in Kashgar, the most Uighur town in Xinjiang. At the western edge of the Taklamakan Desert and near the foot of the Pamirs and the Tien Shan mountain ranges, the city had been a trading post for Central Asians and Chinese for two millennia. The British and Russians had set up consulates in the town in the late nineteenth century as part of their Great Game tussle over the region. Though the British influence had faded, Russians, along with Central Asians, still frequented the city to make deals on carpets, food, and bric-a-brac. But even here the government was doing its best to Hanify the city. They were shutting down bazaars and tearing down old neighborhoods. In their place, modern shopping arcades and towers rose. But still, the remaining parts of the old quarter retained their character. The dusty narrow alleys and the clay exteriors of homes were so similar to a typical Afghan neighborhood that Hollywood producers filmed *The Kite Runner* there.

As I would see in other places along the Silk Road, it was the food that made the neighborhood come alive. I initially thought that visiting Xinjiang during Ramadan was a stroke of bad planning. But, as I learned at Nur's, the holiday highlighted the importance of food, making clear the contrast of life with and without sustenance. In the mornings, the Kashgar neighborhood where I stayed was languid. The baker sat listlessly in front of his hearth, slowly baking large round pieces of *nang*. Wafting from the oven was a scent that reminded me of freshly baked pizza, making me realize it was the dough, not the sauce or the toppings, that provided pizza's essential fragrance. The scent went to waste in the alleys as the sun rose; the *nang* the baker stacked on his table remained untouched. The butcher stared into space next to a lamb carcass hanging from a hook, the price per kilogram written on a changeable placard. At an open-air general store, tea leaves and spices sat in crates undisturbed as the day grew hotter. In one supermarket near the bazaar, most of the aisles were empty of customers except for the drink aisle, where fasters sometimes parked themselves and gazed at cans of Coca-Cola and pomegranate juice as a test of will.

In the late afternoon, the neighborhood began to stir. Vendors appeared on the streets, setting out wicker baskets neatly stacked with flat yellow figs, unloading melons from the backs of trucks, and opening large vats filled with homemade yogurt. They heated up griddles and ovens, preparing to make Russian-style crepes, called blini, and savory breads. After a long, hungry day, shoppers began to arrive, the slow trickle of customers quickly growing to a torrent that swept along motorbikes, dogs, and children. By dusk, the chaos reached fever pitch, the vendors shouting prices and flaunting their wares as shoppers, getting more famished by the second, jostled in messy queues.

Craig and I were drawn to one stand with a very long line of people holding out money and waiting in hungry anticipation. They had gathered in front of a *tonur* that was producing something that looked like cinnamon raisin bagels. When I got a little closer, I saw that the bread was indeed shaped like a puffy bagel, but without a hole, and it was not raisins that flecked the surface but little brown bits of lamb. People were buying them, but as it was not yet sundown, they abstained from eating the fresh buns.

Anticipation was building. Scattered around the neighborhood were little stands set up by the community that offered free slices of watermelon and bread at sundown. We turned a corner and ran into the biggest wok I'd ever seen. It was larger than a kiddie pool and filled with bubbling rice pilaf. Every so often, the chef circled the perimeter of the wok, pouring in broth from a kettle. The pilaf glistened with carrots and lamb, and the scent of cumin and onions wafted in the air. The chef said he'd been cooking since two in the afternoon and, now, just as the sun dropped below the horizon, he doled out large ladlefuls of the pilaf. Everyone had brought their own cups and plates for the food, which anonymous donors sponsored every night during the month. Someone offered us a plastic bag and into it went a ladle of rice pilaf, a dish I was growing more familiar with by the day.

"Allah says that if you do good deeds during Ramadan, you will be rewarded seven hundred times in your afterlife," the chef said.

In Kashgar, Craig and I fell into a pattern that was an adaptation of our life together in Beijing. We would have breakfast together, and then we would pursue our separate work. I would go off for a cooking class or an excursion, and Craig, who'd gotten a few magazines interested in Silk Road articles, would go out to report or stay in to work on his book. In the late afternoon, we would meet and take a walk and settle in for dinner, usually at a restaurant. This became our routine, or as much of one as we could construct on the road.

After breakfast one morning, I met with a beret-wearing Uighur guide named Elvis, who offered to arrange cooking classes for me. "I know a woman who is a very good cook," he said in a nasal voice. "But we'll see if she's willing to cook for you." He was a pessimistic fellow. The guiding business wasn't going so well, he said. The crackdown on Uighurs had scared many tourists away.

I asked him how he'd ended up with a name like Elvis. He told me there was a better-known Han Chinese guide in the city, named John. He wanted to be more famous than John, so one foreigner he'd guided recommended that he name himself Elvis.

Then he talked about my name. "Did you know that Jen means 'the devil' in Uighur?" he said with a laugh. Every so often, as I learned Uighur dishes and he translated by my side, he would brighten. "After you learn these dishes, you can invite your friends to your home and have a Uighur party!" he'd say.

Elvis introduced me to his friend Hayal, who lived in the old quarter. In her late fifties, she was a regal woman with auburn hair, a rosy complexion, and a beak-like nose. She wore flowery frocks that flowed to her ankles, and covered her hair (but not her face) with a head scarf of light brown mesh. She lived in a beautiful walled-in compound on Uzbek Lane, named such because the alley's inhabitants, including Hayal's family, had migrated from Uzbekistan more than a century before. (Uighurs and Uzbeks are ethnically and culturally similar and have moved between China and Central Asia for centuries.) Though the two-story home was built around a courtyard, like other homes I'd seen in China, it felt more European with its rosebushes and fig trees. As in Nur's home, the grandest room was for guests. I spent most of my time there, and on the airy porch before it, where Hayal taught me Uighur noodle dishes.

She began with *chuchura*, small dumplings that reminded me of wontons in soup. As in many places on the Silk Road, the dumpling filling was lamb, or more accurately, mutton, the meat of a mature sheep. She called for her daughter-in-law, a pretty woman named Ana, who appeared in the room with a large ax that Hayal used to hack apart the meat. She separated the gristle, fat, and a large bone and boiled them in an electric rice cooker with tomatoes, onions, and radishes to make soup. With a knife, she minced the tender meat for the filling. The meat was so fresh that it didn't have the gamy smell I associated with mutton. She chopped up coriander stems and onions and added them to the filling, seasoning it with black pepper, ground cumin, and "a little salt," as the Uighur woman described it, dumping in two heaping spoonfuls.

The wrappers were made with flour, salt, water, and egg—making them more similar to Italian pasta. The rolling pin Hayal used, which was larger in diameter than Chinese ones and came with handles, also reminded me more of the West. She rolled out the dough into a thin sheet and cut the sheet into two-inch squares. She took a wrapper, added a tiny dollop of meat to the center, folded it in half, and pinched the two opposite edges together. The dough was so pliable that, like fresh Chinese dumpling skins, it didn't need to be moistened at the edges before being sealed. After we finished wrapping, she added the dumplings to the soup, along with left-over scraps of dough, and boiled them for a few minutes before serving the dumplings, the scraps, and the soup together. The mutton fat had made the broth smooth and silky, and there was just enough filling in the *chuchura* to impart flavor but not take away from the tender wrappers. Hayal was indeed an excellent cook, as Elvis had claimed. It was prescient that she had started with *chuchura* as well—I would continue to see replicas of this dish as I went west, all the way to Italy.

Another day we made *manta*, Uighur steamed dumplings. The name sounded like Chinese *mantou*, steamed bread buns, but *manta* were stuffed like Chinese dumplings, albeit with a higher proportion of meat to dough, a reflection of the importance of meat in the Uighur diet. Hayal placed a pound of marbled mutton on a wooden cutting board and minced it with a curved blade. It was not just meat that gave *manta* its distinctive taste, but fat—she pointed at the white streaks on the mutton and said, "Without fat, the *manta* won't be delicious." After finely chopping the meat, she mixed in the same flavorings as for *chuchura*—minced white onion, ground cumin, black pepper, and a generous dose of salt—the main seasonings of Uighur food, as important as ginger, leek, and garlic were to northern Chinese food.

Hayal ordered her daughter-in-law to roll out the wrappers, using the same dough as for *chuchura*. Ana rolled out a wrapper to about the size of a Chinese dumpling. The mother-in-law grabbed the pin from her daughter-in-law. "You're doing it wrong!" she growled before flattening it into a larger, thinner disk. She placed a large spoonful of meat in its center and pinched together the edges at the top so that the dumpling was shaped like a shoe and the folds resembled laces threaded together. After the *manta* were steamed, Hayal served them with clotted sheep's cream. Gone were the vinegar, soy sauce, and chili oil that garnished Chinese dumplings; in their place entered dairy, the first I'd seen of it other than yogurt. The dumplings were hearty and rich; just a few were enough to fill my stomach.

Hayal was more observant than Nur and his family. She rose every day at six to read the Koran. Even as she taught me how to cook, she abstained from eating. She told me that Islam taught that guests were sent from God; that was why she'd invited me into her home. She saw it as her duty to accommodate me. But her hospitality had limits; she would not allow me to touch any meat in her home because I wasn't halal, which meant I often sat by idly as she worked.

As Hayal was teaching me how to make rice pilaf one morning, her sister came by. She entered the courtyard as a giant blob, her head and face covered by a thick brown burqa, her body enveloped in a long black robe down to her ankles that reminded me of a nun's habit. She lifted the burqa, folding it behind her forehead once the door was safely closed. The first time I'd visited Kashgar, the coverings had startled me. They had seemed so backward, so oppressive—I couldn't quite understand how women would submit to walking around town so veiled, particularly in the heat of summer.

The sister watched as Hayal and I cooked, smiling nostalgically. One of her sons had recently gotten married, so she no longer had to cook. "Now my daughter-in-law does all the cooking!" she said with a cackle.

Hayal groaned. Her own daughter-in-law was useless, she said. She'd been wrong in thinking the girl would be a good match for her son. "Sometimes I have to call her three times before she comes over. And she barely knows how to cook!"

Ana was within earshot. It also didn't seem to matter that Hayal had a maid, a young teenage girl from the countryside whom she treated with equal disdain, or that Ana had just had a baby and was supposed to be resting, on leave from her job as a nurse. ("I can't wait to get back to work," Ana whispered to me in a furtive moment.) During my lessons, as the hired help sat by listlessly, Hayal fired off a litany of orders at Ana: bring the ax, bring the knife, bring the water, roll the dumplings, take the cutting board and knife away.

I asked Hayal's sister why she wore the veil.

"It protects me from the evil eye of strange men outside the home," she said. I'd heard about the evil eye from other Uighurs—a bad spirit that lurked, sometimes in another person whose gaze could inflict damage should it fall upon you.

"Does your husband make you wear the veil?" I asked.

"He prefers that I wear it," she said, but she made it clear that the driving force was her own desire to protect herself.

I asked if any of her daughters wore the veil.

"No," she said, glancing at my capri pants and long-sleeved sweater. "They wear the same things as you. I hope one day they will wear the veil, too, but they will have to choose for themselves."

She turned her attention to the fig tree in the courtyard. "It looks sick," she said. "Somebody must have given it the evil eye."

"We must pray to bring it back to health," Hayal agreed.

I was praying for my own health a few days later, when my digestive tract went haywire from all the changes in my diet. When I told Craig I was going to see a traditional Uighur doctor, he was skeptical. He didn't believe in traditional medicine. I was agnostic but was willing to give it a try.

As at most Chinese hospitals, privacy was a foreign concept at the Uighur clinic. The door to the consulting room remained open throughout my visit, and people waiting for their own appointments watched as the doctor poked and prodded me. At one point, a woman barged in and asked the doctor to write her a note for her employer. ("It would be nice if you could say I was sick for five days," she said.) Fortunately, the doctor didn't require me to undress.

"Stick out your tongue," he said. I obliged, hesitantly. "Stick it out farther!" he commanded. I did my best to channel my five-year-old self. He winced, as if the sight confirmed his worst fears. "You have a lot of *yel.*"

"What's *yel*?" I asked, stealing a glance in the mirror. It was an invisible concept, like the evil eye. As he explained more, it sounded something like *huoqi*, fire-air, a Chinese concept that my grandmother often talked about when I was a child.

The general idea of Uighur traditional medicine, like its Chinese counterpart, and other forms I would encounter along the Silk Road, was of balancing forces in the body—hot and cold, and to a lesser extent, wet and dry—to maintain one's health. Everything a person ate could be categorized as "hot" or "cold"; though temperature might be one factor, it was more about how the food interacted with one's body. Individuals were also diagnosed with "hotter" or "colder" dispositions, which could be balanced out by consuming certain foods. Having too much *yel*, or *huoqi*, meant that I had too much internal heat, which could cause a range of issues, including pimples, rashes, canker sores, or, as in my case, digestive troubles.

The doctor told me to stop showering—exposing my body to torrents of water would exacerbate my problem. (That didn't sound so difficult, given that I'd just gone a week without a shower.) He recommended that I stop consuming milk as well (not a problem, either, as I am lactose intolerant and avoid milk) and fruit (a little harder, given the delicious produce). And noodles. The gluten in the noodles would work my stomach into bigger knots, he explained. That was a complete nonstarter. There was no way I could give up the dish that had inspired my journey. But I decided not to argue and instead nodded politely.

"We have all kinds of medicine that can help," he said. "All you have to do is pay between twelve and fifteen dollars and you'll feel much better."

"Can I feel better for, say, seven dollars?" I asked. I couldn't resist. Bargaining had become second nature, having lived in China for so long.

"Sure," he said, chuckling as he wrote the prescription, which I collected from the pharmacy downstairs.

Back in my hotel room, I unfolded the camping spork that Craig traveled with and sniffed and tasted the various substances. One seemed to be a paste of crushed rose petals and sugar—I imagined it would go quite well on toast—while another was a sugary paste flavored with mint, which I later added to tea. The third jar contained cumin, cinnamon, black pepper, and ginger mixed with a sticky, tarry substance that reminded me of Vegemite, the Australian yeast-based condiment. That jar I could have done without.

The idea of food as medicine was on display all along the Silk Road, and the farther I traveled, the more I wondered how the West had strayed from the idea. Americans could recite the old adage "You are what you eat," but they'd forgotten what it meant as they chowed down on increasing amounts of processed food.

Still, while the concept in general made perfect sense, the specific principles were hard to apply. Despite being raised by Chinese parents and having lived in China for a decade, I was still baffled by what was hot or cold. Oranges, despite the vitamin C, were not to be eaten when you had a cold, because they were hot. Lychees were especially warming—eat one too many and you'd develop blisters in your mouth. Watermelon was cooling, which made intuitive sense, as did the fact that fried and spicy foods were both hot. But then chickens were hot and ducks were cooling—"That's because ducks are often in or near water," one Chinese friend explained.

Along my trip, I received bewildering advice about which foods cured or exacerbated ailments. On one train trip in eastern China, my fellow passengers—who happened to be randomly conversing about food, as Chinese often do—advised me to eat black sesame if I wanted to prevent gray hair. Chairman Wang warned me never to drink cold water, no matter how hot it was outside, because it was detrimental to my overall health. In Xinjiang, Uighurs told me walnuts would make me smarter and that aloe and watermelon, eaten together, would relieve headaches and eye infections. And black sesame? That didn't ward off gray hair in Xinjiang. There it reduced high blood pressure. (Maybe it did both.) And, of course, rhubarb cured constipation, something I'd learned in my research.

Confused by all this, I decided to skip food altogether for a day. I approached the challenge with some trepidation. I'd never fasted before. Fasting was only part of Chinese tradition when it was forced upon you—for example, if you were in a famine. Why would a people who had experienced so much hardship voluntarily fast? Many Chinese I knew ate at regimented times every day, preferring to start their lunches and dinners just before noon and six. And they ate heartily, until every last grain of rice was gone. When I dined with my paternal grandmother, who'd almost starved to death during World War II, she often scolded and goaded me until I finished every last speck off my plate.

But it was Ramadan, and what better opportunity to fast—particularly if I could find a partner. Craig, not wanting to interfere with my work, suggested I fast with a local (he wasn't much of a faster, either). But Elvis wasn't fasting and anyway his glumness had begun to wear on me, along with his strange superstitions that reminded me of Hayal and her sister. He proclaimed how religious he was, despite not fasting (for health reasons, he said) and didn't pray five times a day, as most observant Sunni Muslims do. He explained it was okay, though, because he attended five o'clock prayers at the mosque, the time "when the angels come down every day and report to God."

Craig had asked the question I was too timid to pose. "But aren't you tricking the angels if you only go to prayers at five?" he said, in his journalistic deadpan.

"No, it's not a problem," Elvis said defensively.

Thankfully, around then I'd met Mahmood, a guide who worked in our ragged three-star hotel. As Mahmood took me around town, I was impressed with his decorum. He opened doors for me and poured me tea, and stooped to rearrange chipped blocks on the sidewalk so people didn't trip. I was even more impressed when I found out he was fasting for the entire month, while going about his usual routines. He offered to help me through my fast.

We agreed to start by meeting for a predawn meal of rice pilaf. I'd gone to bed early the night before but hadn't slept well. That evening, Craig and I had eaten at a Pakistani restaurant, opened by a family of women from Pakistan who'd crossed into China several years before and made a steady business out of feeding traders from their country. We'd had a delicious beef and chickpea stew called *queema*, and *chapatis*, grilled flatbread that resembled Chinese ones. We'd washed the meal down with many cups of chai. It must have been the chai. We tossed and turned, and Craig finally inflated his camping mattress and settled onto the floor. When at last I drifted off to sleep, I had strange dreams involving the cooking school. I'd employed a midget and the kitchen had morphed into an ice cream parlor selling soft-serve. I was abruptly jolted from the dream when my alarm went off at four-thirty. In the dark, I went downstairs and found an empty lobby. I called Mahmood to wake him up.

A thin crescent moon shined as we walked toward the restaurant. Apart from a donkey cart that rolled by, the street was empty, but in front of the restaurant, diners in various degrees of wakefulness waited at outdoor tables. A bright-eyed chef stirred an enormous wok of rice pilaf. I wondered why he looked so alert. It turned out that during Ramadan, he reversed his routine, waking up around sunset to prepare dinner, and going to bed only after he cooked the morning meal. "You can come tomorrow at one in the morning if you want to watch me make *polo*," he said cheerfully. I could barely muster a polite response.

The chef poured black tea that was as strong and smooth as Earl Grey, a special treat for Mahmood, one of his regulars. "Where are your friends?" the chef asked him.

They were all still asleep, my guide said. As the month went on, he explained to me, it got harder to stick with the fast.

We started with *nang*—good for an empty stomach, Mahmood said. We followed that with grapes, a salad of tomatoes, onions, and green peppers, and, finally, the main attraction: a heaping bowl of rice pilaf. Though I hadn't been hungry when I sat down, my appetite got bigger as I ate.

Mahmood advised me to adopt the chef's strategy and sleep during the day. "Sleeping is a good way to kill time." He was amused by the expression, which he'd just learned. "Don't exert yourself. Don't use your brain too much." As we gnawed hunks of mutton off their bones, my fasting partner mentioned that he'd recently guided a group of European women who didn't eat meat. He'd never met vegetarians before; the concept was foreign on most of the Silk Road.

I explained that vegetarians avoided meat for health, moral, or environmental reasons, or simply because they didn't like the taste of it. To Mahmood, those reasons were revolutionary. Perhaps some people could do it, he allowed, but not Muslims. "The Koran says that we must eat meat, halal meat, and we should be thankful for it. To not eat meat would affect the natural balance of the world."

I got two-thirds of the way through my pilaf before I was simply too full. My guide finished his before saying, "You're supposed to eat more in the morning, less at night. You will appreciate your food much more tonight!"

We walked to the main square to see how many other people were eating. The night market around the square was emptying out as a small stream of men headed toward the mosque. I asked Mahmood why only men were out. Only men went to mosque, he said, and maybe some of these men didn't have women to cook for them. That figured.

I went back to the hotel, where Craig was still sleeping. I downed half a liter of water just before the sun cracked the horizon, and fell back asleep. But my rest was disturbed by a constant urge to pee. And, annoyingly, when I woke at nine to go to Hayal's for my cooking lesson, I was thirsty again.

"You can't suddenly expect to become a camel just because you're fasting," my husband said as I left for class.

Hayal was disappointed to hear I was fasting.

"It's not going to save you," she said, kneading a large mound of dough for *laghman*, the Hui version of hand-pulled noodles. "You have to study the Koran and accept Islam if you don't want to go to hell." Plus, she'd labored over the noodles for me, stretching them using the same method as the noodle makers I'd seen back east. She hadn't spun them as thin, though, so thankfully they were a little less tempting. But she held out a spoonful of the stew that would top the noodles, like a witch with a potion. "Here, have a taste," she said.

The flavor of Sichuan peppercorns and tomatoes lingered in my mouth for hours, as did a dab of homemade mulberry jam Hayal had offered me. She seemed to take it as her personal mission to persuade me not to fast, as if I was disturbing the natural order of the world Mahmood had talked about.

I went back to the hotel to nap. When I woke, I realized that it wasn't skipping meals that was hard, it was forsaking all liquids, particularly in this arid desert climate at the height of summer. I always carried water with me. I hated feeling thirsty. Some people's worst nightmare was to die by drowning; the idea of dying of thirst was more dreadful to me. I broke down and guzzled an iced tea from the hotel's convenience store. I thought back to the fasters I'd seen in the supermarket near the bazaar, challenging themselves by gazing at soft drinks. That should qualify as an Olympic sport, I thought.

The tea assuaged my hunger until sundown, when Craig and I met up again with Mahmood.

"How was your day?" he asked me brightly.

"Not great," I said weakly.

We drifted around the evening market, trying to decide which item we'd eat at sundown. I came across the buns that looked like cinnamon raisin bagels again. They were baking in a *tonur* in the ground, around which a large line had formed. Little rounds of dough stuck to the inside of the oven to rise and brown, after which they were pulled out with an iron rod, one by one, and placed upon sheets of newspaper that were haphazardly thrust into the hands of the nearest shopper.

"Oh yes, *gush gerde*," Mahmood said. "That bread is so good we have a song about it." He began to sing a song in Uighur that went something like *"Gush gerde, gush gerde, my mother makes gush gerde . . ."* My mouth watered with anticipation as I stared into the oven.

We queued up. By a stroke of luck, sundown hit just as a batch of buns came out of the *tonur*. The baker shoved one into my hands. I juggled it like a hot potato before taking a bite. It was hot and crusty on the outside, chewy on the inside, just like a Lower East Side bagel. Perhaps it was something about the water or the hearth, or something about my hunger, but I could truthfully say that it was the most delicious bread I'd ever tasted. And the memory of that lamb bun would linger with me for the rest of my trip.

CHEF ZHANG'S HAND-ROLLED NOODLES/ANDREA'S PASTA

Serves 4

4 cups all-purpose flour
2 cups water for Chinese noodles or 4 extra-large eggs for
   Italian pasta

MAKE THE DOUGH:

Heap flour on a large, flat surface and make a well in the center.

For Chinese noodles: Pour 1 cup of water into the well and work it into the flour, mixing with your hands. Slowly add more water, about ¼ cup at a time, mixing thoroughly until all the flour has been incorporated and the dough is soft, pliable, and smooth.

For Italian pasta: Pour the eggs into the well and beat them with a fork, working in some of the flour, then continue mixing with your hands until all the flour has been incorporated and the dough is soft, pliable, and smooth. If it feels dry, knead in a few drops of water.

Transfer the dough to a clean surface and knead by hand or with a stand mixer for 3 to 5 minutes, then cover the dough with a damp cloth or wrap it in plastic and let it sit for at least 30 minutes.

ROLL OUT THE DOUGH:

Make sure the rolling surface is clean and dry, then dust it with flour. Break off a quarter of the dough to work with, leaving the rest under the damp cloth or wrapped in plastic. Knead the dough briefly, then flatten and stretch it with your hands into a rectangle. Sprinkle the dough with flour and flatten the dough with a rolling pin, forming a long rectangle about ¼ inch thick and about a third the width of the pin.

Starting with the end closest to you, flatten a small section of the dough, rolling the pin back and forth in a rapid and forceful motion. Pause frequently to sprinkle the rolling surface, the dough, and your pin with flour. Once you've flattened the first section, liberally flour the surface of the dough and roll it onto the pin, then move on to the next section, pushing down on the pin to make the layers thinner and wider (though not wider than the width of the pin). Unwind the dough occasionally and sprinkle it with additional flour to make sure the layers of dough don't stick together. If the dough gets too diffi-cult to work with, cut it in half crosswise and work one half at a time. Once you've flattened all the dough, unfurl it and check that it's uni-formly thin (but not paper-thin), flattening any thicker sections with the pin. The dough should be no more than 2 millimeters thick.

Wrap the dough once more around the pin, then, holding the pin above the board, unroll the dough so that it folds over itself in S-shaped layers about 3 inches wide. With a sharp knife, cut the dough crosswise. For standard Chinese noodles or taglioni, cut the dough into ⅛-inch-wide strands. For fettuccine, cut the dough into ½-inch-wide strands. Shake the noodles lightly with your fingers to separate the strands, then set them aside on a surface or plate sprinkled with flour while you roll out the rest of the dough, a quarter at a time.

COOK THE NOODLES:

Bring a large pot of water to a boil. Drop in the noodles/pasta. Boil Italian pasta for 2 to 3 minutes, Chinese noodles for 4 to 5 minutes.

(Chinese prefer softer noodles.) Italian pasta may also be allowed to dry for 2 to 3 hours before it is boiled, a step that will help to give it an al dente texture.

Remove the noodles/pasta from heat and drain. (Chinese noodles are often bathed quickly in cold water to stop the cooking process.)

Toss the Italian pasta with Arrabbiata Sauce or the Chinese noodles with Chef Zhang's Pork Belly Sauce (recipes follow). Or use another sauce of your choosing. Serve immediately.

ARRABBIATA SAUCE

Serves 4

1 *tablespoon olive oil*
1 *medium yellow onion, minced*
1 *clove garlic, minced*
2 *tablespoons tomato paste*
One 28-ounce can crushed tomatoes
½ *teaspoon dried red pepper flakes*
1 *tablespoon sugar*
¼ *cup red wine*
¼ *teaspoon salt*
¼ *teaspoon freshly ground black pepper*
Freshly chopped parsley

Heat the olive oil in a large frying pan over medium heat. Add the onions and garlic and cook for a few minutes, until the onions are soft. Stir in the tomato paste, crushed tomatoes, red pepper flakes, sugar, wine, salt, and black pepper. Bring to a boil, reduce the heat, and simmer for 15 minutes. Stir in the parsley and remove from the heat. Mix with Andrea's Pasta (p. 96) and serve immediately.

CHEF ZHANG'S PORK BELLY SAUCE

Serves 4

1 pound pork belly, cut into 1-inch cubes
¼ cup vegetable oil
¼ cup sugar
2 tablespoons plus ¼ cup light soy sauce
1 quart water
1 leek, white part only, cut into 1-inch pieces
2 thin, thumb-sized slices of ginger
4 star anise
2 bay leaves
1 tablespoon powdered chicken bouillon (optional)
2 whole dried red chili peppers
½ teaspoon salt

Fill a wok halfway with water and bring to a boil. Add the pork, return to a boil, and simmer for 2 minutes. Drain and set aside.

Place the wok over high heat until it is dry again, then add the vegetable oil and sugar. Stir vigorously until the mixture begins to caramelize. When it is reddish-brown, add the blanched pork, stir to coat with the sugar, then add 2 tablespoons of the soy sauce. Stir-fry for 2 to 3 minutes, then add the water, the remaining ¼ cup soy sauce, the leeks, ginger, star anise, bay leaves, bouillon, if using, red chili peppers, and salt. Bring to a boil, then reduce the heat and simmer for about an hour, until the sauce is thick. Discard the bay leaves.

Serve over Chef Zhang's Hand-Rolled Noodles (p. 96).

CHAIRMAN WANG'S DUMPLINGS WITH LAMB-AND-PUMPKIN FILLING

Makes 80 dumplings

FOR THE WRAPPERS:
4 cups all-purpose flour
2 cups water

FOR THE FILLING:
2/3 pound ground lamb
½ cup chicken stock
1/3 cup soy sauce
1 large egg
½ teaspoon salt
1 tablespoon sesame oil
1 teaspoon minced garlic
1 tablespoon minced leeks
½ teaspoon minced ginger
*2½ cups grated Dickinson pumpkin or butternut or
    other winter squash*

TO ACCOMPANY THE DUMPLINGS:
Shanxi black vinegar
Chili oil
Minced garlic

Make the wrappers: Prepare the dough as for Chef Zhang's Hand-Rolled Noodles/Andrea's Pasta (p. 96). After it has rested, divide it into four equal pieces. Working with one piece at a time (keep the others covered with a damp cloth so they don't dry out), use your palms to roll it into a long rope, about ¾ inch in diameter. Slice the ropes into 1-inch-long pieces and sprinkle them lightly with flour. Roll each piece into a walnut-sized ball, then flatten it against the counter with your palm, so that the center of each disk, thanks to the hollow of your palm, should be slightly thicker than the edges. Sprinkle flour over the dough and work surface.

Working with one piece of dough at a time, place the rolling pin (preferably a thin Chinese-style rolling pin) right at the center of the disk and roll down to the edge, then roll the pin back to the center. Turn the dough a few degrees and roll the pin over the dough in the same manner. Continue rolling, turning the dough in the same direction, until you have made a full revolution. The dumpling wrapper should be flat and round and about the size of your palm, with the center still slightly thicker than the edges. Repeat with the remaining pieces of dough, dusting the bottom of each wrapper with a little flour and stacking them (do not stack more than eight wrappers together, to prevent sticking). Cover them with a damp cloth to prevent them from drying out while you finish rolling the rest of the dough.

Make the filling: Combine the lamb and the chicken stock in a medium bowl and mix vigorously with chopsticks or a fork, stirring in one direction only for 50 strokes. Add the soy sauce and mix for another 50 strokes. Beat in the egg, salt, sesame oil, garlic, leeks, and ginger. Add the pumpkin or squash and stir for another 10 strokes.

Wrap the dumplings: Sprinkle your work surface again with flour. Place a dumpling wrapper in your palm. Using a spoon, scoop roughly 2 teaspoons of filling and place it in the center of the wrapper. Fold the wrapper in half, taking care not to squeeze the filling beyond the center of the dumpling, and pinch the top of the semicircle together. Seal the open sides, pinching the edges to make pleats (keep all the pleats on one side of the dumpling) and sealing them as you work to the top of the semicircle. If folded correctly, the dumpling will have the shape of a fat-bottomed crescent and will sit upright rather than tip over when placed on your work surface. Repeat until you run out of filling or wrappers.

Bring a large pot of water to a boil over high heat. Add a batch of dumplings—no more than 20 or so at a time—and when the water returns to a boil, cook for another 5 minutes.

Remove the dumplings with a spider or slotted spoon. Repeat with the remaining dumplings, serving each batch immediately, accompanied by a small dish of the vinegar, chili oil, and garlic, quantities adjusted to taste.

VARIATION: For pork-and-fennel dumplings, substitute ground pork for the lamb and minced fennel (bulbs and leaves) for the pumpkin. In fact, almost any meat-and-vegetable combination can substitute for the lamb and pumpkin. (Vegetables with high water content should be sprinkled with salt after they are grated or shredded and allowed to sit for 30 minutes, then squeezed of excess water before they are added to the other ingredients.)

LA MIAN (CHINESE HAND-PULLED NOODLES)

Serves 6

To get a sense of how to make these noodles, you have to see the process performed. Please visit my website, www.jenlinliu.com, for video clips.

4 cups all-purpose flour, plus 2 cups additional for dusting
1 teaspoon salt
3½ cups hot water (about 100 degrees Fahrenheit)
2 tablespoons food-grade lye (sodium hydroxide), available online,
    or substitute baking soda
¼ cup vegetable oil

Make the dough: Heap 4 cups flour in the center of a large work surface. Dissolve the salt in the hot water. Make a crater in the center of the flour, then pour in 1 cup of hot water and slowly mix it in with your hands. Add another 1¼ cups hot water, ¼ cup at a time, until the water is fully incorporated. Knead the dough briefly.

Dissolve the lye or baking soda in ¼ cup hot water and set it near your dough. Keep the remaining hot water nearby.

Knead the dough on the floured work surface for 5 to 10 minutes. When it has softened to the consistency of putty, stretch it out about one foot into a long rope and add a few dabs of the lye solution, working it in with your fingers; this will make the dough more flexible. Knead for another 5 to 10 minutes. Cover the dough with a damp cloth or wrap in plastic and set aside for at least 30 minutes.

Form the noodles: Break off a quarter of the dough to work with, leaving the rest under the damp cloth. Knead the dough for 4 to 5 minutes, working in a few drops of hot water at a time to soften the dough. Grasp the dough by each end, then stretch it out in front of you. Roll it on the counter into a long rope an inch or so in diameter and a foot long. Holding each end of the dough in either hand like a jump rope, swing it up and down to loosen the gluten and further lengthen the rope to about 2 feet long. Slap the rope of dough against the counter, stretch it until it's about 3 feet long, double it over, and twirl it so the strands twist around each other like a cruller. At this point you are stretching and doubling and twirling just to get the dough to the right degree of stretchiness and pliability, not to form separate strands. Dust the dough with flour and repeat the stretching, swinging, and twisting for 5 minutes. Then gather the dough into a ball, rub a clean portion of the counter with vegetable oil, place the dough on it, and cover with plastic wrap while you repeat the process with the remainder of the dough, working with a quarter of the dough at a time. Let the dough rest, covered, for 15 minutes.

Return to the dough and once again swing, twirl, and twist each mound. If the dough isn't able to stretch to full arms' length without breaking, dab on more lye solution and work in another sprinkling of hot water. Divide the dough into portions about the size of a tennis ball. Roll them into long ropes and cover with a damp cloth.

Working with one rope at a time, dust it and your work surface liberally with flour. Loop the dough around the index finger of your dominant hand, holding the ends of the rope in your other hand and stretching your hands apart to lengthen the dough. Then drape the resulting double strand over the middle finger of your nondominant hand and stretch out the now-quadrupled strands of dough again (experience with the children's game of cat's cradle comes in handy here). Repeat this motion of hanging the multiplying strands of dough over the finger of one hand and stretching with the other, taking care that the noodle strands do not stick together by periodically passing the noodles through the flour on your work surface. When the strands have reached the thinness of angel hair pasta, yank your finger through the looped ends to separate the strands.

Cook in boiling salted water for 3 minutes and serve with the sauce of your choice, or with broth, as in the following recipe.

HAND-PULLED NOODLES IN BEEF SOUP

Serves 6

2 pounds beef rump or round steak

1 pound beef bones

1 thumb-sized knob ginger

3 celery stalks

8 cups water

3 cinnamon sticks

3 to 4 black cardamom seeds

1 teaspoon Sichuan peppercorns

1 teaspoon whole white peppercorns

3 bay leaves

1 recipe La Mian (Chinese Hand-Pulled Noodles) (p. 104), or
      1 pound thin variety of dry Chinese noodles or angel hair pasta

1 bunch cilantro, chopped

Chili oil

Shanxi black vinegar

Place the beef, beef bones, ginger, celery stalks, and water in a large, heavy stockpot and bring to a boil. Tie the cinnamon sticks, cardamom seeds, Sichuan peppercorns, white peppercorns, and bay leaves in a cheesecloth sachet and add to the pot. When the soup comes to a boil, reduce the heat to medium and partially cover. Let the broth simmer for 3 hours, skimming the impurities occasionally.

Remove the soup from the heat and strain the broth, then return it to the pot and keep it hot. Reserve the beef and discard all the other solids. Cut the beef into thin, bite-sized slices and set aside.

Fill a large pot with water and bring it to a boil. Add the noodles. Boil the freshly made hand-pulled noodles for 3 minutes. Premade noodles should be boiled according to package directions. Drain the noodles and divide them among 6 soup bowls.

Ladle the hot broth over the noodles, top with the sliced beef and serve immediately, accompanied by cilantro, chili oil, and vinegar.

MIAN PIAN (NOODLE SQUARES WITH SPICY TOMATO SAUCE)

Serves 6

¼ teaspoon salt
4 cups all-purpose flour
2 cups warm water
1 tablespoon vegetable oil
1 recipe Spicy Tomato Sauce (p. 111)

Combine the salt with the flour in a bowl. Make a well and add the water gradually, following the instructions for mixing, kneading, and rolling out the dough for Chef Zhang's Hand-Rolled Noodles/Andrea's Pasta (p. 96). While the dough is resting, make the Spicy Tomato Sauce.

Bring a wok or large pot of water to a boil.

After you have rolled out the dough and unrolled it into S-shaped layers, cut it into strands 1 inch wide. Dab your fingers with a little vegetable oil. Working with one strand of dough at a time, hold one end between the thumb and index finger of your nondominant hand and drape the other end of the strand over the wrist of that same hand so that the noodle doesn't dangle too much. Position yourself before the pot of boiling water. With the thumb and forefinger of your dominant hand, rapidly pinch off the strand of dough into 1-inch lengths, using the index finger of your nondominant hand as a cutting edge, and drop them into the boiling water. Once you've torn several strands of dough into squares this way, stir, and boil for 3 minutes.

Remove the noodle squares from the boiling water with a slotted spoon and plunge them into a basin of cold water, then quickly drain them in a colander. Continue forming and boiling the rest of the noodle squares in batches this way. When the last batch is boiled, return the previously cooked noodles to the pot to reheat for a minute, then drain and serve immediately, topped with the sauce.

SPICY TOMATO SAUCE

To top 1½ to 2 pounds pasta

¼ cup vegetable oil

3 cloves garlic, minced

1 red onion, diced

½ pound beef or lamb tenderloin, thinly sliced into 1-inch
squares

2 tomatoes, diced

2 cups roughly chopped Napa cabbage

1 cup garlic scapes, chopped into 1-inch pieces (optional)

1 poblano or other mildly spicy green chili pepper, chopped, or
substitute a mixture of bell pepper and jalapeño

2 celery stalks, leaves discarded, chopped into ½-inch pieces

¼ cup soy sauce

2 tablespoons ground dried chilies

2 tablespoons sugar

3 ounces tomato paste

¼ cup Shanxi black vinegar

¼ cup chicken stock

Salt and freshly ground black pepper

Place a wok over high heat and add the vegetable oil. Add the garlic and onions and stir-fry for about 2 minutes, until they are soft and fragrant. Add the beef squares and stir-fry until lightly browned, about 3 minutes.

Add the tomatoes, cabbage, garlic scapes, chili peppers, and celery and stir-fry for an additional 3 minutes. Add the soy sauce, chili powder, sugar, tomato paste, vinegar, chicken stock, and salt and black pepper to taste, stirring between each addition. Reduce the heat and simmer for 10 to 15 minutes, adding ½ cup water if the sauce begins to dry out. Remove from the heat and serve with Mian Pian (p. 109).

CHUCHURA (UIGHUR WONTONS)

Serves 5

FOR THE DOUGH:
5 cups all-purpose flour
1 extra-large egg
Pinch of salt
2 cups water

FOR THE STOCK:

2 quarts water
1 large sheep bone (such as the
    leg bone, or several ribs),
    with gristle and fat
2 tomatoes, diced

1 medium onion, diced
1 white turnip, diced
Salt and freshly ground
    black pepper to taste

FOR THE FILLING:

¾ pound ground mutton or lamb
1 small onion, minced
1 bunch cilantro, stems minced,
    leaves reserved

2 teaspoons ground cumin
2 teaspoons freshly ground
    black pepper
1 teaspoon salt

Make the dough: In a large bowl, combine the flour, egg, and salt. Mix with one hand while you slowly add the water with the other. When the water is fully incorporated, place the dough on a large, floured surface and knead for 3 to 5 minutes, until the dough is soft, pliable, and smooth. Cover with a damp cloth or wrap in plastic and let sit for at least 30 minutes.

Make the stock: Place the water and sheep bone in a large pot and bring to a boil. Skim off the impurities. Add the tomatoes, onions, and turnips. Season with salt and pepper. Return to a boil, reduce the heat, and simmer for 1 hour.

Make the filling: In a bowl, combine the ground mutton or lamb with the onions, cilantro stems, cumin, black pepper, and salt.

Form the dumplings: Working with a quarter of the dough at a time, follow the instructions for rolling out the dough in Chef Zhang's Hand-Rolled Noodles/Andrea's Pasta (p. 96). Unwind the dough in one long sheet and cut it into 2-inch squares. Stack the wrappers in a few separate piles, taking care to dust each wrapper with a little flour before stacking so they don't stick together.

Place a dumpling wrapper in one palm and place about a teaspoon of filling in the center. Fold the square in half and seal all the edges, forming a rectangle. Fold down the long sealed edge of the dumpling like an envelope flap. Bring the bottom corners of the dumpling together and pinch them closed, forming a ring. Repeat with the rest of the wrappers.

Roll out another quarter of the dough and repeat the process until you run out of dough or filling or both.

After the stock has simmered for at least 1 hour, raise the heat and add the dumplings and any scraps of leftover dough, along with the reserved cilantro leaves. When the soup comes to a boil, cook the dumplings for another 5 minutes, then remove the pot from heat. Divide the dumplings among 5 bowls, add a couple of ladles of soup, and serve immediately.

central asia

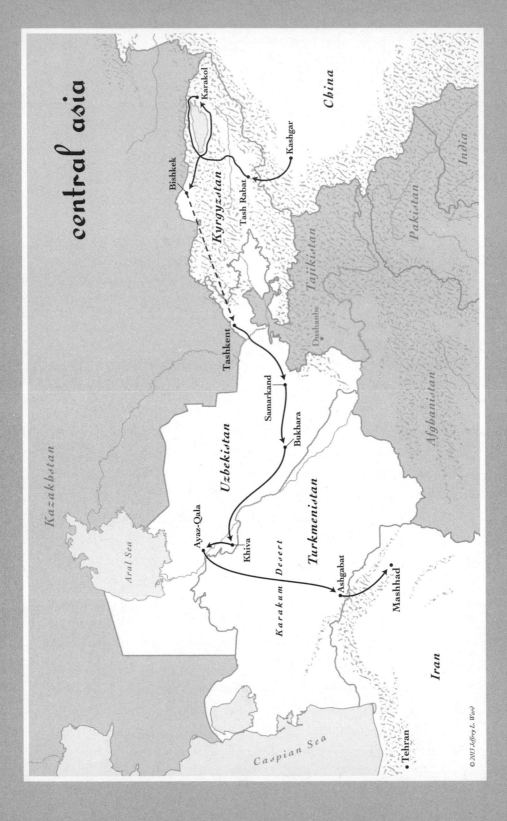

central asia

China
Karakol
Bishkek
Kyrgyzstan
Kashgar
Tash Rabat
Tajikistan
Dushanbe
Tashkent
Samarkand
Uzbekistan
Bukhara
Afghanistan
Pakistan
India
Kazakhstan
Aral Sea
Ayaz-Qala
Khiva
Karakum Desert
Turkmenistan
Ashgabat
Mashhad
Iran
Tehran
Caspian Sea

© 2015 Jeffrey L. Ward

5.

A sandstorm swept through Kashgar the morning we left, blanketing everything with a fine layer of dirt, including the inside of our hired car. The driver, apparently used to the storms, left his window partially rolled down, turning our throats hoarse and our eyes watery. We drove two hours through dry hills marked by nothing but the occasional wild camel before reaching the border.

The Han guard on the Chinese side was unusually friendly, probably out of boredom. I asked what time it was; he quoted me what the clocks said in Beijing. "We all go by Beijing time. It saves time," he declared. He examined my Han face, then my American passport, and, confused, asked where I was from. I gave him the pat answer I'd developed over many years: Yes, my ancestors were from China and my parents from Taiwan, but I was born and raised in America. After my complicated explanation, the inquirer would usually conclude, "So you're Chinese." This one nodded in admiration, as if being born in America was a hard-earned achievement.

"It's a long crossing, isn't it?" he added. "We have to make it this wide because otherwise the shepherds might lead their sheep into the other country!" The stamp came down on my passport with a loud *thunk*. I was finally out of China, the country where I'd lived for a decade. It was a strange feeling, even though China hadn't felt "Chinese" for the last thousand miles.

We switched to a new car and a Kyrgyz driver and went on for a couple more hours before we reached the border post for Kyrgyzstan. It was only after more bureaucratic stamping and crossing over a high pass that we officially entered Central Asia. Rain, rather than dirt, now fell from the sky. Men rode horses across pastures dotted with the occasional wooden cottage. The land became green and mountainous—scenery that was different from most of the Silk Road and, as it happened, the kind of terrain my husband loved.

In the early evening, we reached Tash Rabat, a caravanserai, or a camel way station where travelers once hitched their animals, ate, and slept. Hundreds of caravanserai dotted the Silk Road, though this one, more than a thousand years old, was particularly beautiful: the domed stone building sat in an emerald green valley. A caretaker unlocked the gate, and, with a flashlight illuminating the way, we wandered around the well-maintained cavernous building, in which I envisioned traders and explorers sitting down for a communal meal in one of its long halls. Marco Polo had wandered through this very area, in fact, and dined on prairie dogs, animals that still darted through the grasslands.

We'd sleep in cozier quarters nearby, in a camp of yurts, the round, tent-like dwellings of Asian nomads. We shivered as we entered through a heavy straw curtain; it had gotten so cold that I'd donned two fleeces and a raincoat. Inside, we found a stove, a pile of duvets, and a floor of felt carpets with swirling patterns of red, brown, and purple. An entire family usually occupied a single yurt, which they could take apart and reassemble in just a couple of hours. But nowadays, few Kyrgyz lived in yurts, because most were no longer nomads. Even the yurt camp owner, Borul, didn't live in a tent. "They're just for tourists," she said with a laugh. She pointed to her dwelling, a blue trailer made of scrap metal. She and her husband spent their summers in the "wagon," as they called it, and their winters in a wooden house in a nearby village.

Borul looked older than her mid-forties, her face leathery and dark from the high-altitude sun. But she dressed younger than her years, in a flowery purple skirt over black tights and a yellow fleece emblazoned with the logo for Dolce & Gabbana. Flashing a smile that revealed a set of gold teeth, she invited me into the trailer where she was making dinner.

In the simple kitchen, two pots simmered on a gas stove. Borul invited me to sit on a loveseat before a coffee table littered with an odd assortment: a jar of Nescafé, a plate of Russian candies, clotted sheep's cream in a tin, and, disconcertingly, a raw lamb's leg. Like many of the homes I'd come across, this one didn't have a refrigerator.

I asked Borul if I could help with dinner, and with a shrug and an easy laugh, she handed me a potato to peel. We were her only guests for the night, the last ones having departed the week before.

"Windy," said Borul, looking at the gray skies through the thin windows, steamy from the cooking. Yesterday it had been sunny.

"What about tomorrow?" I asked. She shrugged. Without television, phones, or the Internet, she never knew.

She scooted me out of the trailer and into a yurt that doubled as a dining room. Craig and I sat across from each other at a long table, under a generator-fueled lightbulb that flickered like a candle. Borul set down a round of *nang*, softer and denser than the ones in Xinjiang, and the tin of clotted sheep's cream called *kaymak*. It tasted gamy until I added a layer of homemade apricot preserves. Washing the appetizer down with black tea, I was reminded of a European tradition: tea and scones. Borul also brought out coleslaw and a vegetarian borscht, enlivened with freshly chopped dill, the herb's first appearance on my journey. The lamb's leg, thankfully perhaps, never appeared.

Our stomachs pleasantly full, we retired to our yurt. Borul's husband lit the stove, fueled with kerosene and dried rounds of odorless dung. The room was cold at first, but as the stove got cranking and we piled on the padded blankets, that yurt—in the isolated mountains of a country barely known to the world—became the coziest of our accommodations so far. We woke after ten hours of peaceful slumber to find warm blini in the dining yurt. These crepes were thinner than the ones in Kashgar, and folded into quarters and smothered with the same clotted cream and apricot preserves from the night before. Central Asian dining was getting off to an unexpectedly fortuitous start.

Kyrgyzstan's tourist traffic had slowed to a trickle ever since a revolution had swept through a few months before. We'd heard about the turmoil while we were still in Cambridge, just as I'd decided to journey the Silk Road. It was the lead item on the evening news: images of protesters running from the military flashed on our television to the sound of gunfire. My husband raised an eyebrow. Did I still think I would be safe on my own? he asked. I considered other routes, but since my travels began, the revolution had died down and the country had installed a new transitional government.

Still, the instability was one more reason Craig had joined me before I reached Central Asia. We abandoned a plan to travel through southern Kyrgyzstan, because even as the rest of the country regained calm, riots had broken out there between ethnic Kyrgyz and the Uzbek minority, resulting in dozens of deaths. Instead, we stuck to the north, a mountainous, peaceful area. I even decided to set aside my culinary mission for a week to go trekking with Craig, something I wanted to do for him since he was accompanying me on the Silk Road for long stretches.

We drove to a small town called Karakol near a beautiful lake of the same name. At a trekking agency, we decided on a route and paid for the necessary support. For seven hundred and fifty dollars, a guide, a cook, and two porters would accompany us. Food and gear were included. Craig and I usually preferred to hike independently, but Kyrgyz trails weren't marked and a large crew was the standard offering at the agencies, many of which were nonprofits aimed at employing youth in the poor region.

At the bed-and-breakfast we stayed in before the hike, we met an American couple in their seventies. Hans and Jane arrived late one evening, the headlights of their hired car shining through the living-room window. The car waited while Jane, in a brown vest and hiking boots fitting for a war correspondent, bargained with the innkeeper. I was impressed with her boldness. It was past nine and there weren't many guesthouses in this forlorn little town.

After they settled in, we struck up a conversation with the couple. They'd just come from Tajikistan, where they'd taken a weeklong trip on the Pamir Highway, one of the region's most scenic drives, which runs along steep mountains dotted with villages and lakes. We invited them to join us for dinner the next evening at a nearby home occupied by Dungans, the ethnic minority known as the Hui in China. The minority had migrated to Central Asia after a Muslim rebellion in the 1800s, and their descendants were a sizable minority in Kyrgyzstan. I was intrigued to learn that Dungans had brought many of their dishes with them. But while the Dungan family served us delectable fruits, nuts, and pastries, the main course was lackluster—the hand-pulled noodles were unpleasantly thick and floated in a watery sauce. And then there was the trouble with the seating.

In what I was learning was typical for Central Asia, dinner was served on a low table set on a raised platform on one side of the living room. Jane, Craig, and I slipped effortlessly onto the platform, placing our legs beneath the low table. But Hans squatted precariously, legs trembling. "What's wrong, Hans?" Jane asked loudly. "I—can't—sit!" he said finally. Our hosts moved us to a Western-style table nearby. Many Westerners, it turned out, had the same problem.

Hans also had trouble hearing. So Jane did most of the talking, telling us that her husband had been an accomplished neurosurgeon who'd practiced in Boston, not far from where Craig grew up, while Jane was a teacher. After retirement, they split their time between San Diego, where I'd lived in my youth, and Sydney. But most of the time they were on the road, visiting their grandchildren and seeing the world. Jane reflected fondly on their younger years, even when they'd struggled before Hans had settled into his career. She gushed nostalgically about trips she'd taken to China. She told us, too, about a trip to Nepal she would take later that year, not with Hans but with a girlfriend, a several-week-long trek on the Annapurna circuit, which piqued my husband's curiosity—he'd always wanted to do that very hike. Despite the difference in their physical abilities, she and Hans seemed to get along well, and it was encouraging to see a couple whose adventurous spirit hadn't diminished with age.

After dinner, I asked Jane what she thought was the key to a happy marriage.

She paused for just a second before she said, "Always support your partner's dreams and ambitions."

And with that, I braced myself for a week of high-altitude hiking with my mountain-loving husband.

In the morning, we drove to the trailhead with our large support crew. Our guide, a recent college graduate named Anarbek, told us we would travel over two twelve-thousand-foot passes in the coming week. He and one of the porters were ethnic Kyrgyz, with features that seemed a blend of Han Chinese and Tibetan. Meanwhile, the cook and the other porter had the fair skin and light hair of their Russian ancestors. As it turned out, the large crew would come in handy—I hadn't quite wrapped my head around the challenges of the hike.

The trek began leisurely enough. We ambled through a valley that cut through red sandstone cliffs and stopped for refreshments at a nomads' yurt. A pair of sisters paused in milking cows to bring us mugs of thin, milky *koumiss*, cow's and mare's milk fermented for days until it became slightly carbonated and alcoholic. It was the national drink of Kyrgyzstan, even given to babies, and a tradition old enough to have appeared in Marco Polo's travelogue.

Polo had likened the beverage to a fine wine, but I had another reaction. Craig snapped photos of my response: an undeniable look of horror spread over my face as I took my first sip. I'd never ingested anything quite like it. The *koumiss* evolved from sweet to sour to salty on my tongue, and it was not wine that it tasted like, but some kind of moonshine, spiked with soda water and spoiled milk. It was "complex," I said to my host, hoping she'd interpret my grimace as a smile. Thankfully, Anarbek finished off my mug and filled his large water bottle with the liquid. "It'll give me strength for our hike," he said. Evidently *koumiss* was to Kyrgyz what Gatorade was to Americans.

Still, it was a gift, and I showed my gratitude by offering the sisters a handful of dried apricots. In return, they produced something that resembled a Ping-Pong ball. "That's *kurut*," Anarbek explained. "It's dried yogurt. It's very portable and good for hikes." Expecting it to taste like the dried yogurt that covered raisins, I eagerly popped the *kurut* into my mouth. My mouth puckered instantly from the acid, and my tongue was coated in a chalky substance that reminded me of a Pepto-Bismol tablet. Tucked into my backpack was a chocolate bar, but I decided to halt the trading then and there, not willing to cede it for another surprise.

The food the cook prepared that night was only marginally better. He'd brought many water-heavy vegetables like cabbages and tomatoes that I'd never lug on a hike, along with forty pieces of *nang*, as important to Kyrgyz as it was to Uighurs, and copious amounts of Russian smoked cheese and beef sausages. Dinners usually consisted of simple renditions of dishes we'd tried in Xinjiang, like rice pilaf, now called *plov*, or soups like borscht with boiled dried pasta. He cooked with a heavy cast-iron *kazan*. (No wonder two porters were needed.)

The food was why I was lukewarm about hiking and camping; I never felt fully satisfied. I hadn't hiked much before Craig and I met, and I'd never camped. (My father was skeptical of the activity, like many Chinese— why subject yourself to the pain and hardship?) But with Craig, I gamely trekked through the Sierra Nevada and pitched a tent on the coast of Maine. It was only after we married that Craig found out the truth. On the second morning of our honeymoon, he roused me at eight in the morning for a hike on the Na Pali Coast Trail. Though I'd agreed to it enthusiastically some days before, that morning I was reluctant and bleary-eyed. He prodded me into the rental car and drove us to the trailhead. As we ascended the slippery path, my new sneakers becoming caked with mud, I could no longer hide my ill humor.

"But I thought you liked hiking," Craig said.

In my defense, my enthusiasm hadn't been a charade. It was just that I'd been falling in love and would have done anything he'd asked. Over time, though, I developed a grudging tolerance—and later even a secret fondness—for my husband's hobby. But always a stubborn one, I never readily admitted to enjoying it, of course.

In any case, despite the terrible food, I was beginning to enjoy our Kyrgyz trek. The mountains were just as beautiful as Yosemite and they didn't come with the crowds—in a day's worth of walking, we usually came across just one group of hikers or a nomadic family. At night, we camped in valleys surrounded by alpine forests and drifted into slumber with our sleeping bags zipped together. After noisy, chaotic China, the mountains restored us and helped reset our tempos to a slower beat.

On our second morning, we peeked out of our tent to find white covering the valley.

"It snowed?" I asked, aghast.

"Frost," Craig said, his face aglow. "Just frost."

So it wasn't as comfortable as the five-star hotels I liked. But I couldn't begrudge him his happiness, as he stared out of the tent and sipped his instant coffee with pleasure. He was more at home here than he seemed elsewhere on the road, and that made me content as well.

After I'd forced smiles through many miserable meals, in the middle of our hike one afternoon, we came across a nomad simmering a *kazan* full of milk outside his yurt. He strained the liquid through cheesecloth and poured it through filters that turned it into thick cream. He invited us into his tent for a sample.

We crossed our legs underneath a table low to the floor and dipped pieces of *nang* into the creamiest of creams, better than the fresh ones I'd bought at specialty markets and whipped into stiff peaks, and superior even to the crème fraîche that topped desserts in fancy French restaurants. The nomad also treated us to bowls of yogurt that reminded me of the crème brûlée–like yogurt I'd eaten in the Tibetan region of China.

The cows that had produced the amazing dairy, though, were conspicuously absent. It turned out that they were grazing freely in the mountains and would wander back on their own, or a shepherd would later round them up. The cows' freedom to roam created such luscious cream and yogurt, Anarbek explained. "Different pastures and different grass give the cream a special taste," he said. This unexpected gem in the middle of our hiking trip felt like an affirmation that Craig and I, with our differing interests, were as compatible as I'd hoped.

But on our last full day of hiking, the weather turned. As we donned our backpacks, snow began to fall. We passed a nomadic family who'd packed up their yurt and were transporting it, by horse-drawn wagon, in the opposite direction. Most nomads had already left; even though it was only early September, winter was coming on. By noon, we found ourselves in a near blizzard at a lake just below the highest pass of our hike.

"Ala-Kol crazy!" our cook said, referring to this stretch of the hike. He overtook us, his bloated backpack bouncing behind him as if it were light as a balloon. The lakeside was barely visible in the snow, but I was more concerned with the visibility of my feet, as I tried not to slip on the icy rocky path, lagging farther and farther behind Craig and our guide. It was at moments like this that I wanted to curse my husband's rugged spirit. I'd had this feeling before, not just on hikes but in large natural bodies of water he wanted us to swim across, or plunge deeper into when we went scuba diving. Why did he always have to push me to my limit?

Panting and huffing, I finally joined Craig and our guide at the top of the pass. I sighed with relief, until I looked down. If the mountain had been a ski slope, it would have been a double black diamond. On a clear day, the descent would have been difficult, but the snow seemed to make it impossible.

"Hm," Anarbek said. The snow was coming down even more rapidly now, and there was no sign of our cook and porters. Had the snow covered their tracks? Or had they slipped off the mountain? Anarbek had mentioned this very spot before we began, when I'd asked him about the most dangerous situation he'd found himself in. On one hike, a two-hundred-pound woman had lost her balance here and had careened down the mountain for several hundred feet; our guide grasped her for dear life and saved her from slipping off the mountain.

He began taking slow steps across the ridge, digging each foot into the snow and rooting it in the loose, rocky soil beneath. Craig followed, but I decided not to take any chances and instead planted my bottom in the snow, inching along the path they'd created. The incline eventually flattened out and we saw footprints left by our crew. But more challenges lay ahead: we had miles of hiking left as the snow gave way to rain. I wasn't sure which was worse, now that my feet were drenched to the bone and my raincoat and waterproof pants offered only marginal protection. At a river, I prayed as I shimmied across a log that had been laid over the fast-moving current.

At dusk, we finally reached a small guesthouse, where we found the rest of our crew relaxing and not looking the least bit tired. We'd traversed twenty miles that day, and more than sixty miles over the week. A driver, thankfully, would pick us up the next day. After we bathed in a grungy pool filled with hot spring water, we sat down to something our cook called *laghman* even though it bore little resemblance to hand-pulled noodles. He'd thrown ramen and our remaining vegetables into the pot and added packaged spices. But that dinner reminded me of something Craig said about meals after an especially difficult day of hiking: I'd never tasted anything so good.

After a week in the wilderness, Craig and I made our way to Bishkek, Kyrgyzstan's capital. Though strife had besieged the place just a few months before, it seemed peaceful, even cosmopolitan, with parks and Soviet-style buildings that reminded me of Moscow. The young women looked like extras on *Sex and the City*, with their off-the-shoulder T-shirts, tight jeans, and stiletto heels. Posters of Gisele Bündchen and other supermodels decorated store windows showcasing fashions you'd expect to see in Paris or New York, and Mercedes-Benz and BMW sedans cruised the streets.

We settled into a bed-and-breakfast down a quiet alley. Our room was in the cozy attic of a sprawling wooden house that reminded me of a ski chalet, and I was delighted by my first proper bath in a week. The lodge featured a comfortable dining room where every morning the staff set out a Russian-style breakfast buffet with blini, fresh fruit preserves, and creamy yogurt. At breakfast, we met other foreigners, but few, if any, had come to Bishkek on vacation. International officials had come to oversee the upcoming election, diplomats had arrived on hardship postings, and American military contractors worked on a large air base that supported U.S. operations in Afghanistan. One morning, I chatted with one contractor, a middle-aged Midwesterner with a gruff but folksy demeanor. He asked what Craig and I were doing in Kyrgyzstan. I replied that we'd just finished a weeklong hike. "You did what?" he said, his eyes bulging.

He asked what we planned to do that day. I'd discovered that Bishkek had an international dining scene, I told him, and we were planning to eat at an Italian restaurant that night.

"Get out of here! Italian? Here?" He chuckled with amusement. He told me that he shuttled directly between the military base and the guesthouse every day. "Oh no, I'm not leaving the hotel tonight. Especially after that crazy redneck in Florida announced he was going to burn the Koran on September eleventh. All hell's going to break loose if he does that!"

As it turned out, the Florida pastor backed down on his threat, and even if he hadn't, I imagine we would have had the same uneventful evening eating the same passable, locally produced cheese and ravioli.

Kyrgyz food and Italian cuisine had similarities, I discovered, starting with the quantity of dairy and noodles both cultures ate. The Kyrgyz, in fact, ate more pounds of flour per person than any other people in the world, including Italians. I saw evidence of this at my friend Gulzat's home in the Bishkek suburbs.

I'd met Gulzat at a talk on Central Asia during Craig's year in Cambridge. A globe-trotting sociologist, she'd also been on a fellowship. I immediately liked her. She was straightforward and serious, but she didn't have the typical professorial appearance. Like many young women in Bishkek, she wore splashy dresses, form-fitting blouses, and plenty of makeup on her pretty, angular face.

Gulzat invited Craig and me to her home for a meal one evening. I went early with her to cook. On the way to her apartment, we stopped at a stand in her apartment compound that specialized in dairy products. Dairy was so vital that most neighborhoods had a little stall like this nearby, she said. She picked up a carton of *ayran*, a watery yogurt drink, and handed me something that resembled a candy bar: chocolate-covered cheese curds, which I unwrapped and demolished in a few bites.

Gulzat lived with her husband, their two-year-old daughter, and her mother-in-law in a small one-bedroom apartment. "We're not very, uh, technologically advanced," the sociologist said as we made our way up a darkened stairwell. She'd also told me on our way over that she wasn't a very good cook. "I apologize in advance," she said. In the apartment's narrow vestibule hung a replica of a famous oil portrait of an elegant Russian lady that I recognized from the paperback edition of *Anna Karenina* I'd read in high school. Gulzat introduced me to her "mom-in-law," a woman named Roza with short, curly hair and a tanned complexion. She was frying *boorsok*, little squares of dough that she then drained and sprinkled with powdered sugar. "They're used for greeting guests," Gulzat said, serving the snack with black tea poured into *piala*s, handless teacups that resembled Chinese rice bowls. She filled them only halfway, as was the tradition in Central Asia. "It's considered rude to fill to the top," she said. The custom kept the contents of the teapot hot and also was a sign that the host would pay constant attention to the guests, refilling their cups whenever necessary.

After sipping tea, we set to work on the noodles. "Kyrgyz cooking is basically meat and dough," Gulzat said, a statement that would echo in my head as I traveled farther west. She added a dash of salt to the flour and water before I took over the kneading, my years of noodle- and dumpling-making coming in handy.

After I kneaded the dough, Gulzat wrapped it in a bathrobe and placed it on a balcony near the kitchen. She lined up the rest of the ingredients she needed to make the meal. "I gather up everything, otherwise I forget to add things sometimes," my host said. As we cooked, she told me she had been disappointed with the food in America. The yogurt was terrible. The meat didn't have any flavor. The produce wasn't fresh. "I tried to buy organic but it got too expensive," she said, sounding like my husband. In Kyrgyzstan, farms remained small and everything was grown without chemicals. Every family pickled their own vegetables and made their own preserves. She brought in a jar from the balcony and opened it, handing me one of her pickles, which was crisp and just sour enough to make me reach for another. She dropped a spoonful of berry preserves into my tea, which enlivened it with the flavor of summer. "Right now, at my university, the most popular topic of conversation is 'What did you conserve?'" she said.

When the dough was ready, Roza sprinkled flour on a wide table and picked up a long rolling pin. The mother-in-law rolled out the dough into a sheet as wide as the table and cut the sheet in half. She sliced half of it into handkerchief-like squares, while she cut the other half into fettuccine-like strips. She set about making the accompanying toppings. She sautéed vegetables, mutton stock, and dill for the squares, a dish called *gyulchetai*, and she placed boiled mutton and onions over the fettuccine, a dish called *beshbarmak*.

Beshbarmak was Kyrgyzstan's most important dish and, as one that was used for greetings, carried the same symbolism as Uighur *polo*. And just as Chinese had renamed *polo* when they saw locals eating it with their hands, the Russians, after seeing Kyrgyz eat the dish without implements, called it "five fingers," the literal translation of *beshbarmak*. To make it properly, a family purchased and slaughtered an entire sheep. After boiling the animal, the hosts bestowed various parts upon guests, depending on their age and relationship to the host. It was a dish that caused friction between the generations in her family, Gulzat said. While Roza and her parents insisted on preparing the dish whenever important guests came, Gulzat and her husband argued that it was too expensive a formality. Given that Craig and I were ignorant of the tradition, Gulzat had been able to convince Roza that slaughtering a sheep wasn't necessary, and the mother-in-law had contented herself with cooking a few pounds of mutton. She did, however, include one important part of the sheep—*koiruk*, the fatty tail of a special breed that had two pom-pom-shaped rumps. It was the sheep's most expensive cut, a prized delicacy. Eating the fat gave women a good complexion, Roza told me.

As the noodles cooked, Gulzat kneaded still more dough, for baked pastries. All the while, her toddler, a spunky two-year-old named Aybike, bounced on a sofa in the kitchen, vying for her mother's attention. As the food simmered, Gulzat's husband, Joldon, and Craig arrived and moved the large prep table into the living room where we would eat. Joldon was a clean-cut man of medium height with a laid-back air. Like Gulzat, he was an academic, a political scientist, and he ruefully admitted that he did none of the cooking. That was the domain of his mother and his wife.

Still, Gulzat and Joldon agreed, Kyrgyz women had it better than most women in Muslim countries, a result of the Soviet and nomadic past. Communism had made women as educated and gainfully employed as men. Roza had earned a master's degree and worked as a magazine editor until she retired. And Gulzat had a career that rivaled Joldon's in prestige.

"There's something about Kyrgyz culture that makes things less conservative," Joldon said.

"Traditionally, we have lived in circular yurts that are hard to divide," Gulzat added. The freedom and independence of living outdoors also meant that Islam did not take a strong hold. "Also, it isn't easy to have more than one wife when you're a nomad."

I'd noticed the mild Muslim influence in Kyrgyzstan. The day Gulzat invited me over happened to be Eid, the holiday that marks the end of Ramadan, but the family didn't celebrate it, nor had they fasted. That was the case for most Kyrgyz. The national drink, *koumiss*, contained alcohol, and almost everyone we met drank beer and vodka. And while pork was not common, both Gulzat and Joldon had tried and liked it.

After Gulzat and Roza finished the cooking, we sat down at a table crowded with dishes. I started with the *beshbarmak*, using a fork, a new

Kyrgyz custom. The sheep's tail fat tasted like the juicy blob of fat on a rib-eye steak. *Beshbarmak* seemed to be one of those dishes, like turkey on Thanksgiving, that was eaten for tradition's sake rather than for taste. Better was the *gyulchetai*, which, with its tender pasta squares and fresh dill and parsley, rivaled the noodle dishes I would later have in Italy. The raisin scones Gulzat baked were delicious, and a marker of Russian tradition.

Why didn't Gulzat think she was a good cook? The food had been excellent, I told her. "Well, it's not that I'm not a good cook. I just don't like to cook much," she said with a shrug. But when she did, she attacked the duty with her serious, type A personality that guaranteed a good meal.

Like other aspects of the Kyrgyz capital, Bishkek's dining scene was cosmopolitan. Along with the Italian trattoria, Craig and I came across a Mexican cantina, European sidewalk cafés, and several hamburger stands reminiscent of In-N-Out Burger. As Gulzat showed me the capital's various offerings, she noted that the nomadic lifestyle, more open and less wedded to tradition, had also made Kyrgyzstan the most international part of Central Asia.

I was most interested, though, in Kyrgyz food, which was inherently international; after all, we were at the crossroads of nomadic, Russian, and Chinese culture. I'd seen the nomadic influence during our hike, in the delicious cream, yogurt, and salty yogurt balls, and at Gulzat's in the hunks of mutton and sheep-tail fat. The Russian influence, from more than a century of colonization, showed in the blini, the beer and vodka, and the cheeses and sausages.

But the food became even more interesting when Kyrgyz cooks fused Chinese and Russian ingredients. Gulzat told me that Dungan restaurants had become so popular that they were now a part of mainstream Kyrgyz culture. Though the Dungan meal we'd eaten with Hans and Jane had been disappointing, I was willing to give the cuisine another try.

Gulzat took me to a restaurant buried in the narrow alleys of Dordoy, an enormous wholesale market where Chinese goods still went west over-land. Fatima, the head chef, had dark hair and small eyes, a stout body, and a white head scarf that reflected her Muslim beliefs. I tried a few words of Mandarin on her. She shrugged. She knew a dialect of Chinese that I couldn't understand, and like everyone else in Central Asia, she spoke mostly in Russian.

In her kitchen, an all-female staff rushed to fill orders—a refreshing sight, given the male-dominated restaurants I'd seen so far. Dungan restau-rant chefs were mostly women, Fatima said. "We work harder than men!"

A dedicated *laghman* chef rolled out dough. The sauce for the hand-pulled noodles bubbled next to a pot filled with beef goulash. Another chef filled an order for a Chinese dish, stir-fried beef atop steamed rice, which ended up on the counter next to a Russian dish, beef cutlets with mashed potatoes. Certain menu items blended both cultures, fusion food that had come from decades of cross-pollinating cultures rather than the hare-brained notions of cocky chefs in New York or London. One of the most delicious was *ashlyanfu*, which blended traditional wheat noodles, some-times called *ash* throughout Central Asia and Iran, with the almost trans-parent strands made of starch from beans, corn, or sweet potatoes that were popular in China. The starchy strands' Mandarin name, *liangfen,* sounded like *lyanfu.* Fatima mixed the *ash* and the *lyanfu* with a stir-fry of minced vegetables and scrambled eggs. She tossed in the traditional Chi-nese seasonings of chili oil, vinegar, and soy sauce. And then the clincher: freshly minced dill, an ingredient completely foreign to Chinese food but one that was ubiquitous just across the border.

The noodles thoroughly mixed, Fatima ushered us out of the kitchen and into the busy dining room. On each long communal table was a com-bination of accoutrements that could be found nowhere else: tea in a large thermos, a bowl of sugar, a small bin of rye bread, Chinese chili oil in cup-cake tins, and black vinegar in plastic bottles. Gulzat gave chopsticks a try, fumbling around with them before giving up and picking up the usual Eu-ropean flatware. (Chopsticks appeared with noodles only in Kyrgyzstan and disappeared entirely when we crossed into Uzbekistan.)

A pair of men sitting next to us inquired about my provenance.

"She's from America," Gulzat told them.

"But she doesn't look American," one of them said.

"Her background is Chinese," Gulzat explained.

"So why does she think she's American?" the other replied.

Rather than argue, I focused on the noodles before me. The mutt of a dish worked, the chewy wheat noodles contrasting with the slick, gelatinous starchy strands that I'd learned were not considered noodles in the East. I devoured the entire dish, which was at once comfortingly familiar and yet enthralling with the addition of dill. In other dishes, I'd noticed that the fusion had produced some oddities—for example, *dapanji*, or big-plate chicken, the spicy stew of chicken and tagliatelle noodles I knew from China, had somehow morphed into the name for a beef stir-fry. But I decided all could be forgiven when, at the end of the meal, Fatima brought us a plate of golden fried wontons with sour cream. It was a combination so simple, yet so completely ingenious and mouthwatering that, with Gulzat's help, I devoured the entire plate. It was the crowning reflection of a cuisine that had straddled Asia and Europe for eternity.

Craig and I ate twice more at Gulzat's home. Each time, I learned a little more about Kyrgyz culture. One evening, I cooked for Gulzat and her family, who were eager to try a few of my Chinese dishes. As I prepped and stir-fried, Gulzat took prodigious notes, while Roza occasionally popped into the kitchen. "She told me to take careful notes so I can prepare a meal for her friends," Gulzat said.

It wasn't always easy living with her mother-in-law, she added. As I'd seen in western China, mothers-in-law exerted full control over Central Asian households. (And actually the tyranny of mothers-in-law went farther back East, and was part of Han Chinese culture, too.) Gulzat and Joldon lived with her not out of tradition but because they couldn't afford their own apartment on their small academic salaries. But still, it meant that Gulzat was subject to the same rules as other daughters-in-law. Roza was kinder than most matriarchs, Gulzat allowed, sharing the cooking and housekeeping responsibilities most of the time. But when Roza invited her friends over, Gulzat was expected to cook, to demonstrate her obedience.

I asked Gulzat what the situation was when she invited her friends over for dinner.

"I never have friends over," she said, adding that it would not be considered appropriate. "You're a special exception."

Gulzat's own mother believed in the same rules, she said. When Gulzat had lived in Massachusetts, her mother had visited and they'd gone to a dinner party. The host did most of the cooking, while the host's son and daughter-in-law socialized. Gulzat's mother was floored. "What is going on?" she asked her daughter. "Is the daughter-in-law playing an evil trick on her mother-in-law?"

For our last meal at her house, Gulzat prepared the largest feast yet, with Russian specialties like pickled herring and plates that were local but reminded me of the far-off Mediterranean: batter-fried eggplant slices, and tomatoes and onions sprinkled with basil, all ingredients common in Central Asia. Gulzat also served a nomadic dish of boiled horsemeat, which Marco Polo had written about in his diaries. It was less exotic than it sounded and was, in fact, rather unmemorable.

Over the meal, I asked Gulzat and Joldon how they'd met. They told me they'd studied at the same university and dated for two years before they married. Or actually, Gulzat said, correcting herself, before she was kidnapped.

"Kidnapped?" I asked.

Bride kidnapping was a tradition that often preceded a Kyrgyz wedding, they explained. On the day of the wedding, the suitor's deputies would accost and blindfold the bride-to-be and whisk her off to the ceremony. The groom's family would have the meal, bridal wear, and gifts ready. The groom and his friends and family usually plotted the kidnapping and the wedding without the consent or consultation of the bride, although her parents might be part of the scheme. Sometimes, in fact, the suitor could be a complete stranger. Gulzat noted it wasn't unusual to hear of women, even educated, worldly ones, who'd been victims of this barbaric-sounding tradition. In villages, the situation was often worse and could involve violence.

Gulzat's case was less extreme. She and Joldon had spoken about getting married for months before the wedding, and she'd expected the kidnapping. Joldon added that if he hadn't carried out the custom, they would have been forced to go through a formal, Western-style engagement and wedding, which would have taken longer and been more expensive.

Gulzat, in fact, had gotten impatient waiting for Joldon to abduct her, the way that women get antsy for a formal proposal. "When are you going to kidnap me?" she'd impatiently demanded several times.

But she was still caught off guard when Joldon's relatives showed up one morning, blindfolded her, and forced her into a taxi. "I didn't have any control over the situation," she said. She cried on the way to her wedding. But that was one of the hallmarks of the tradition—a crying bride was an auspicious sign.

At the end of the meal, Gulzat and Roza presented me with a gift—a beautiful dark red satin gown, an outfit that a Kyrgyz bride would wear in her first days of marriage. "I'm going to miss having you around," Gulzat said, giving me a hug. I was touched by the gift and the hospitality. But as we left Kyrgyzstan, I wondered how she'd fare with her mother-in-law.

Months later, I received a note from her saying that she and Joldon were moving to—of all places—Italy. Joldon would further his studies in Florence, and they'd finally have a place of their own.

6.

was sorry to miss Osh, a Silk Road post with an alluring bazaar in Kyrgyzstan's south, but we'd heard that after a spate of ethnic violence, the government had imposed martial law and turned it into a ghost town. So we decided to fly on to Tashkent, the capital of Uzbekistan.

After having traveled overland for most of the trip, I found the swift transition from one country to the next jolting. In the Tashkent airport, we scrambled to find money, a phone, and a driver. The ATMs seemed to dispense only bills worth about three dollars each. We used hand gestures and our Uzbek and Russian phrase book to communicate with our driver, whom we'd chosen out of an aggressive throng for seeming more mild-mannered than the rest. The receptionist at the hotel couldn't find our reservation. When we finally opened the door to our hotel room, we were exhausted. But Craig, as he tipped the bellhop, seemed to have gotten a second wind. Where, he asked, could he find a hamburger?

"A hamburger?" I yelped. "After all that, you want a hamburger?"

"I was just kidding," Craig said. "Can't you take a joke?" He suggested we take a walk to get a feel for the neighborhood. He would lead the way. "I bet I'll find some good food for you."

The hotel was located in the capital's center, where the wide boulevards and widely spaced buildings, empty sidewalks, large parks, and plentiful monuments gave the city an imposing, Big Brother feel. It wasn't an accident. Uzbekistan was one of the most repressive countries in the world. Ever since the country had become independent of the dissolved Soviet Union, one man had ruled. Over his twenty-plus years as president, Islam Karimov had won reelections by a handy margin of more than 85 percent, making the country's supposed democracy a farce. He'd cracked down on activists and journalists and, in 2005, he was responsible for massacring several hundred people who'd participated in peaceful protests in the Fergana Valley.

We walked the eerily quiet streets a little on edge, unsure of our surroundings. But as we got a little farther away from our hotel, we saw a large covered structure in the distance from which came a rumble. We got closer and stumbled into an enormous bazaar. The aisles were filled with the most beautiful produce I'd ever seen. Cashews, almonds, and pistachios were carefully arranged in plastic tubes that formed geometrical patterns like the decorative tiles on the facades of mosques. Pristine pears, greenish-red like autumn leaves, formed cylindrical towers. Split pomegranates hung on wooden posts, their pink pearls spilling out of the peel. Even ordinary staples like eggs looked alluring, the white ovals arrayed in perfect squares. Vendors polished tomatoes and lemons. In an aisle full of salads, sellers rapidly chopped purple, yellow, and orange carrots into sticks and shreds behind colorful heaps of jade cabbage and magenta beets. The vendors offered us samples of anything we wished, including a taste of a large watermelon, into which one vendor inserted his knife and pulled out a juicy red rectangular piece. When we affirmed it was one of the sweetest we'd tried, he plugged the rind back in and sold the melon basically intact.

Along the market's edge, a row of butcher stalls with cool marble counters sold fresh, bright cuts of mutton and beef that hung on hooks. Just beyond was a small eatery from which a heavenly scent seemed to be drifting. At the front of the shop, we peered into a beehive-shaped oven, similar to ones we'd seen in Xinjiang. Stuck to the inside were buns like the ones we'd tried in western China, but with a drier, more pastry-like dough and a chunk of juicy lamb filling embedded within each. Called *samsa*, the dish was a cousin of the Indian samosa. It was the closest I'd come to finding the lamb buns I'd loved in Kashgar, the closest Craig would get to a hamburger, and it satisfied both of us immensely.

Craig's parents joined us in Uzbekistan. When we picked them up at the Tashkent airport, they seemed only a notch less energetic than usual after twenty-four hours in transit from their home in Massachusetts.

Craig's parents had lived in Beijing for several years, overlapping with the beginning of Craig's and my relationship. David had taken early retirement after a career with the lighting company Sylvania, which had moved the family several times. He left their next move up to Caroline, a psychologist. They'd lived in Europe early in their marriage, and the idea of living overseas again was appealing. They'd never lived in Asia, and Beijing was enticing with Craig there. Caroline accepted an offer from an international hospital, and they adapted to Chinese life over five years. They bicycled most places and otherwise used the buses and subways. They'd learned enough Mandarin to get by, and David raised birds and crickets, as did many retired Beijingers. Like Craig, they were adventurous and enjoyed the outdoors. On the weekends, they often went for hikes.

Not long after Craig and I started dating, the four of us climbed an unrestored part of the Great Wall. As we trucked on at a clipped pace, the wall seemed to get steeper and steeper, the ridge dropping off precipitously on either side. Huffing and panting behind them, I finally caught up, only to discover that we'd reached a point where the path dropped away altogether.

"*Mei wenti*," David said, using his favorite Chinese expression, which means "Not a problem." He called to Craig's mother to pass the rope. Donning a pair of gloves, he swung it around a tree jutting from the steep ridge and, holding both ends, stepped around the impassable bit in the blink of an eye. Caroline and Craig navigated the section with the same confidence. They turned to pass the rope to me and waited expectantly. Mustering up the courage, I gingerly followed, my legs shaking. The few steps seemed to take an eternity, but finally I made it across and stopped to wipe my brow. Until that excursion, I had no idea that gloves and ropes were standard hiking equipment.

Despite the hiking, I got along well with Craig's parents and I was happy they'd flown halfway around the world to see us. And it seemed only appropriate to have my mother-in-law around, given the status of matrons in Central Asia.

One night shortly after they'd arrived, however, we went out without Craig's parents to attend a stranger's wedding. We'd gotten invited on the fly, when I called up the head of Uzbekistan's chapter of the international organization Slow Food, to which I belonged. "What are you doing tonight?" Marina asked over the phone. "Would you like to come to a wedding?" She spoke conversationally, as if we were long-lost friends, even though we'd never met. I'd initially thought the Slow Food connection explained her friendliness, but nearly all Uzbeks showed us the same hospitality.

Marina herself would be late to the wedding, so she arranged for her mother to pick us up. We prepared a cash gift and dressed in our best clothes, still wrinkled from our backpacks. At the appointed hour, the mother, an equally friendly woman of Ukrainian heritage, whisked us in her small sedan to an enormous hall in a park, where the wedding was already under way. "Who's getting married?" we asked, en route. The groom was the son of a successful melon farmer who was also a Slow Food member, she told us.

On the surface, it almost could have been a wedding in America. Hundreds of guests were gathered in a hall filled with round tables. Dapper men in suits and raven-haired women in pretty dresses danced to a live band with a disco beat. The bride and groom sat before everyone, she in an off-the-shoulder white wedding dress, he in a tuxedo. Next to them was an enormous tiered cake. Young girls in miniature wedding dresses pranced around the hall. As in much of America, and many other countries, the aspiration to become a bride began early.

And as at most American weddings, the food wasn't particularly good, though you could say Asian and European culture were represented, with a little Americana thrown in. Waiters served bowls of *manpar*, a soup reminiscent in name of *mian pian*, the Chinese noodle squares I'd adored in China's Tibetan areas. The content of these bowls also approximated the Chinese dish, though not as successfully: the doughy squares were brittle and floated in a watery soup. Communal platters of Russian foods, including salads of beet and potato, rye bread, cheese, cold cuts, and fruit, sat in the center of each table. And after the waiters cleared the *manpar*, they served up plates of fried chicken with limp French fries. This was washed down with orange Fanta and Coca-Cola, two soft drinks I saw all along the Silk Road, and for the more Russified, vodka and red wine from the republic of Georgia. Oddly, the enormous cake went untouched.

While the wedding aspired to Hollywood, one element struck me as completely out of sync: the expression of the bride. As the groom glowed, she gazed downward for the entire evening, looking solemn and distressed. This was a custom, a guest told me. Uzbek brides were supposed to appear demure, modest, and chaste, and looking happy was antithetical to that.

A few days later, I attended a post-wedding party for another bride. This *bibi sayshami* took place several days after the wedding, at the groom's family home, where Uzbek newlyweds typically live after marriage. A female mullah sat cross-legged on the floor, singing and offering her blessings. During the breaks, the mother-in-law's relatives and friends, sitting in a circle, gossiped and ate at the women-only ceremony. The bride, bowing before her elders, looked just as gloomy as the one at the wedding. She wore an elaborate medieval-looking headpiece and a velvet dress, like the one Gulzat and her mother-in-law had given me. On the walls hung dozens of other outfits all selected by the groom's family, which she'd wear during her first forty days of marriage. On the floor, the host had laid out snacks of dried nuts and pastries while the main dish simmered in the home's courtyard: *plov*, the rice pilaf that seemed quite popular in Central Asia.

"I don't usually attend these ceremonies," Lola, my Uzbek translator, told me as we sat down.

"Why?" I asked.

"Because once they know I'm not married, they will make my life very difficult."

And just as she predicted, not long after the event was under way, the ladies began their inquiry. How old were we? Were we married? Did we have children?

One woman looked miffed when Lola told her I had been married for almost two years but was not yet a mother. "Why don't you have children?" she asked, aghast. "Your husband must be unhappy with you!"

When Lola told them she was twenty-three and unmarried, they demanded her phone number and address. They'd been looking for a woman her age for the mullah's nephew, who'd just graduated from law school. Lola didn't even bother telling them she wasn't interested—there was no point. She grumpily tolerated their questions: Was she a student or did she have a job? What did her father do for a living? Did her mother stay at home? And wait a moment . . . why was she twenty-three and *not* married? Finally, it all became too much for her and we decided to flee before the main course arrived. I had a feeling the next opportunity to eat *plov* would come up soon enough.

I learned more about Uzbek marriages when I took cooking lessons in a Tashkent home. The man of the house, Murad, was middle-aged and of average build, with a domineering attitude that reminded me of Al Pacino's character in *The Godfather*. Even though he didn't cook, he was always present at my lessons, lording over them while his dark-haired wife, Shaista, did all the work. They had two grown children and lived in a pleasant single-story house around a courtyard that reminded me of Uighur homes.

The food, too, reminded me of Xinjiang. In fact, Uighurs and Uzbeks, both sedentary, Turkic-speaking people, were more culturally and ethnically linked than other ethnicities in the region. We began with something

Shaista called *manti*, the name of which sounded similar to *manta*, the dumplings I'd learned to make in Kashgar. *Manti* was also a filled pasta dish, Shaista said. She started by mixing together minced beef, ground cumin, black pepper, onion, and salt before moving on to the dough. In a large bowl she combined warm water, salt, flour, and one egg and kneaded it into a smooth mound. She flattened the dough into a large, thin sheet with a long, narrow rolling pin—the longer the pin, it seemed, the more experienced the noodle maker. Shaista swiftly rocked the thin baton back and forth, folded the dough over itself, and cut it into three-inch squares. She took a square, added a generous dollop of filling, and brought diagonal edges together to form a loose box.

The dish had crossed the continental divide. The fillings' seasonings were identical. Though Shaista had used beef, she said lamb and pumpkin were just as often the main ingredients, as they were in Xinjiang. The dough was the same, except for the egg, which linked *manti* to Italian pasta. While the folding method varied slightly, the dumplings were roughly equal in shape and size. They were both steamed and served with dairy (clotted sheep's cream in Xinjiang, thick yogurt at Shaista's). And, following protocol, I ate them both with my hands.

After a lesson one day, Craig and his parents came to the house for lunch. Murad did a double take when he saw my fair-skinned husband and in-laws. "You two are married?" he asked as we sat down on a divan in their courtyard. "Do you love each other?" His wife, who emerged from the kitchen every so often but did not sit with us, was also curious.

"Sometimes," Craig answered drily.

Murad was confused because parents arranged most marriages in Central Asia, my translator explained. Despite the mixing that had gone on in Eurasia for centuries, it was apparently still uncommon for people of different ethnicities to marry. The few East Asians in Central Asia were mostly of Korean descent, and they stuck to themselves.

Aside from providing cooking lessons, the Uzbek couple also offered up rooms in their sprawling home for tourists. Occasionally, when the rooms were full, backpackers set up their tents and slept in the yard. During one lesson, Murad commented that he'd seen the strangest thing that morning. Two European men were washing their clothes in the yard while their respective female partners were still asleep in the tents. What was that all about? He'd never seen men do housework. And even worse, the women had been resting!

Later, I asked Shaista what she thought the role of an Uzbek woman ought to be.

She hesitated before saying, "Family is the most important. Everything else is secondary. Uzbek women live selfless lives, thinking about their husbands and their families before themselves."

I met more brides at Tashkent's Mashhura School, a cross between a girls' finishing institution and an adult education center. I'd learned of the place from an Uzbek woman I'd met in Beijing while planning my journey. When I contacted the school, the administrators invited me for a visit. Before showing me around the school, though, the school's accountant, Maruf, and several other staff—all of whom seemed to be men—treated me to a meal nearby. In the kitchen, a chef stirred a delicious-looking sauce for *laghman*, another noodle dish—the hand-pulled variety—that crossed over from China. My mouth watered in anticipation, but it was not noodles I was treated to when we sat down. Over a meal of tea and that familiar dish of *plov*, they told me that the school was named after the woman who founded it. The school offered some vocational classes, like tailoring, makeup artistry, and word processing, aimed at women looking for work in a rather old-fashioned job market. But the main focus seemed to be preparing women for marriage. Cooking classes were the most popular, since a wife's most important duty was to feed her husband and the rest of the family. The administrators offered to let me sit in on the classes if in return I would give the students a lesson in Chinese cooking.

In the classroom I sat next to students who ranged from wide-eyed teenagers to women in their mid- to late twenties who appeared already jaded by marriage. They all dressed in long, conservative skirts and dresses. Some wore heavy makeup. The sessions reminded me of the cooking school where I'd learned to cook in China, if you swapped out the men preparing for professional chefdom with women who were, or aspired to be, housewives. The teacher dictated the recipes in a monotone. The women copied down the recipes. The teacher demonstrated the dish while everyone watched silently from their desks.

International cuisines—or at least what Uzbeks thought of as international—were part of the curriculum. I'd seen some dishes on Uzbek menus with names like "Canadian meat" and "Mexican salad." The Canadian meat was no more than a steak, and the Mexican salad had only a sprinkling of chopped tomatoes and cheese. In one class, a teacher demonstrated "Chinese meat," sliced beef stir-fried with the Central Asian staples of onions, black pepper, and cumin. Even so, the unmarried students hoped improving their culinary repertoires would help them land good husbands. The process could be competitive. Bachelors and their family members often scrutinized a prospective bride, even interviewing her neighbors, relatives, and friends to evaluate her chastity, obedience, and talents.

When it was my turn to teach, I was flustered. The students sat silently and expectantly, the older ones raising their eyebrows. I was exactly the wrong person to teach them how to be good Uzbek housewives, what with my independence and wanderlust. I'd decided to cook *kungpao* chicken, and nervously began chopping leek, ginger, and garlic on a cutting board. As I prepped, I inquired about the board, which was slightly concave.

The students explained that the boards had warped from the volume of carrots they had to cut. "And if we're angry at our husbands, we chop even harder!" one woman piped up. "And the more curved the board is, the angrier we are at our husbands!" said another. The room, eerily quiet just minutes before, erupted in laughter.

I mentioned that I'd heard a lot about the qualities of good Uzbek wives but hadn't heard much about the attributes in a good husband. "What do you look for in a man?" I asked.

The class stirred and mumbled among themselves before one student replied sullenly, "We don't have any good men. They've all gone abroad to work!"

Others protested. "No, that's not true. We do have good men!"

"Do husbands have to make money?" I asked.

Of course, that went without saying, the women unanimously replied.

Another student volunteered her thoughts. "What I look for is someone who doesn't put his mother above me." That garnered a number of nods but a couple of smirks that said, Was that really possible?

Our conversation was interrupted when Maruf, the accountant, stopped by to check on the class. Everyone fell silent as I stir-fried the chicken, added the seasonings, and displayed it on the table.

"Wow, that was fast," a student said, as everyone huddled around. "Uzbek cooking takes much longer."

"That's strange you added sugar," another observed. "We don't add sugar to our cooking."

"Looks like our kebabs, but so much smaller," the accountant said. He poked the chicken with a fork and held it up for inspection, then tasted it, nodded, and left.

The women giggled. "Did you see his glasses?" "Funny." "What a dork!" More laughter.

After I finished demonstrating my dish, the teacher took over and began slicing a cucumber, fanning out the pieces as she chopped.

"Are you thinking about a particular man when you're cutting that?" one bold woman asked. The class roared again.

The teacher stared stonily ahead. "Uzbek rice salad," she declared, reading from the textbook. "Four hundred grams of rice, one hundred fifty grams of water . . ."

One of the women at the Mashhura School stood out. Fara was an assistant teacher for the class I guest-taught. She had come to Tashkent for just a few months to teach, then she'd return to her home in Samarkand, a legendary

Silk Road post that was the next stop on my journey. She was a pretty, petite woman with curly brown hair, high cheekbones, and a perfect button nose. Her parents were Tajik, an offshoot of the Persian ethnic group who were Uzbekistan's largest minority and whose imprint on the food culture could be seen in the dolmas, the meat-stuffed peppers and eggplants that were found from Central Asia to the Mediterranean.

One afternoon during a class, she made baklava, another dish that extended several thousand miles, from Central Asia to Greece. (Some food experts believe that baklava originated in Central Asia.) But this particular baklava was different from what I was familiar with: it consisted of layers of thick pastry and meringue, rather than the usual crushed nuts sandwiched between paper-thin layers of buttery, syrup-soaked phyllo. While she mixed flour and butter for the dough, Fara turned her attention on me as the rest of the class listened. She asked how I liked Uzbekistan and if the food was to my taste. I complimented the beautiful bazaars and said I'd enjoyed *plov* a number of times. In turn, I asked her how she'd found her job.

Through a friend, she replied. She'd recently returned to work after taking a three-year maternity leave, a length not uncommon in Uzbekistan. She'd worked at a bakery as a teenager and enjoyed kitchens. While she only earned about three hundred dollars per month at this job, chefs' salaries could climb to ten times that at fancy hotels. I found it strange that she had traveled for work alone, especially since she had a three-year-old daughter. From what little I'd gleaned about Central Asian culture, she didn't seem typical. And her dreams were actually bigger: she wanted to become an Uzbek chef in the United States, she said. Were there many good Uzbek restaurants in America?

As I fumbled to reply, she asked me another question, even more difficult to answer: "Do you think you could help me get to America? I would really like a visa," she said. She waited earnestly for my response as she whipped the meringue. The students, too, looked on curiously.

"But it's far away," I said finally. "What about your family?"

She shrugged, looking down at the fluffy egg whites. "I can leave them behind."

. . .

We left the wedding parties and the brides-in-training behind in Tashkent and went on to Samarkand. Guidebooks waxed lyrical about the town, calling the former capital of the Timurid Empire "the Mirror of the World" and "the Pearl of the East." Marco Polo had described it as "a noble city, adorned with beautiful gardens and surrounded by a plain, in which are produced all the fruits man can desire." At the height of the Silk Road, Samarkand was one of the most cosmopolitan centers in the world, a melding of East and West. It had been a locus for centuries, beginning with the conquests of Alexander the Great, the Macedonian who swept through the region in 329 BC. More than a thousand years later, the Mongol emperor Genghis Khan plundered the city as he and his army galloped west. But only one century after, the homegrown conqueror Tamerlane rebuilt Samarkand into a major capital of a kingdom extending from India to the western fringes of China. Uzbeks I met were enormously proud of Tamerlane. "If he'd gotten any farther, you'd be Muslim!" said Murad, the Godfather-like husband in Tashkent. Throughout the centuries, merchants in Samarkand traded pistachios and saffron from Persia, silk and rhubarb from China. Golden peaches, grapes, and watermelons from nearby orchards were packed on ice and sent to Chinese emperors.

But most of Samarkand's allure had disappeared long before we arrived. From the 1500s on, traders began to bypass Eurasia, opting to move goods by sea. In the 1800s, British and Russians battled for control over the no-man's-land. The Russians won out. They brought their vodka and blini and sausages, and planted cotton everywhere, turning bland cottonseed oil into a staple. The decades of heavy-handed Soviet and post-Soviet rule further diminished Samarkand's allure. In recent years, the Karimov government had bulldozed old neighborhoods to build a downtown district where rows of new storefronts sat empty. They'd also spruced up the Registan, a trio of fifteenth-century madrassas that was the country's biggest tourist draw. It had been renovated so overzealously that it was as authentic as a castle at an amusement park. In the blue-tiled buildings with tall spires where young men had once studied mathematics and Islam were a series of tacky gift shops. In front of the Registan, where old travelogues had described a bustling market, sat a soulless, empty square.

To add to that, Samarkand, like the rest of the country, had a dismal food scene. Somehow the bounty and beauty of the bazaars did not translate into a vibrant cuisine. Much of the food reminded me of Uighur cooking. I'd been touched when Nur's sister Malika had made rice pilaf on the western fringes of China, knowing that she'd cooked it as a token of appreciation for an honored guest. But little had I known that the dish would stalk me from Malika's all the way to the border of Iran, with hardly a variation on the litany of rice, mutton, carrots, and onions. Once in a great while, a cook would break the orthodoxy and throw in a few chickpeas or raisins. "We never get sick of *plov*," Murad of Tashkent told me. "We never say, 'Oh, no, not again, no *plov* tonight.'" But as our time in Central Asia went on, that sentiment expressed exactly how I felt. Even Craig, who could survive for days on saltines and peanut butter, began turning up his nose at the dish. Our only solace was that, given the number of times we'd been served the pilaf, we ascertained that we were very, very important guests.

The more meals of *plov* I ate, the less convinced I was of the theory that noodles had originated in Central Asia. I'd been enthralled with the *gyulchetai* noodles that Gulzat had cooked in Kyrgyzstan, but it was unlikely that Kyrgyz had invented the staple, because nomads didn't have a tradition of raising wheat or other crops. And in the rest of Central Asia, many of the noodles—the *laghman, manti,* and *manpar*—sounded and looked like offshoots of Chinese ones. As we pushed west, the steamed *manti* dumplings took on a gristlier filling and the hand-pulled *laghman* noodles became coarser and were served in more watery soups.

And few Central Asians subscribed to the theory that they'd invented noodles themselves. Also, few knew the story of Marco Polo bringing noodles from China and Italy, and nobody related any homegrown tales or legends about noodles in its place. Some Uzbeks believed that Uighurs, whose cuisine they knew from the occasional eatery, were the inventors of noodles. Though Uighurs back in China had denied that credit, they had served as go-betweens for Han Chinese and Central Asians, and given the likeness between Uighur and Central Asian noodles, perhaps the Uighurs, after learning them from the Hui and the Han, had transmitted them westward.

It seems that Chinese were eating noodles earlier than Central Asians, since the first recorded mention of noodles in Central Asia appeared centuries later than it did in China. The *Book of Victory*, by a Persian historian named Sharaf ad-din Ali Yazdi, describes how Tamerlane ordered his troops *not* to make noodles during a war in the late fourteenth century. It was also noted that Turco-Mongolians, who'd first arrived in the territory with Genghis Khan's armies, primarily ate noodles. Also around then the Florentine merchant Pegolotti wrote of how Central Asians made a noodle dish called *burhani*. Cooks sliced dough into small pieces and punched each with a hole, then placed them in a pot of water. "When the water boils, they add sour milk and eat it," concluded the description, reminding me of the medieval noodle preparation in the Mongolian encyclopedia. Perhaps Mongolian conquests, nomads like the Kyrgyz, Dungans escaping religious persecution, and Uighur traders had all played a role in spreading noodles.

But noodles aside, I didn't see much Han Chinese culinary influence in Central Asia. With few Dungans or other ethnic Chinese populating Uzbekistan, the East Asian influence was largely left to ethnic Koreans, whom Soviets had deported from their homeland during World War II. At the bazaars, Koreans sold a freshly shredded carrot salad tossed with garlic and vinegar, a dish they'd improvised after arriving in Central Asia. But however delicious, it, too, became repetitive.

Of all outsiders, Russians had the biggest imprint on Central Asian food, the influence becoming more pronounced in Uzbekistan. Meals often began with mayonnaise-laden salads bearing fanciful names like "Lady's Whim" and ended with shots of vodka. Food quality aside, the atmosphere of the eateries bothered me. Because restaurateurs built establishments to accommodate weddings, dining rooms tended to be cavernous and full of large, round dining tables. Few invested in decor because occasionally the police conducted sweeps and inexplicably shut down restaurants that didn't meet their mysterious standards. A few eateries pirated the look, feel, and taste of McDonald's, filling the demand for Western products in an area devoid of international franchises. Hamburgers and fried chicken seemed to have an appeal that had so far crossed every border.

I was all the more grateful, then, to reunite with Fara, who'd returned to her home in Samarkand to teach at a local branch of the Mashhura School. She introduced me to her cousin's *chaikhana*, a traditional teahouse that was a refreshing change from the echoing restaurants most Uzbeks, bafflingly, preferred. Her cousin Alisher had converted part of his home in a quiet alley into a charming outdoor dining room featuring raised divans atop which elderly men lounged, drinking tea and dining. Caged birds chirped pleasantly in the covered patio. Even here, though, I could not escape the ubiquitous *plov*.

Alisher eagerly summoned me to the pilaf, cooked in front of the restaurant in a *kazan* as large as the ones I'd seen in Xinjiang during Ramadan. He began to explain how it was made. I didn't have the heart to tell him or Fara that I'd already seen it cooked a dozen times, so I mustered the energy to pretend I was fascinated. Like most Samarkanders, Alisher insisted that his *plov* was totally distinct from that served elsewhere. The only difference I could see was that he had scattered a few whole chili peppers along the edges of the *kazan*. Alisher went on to explain that Samarkand *plov* was less salty than Tashkent *plov*, as well—Samarkanders couldn't understand why Tashkenters made such salty *plov*! But the most important difference—and this was key—was that in Samarkand, the ingredients were cooked in *layers* rather than in a haphazard mix. The meat sat at the bottom of the *kazan*, atop which lay the carrots and the rice, each layer undisturbed like a giant *plov* parfait.

While the rice simmered, Alisher seated us and brought a procession of side dishes that I was thankfully able to make into a meal itself—an onion salad, fried eggs, and beef sausages. Fara told Alisher where I was from, which prompted a conversation about the United States. While Fara desperately wanted to go, Alisher did not.

"What would I do there?" he said. "All my work, my family, is here."

"I don't know what I'd do, but I just want to leave this place," Fara murmured, keeping her voice low so other diners wouldn't hear.

"But Samarkand is beautiful. You can go to the mountains, you can see the old historic sights," he said.

"But there are so few opportunities here," Fara argued.

He agreed. "It is true that much depends on connections."

"It's just not easy to make enough money to make ends meet," she added. But there were other reasons she wanted to go, things that she couldn't quite express.

The sound of a collision in the alley interrupted the conversation. We went out for a look. A wedding procession had come to a halt as one car had rear-ended another. The drivers hopped out to examine the dent. They exchanged a few words before getting back into their cars and tearing off, kicking up a fine dust outside the teahouse.

"I had a fancy wedding once," Fara said wistfully.

While Alisher went to check on the *plov*, Fara explained why she wanted to leave for America so badly. Not long before, she'd gotten a divorce. She hadn't told me when I first met her because no one at the school knew; divorce was taboo in Uzbekistan.

She'd never wanted to marry her husband in the first place, she continued. Before her wedding, she'd been in love with someone else. He was tall and attractive, with thick eyebrows and dark hair, and worked as an exporter, often flying to Dubai for his job. She'd met him through friends and liked that he was more modern than most Uzbek men. He didn't want to control her, and he didn't mind if she wore pants.

Meanwhile, her parents began to bother her about getting married. She kept the relationship a secret, since families usually arranged marriages and he hadn't proposed. He promised to, after his work slowed down. But for whatever reason, he continued to put off a proposal, saying that he needed more time.

Tired of waiting, Fara gave her boyfriend an ultimatum: she'd have to consider offers of marriage when they came up. One day, two women came knocking on her parents' door. They were the mother and aunt of a nearby bachelor. The man had often seen Fara walking in the neighborhood and proclaimed his love for her through his relatives. Weary of her parents' pressure and impatient with her boyfriend's stalling, she agreed to meet him.

The new suitor was okay, in Fara's estimation. "He didn't drink much, he had a decent job, and he was kind," she allowed. They went on several dates, usually outings to parks or gatherings with relatives. And before she knew it, without her consent, in the same manner that brides were kidnapped in Kyrgyzstan, the families had agreed upon a date and place for the wedding. No wonder Lola, my translator, resisted introductions to prospective suitors. Once an introduction was set in motion, the wheels often turned so quickly that a woman was no longer in control of her future.

Worse yet, the prospect of losing her didn't spur Fara's boyfriend to action. There was no way to stop the impending marriage. "I felt like I was in a trap I couldn't escape," she said, tensing up as she recalled the wedding.

After getting married, she moved in with her husband and his family and was soon left alone with her mother-in-law when her husband took a job in Russia, a common pattern among Uzbek men. Her mother-in-law quickly turned her into a slave, making her clean and cook meals for the household, which included another son and his family. The tasks kept her busy from the early morning until late at night. At the end of each evening, her mother-in-law expected Fara to give her a massage, and she was only permitted to bathe and get ready for bed when everyone else had retired. The matron forbade Fara to wear pants or leave the house without a head scarf. When Fara's husband sent money back home for her, the mother-in-law withheld it.

Fara had wondered about her mother-in-law before the marriage. "I knew something wasn't right," Fara said. Though she was polite enough, there was something phony about her, something Fara couldn't quite trust. Fara had always noticed her large hands. One day, after Fara had moved in and tensions grew between the two, Fara said that her mother-in-law lifted up her hands and said, "My hands are made for hitting. When I hit you, you'll never get up."

Even after Fara became pregnant, her mother-in-law still demanded the same duties of her. Fara began to resist, resulting in many arguments that continued after she'd given birth prematurely to an underweight girl and her husband returned from Russia. One day, the fighting turned physical: her mother-in-law hit her. Worse, her husband watched. And then they locked her in a closet for several hours.

Fara fled to her parents' home and filed for a divorce. It wasn't an easy decision, despite the abuse. Divorce carried immense social stigma—she would be seen forever as "damaged goods"—and it cost a small fortune. Thankfully, her husband consented; if he hadn't, the divorce wouldn't have been possible. His parting words were, "I love you. But I love my mother more." And once the divorce was final, he renounced any responsibility for his child. When Fara and her daughter, now three, ran into him in the neighborhood, he ignored them.

After the divorce, Fara fell into a deep depression. She sat for months at home before a friend recommended her for a job at Mashhura. When I met her, it had still been less than a year since the divorce, and the experience remained raw.

Two things had sustained her, she told me: the Koran and her dream of America. "Whenever my heart turns cold, I read the Koran and it makes my life bearable," she said. Her dreams of the West were more complicated: she admitted that she wanted to see her first boyfriend, who now lived in New York. They'd recently reunited on one of his visits home, and their connection was every bit as strong, she said. They'd continued to keep in touch after he returned to the United States and she held out hope that she'd be able to move there someday, even after she learned he had a wife and daughter. All I could do was cringe and wish her the best. Another thing you could find across cultures besides fried chicken and burgers, I thought, was women who fell for the wrong men.

The more I learned about mothers-in-law on the Silk Road, the more grateful I was for Caroline. She neither expected nor wanted us to live with her and David. When we went to their house, I didn't have to cook or clean. She never inquired about plans for children, much less put pressure on me to have them. She treated Craig and me as equals and gave us a good amount of space.

In Central Asia, I also appreciated her presence because it gave me a creative way to dodge questions. When Murad of Tashkent asked me why we weren't staying in his guesthouse, I feigned regret and told him it was "because of my mother-in-law." I didn't have to explain more. When taxi drivers and travel agents pestered me, I said that I would first "have to check with my mother-in-law." They fell silent. With Caroline at my side, I was armed with a response that no one, not even the most aggressive of touts, argued with.

But as we traveled through Uzbekistan, I discovered one tension point with Caroline. Though she was adventurous in general, she was usually cautious about eating. Like Craig, my mother-in-law didn't share my degree of passion for—okay, my compulsive obsession with—food. Caroline had read that food poisoning was common in Central Asia. At meals, she invariably pulled out a bottle of hand sanitizer. She avoided raw vegetables. Walking together in Samarkand, she noted with concern that vendors shined round loaves of *nang* with what appeared to be dirty rags. She winced at the bazaars as I sampled delicious creams and yogurts with my fingers before swaggering to a beverage stand to take shots of mulberry juice.

One afternoon, Craig's parents and I visited a *chaikhana* for lunch while Craig went out to report. Like the one Fara had taken me to, this airy teahouse was packed with locals lazing on divans, chatting, sipping tea, and snacking the afternoon away. I ordered a large meal in Uzbek fashion, covering the table with rounds of *nang*, meat kebabs, various salads, cups of fresh yogurt, and bowls of *laghman*, the hand-pulled noodles that were still popping up here, far from western China.

We ate the *laghman*, awkwardly making do with the spoons we'd been given. (Chopsticks had disappeared after Kyrgyzstan.) But Caroline eyed a tomato-and-cucumber salad suspiciously. How could I be sure that the veg-etables had been washed in clean water? "I'm not going to have any salad," she declared.

"Look, I haven't been sick since I left China," I said defiantly, though I knew that challenging a mother-in-law was forbidden in Central Asia. I scooped a dollop of yogurt and mixed it with the raw salad. I took a sip of lukewarm tea. "The food is perfectly safe! All the kitchens I've visited have been spotlessly clean." As I recounted some of the eating experiences I'd had—the delicious tea and scones at the yurt camp, the fried wontons with sour cream at the Dungan restaurant, and the long, endless meals at Gulzat's—Caroline began to relax. She even reached over and stabbed a few rings of raw onion before inspecting a mutton kebab. She liked onions, and the meat was well done. The salad and yogurt, though, she still eyed suspiciously. As I crunched away, she looked at me disapprovingly. To Caroline, I was playing a dangerous game of roulette.

The next morning, I woke up with gas so terrible that I was sure it could be grounds for divorce. Craig reassured me that if my bodily functions were the worst of our problems, we were doing pretty well. He started getting ready for his day, having planned to meet a few contacts, but as I mumbled and moaned, he reconsidered. "Are you sure you're okay without me?" Of course, I said.

"If you need them, my parents should be around," he said.

"Don't worry. I'll be fine." I hid a grimace. And with that, he pecked me on the cheek and left.

I rolled over and tried to go back to sleep. The pain went away for a while but then it got much worse. My stomach knotted in cramps as I curled up in fetal position. And then a thunderous sound echoed in my stomach, as if a bolt of lightning had struck. I lurched toward the bathroom.

Somehow, before I'd realized the gravity of my condition, I managed to creep outside to join Craig's parents in the dining area.

"You missed a delicious breakfast!" David said. "First, we had yogurt and muesli with these very plump raisins—"

"Jen might not be in the mood to think about food," Caroline gently interrupted.

It was true. I'd never felt so repulsed by the idea of eating. I did my best to look away from the breakfast buffet. Even the innocent Russian blini were nauseating. I could suddenly relate to Caroline's amoeba-in-a-petri-dish queasiness about everything on the table.

She looked at me sympathetically and asked if there was anything she could do. But I also noticed a little smile doing battle with her motherly expression. She leaned forward in her seat. "So you still think all the food is safe?"

I shook my head wearily and returned to my room, where I developed a case of chills and sweated through my sheets. "I'm fine!" I called out to my in-laws when they later knocked on my door, as I hid under the comforter. But I did let the housekeepers in later. They'd heard the constant flush of the toilet, and they sympathetically held out rolls of toilet paper when I weakly opened the door. Later, another staff member came knocking, jovially declaring, "I have tea for your diarrhea!"

So yes, I could admit it: sometimes mothers-in-law knew best. And yet, I wasn't going to change my eating habits. I couldn't. While it wasn't as valiant as dodging bullets as a war correspondent, reckless eating came with the territory of being a food writer.

I never established whether what I'd contracted had been food poisoning or an airborne virus. We suspected the latter when Craig came down with a similar ailment a few days later, after which my father-in-law succumbed to it. The only one who managed to avoid the bug was Caroline, which I attributed less to her careful eating than to the powers bestowed upon mothers-in-law in Central Asia.

I recuperated at Antica, our charming bed-and-breakfast, under the care of the two sisters who ran the place. The house had belonged to the family for four generations. The younger sister, Aziza, told me that their great-grandfather, a textile merchant who'd traded with Persia and Europe, had become successful enough to buy the sprawling home with more than a dozen guest rooms. A beautiful courtyard featured fruit trees and an herb garden. Grape trellises hung over a set of dining tables. Under a covered area near the tables was a desk where Aziza took care of the books. Nearby, her older sister, Oyti, ran the open-air kitchen. The pair looked as different as two sisters could. Aziza was petite with curly hair and a dark olive complexion. Oyti looked European, with a fair complexion and a stocky build. Their frail parents were usually around, strolling in the sunny courtyard or resting in the shade on a divan.

Aziza ran the place smoothly, taking care to be friendly and helpful, doling out a wealth of recommendations to guests. I admired her for more than just her business acumen. In a country where most people feared speaking out, she railed against the government's program to force teachers and students into the fields each fall to harvest cotton, which was just ripening as we traveled through. A single woman, she had also been smart enough to avoid the obligations that came with a Central Asian marriage. She had managed to even avoid cooking, leaving that to Oyti, venturing into the kitchen only to check on things. "I can do many things but I can't cook," she said, feigning remorse.

I was impressed with Oyti, too, esecially after she showed me a number of Uzbek specialties that at last warmed me up to the cuisine. Oyti—the nickname means "elder sister"—had gone through a traumatic divorce that had also separated her two children. She'd taken her daughter while the ex-husband gained full custody of her son. What made it more painful was that her ex had opened a competing guesthouse just around the corner. They didn't speak, and her relationship with her son was distant. Instead, she found solace in the family she and Aziza had formed with their mostly female staff. When I was sick, the sisters had the staff bring me *nang* and a delicious, sweet blend of black tea leaves, crystallized sugar, pomegranate seeds, quince leaves, and fir twigs. It reminded me of the desert tea I'd sipped in Xinjiang, but this one had special antibacterial powers, the sisters told me. "Sometimes you will see the gypsies at the market burning the twigs for luck," Aziza said.

Some of the ingredients were optional, Oyti noted.

"No, they're not," Aziza argued. "Especially when the tourists are in bad shape!"

From hearing the sisters talk about the tea and other dishes, I learned why Uzbek food tended to be bland. Spices and seasonings, which I saw at the markets but not in the food, were generally reserved for medicinal or cosmetic uses, as they had been for centuries. The vision-impaired consumed saffron in soups to improve their eyesight, while diabetics consumed dried barberries to regulate their insulin levels. Elders spiced their tea with cinnamon to help their kidneys. Parents washed their infants' hair with basil for healthy locks.

Whatever was in the tea helped, along with a dish called *atala*. It was a typical breakfast, but the sisters rarely served it because foreigners didn't like it. But I was intrigued by this ancient wheat dish that preceded noodles. In a hot *kazan*, Oyti heated a cup of cracked wheat flour with a bit of oil, mixing constantly, allowing it to clump. The flour browned and turned pasty. She added a little water and a generous amount of sugar and stirred until it became dark and sticky like caramel. She took it off the heat and let it cool slightly. I had a taste. It was like a gooey cream of wheat, rich yet simple, and gentle enough for my delicate stomach.

As my health improved, I sampled more of her cooking. She made delicious pumpkin pastries. Finely diced pumpkin and onions were mixed with salt, sugar, cumin, and black pepper. She wrapped the filling in long strands of pastry dough, crisscrossing it so that it resembled the lacing of a bustier. The hot oven melted the sweet-savory filling and crisped the exterior. I reached for several more, my appetite suddenly fully awakened.

The bed-and-breakfast had been so comforting that I was reluctant to leave. It felt like home, being under the care of the sisters and with my in-laws around. But Caroline and David packed up and headed home, leaving Craig and me to prepare for Turkmenistan and Iran. I felt a pang of sadness as I thought about the untethered life, far from family, that Craig and I would return to—for the rest of the trip, and perhaps beyond.

On our final day in Samarkand, the staff, who didn't usually cook anything but breakfast for guests, made us an afternoon meal of you-know-what. Aziza was aware that I found *plov* tiresome but wanted to show me a more creative version. I volunteered to go to the bazaar. When I returned, Oyti was battling with the stove—it was Sunday morning, and because families cooked more on the weekends, the gas supply in the neighborhood was lower than usual. She finally got the fire going and prepped the ingredients in the order they'd be added to the *kazan*. If a cook was adept, Oyti said, she wouldn't have to prep anything but the meat ahead of time, using the spare moments as the dish simmered to chop and add the other ingredients.

The dish looked appetizing enough when it was done, with pomegranate seeds, radishes, and whole heads of garlic decorating the rice. Craig helped set the table. "Are all American men like that? Is he always that helpful at home?" the staff asked. Another inquired, "Where did you find him?" Aziza said a prayer after the meal: "Thanks be to Allah for bringing everything to us. We are grateful for this food, for those who grew it, and for those who brought it here. *Omin*." They each ran a hand over their face in a downward motion, a Central Asian gesture of prayer.

The result of Oyti's labor was delicious. The pearly pomegranate seeds gave the rice a festive look and tiny bursts of sweetness, while the radishes added bite. The garlic cloves had dissolved like butter, and slices of quince had softened like baked apples. I made my peace with *plov*.

The food got steadily worse after we left Samarkand and moved across the rest of Uzbekistan. As the miles ticked on, the *nang* became smaller and drier. The pomegranates paled. Even the bazaars became less attractive and more ragged—rather than taking time to carefully arrange their produce, vendors haphazardly dumped stunted fruits and vegetables atop crumpled blankets on the ground. In Khiva, a walled trading post Disneyfied for European tourists, we had the worst noodles of the trip. Limp green strands sat underneath a flavorless mush of mutton, tomatoes, and potatoes. Even after I seasoned it with a good amount of salt and paprika (the inexplicable stand-in for pepper), it was still inedible. I looked longingly at the imported junk food that lined the shelves at a dusty little shop, then broke down and forked over the cash for an expensive canister of Pringles.

In this wasteland, Craig and I celebrated our second wedding anniversary. With culinary and recreational options slim, I suggested that we focus the evening around a bathhouse, an age-old Oriental tradition that extended across China through the Middle East. We'd heard that one in particular, in the historic town of Bukhara, was good.

My first warning should have been the staff—hairy men lurked at the entrance, wearing nothing but shower caps and loincloths. They sullenly handed us thin sheets and ordered us behind a curtain. After we emerged with the sheets wrapped around us, they corralled us into a dungeon-like corridor choked with steam. "Stand here!" one masseuse barked. The vapors smelled faintly of urine. Next, while Craig remained in the main corridor with one masseuse, another therapist led me to a separate chamber. "Lie down!" he snapped. Face down, I went onto a hard marble surface. He commanded me to remove my sheet, an order I resisted. "Suit yourself," he replied, and promptly dumped several buckets of scalding water over me. With a rough cloth, he proceeded to sand my arms and legs down, so forcefully that enormous dark clumps of dead skin rolled off, leaving me as red as a boiled lobster. Then he applied a scrub of honey and ginger over my raw skin that penetrated and stung my pores. More torrential buckets of water followed, this time icy cold. "Jen?" Craig asked tentatively from the main room. I limped back to find my husband as bright red and ruffled as I was. We almost slipped on the wet floors as we exited, just as an enthusiastic group of topless Italian women traipsed in. That was our first and last bathhouse of the trip. So much for a romantic anniversary.

Just before reaching the Turkmenistan border, we stopped at a yurt camp near Ayaz-Qala, the remains of a walled city from the sixth century.

We wandered through the ruins, an enormous sand pit divided by mud walls, before settling into a yurt on a concrete foundation: the Central Asian equivalent of a mobile home. The advertised lake where we could supposedly swim was a salt marsh. Tumbleweeds blew in the valley below us. And throughout the day, camels tethered to wooden posts nearby groaned unhappily.

After settling in, we ran into a retired American whom we'd met in Samarkand several weeks before. Jeffrey, sprightly despite being in his seventies, was traveling alone through Central Asia. "You look familiar!" he said, pausing in between the yurts and tilting his head toward us. Since we last saw him he told us he'd done "a figure eight" through Uzbekistan, stopping at the inland Aral Sea, which was drying up due to environmental damage, and Nukus, a forlorn border town. The Aral Sea was "not as depressing as I imagined—it was kind of fun!" Nukus had a great art museum, he added. When I shared my disappointment with the yurt camp, he nodded. "When I first got here, I had the same feeling," he said. "I thought, what *is* this place? But it grows on you. And it doesn't hurt that the bathrooms are pretty clean!"

I was dubious, but it turned out Jeffrey was right on several accounts. We later went to Nukus, which had a good museum featuring priceless modern art smuggled out of Russia. The yurt camp wasn't so bad; the bathrooms were indeed quite nice. And in the early evening, the place became magical, as the sun went down in the valley, lighting up the sky in pink and orange streaks like a Hawaiian sunset without the ocean.

In the dining yurt, we ate bland rice pilaf with Jeffrey, who asked how my food research was going. I told him I'd been dismayed by the food in Uzbekistan. It wasn't that the dishes were terrible, it was the monotony of the cooking that bothered me. Why did *plov* have to be cooked with the same five ingredients? Why were there only a few basic fillings for *manti* and *samsa*, the steamed and baked dumplings? Where was the imagination when it came to cooking?

"Well, you know, what you're describing reminds me of what eating was like when I was growing up in Michigan in the 1950s," Jeffrey said. The mains at dinner alternated between steak, lamb chops, baked ham, roast chicken, and spaghetti, he said. (As I learned in my research, Italian pasta was relatively new to America, only having been mass-marketed in the 1920s and '30s.) "When we had spaghetti, my father would uncork a bottle of Chianti, the only wine we drank, and which we only drank with spaghetti," he added. "I grew up in *Leave It to Beaver* America, and we were delighted with our food." On the very rare occasion, they went out for an exotic taste of the East at a humble Chinese restaurant.

I thought about my own childhood in 1980s Southern California. I'd grown up largely on Chinese food, a carryover from my parents' upbringing, and the standard American fare: macaroni and cheese, hamburgers, pizza, and—like Jeffrey—spaghetti. There hadn't been much imagination, nor was anyone particularly concerned about it. It was only when I was in my teens and twenties, as America changed and I moved around more, that I was exposed to different cuisines. By the time I left for college, San Diego restaurants, along with those in many cities across America, had begun to change. More ethnic eateries opened, aside from the standard Mexican taco joints and Chinese takeouts. I still remember eating pad thai and gyros for the first time. When I moved to New York, my horizons broadened significantly. I encountered Indian chicken tikka masala, Middle Eastern falafel, and Vietnamese *pho* downtown; uptown, near my university, I tasted Korean rice cooked in a stone pot called *bibimbap*, Cuban *arroz con pollo*, and Jewish bagels. While much of this is hardly considered exotic across a large part of America these days, there was a time, not long ago, when it was.

Of course, I couldn't hold Central Asia to my standards, which had evolved over years of eating widely, obsessed as I was with food. Talking to Jeffrey was a reminder that I should appreciate what came to me—not that I was going to love every meal of *plov* that would pop up, but that I might cultivate not only tolerance but respect for it.

That reminded me of how bread was treated in Central Asia, a lesson I'd learned from an Uzbek baker. After he mentioned he'd once tried Italian bread, I asked him to compare it to his *nang*. He paused. "In Central Asia, we cannot criticize bread. No bread is bad," he said. It wasn't censorship—it was a cultural difference. As in Xinjiang, bread was treated with the utmost respect and never thrown out, no matter how old it got. The baker told me that whenever Central Asians discovered bread on the ground, they picked it up, kissed it, and held it over their forehead before placing it on a table or a counter, somewhere higher than it was found. Those were the Prophet Muhammad's orders, a reminder that sustenance was sacred. After the journey, at the end of meals out, I would ask waiters to box up leftover bread along with everything else, a request that might have sounded miserly but seemed just right to me.

We had one more Central Asian country to get through: Turkmenistan, a country that lived up to the caricature of the wealthy desert autocracy that Sacha Baron Cohen created in *The Dictator*. After we crossed the border, we drove along a road that cut through endless sand for hours until we came upon the first sign of the country's vast natural gas reserves. In the middle of rolling dunes appeared an enormous bowl-shaped depression in the earth engulfed in flames. As we pitched a tent for the night, we stared agog at the Darvaza Gas Crater. It was as large as a high school running track. Fires burned within its endless nooks and crannies, and from deep in its center, the occasional spiraling fireball shot out. It looked like the gates of hell. Craig walked to its very edge and peered in while I stood yards away. "Don't get too close! I don't think this is the sort of place where anyone is going to save you," I yelled nervously. Our guide had told us that camels and sheep occasionally wandered off the edge. But Craig could barely hear me over the continuous rumble, which got louder as the evening air cooled. In the winter, our guide told us, the fire was so loud it sounded like a rushing train.

A number of friends and acquaintances who'd traveled the Silk Road had told us that the site was too weird to pass up. Few Turkmen knew about it. Pipes jutted from the edge; natural gas was one of the country's biggest industries. Had a gas exploration project gone wrong? How long had the fire burned? Had there been an effort to stamp it out? Our guide didn't know anything. "We have no information on that," she said, lowering her head. Across Turkmenistan, it would be a common refrain, the answer to nearly every question we posed.

We packed up the next morning and drove through more barren desert. We stopped in a small village devoid of cars, running water, and electricity. But they had natural gas, plenty of it, so the fires of outdoor ovens burned all day. As we walked through the village, its inhabitants pretended not to see us. It was as if we were creatures in some other dimension.

We got back into our four-by-four and, several hours later, arrived in a place that couldn't have been more different—a tacky, modern city rising out of the desert like Las Vegas. The capital, Ashgabat, was filled with new marble buildings, gushing fountains of water, and soaring gold statues of the former dictator, a megalomaniac named Saparmurat Niyazov. He'd died in 2006, after ruling the country for fifteen years, during which he renamed himself Turkmenbashi—the leader of all Turkmen. During his rule, thousands of Turkmen were jailed, tortured, or exiled for expressing dissent. After he died, his loyal dentist, who was rumored to be his illegitimate son, replaced him in a sham election.

Over the next few days, we toured the capital's eerie sights. The National Museum was dedicated to Turkmenbashi, with room after room detailing his biography and filled with his possessions. At the National Library, bookshelves were sparsely filled, though there were plenty of copies of a monthly magazine, the cover of each edition featuring the image of the new president. The library's most important room, under the building's dome on the top floor, was dedicated to the *Ruhnama*, a book in which Turkmenbashi spouted his philosophy and rewrote history to his liking. While other books were scarce, dozens of copies of the *Ruhnama* lined a shelf, along with an enormous model of the work, painted pink. Back on the streets, we walked through a new section of Ashgabat paved with wide thoroughfares and tall new buildings, created from the fortunes of the country's natural gas bonanza. We approached a local to ask for directions; he, too, pretended not to see us and continued on. Across the country, everyone averted their eyes. Though Sacha Baron Cohen had created farce out of a place like Turkmenistan, what we experienced was more like science fiction.

Finally, we met a warm Turkman. A friend of a friend, he was even willing to meet us for lunch. While we ate, he explained that many locals gave a chilly reception out of fear. The government ordered locals not to talk to foreigners—university students, for example, were required to sign a contract that promised they would not interact with anyone but Turkmen. And despite his hospitality, even Michael was on edge. He asked me if my book was political in nature, taking care to inquire in the restaurant's parking lot, where he was sure that our conversation wouldn't be bugged. I paused—his question reminded me of something the writer George Orwell had once said: all writing is political. I decided not to bring that up.

"No," I said. "I'm mostly interested in food."

"Oh, good," he said. "Because I could get in a lot of trouble if it was."

Michael treated us to a meal at Pizza Haus. Despite its xenophobic policies, the government had okayed restaurants serving foreign food. Though international fast-food chains hadn't opened in Turkmenistan, a number of copycats like Pizza Haus did brisk businesses. The owner had managed to replicate Pizza Hut's feel, with a den-like setting and a salad bar. The pies were just as dismally bland.

Michael dressed and talked in a Western manner, wearing a button-down and khakis. He'd studied in America for a master's degree before returning to Turkmenistan to marry, and he was the father of two children and counting. His wife, he said, was pregnant again. He invited us to his home to have a meal with his family.

"I just finished building a yurt in my yard," he said in a British lilt he'd

picked up from his foreign coworkers. Turkmen, like Kyrgyz, were traditionally nomads. He planned to use the yurt for entertaining and housing
guests. He would have invited us to stay at his home, but the government
didn't permit tourists to stay anywhere besides a few designated hotels.

Michael asked me what Turkmen dishes I wanted to try. As I'd drifted
farther from China, I discovered that noodles were no longer commonly
made at home, and even dried noodles were rarely eaten. Not long after we'd
entered Turkmenistan, I'd come across plastic bags of noodle fragments in
a small grocery store. Our driver had told us that they were a convenience
food of last resort, and they'd probably sat in the store for two years.

Our Turkmen friend confirmed that his family rarely made noodles at
home, and given the lowly status of the foodstuff, they would absolutely not
serve them to guests. With no noodles to try, I inquired about a traditional
sheep-and-bread soup called *dograma*. The foreign friend who'd introduced
us to Michael had mentioned that it was delicious.

"That's a very good dish," Michael said. "We'll have to slaughter a whole
sheep to make it." The sheep needed to be fresh, he said. And not a single
bit of the animal would go to waste. The head and feet would be saved for
another meal. His family would use the wool for clothing. The skin could
be used for jackets and shoes. "We eat all parts, including the testicles and
the brain. The brain is terrifically juicy and good for your health. I eat it
once a month to keep my brain sharp."

The brain didn't sound so appealing. But still, I perked up. The idea
of witnessing an animal slaughter inspired morbid curiosity. I'd had the
chance in Kashgar when I visited a live animal market, but I'd side-
stepped the slaughterhouse at the last moment. Over the past month,
however, I'd become more aware of the importance of sheep to Central
Asian cuisine. The more I thought about it, the more I realized that there
was something hypocritical about enjoying meat without watching how it
was produced, from start to finish. "How about it?" I asked Craig. He
was game. After all, it wasn't every day that someone offered to slaughter
a sheep in our honor.

.   .   .

On the appointed afternoon, Michael drove us out of Ashgabat in his shiny sedan to his home an hour away. His family, both immediate and extended, lived in a small village of neat, rectangular plots that reminded me of how homes were often divided in American suburbs. But his dwelling was far from luxurious. The four rooms were small, and the kitchen, adjacent to the main building, had been built of flimsy material, like a toolshed. In a large yard, near an outhouse and a barn, sat the circular yurt that Michael had recently pitched.

Craig and I greeted Michael's family, which included his two toddlers, who frolicked next to his wife. She was a shy woman who was eight and a half months pregnant and looked ready to go into labor at any moment. Semsa looked as traditional as Michael looked modern. She wore a formless smock down to her ankles and a long head scarf, which swept up her hair into a bundle of fabric atop her head, the typical hairdo for Turkmen women. I said hello, only to learn that she didn't speak English. She hung back in the kitchen as the slaughter got under way.

Two of Michael's relatives carried a sheep out of the barn. They held it by its legs, upside down. The stunned look on its face seemed to be not one of fear but of confusion. Twenty-four hours before, it had been grazing on a patch of weeds in the Turkmen desert when it had been rounded up with its flock to a nearby bazaar. Michael's relatives had gone to the bazaar that morning and, after inquiring about its age (it was a year old), checking for healthy eyes and teeth, and feeling its round but not oversize midsection, they plucked it out of the crowd.

It was best for the sheep to be slaughtered as soon as possible after purchase, Michael told us. If it didn't adjust to its new surroundings, the animal was numbed against its imminent death.

As one relative held the sheep, the other used a sharp knife to slit its throat in one quick motion. Blood gushed into a shallow hole that had been dug in the ground, staining the dirt. The sheep's legs twitched while its bladder relaxed, releasing a steamy stream of urine. The butcher made an incision in the spine and washed off the knife with water from a tin ewer, pointing its spout to Mecca as he set it down. The sheep stopped twitching and its eyes took on a glassy hue.

The butcher began to skin the sheep. He started at its feet, flaying with his knife before using his hand to massage skin away from flesh. The front leg wagged up and down as he worked his hands up it. His cell phone rang. He stuck his knife into a wooden post nearby and answered the phone with a bloody hand. When he hung up, he resumed the work, his hands fully immersed in the sheep's body, making it look as effortless as pulling a duvet out of its cover. The sheep fully skinned, he sliced off the legs, then knocked off the head in one quick swoop. He hung the carcass upside down on the post and began the dirtier work: pulling out the intestines, which were as endlessly long as a fire hose. "Not my favorite part," Michael said, grimacing. The rest of the internal organs were swiftly removed and the veins of the heart were cut to let the blood run out. The butcher slapped some cartilage onto the wooden stick. "We have to share something with the post," our Turkmen friend explained. The butcher carved the meat away from the ribs and spine and removed the precious fat from the tail, leaving the skeleton hanging. I glanced at the clock on my cell phone. The whole slaughter had taken less than half an hour. "End of story," Michael said.

I'd chopped plenty of meat and boned chickens and fish, but I'd never seen an animal this big slaughtered and butchered. I was surprised that I wasn't traumatized. I'd felt a little queasy when the butcher removed the internal organs, but the slaughter hadn't disturbed me, nor did it seem cruel. When it had been killed, the animal hadn't made so much as a peep— "like a lamb to slaughter" was an apt phrase. The sheep would provide sustenance for the family for the rest of the month. The butcher had worked so smoothly and quickly that we could get on to the cooking without much thought.

Everyone sprang into action. Inside the yurt, Michael's sister-in-law kneaded dough to make bread, kneeling before a large mound and pushing her knuckles into it. Another female relative flattened the dough into oval sheets, after which she made a dotted line pattern around the edges with a spear. The bread was placed into yet another beehive-shaped oven and baked until crisp. Once it had cooled, we broke each sheet into little bits, a task that frustrated my husband with its repetitiveness. "That took a long time," he said later. "Why didn't we just dip the bread into the soup?" Had it not been crumbled, though, it wouldn't have reminded me of the bread-and-mutton soup I'd eaten earlier on the Silk Road, in Xi'an. The bread, I remembered the Chinese food writer telling me, had originated somewhere in or around Persia. The connection was uncanny. But here there was an extra step. Michael placed the bread crumbs on a plastic sheet, sprinkled finely minced onions over it, and wrapped the plastic over the mixture. It was kneaded so that the onion juices and vapors permeated the bread.

Meanwhile, Michael's father made the broth, firing up a huge *kazan* in the yard to boil the rib meat and assorted scraps. After the broth had simmered, he added tomatoes pushed through a food mill. The meat was cooked until it was firm, after which it was shredded by hand and divvied among the bowls, along with the bread and onions and the rich broth. I was impressed at the communal effort the feast had inspired. The entire family was helping, and for once the men seemed equally involved.

As this was going on, I went into the kitchen, where Michael's wife, Semsa, was making . . . *plov*. Though I'd mentioned the copious amounts of rice pilaf I'd already eaten, our host told me it didn't seem right not to have the dish when he was showing off his best hospitality. Semsa stirred the rice, her enormous belly nearly touching the stove. I chatted with her with the help of a neighbor who'd come for the feast. I learned that she, like many Turkmen women, was a stay-at-home mom. She'd never worked, in fact, and though her husband had gone off to college and received an advanced degree in America, she'd never gotten anything higher than a high school education and had never left Turkmenistan.

As she cooked, I noticed an odd habit of hers. Every so often, she looked around demurely and covered her mouth with the end of the head scarf that hung around her shoulders. She held the scarf in her mouth, biting it almost coyly. Seeing the puzzled expression on my face, she tried to explain by pointing outside the kitchen and then at the head scarf. Just then, Michael and Craig happened to saunter in.

"It's a sign of respect," Michael said.

"Respect?" I asked.

He explained that it was customary for a Turkmen woman to cover her mouth whenever a man who was not her husband nor related to her by blood was in her presence. It sounded too bizarre to be true. But sure enough, each time a man walked by the kitchen, Semsa and any other women nearby stuck their head scarves into their mouths.

Women were also not allowed to talk to these men, our host added.

"Wait," Craig said to Michael. "What if there's something important she needs to say?"

"Well, actually, just a while ago, for example, my father asked her where the tomatoes were," he said. I remembered: she'd replied by pointing. She could also gesture or tell one of her children to pass on the message. Naturally, that was a practical solution, because her children were never far.

"But what if there's a fire? Or an emergency?" Craig asked.

"If there is something really important, like a fire, she can whisper, *like this*," he said, lowering his voice to a faint echo.

Craig and I fell as silent as his wife.

"It's a sign of respect for elders, for men," he repeated, seemingly ignorant that we were becoming more disturbed by the minute. "You know, women should learn to shut up—" He stopped abruptly and laughed lightly.

All I could do was feign a chuckle, as I tried to figure out an appropriate response as an honored guest. I inquired more. He acknowledged that things were different in America, as he'd seen when he was there. But he'd reconciled it very sharply. That was America and this was Turkmenistan. Yes, it was true that his wife didn't have a say in many matters. But in exchange for her silence, he would take care of her and the family. "You can't really live a modern life and be *the man*," he said. So naturally, he'd chosen to be the man.

Michael ushered us into the yurt, where with great fanfare he opened a fancy bottle of red wine from the Caucasus. His family toasted us. The meal began with a mouthwatering cucumber, tomato, and mint salad, and slices of juicy melon. The *dograma* was hearty and delicious, while Semsa's *plov* was better than most, with fresh mutton and apricots. Michael carried on an interesting conversation about world politics. The family toasted us some more. But still, the meal was indigestible. Not only because of the outrageous custom we'd just learned about, but also because the women sat outside the yurt in the cold, while Craig and I dined with the men. Apparently, my status as a foreigner made me an honorary man.

Of all the spectacles we'd see across Turkmenistan, the most alienating was Michael, who seemed so familiar, so kind, so Western, until we saw him at home in this land of unjust dictatorship, with his silent wife.

In Central Asia, I'd met women who'd cried and were unhappy at their weddings, an abused bride, and now a mute wife. If this was what it was like to be female in Central Asia, what about Iran, into which we would be crossing the next day?

GYULCHETAI (KYRGYZ NOODLE SQUARES WITH VEGETABLES)

Serves 6

FOR THE MEAT AND VEGETABLES:

3 pounds lamb, beef, or horsemeat in several pieces, bone-in

2 quarts water

2 bay leaves

Salt and freshly ground black pepper

2 onions, peeled and sliced ½ inch thick

4 large carrots, cut diagonally into thirds

6 small potatoes, halved

FOR THE DOUGH:

1½ cups water

1 egg

1 teaspoon salt

4 cups all-purpose flour

Minced parsley and dill for garnish

Prepare the broth: Place the meat in a large stockpot and add the water. Bring to a boil and skim off the impurities. Reduce the heat, cover partially, and let simmer for an hour, skimming off the foam from time to time. Add bay leaves and salt and black pepper to taste, and let the broth continue to simmer for another hour.

Make the dough: In a large bowl, combine the water, egg, and salt and mix thoroughly. Add 1 cup of flour and mix it in with your hands. Then add the rest of the flour, ¼ cup at a time. Mix thoroughly until all the flour has been incorporated. Place the dough onto a clean surface and knead for 3 to 5 minutes, until the dough is soft, pliable, and smooth. Cover with a damp cloth or wrap in plastic and let it sit for at least 30 minutes.

Roll out the dough: Follow the instructions for rolling out the dough in Chef Zhang's Hand-Rolled Noodles/Andrea's Pasta (p. 96). Cut the dough into strips 4 inches wide, then cut the strips crosswise into 4-inch squares. Sprinkle the squares with flour so they don't stick together and make several stacks of them. Roll and cut the remaining dough the same way.

Finish the dish: Add the onions, carrots, and potatoes to the stockpot. Continue to simmer for about 20 minutes, until the vegetables are tender but not too soft. Remove and discard the bay leaves. Using a strainer or slotted spoon, remove the meat and vegetables from the pot and set aside. Add some of the pasta squares to the stock, being careful not to crowd the pot. Boil for 7 to 8 minutes. Then remove the noodles with a strainer and place on individual plates. Repeat until all of the noodles are cooked and divided among the plates. Slice the meat thinly and place some on each portion, along with the vegetables. Garnish with minced dill and parsley and serve immediately.

SAMSA (UZBEK BAKED DUMPLINGS)

Makes about 30 dumplings

FOR THE DOUGH:

1 cup cold water

1 teaspoon salt

2¼ cups flour

FOR THE FILLING:

½ pound ground beef or lamb (30 percent fat)

1 medium onion, minced

1 teaspoon salt

1 tablespoon ground cumin

1 teaspoon freshly ground black pepper

½ cup vegetable shortening or margarine

2 egg yolks, beaten

Make the dough: Place the water and salt in a large bowl, and add 1 cup of the flour. Mix thoroughly, then add the rest of the flour, ¼ cup at a time, until all the flour has been incorporated. Transfer the dough to a clean, lightly floured surface and knead for 3 to 5 minutes, until the dough is soft, pliable, and smooth. Cover the dough with a damp cloth or wrap it in plastic and let it sit for at least 30 minutes.

Make the filling: In a medium bowl, combine the beef or lamb with the onions, salt, cumin, and black pepper and mix thoroughly.

Preheat the oven to 350 degrees Fahrenheit.

Make the dumpling wrappers: Follow the instructions for rolling out the dough for Chef Zhang's Hand-Rolled Noodles/Andrea's Pasta (p. 96), rolling each portion of the dough into a single, very thin sheet—it should be almost translucent. Smear a very thin layer of shortening or margarine over the sheet of dough. Fold it in half. Smear another very thin layer of shortening or margarine over this surface and fold it again. Place the dough in the center of your working surface and roll it out into a square about 2 millimeters thick. Sprinkle flour over the dough and cut into 3-inch by 3-inch squares.

Shape the dumplings: Place a dough square in the center of your palm and add approximately 2 tablespoons of filling. Bring one pair of diagonally opposed corners together and press to seal, then bring the other pair together and press again. Seal the dumpling completely along the edges to make a pyramid shape with a square base. Brush each dumpling with a thin layer of beaten egg yolk.

Bake the dumplings for 10 minutes. Then raise the oven temperature to 425 degrees Fahrenheit and bake for another 10 minutes. Remove from the oven and serve immediately.

Alternative vegetarian filling:

Substitute 2 cups finely cubed pumpkin for the ground meat, and dot the filling generously with butter before folding and sealing the dumplings.

MANTI (UZBEK STEAMED DUMPLINGS)

Makes about 30 dumplings

FOR THE DOUGH:

1 cup warm water

1 extra-large egg

1 teaspoon salt

2½ cups all-purpose flour

Meat or pumpkin filling as for Samsa (p. 174)

Ketik, or whole-fat plain yogurt

TO COOK THE DUMPLINGS:

3-tier steamer pot or large, covered pot with a steamer insert

1 tablespoon vegetable oil

Make the dough: Place the water, egg, and salt in a large bowl, and add 1 cup of the flour. Mix thoroughly. Then add the rest of the flour, ¼ cup at a time, until all the flour has been incorporated. Transfer the dough to a clean, lightly floured surface and knead for 3 to 5 minutes, until the dough is soft, pliable, and smooth. Cover the dough with a damp cloth or wrap it in plastic and let it sit for at least 30 minutes.

Follow the instructions for rolling out the dough for Chef Zhang's Hand-Rolled Noodles/Andrea's Pasta (p. 96). Cut the dough into 3-inch strips, then cut the strips crosswise into 3-inch squares. Make a few stacks of the squares, dusting them with flour before stacking to keep them from sticking.

Shape the dumplings: Place a dough square in the center of your palm and add approximately 2 tablespoons of filling. Bring one pair of diagonally opposed corners together and press to seal. Then bring the other pair together and press again. The dumpling will take the shape of an open box. Repeat until you run out of wrappers or filling.

Slick the bottom of a steamer insert or tiers with a little oil. In a pot large enough to fit your steamer insert or tiers, bring 1 inch of water to a boil. Place as many dumplings in the steamer insert or tiers as will fit without touching and steam each batch for 15 minutes. Serve with *ketik* or whole-fat plain yogurt.

ANTICA BED-AND-BREAKFAST PLOV

Serves at least 10

1 cup canola oil

3 pounds bone-in lamb or beef shank, cut into 4 hunks, or 2 pounds
    boneless stew lamb or beef

3 large onions, diced

4 large carrots, peeled and cut into sticks about 2 inches long by
    ½ inch thick

1 tablespoon salt

1 tablespoon ground cumin

1 tablespoon freshly ground black pepper

5 cups rice, medium grain, Thai jasmine, or Indian basmati, rinsed
    and soaked in hot water

3 cups water

½ cup chopped raisins or other dried fruit

1 white turnip, cut into eighths

1 kohlrabi, cut into eighths

4 heads garlic

2 quinces or apples, peeled, cored, and cut into eighths

Pomegranate seeds, for garnish

Place a large wok or stockpot over high heat and add the canola oil.
When the oil is smoking, add the meat and onions and cook for 3 to
4 minutes, turning the meat until it has browned on all sides. Add
the carrots and continue to cook, stirring occasionally, for 2 to 3
minutes. Add the salt, cumin, and black pepper. Drain the rice and
add to the wok or stockpot, allowing the rice to fully cover the meat
and vegetables. Add the water and cover the pot. After 5 minutes,

reduce the heat to medium-low and allow the mixture to simmer for 15 minutes.

Uncover the pot and remove the meat. Add the dried fruit to the pot and mix with the rice. Then place the turnip, kohlrabi, garlic, and quinces (or apples) atop the rice mixture, cover again, and allow it to steam for about another 25 minutes, until they are tender. Meanwhile, cut the meat into 8 portions and place each portion on a plate. Divide the *plov* among the plates and garnish with pomegranate seeds before serving.

iran

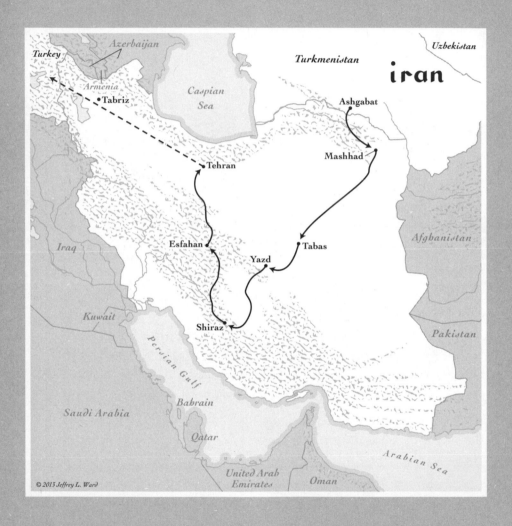

7.

The morning we left for Iran, I dressed carefully, in a turtleneck, baggy pants, and a long black sweater jacket. As our van snaked up a sloping road that cut through barren yellowed hills, I unfurled a purple scarf and draped it over my head. Our ethnic Russian guide chuckled from the front passenger seat: "Soon you'll have to wear that everywhere! These are your last moments of freedom."

I shivered, despite the warm autumn sunlight that filtered into the van. Though Craig and I were happy to leave Turkmenistan, we approached Iran with mixed feelings. For the next three weeks, we would lie about our identities. I was no longer a writer, just a chef interested in Persian cooking; Craig was not a journalist but the owner of my cooking school. We'd sent our notebooks, laptops, and video camera back to Beijing, lest they arouse suspicion from authorities. Part of me felt ridiculous for making such efforts—after all, what authorities imprisoned someone for reporting on kebabs and *khoresht*s? But the Islamic government had locked up and tortured many innocent foreigners.

I'd been hesitant about Iran from the start. Even after we'd gotten our visas and I'd set out on my travels through western China and Central Asia, Craig and I had continued to talk about Iran as if it were a hypothetical ("If we get to Iran, we'll . . ."). But somewhere along the way, the idea had gained so much momentum and the country's allure was so strong that by the time we were at the border, it seemed impossible to back down.

As we went through bureaucratic formalities to get stamped out of Turkmenistan, the border guard seemed to hold on to our passports for longer than usual. Craig and I exchanged glances, hesitating for a split second. Were we really just about to enter the Islamic Republic of Iran?

"There's still time to turn back," Craig said.

But our guide had said good-bye, and our van had dropped us off and pulled away. We were stranded.

"I guess we'll have to go on," I said, sucking in my breath.

"Truthfully, you've always seemed more concerned about getting *into* Iran than getting out," Craig noted as the Turkmen official handed us our passports.

"Trust me, it will be totally fine," I said. I tried my best to slip into a Zen-like state despite having tossed and turned all night.

At the gate on the Iranian side, we handed our passports to a border guard—our first contact with an Iranian. He examined them carefully, slowly turning each page as if he didn't believe the documents were real. After he handed them back, we went on, crossing paths with a group of Iranian men happily heading the opposite direction. In Turkmenistan, we'd heard that Iranian men often went there for rollicking weekends filled with liquor and women. If Iranians went to that wretched country for fun, what did that say about their own nation? We were exchanging one crazy authoritarian leader for one more sinister, who spewed vitriol against America, Jews, and the West in general. Resisting the urge to turn back, I adjusted my scarf, and into the border control office we went.

Our first peek of Iran surprised me: it was as mundane as a Department of Motor Vehicles. Waiting in rows of plastic bucket seats were a couple dozen Middle Eastern men, mostly in Western clothing, and head-scarfed women. Before we could join the line, though, an official with a warm, grandfatherly smile waved us to the front, as if he'd been anticipating our arrival. Standing next to him was a man who introduced himself as Mr. Sanjar, the guide who'd escort us for our entire Iranian sojourn. With a backpack slung over one shoulder, he greeted us with a toothy smile. "Welcome to Iran!" he said joyously in remarkably clear English.

Despite the warm reception, we remained on edge. The border guard pulled out two yellow cards labeled "Interpol Iran Police" and asked us to fill in our details. Then he had us dip our fingertips into ink and press them against the back of the card. Was this part of a plot? Were they going to incriminate us now that they had our fingerprints? From the corner of the room, a poster of the Ayatollah Khomeni, the leader of the Islamic Revolution of 1979, and the current leader, Ayatollah Khamenei, stared down as if they were sternly admonishing us. Hadn't one of them issued the death decree against the writer Salman Rushdie?

The guard stamped our passports and looked at us, brow furrowed. It seemed as if there was a problem or a question. Our passports still in his hand, he told us he had one further request. We tensed and nodded.

"He wants a ride to the next town. Would you mind if we take him?" asked Mr. Sanjar.

As Craig and I left the office with our new Iranian friends, the aroma of turmeric and onions wafted from a food stand next to the exit, rousing my nose from its Central Asian dormancy. We celebrated our arrival in Iran with a ground kebab called *kubideh* on grilled flatbread, garnished with tomatoes and cucumbers, washed down with a can of alcohol-free beer made from lemon malt. (Iran was the one place on our journey where liquor was banned by law.) All for just over a dollar. That was the first promising sign that Iranian food would be better than Central Asian.

Forget the possibility of being tortured *in* Iran; arranging to go there had been torture itself. Fellow journalists and Iran experts I spoke with said Craig and I were outright crazy for wanting to go. America and Iran had cut off diplomatic relations in 1979, when protesters overthrew the shah and stormed the U.S. embassy, taking dozens of American diplomats hostage for more than a year. Since the revolution, Islamic religious fanatics had governed the country, and the hard-liner Mahmoud Ahmadinejad had been elected president in 2005. When he was reelected four years later, thousands of protesters took to the streets, accusing the government of rigging the election. Iranian authorities in turn blamed Europe and America for instigating the instability as they had in the past. Months later, antiforeign sentiments still ran high, with Ahmadinejad continuously denouncing America. The West suspected Iran of building nuclear weapons, and the Israelis were threatening to bomb Iran. In the midst of the tension, Iran had jailed dozens of Americans, including three hikers who'd unknowingly crossed the border, accusing them of spying. Whether Iran believed the accusation or simply regarded them as bargaining chips hardly seemed to matter.

I could have bypassed Iran; Azerbaijan, a sparsely populated country once part of the Soviet Union, also offered passage to the West. But Iran stood at a pivotal place on the Silk Road, a major empire between the Chinese and the Romans. The Parthians, a nomadic tribe who rose to power around the second century BC, first established formal links between East and West to transport silk, a fabric they were as enamored with as were Europeans. After the Parthians, Persia (as the nation was known before the early 1900s) had been conquered by an assortment of leaders from east and west, as in Central Asia. Alexander the Great swept through in the third century BC, sacking the famed city of Persepolis. Arab Muslim invaders followed in the seventh century AD, bringing Islam with them, only to be knocked out of power by the Seljuk Turks of Central Asia and the Mongols in the Middle Ages. In the sixteenth century, Persia reestablished itself as a formidable empire, its influence spreading through Central Asia and Turkey at the height of the Safavid Dynasty.

Through the centuries, Persia served as a transit point for goods moving east and west. Ancient caravanserai still dot the desert, spaced about twenty miles apart, the distance camels could cover in a day. Persia produced its own alluring ingredients that dispersed in either direction. Saffron, grown in the arid region of Khorasan, made its way westward, where it found a strong following among Egyptians, Spaniards, and Greeks; going eastward, the ethereal red threads also gained popularity in Central Asia and China, where they were used as medicine. Iranian pomegranates and pistachios became so widespread that I found them all along the Silk Road. Some suspected that noodles, too, came from Iran. Though noodles aren't central to the Iranian diet nowadays, wheat had long been consumed in the country. The more I learned, the more I wanted to go.

Besides, we had friends in the Iranian diaspora with family in Iran, and they told us stories of how accommodating the people were. And once we'd started our travels, we'd met numerous Silk Road tourists who said that Iran had been the highlight of their trip. Unlike its neighbors Iraq and Afghanistan, Iran wasn't embroiled in war (not yet anyway), making it a much safer destination. I took comfort in knowing that the upside of repressive governments was less crime.

I wanted to go to Iran, despite—or because of—the supposed dangers. The same urge had drawn me to China more than a decade before. Part of it was my contrarian, independent streak. But also I wanted to get behind the rhetoric. I thought there was more to gain from going to a foreign place—from learning firsthand of its complexities—than staying home and letting my ideas about it harden into the image the media conveyed.

So several months earlier in Beijing, I'd gone through the complicated process of applying for Iranian visas, made extra difficult for Americans, especially those of non-Persian descent. We would have to join a tour group and be escorted at all times. Officials occasionally googled applicants to confirm their identities and determine their motivations for visiting. Sometimes visa applications were rejected for no particular reason at all. I'd managed to find one Iranian travel agency that had a good record of getting Americans in, and we agreed to a six-thousand-dollar private tour for two, should our visas be granted. I hoped that it would help that we were applying for visas in China, which had better relations with Iran than the United States. But still, I was doubtful about our chances.

As our visas went through the cryptic Iranian visa system, I visited Rumi, a Beijing restaurant where I'd first eaten Persian food. After opening several years before, it had acquired a loyal expatriate following, drawing not just Iranians and other Middle Easterners but Westerners and Chinese as well.

Fariborz was the thirty-nine-year-old owner, with knitted eyebrows, expressive dark eyes, and a round face. At a table on the second floor of the airy, white-walled restaurant, he told me his story. He was born to an affluent family in Tehran and lived there until he was nine, when the Iran-Iraq War broke out. He and his family happened to be vacationing in Germany. His father, already troubled by the Islamic Revolution the year before, decided to relocate the family to their summer home in Britain, where they eventually gained citizenship. After graduating from college and marrying the daughter of another Iranian family in exile, Fariborz and his new wife moved to New York, where he worked as a buyer at Bloomingdale's. The rat race eventually tired him out, and when a relative who'd been doing business in the Far East persuaded him and his wife to move to China, he could finally realize his lifelong dream to open a restaurant.

Fariborz treated me to an enormous feast. "Please," he said, gesturing to the dishes as they arrived and saying he'd already eaten. I started with a delicious eggplant dip called *kashkt badenjum*, richer than Middle Eastern baba ganoush. Then came *gormeh sabzi*, a savory stew made of lamb, kidney beans, powdered dried limes, and a trio of greens: dill, parsley, and fenugreek, a sweet herb that originated in the Middle East but is also used in Chinese medicine. The fluffy saffron rice made me reconsider the grain, the most mundane of Asian foods. Fariborz instructed me to smother butter and a roasted tomato over it. The buttery rice mixed with the condensed sweet-and-sour flavor of the fruit could have been a meal in itself. But a rack of lamb, juicy and succulent, accompanied the rice. I complimented the food, and Fariborz beamed with delight.

As we ate, I told him about my plans. The delicious food filled me with anticipatory regret for what I'd miss if our visas didn't come through, I said.

"Oh, you'll get your visas all right," he said.

"You don't think the embassy will do a background check? Or at least google us?" I asked.

"I don't think they know what Google *is*," he half-joked, shaking his head. "But the real question is, *why* do you want to go there?"

Fariborz hadn't been back to Iran since he was a child. He was Baha'i, a banned religion in Iran, and the persecution of its followers (along with Jews and Shi'ite Muslims) had escalated after the Ayatollahs gained power. Since the revolution, the government had jailed and killed hundreds of Baha'is because of their beliefs, virtually wiping out the religion in Iran.

Though he'd built a life overseas, Fariborz felt the deep pain of exile. He told me he'd recently applied for an Iranian passport and thought about visiting the country, but his wife objected. He stayed in touch with Iranian friends and family, who shipped him ingredients and updated him on the news. He'd heard that the government had gotten even crazier lately. He wished Craig and me well on our trip, but warned me: "Do you realize that if you're walking on the street with your husband, they could arrest you if you can't produce evidence that you're married?"

I thanked Fariborz for the delicious meal and the leftovers, which he'd boxed up and insisted I take home. I forgot his warnings and was heartened by his prediction that we'd get our visas. Sure enough, a week later, when I went to collect our passports at the Iranian embassy, they slid effortlessly through the hole under the glass window. I flipped through my passport to find an actual Iranian visa, gleaming with a hologram.

After dropping off the man who'd stamped our passports at a small town just beyond the border, Mr. Sanjar drove Craig and me on to Mashhad, the first city on our itinerary. As we cruised through dry mountains that gave way to a wide highway in a flat desert, he told us about himself. He looked vaguely Mediterranean, with olive skin and curly brown hair rumpled with gel. The singsong cadence of his Farsi seemed to echo the lilt of an Italian speaker: *"Ba-lay! Ba-lay!"* he'd say when he reached agreement after a lengthy negotiation with a hotel clerk or a street vendor. Like many Iranians we met, he'd been exposed to the West: he was fluent in English and Italian and had studied architecture in Rome, where he'd passed as a local. He told us that Iranians and Italians had many things in common, including pride in their history and architecture, a proclivity to eat late into the

night, and joie de vivre. I asked if he'd enjoyed Italian food. He'd tried
pork, he told us—the flavor of prosciutto was incredible! And wine: "Yesh,
I drank red wine! Why not?"

Mr. Sanjar married a woman through family introductions and recently
she'd given birth to twins, a boy and a girl. "We were blessed by Allah!
What about you? Do you have plans to have children?"

Not quite yet, Craig and I answered from the backseat.

He scrutinized us in the rearview mirror, his eyes darting from me to
Craig. He brightened. "You look so European and she looks so Chinese!
Your children will be beautiful. You take one apple tree and you put it on
a different one and you get . . ." Searching for the word, he held his hands
above the steering wheel, connecting two imaginary branches, as we sped
down an expressway at seventy miles an hour.

"A hybrid?" Craig offered.

"Yesh!" he shouted, thumping his hands on the steering wheel. "And
you get better apples!"

It was late afternoon by the time Mr. Sanjar exited the highway and
steered us through Mashhad. Iran's second-largest city was known for a
shrine where the religious figure Imam Reza was buried. Just as we arrived
at our hotel, our stomachs began to rumble. Craig asked if our guide could
recommend a good restaurant—maybe even a teahouse, which we'd heard
were popular places to eat, as in Central Asia.

"Oh no," Mr. Sanjar said. "Teahouses are not for ladies."

"Why not?" I asked.

"Men might give you the 'evil eye.' You might feel uncomfortable. They
are not family establishments," he declared. "I know of one teahouse in
Iran that is acceptable for ladies. Later in the trip, I will take you there."

There was one teahouse in the country acceptable for ladies? This
seemed to affirm my fear that Iran was worse than Central Asia. Across
Asia, I'd noticed that teahouses were mostly the domain of men, a reversal
of the European tradition, but Mr. Sanjar was the first person to tell me that
I should not visit one. Though it sounded more like a strong recommenda-
tion than an outright order, it made me wonder exactly how much authority

our guide had over us. Our travel agency had connected us with Mr. Sanjar, but we suspected he worked for the government, too.

Mr. Sanjar discussed "the program," which I'd arranged with the travel agent. After Mashhad, we would make a V across the country, stopping at the desert oases of Yazd and Shiraz before visiting the key cities of Esfahan and Tehran. From the capital, we would fly back to Beijing for the winter. Sometime earlier in the trip, I'd decided to break up the journey and would continue with Turkey in the spring. In all, we would travel more than 1,400 miles in his small sedan.

At first, my travel agent, Bahar, didn't know what to do about my request for cooking classes. She'd never had a tourist interested in Persian cuisine. Foreigners wanted to see points of historic interest, like ancient Persepolis or the iconic Imam Square in Esfahan, Bahar said. But it had taken just a quick explanation that I was an experienced cook and a few words of lavish praise for Iran's culinary offerings before she agreed to help arrange classes across the country. Mr. Sanjar said he would be available to translate during them and to guide us around town. He added that he often ate meals with his guests, but he would give us some "free time." Having almost always traveled independently, neither Craig nor I was enthusiastic about having a guide, let alone a government minder.

After we checked in, Mr. Sanjar yawned and told us he'd ordinarily accompany us to dinner but that he was tired from the driving. We quickly assured him we'd be fine on our own and hit the streets of Mashhad. It was a densely built city, and its streets bustled with people of all ages and range of dress, particularly the women. The more conservative wore the chador, the black head and body covering that reminded me of a nun's habit. They looked like giant ink blots, their smocks covering even their handbags. But other women seemed to take the restrictions on dress as a challenge in creativity; they wore tight jeans and high-heeled sandals that revealed their painted toenails, a suggestive contrast with their head scarves and trench coats. Many of the women managed to look elegant and stylish. Some store windows displayed mannequins that wore dresses with spaghetti straps and even lacy lingerie.

The food shops attracted my attention, too. From a spice shop wafted the scent of cinnamon and black pepper. A butcher hacked away at large chunks of lamb fat. Rows of lamb and beef skewers took up the window of one shop, while across the street, people waited for freshly baked flatbread to roll out of an oven's slow-moving conveyor belt. Specialty shops carried small containers of red saffron threads and dried fruits like barberries and apricots.

As we gawked at our surroundings, passersby in turn stared at Craig and me. We were no longer in a place where at least one of us appeared to belong. Through most of China, I could blend in, while in Central Asia, Craig, with his sandy brown hair and blue eyes, could pass as Russian. But here the prevailing features were thick eyebrows, pronounced cheekbones, and large, dark eyes, though more often than I expected, locals had fair skin or green eyes.

"Where are you from?" an old man buying nuts in one store asked in fluent English. We hesitated for a moment, wondering if we should say, before the word "America" fell from my lips.

"America!" he said. "I love America. I have relatives in Canada." He told us about his visits to North America. It was the first of numerous times we were asked the question, and each time we answered it we were met with thumbs-up, smiles, even the occasional hug. Not once did we encounter a hostile reaction, even on the anniversary of the day the Iranians had stormed the U.S. embassy and taken Americans hostage, a day when the government organized anti-American rallies.

After window shopping, we looked for a teahouse listed in a guidebook, ignoring Mr. Sanjar's warnings. We went down an alley and a set of stairs to an unmarked basement with a locked door. A few knocks later, the door opened and, lo and behold, two fashionable ladies sat inside, trading puffs on a hookah, sitting on a carpeted divan. It was around six o'clock, too early for dinner and too late for tea, but we ended up having both.

We sipped strong black tea floating over sugar syrup in tulip-shaped glasses. Waiters brought us plates of novel snacks. Dried dates melted in my mouth like honey and changed my mind about a fruit I'd been lukewarm about before. Rosewater pudding was sprinkled with crushed pistachios, which in Iran were roasted to perfection, exuding equal notes of sweetness, saltiness, and butteriness and killing my ability to enjoy them anywhere else. Addictively crunchy dime-sized cookies called *hajji badam* flavored with cardamom and nutmeg complemented the tea as well.

Dinner began with *dizi*, a traditional Iranian soup served in a heavy stone bowl. The waiter fished out fatty chunks of mutton, potatoes, and chickpeas and mashed them into a paste to make a dip that tasted like a meaty hummus. With many weeks of encountering it in *plov* behind me, I appreciated this new incarnation of sheep's fat. The dip was served with *sangek*, long sheets of flat, thin dough baked over pebbles to form bumpy ridges. After limited Central Asian seasonings, we were happy to encounter dried oregano, which I'd mostly associated with Italy, sprinkled over a salad of tomatoes and cucumbers. A plate of leafy herbs, including basil (native to Iran), tarragon, and mint, and slices of *paneer*, a white and crumbly sheep's milk cheese similar to feta, completed the meal.

Having eaten to our hearts' content, we lounged on the carpeted divan, taking in the surroundings. The subterranean room was cluttered with oil paintings of landscapes, ewers, and vases. Watermelons were decorative objects, hanging in mesh bags on posts like counterbalanced weights and floating in a shallow fountain, where the trickling of water competed with birds chirping in a cage and a rhythmic string tune that played through a set of speakers. As we digested our meal, we tried to process everything that had happened that day, still in disbelief we'd made it to Iran. But with every sip of strong black tea and every bite of food, it was becoming real.

Tense as I'd been about going to Iran, I hadn't initially wanted Craig to come. I'd thought it might be safer to venture there on my own, given how obviously Western he looked, not to mention his years as a serious journalist who covered politics. Of all the places on my itinerary, though, the Islamic Republic was the place Craig had been most insistent about accompanying me. Certainly he'd never wanted to go to Iran, which offered few outdoor activities and had the distinct reputation of being a pariah state. But he worried about my safety.

How did he know his presence would guarantee my safety? I argued.

He didn't know, he admitted. But if I got thrown into prison, at least he would be there with me.

I should have appreciated the romantic sentiment. But instead I ungraciously replied, "You think they're going to put us in the same cell? All institutions in Iran are segregated by gender! Why would a prison be any different?"

My husband disagreed. We were married. Of course they'd put us in the same cell.

When we'd planned previous trips, we'd discussed what to see, what to pack, and where to eat and stay. This was the first time we'd discussed sleeping arrangements in a prison. After hours of argument, it was settled: if I was going to be detained, tortured, and imprisoned, my loving husband would be there for the memories.

Toward the end of our time in Central Asia, the suspense about what we'd encounter in Iran spilled over into tension. The paranoia-inducing atmosphere of Turkmenistan didn't help. We argued about what to send back to Beijing before crossing into Iran. I wanted Craig to ditch his expensive camera along with other electronics, lest authorities think he was a photojournalist; he resisted, saying that plenty of tourists nowadays carried professional-looking cameras. (He turned out to be right.) We argued about how we'd represent ourselves. I finally agreed that he could say he was the owner of my cooking school, a suggestion I'd initially bristled at.

But we'd made it to Iran somehow, and we hadn't been thrown in jail so far. The vibrancy and bustle was a stark and welcome contrast to the often stultifying atmosphere of Central Asia. We were glad, too, that Mr. Sanjar had let us venture out on our own, and hoped it was a sign that we wouldn't be monitored too carefully. Plus Craig had been right to come along; I was grateful that, despite my obstinacy, he'd accompanied me.

But still, there was one thing that irked me: the *hejab*. I was resentful that I had to wear a head scarf for the whole trip while Craig was free of the constraint—yet another privilege men were given in this world.

"It's only for a few weeks," my husband said, trying to make me feel better. And hadn't I commented just a few hours earlier on how elegant the women looked? Plus, my husband continued, in the West, the trend toward wearing less, at younger and younger ages, wasn't necessarily a good thing.

"Wait a second," I said. Was he actually expressing sympathy with the Islamic clerics? I did share his concern about scantily clad young girls in America. But having just spent the evening with an annoying scarf over my head and knowing I'd have to wear it for our entire time in Iran, I was in no mood to agree.

"You're not the one who has to wear this stupid thing!" I protested, waving the scarf at him in frustration.

"Sorry," he said, surprised at my vehemence. "I was just trying to make you feel better." He reminded me that men had to follow a dress code as well.

It wasn't nearly as stringent, I argued. So men weren't allowed to wear shorts. Big deal!

"Well, who chose to come to this country?" he said. He had me there. And not only had I chosen, but my decision had dictated his: he felt he hadn't had any option but to come along. I couldn't exactly argue that *that* was chauvinist.

The next day, we faced another challenge: gaining entry to the dining hall of Iran's holiest site. We'd learned about the cafeteria by chance as we toured the Imam Reza shrine that seemed as large as the Vatican, with a library and museum among the endless courtyards and buildings. Imam Reza was an eighth-century leader of Shia Muslims, the minority branch of Islam to which most Iranians belonged. After being killed by an Arab rival, he became a martyr. The shrine attracted more pilgrims than any other Muslim site except Mecca. Middle Easterners and Asians swarmed the complex, ranging from Saudi men with checkered kaffiyehs and flowing *thawb*s to Afghan women whose black *hejab*s revealed only weather-beaten faces.

Authorities limited parts of the shrine to Muslims. Non-Muslims could tour the unrestricted areas only with a shrine employee. So Mr. Sanjar happily deposited us and disappeared, relieved of babysitting duty. Our guide was a friendly young woman named Shirin, whose plump cheeks were accented by the chador tightly pulled around her face. As a covering like hers was required for entry, she threw a chador over me and adjusted it. I felt as if I'd donned a crude Halloween costume. At the gates, a black-clad female security guard frisked me more thoroughly than the most zealous of airport personnel.

"Mussulman?" she barked.

I shook my head no.

She shook her head back at me and crossed her arms. No Mussulman, no entry.

Shirin, who'd already made it through security, poked her head back through a heavy curtain, argued with the guard, and pulled me past the curtain. "Don't mind them," she said. "They don't understand the rules."

Once past security, we entered a complex that brimmed with spirituality. Pilgrims kissed the walls, closed their eyes, and murmured prayers as they walked. In some halls they knelt on the ground and cried over the martyr's death as if it had happened just yesterday. Sermons blared over loudspeakers. Shirin was an excellent guide, giving us a thorough tour of the complex. Occasionally, a guard would stop us from entering a certain area. Whenever that happened, Shirin berated the guard and pushed brusquely through, pulling us along. She took us as close to the truly restricted area where Imam Reza was entombed as she could. As we walked, she told us about herself: she was a master's student in English literature at a nearby university, and her latest paper was about Shakespeare and feminism. Like many young Iranian women, she was more focused on her career than on getting married and having children—a point of view that made Iran seem more similar to the West than to Central Asia.

She led us into the shrine's main courtyard just as the sun drifted behind the gold minarets and the sunset service was about to begin. More than a thousand worshippers sat in neat lines on the ground, men on the right, women on the left. Both genders prostrated toward Mecca as the muezzin sang the call to prayer with an undulating, hypnotic voice. Despite all the differences, we felt as comfortable in the mosque as we would have in a church in the American Bible Belt.

During the service, Shirin asked why we'd come to Iran, given how few Americans did. When I told her I'd come to learn Persian cooking, she eagerly launched into the intricacies of her favorite dish, *gormeh sabzi*, the lamb stew with minced green herbs that I'd first had at Fariborz's restaurant in Beijing. "And have you been to the shrine dining hall?" she asked. "You must go there for a meal."

The dining hall wasn't your average tourist-site cafeteria, Shirin told us. It had an important purpose. Every day, pilgrims donated cash to the shrine for the sacrifice of sheep and cows in their name, an important Muslim tradition. Chefs at the dining hall received the lamb and beef and cooked it, serving it to pilgrims for free. The four-story building fed more than six thousand people a day, but the mosque authorities were building an extension to accommodate more visitors because meat was still going to waste. Pilgrims attached special significance to dining at the shrine. Usually tickets had to be procured a day in advance, Shirin said, but she said she'd take us there to try our luck. When the guards stopped us at the door, she pleaded with them while we awkwardly stood by, but they remained firm— the dining hall was restricted to ticket holders. Finally Shirin gave up, but she told us to come back the next day, when she would get us in.

I woke up early the next morning and, as Shirin instructed, met her at seven o'clock at the shrine's main gate. The night before, we'd told Mr. Sanjar that we planned to revisit the shrine for lunch; he was surprised, and doubtful that they'd let us in. A stop at the dining hall was never part of "the program," he said. And as Shirin and I walked to the office where tickets were distributed, she warned of a possible issue. The man on duty that day was especially religious and uptight, and he might be reluctant to give out tickets to non-Muslims. But not to worry, she continued briskly. If anyone asked, I should say that I was a Muslim. And if they asked if I was Sunni or Shia, I should tell them that I was Shia.

"Anything else I should mention?" I asked her skeptically.

"Well, they might look at your passport photo and see that you're not wearing a head scarf. If that happens, tell them you recently converted and you haven't had time to get a new passport," she said. She'd given the scheme quite a bit of thought. My passport photo showed my hair and my uncovered neck, making it downright risqué. Before I could object, she added, "Tell them your new name is Fatima and your husband's name is Ali." Those were the names of the Prophet Muhammad's daughter and son-in-law.

With that, we found ourselves in the office. Shirin led me past a long line of pilgrims and directly to the front, where a colleague took Craig's and my passports. They glanced nervously at each other before the co-conspirator passed the passports on to their uptight coworker. *Fatima, Fatima*, I mumbled to myself. He examined the passports, flipping through the pages, reminding me of the guard at the border. But without much hesitation, he stamped our passports and returned them to Shirin, along with the tickets.

"I'm glad we didn't have to lie," she said with a sigh of relief. She apologized for not being able to accompany Craig and me to lunch, as she had to guide a European group. She kissed me three times, on alternating cheeks, and said good-bye.

A few hours later, I lined up with Craig in front of the dining hall. It was ten-thirty in the morning and already a line of several dozen people stretched along a fence. An Iraqi woman behind us helped adjust my chador while an Afghan woman from outside the line approached us and asked for my ticket. I considered her request briefly, feeling guilty, but then again, I hadn't gotten up at six in the morning to miss this. I held on firmly to my ticket. So did the others: as the queue began to move, one man kissed his voucher and held it to the sky.

Before long, we were seated in a dining room on the top floor. Rows of tables stretched across the room. We sat with a group of Iraqis from Najaf, the men wearing ragged suits while the women were clad in black. As we'd experienced elsewhere, they nodded and smiled politely when we said where we were from. Waiters unloaded large carts filled with food trays and had everyone slide them down the tables so that every diner started eating in five minutes flat. Juicy lamb kebabs came with saffron-flecked rice and a roasted tomato, reminding me of the meal at Fariborz's restaurant in Beijing. Yogurt and flatbread—the two items that had followed us all the way from China—accompanied the meal. After eating most of the food on their plates, the Iraqis scooped the leftover rice into the plastic bags the cutlery had come in, telling us they were taking it back to Najaf.

Reluctantly, we left the dining hall to meet Mr. Sanjar. At the gates, I took a last look at the shrine. A few pilgrims handed out toffees and raisins to others, almost pleading with them to take the food. Others were fully absorbed in the moment, turning around and walking backward in a final good-bye to Imam Reza. Even though I wasn't Muslim, I was moved.

I began to learn the basics of Persian food with Mr. Sanjar. Like most Iranians, he drank black tea from early morning until late in the evening. Every morning before we set off, he made a thermos of the drink, brewed to a dark, tangy brown. While driving, he bravely poured the steaming liquid into a mug wedged between his legs, then handed it to us in the backseat to share before he sipped his own mug. Like many Asians, Iranians didn't add milk to their tea, but they did consume it with generous amounts of sugar. We saw cubes of it everywhere—on restaurant tables, in our hotel rooms, on shop counters. Iranians often held a sugar cube between their teeth while sipping tea, for an optimal sugar rush. After accidentally gulping many cubes, I decided to drop the sugar directly into my cup.

At meals, Mr. Sanjar explained the order in which to eat things. He began with unsweetened yogurt sprinkled with oregano. That would aid our digestion. Next he took pieces of flatbread and placed the feta-like *paneer* atop it, along with fresh dill, tarragon, and basil. Bread was served at every meal, as important to Iranians as it was to Central Asians. Most varieties were consumed just out of the oven, Mr. Sanjar told us, and as we drove the streets before mealtimes, he pointed to the especially long lines in front of bakeries. The bread came in endless varieties, my favorites being *sangek*, the impossibly long sheets of whole-wheat bread that locals draped over their arms like beach towels, *barbari*, shaped either round or oblong and reminding me of *nang*, and *lavash*, thin and chewy, like soft tortillas. Beginning the meal with bread, cheese, and fresh herbs was a ritual I enjoyed, and one that reminded me of the West.

Only after that would we turn to the main course, usually kebabs or long-simmered braises called *khoresht*s, both invariably served with rice. Mr. Sanjar brought me into the kitchens of our hotels, introduced the chefs, and translated as the chefs demonstrated. The lessons began with rice, something I'd taken for granted in China and wearied of in Central Asia, thanks to the continuous onslaught of *plov*. In Iran, the simplest preparations involved many time-consuming steps. A chef in his twenties named Chennari explained he used fragrant, long-grain rice cultivated in northern Iran, near the Caspian Sea. (Thai and Indian varieties were also popular.) He washed the grains thoroughly several times and soaked it overnight to remove the starch. Then he boiled it with salt for several minutes like pasta until it was just *al dente*—he tested it by placing a grain between his front teeth. He drained the rice and rinsed it with cold water, then transferred it to a pot lightly slicked with oil. Over an extremely low fire, the rice slowly simmered, the excess moisture absorbed by a layer of cloth under a lid or a pillow. He added a few drops of saffron water, giving the granules a golden hue. Persians found perfection in the dish when the grains were plump and fluffy, completely different from their sticky, slightly mushy Chinese counterparts. And this was the most basic of rice preparations.

Kebabs were usually made of ground lamb and beef seasoned and flattened into narrow patties and grilled over charcoal. Though Iranians enjoyed sheep almost as much as Central Asians do, they preferred lamb to mutton and had a greater appreciation for poultry and other meats. Chicken, which had almost disappeared after China, came in many forms in Iran. It was marinated in yogurt, turmeric, and onions and skewered on wide metal sticks. Or it was stewed with tomatoes, turmeric, and onions and served with rice flecked with barberries, a cousin of the cranberry. Still more exotic stews featured chicken with pistachios, almonds, and apricots. But none could compare to *fesenjun*, my favorite of all dishes. Ground walnuts were toasted in a pan until they formed a fluffy paste, then pomegranate molasses was added. Chunks of chicken were put to simmer in the sauce, which thickened into a gooey, tangy reduction enlivened with a sprinkle of cinnamon and saffron.

While I was learning plenty about the food, the people who cooked it remained a mystery. It wasn't just the language barrier; it was Mr. Sanjar, a lackadaisical guide and translator. True, his laziness was a mixed blessing. When I wasn't cooking, I wanted him to leave us alone. But in the kitchen, I needed him to translate and explain the cultural subtleties. He wasn't bad when he tried, but he was impatient and indolent, accustomed to a life of luxurious hotel rooms and meals—and foreign guests far less demanding than I was. His attention was usually somewhere else during my cooking classes. He was on the phone, speaking in rapid Farsi, supposedly checking on "the program." He was at the samovar, a fixture in Iranian and Central Asian kitchens, refilling his tea. He stepped outside to smoke. He scoured the kitchen for snacks. "Just a moment!" he would yell across the room as a chef and I struggled to communicate. He sauntered over to answer a few questions before disappearing again. When I tried to pin him down longer during one session, he gave me a pained look. It was too hot by the stoves! "Can I please take a rest?" he begged, as if I were subjecting him to cruel punishment.

And he was a chauvinist. During one cooking session with a female chef, Mr. Sanjar turned to the male hotel manager and said with a laugh, "But we know men are better chefs!" After another lesson one morning, he got off his phone as we climbed into his car. "That was my wife calling. She's at home. She's a housewife. She doesn't have a choice now because God gave her twins!" he said, howling. His laughter was beginning to make the interior of his compact sedan feel smaller by the day.

. . .

I developed a bout of a condition I dubbed "traveler's paranoia." Like traveler's diarrhea, it sometimes afflicted me in foreign places where I wasn't used to the conditions and standards. Onset could be sudden: one moment I'd be coasting along just fine, taking in the sights or luxuriating over a delicious meal, then out of nowhere, it would strike. I'd seize up in panic, and that awful feeling would persist. Unlike diarrhea, there was no immediate relief.

In Iran, our visas triggered my paranoia. Back in Beijing, just before my journey began, I'd checked my passport and noticed that the Iranian visa looked like it might expire in the midst of our Iranian sojourn. I wasn't sure if the date in the visa referred to the last day we had to enter the country or the final day we were permitted to stay in the country. The embassy, oddly, didn't know either, and our travel agent, Bahar, said it was *probably* the date of entry, but she wasn't sure herself. I considered reapplying, but there was no time to start the arduous process again. Bahar said that even if the visas expired after we entered Iran, we could always apply for extensions inside the country. Besides, Iran was such a hypothetical that I figured I'd worry about it *if* we got in. My husband was right: I'd been more concerned with getting in than getting out, and now I was sorry.

The border guard had told us that the visas were good; an extension wasn't needed. That set us at ease for several days, until our paranoia caught up with us again. Could we trust a single border guard? Mr. Sanjar reassured us several times that the visas were fine, but we didn't trust him either, especially because his surveillance seemed to be increasing. After warning us not to visit teahouses, he'd instructed us not to talk to locals. If we did talk to them (an inevitability given how friendly people were), we should certainly not believe anything they said, nor accept invitations to their homes. We'd hoped to see an Iranian-American friend's family in Tehran, but reconsidered after we learned Mr. Sanjar would report the visit to the police. In fact, every day he filed reports about us to the authorities, he fi-

nally admitted. Also, he tagged along more, deciding that we needed his
expert narration of certain tourist sites even when we assured him we'd
be fine without him. When we went hiking one afternoon, he slowly drove
behind us for several miles, like a stalker in a horror movie. He often showed
up just as we sat down for meals. One evening after we'd checked into a
caravanserai that had been remodeled into a romantic hotel, Craig and I
went for a sunset walk through the desert. Returning to the hotel, we strolled
to the dining room to find Mr. Sanjar waiting at a candlelit table for three.

"Shall we eat?" he asked with his goofy grin.

The evening before the date shown on our visas, we decided that we
needed to ascertain that the visas would not expire the next day. I called
Bahar in Tehran. "How's the program?" the travel agent asked warmly.
"Are you enjoying the food?" I told her that all was well, but that I was worried about the visas. If they were to expire and we didn't leave the next day,
authorities could levy large fines and even imprison us. The consquences
seemed more real after Uzbekistan, where a friend had misread her visa
and, after parting ways with us, had been detained for several days. Bahar
listened sympathetically and told Mr. Sanjar to take us to the nearest visa
office the next day.

We spent the night in Tabas, a barren oasis town consisting of several
streets and a few ramshackle buildings. Having arrived late that evening,
we'd eaten at the only open restaurant, which served limp submarine sandwiches of shredded chicken smothered in ketchup and mayonnaise. Our
motel was rows of ugly military-style cement blocks plunked in the sand.
Our room—a suite, Mr. Sanjar called it—contained two lumpy single beds
and ragged carpeting. We settled into bed with some reading. In the morning, we would make the six-hour drive to Yazd, where the nearest visa office
was located.

Just as I was about to nod off, a detail in the guidebook jumped out at
me: the visa office in Yazd was open only until noon. I shook Craig awake,
my pulse quickening.

I threw on a head scarf and we rushed over to Mr. Sanjar's room. He was

rustling around, the lights and television still on. "Just a moment!" he called
before answering the door, his phone cradled to his shoulder. He was wearing only a shirt and a pair of tight black briefs. I cringed, and it was not
from having acclimated to Iran's social norms. Answering the door in that
outfit would have been inappropriate anywhere.

"Yesh?" he said with a big sigh, dropping the phone from his ear.

"It's an emergency," I said firmly. If our visas were going to expire tomorrow, we'd need to start our drive much earlier. I pointed to the paragraph in the guidebook that listed the closing time for the office.

Unfazed, he gave me a look that said something like, *You are a stupid
foreigner waving a ridiculous guidebook written in English at me.* Then, re-
verting to tour-guide mode, he assumed his most soothing parental tone,
stifled a yawn, and said, "Everything will be fine, don't worry. I'll even go
and check your passports for you."

He pulled on a pair of jeans and walked us to the gatekeeper's office. The
guard, sitting on a mattress, barely looked up from his game of solitaire.
After plunking down a few more cards, he got up reluctantly and fetched
our passports. Mr. Sanjar flipped through the pages of one to find the Iranian visa. "You see, everything is fine—" He paused and examined the
passport a little more closely. There was something strange about it. On
second thought, he decided, we should leave at five in the morning.

The sun was just starting to rise when we left the dingy rattrap of a motel.
A band of fog hovered above the desert floor. Mr. Sanjar sacrificed his frequent smoking breaks so we'd make it to the visa office before noon. Craig
and I sat nervously in the backseat.

Along the way, we happened to pass the site where U.S. forces, attempt-
ing to end the Iran hostage crisis, had flown into the desert to stage an
operation to free the Americans held in Tehran. In the desert, military
aircraft, already running low on fuel, became engulfed in a dust cloud and
crashed, killing several Americans. The rescue mission, needless to say,
was aborted. The Islamic government had commemorated the event with a

large billboard and a mosque. As we passed the site, we asked Mr. Sanjar
how he saw the Iran hostage crisis.

"Well, all I know was the government held the diplomats for one week
and they were treated very well," Mr. Sanjar said. "They were our guests."
This account only increased my alarm. The hostages, in fact, had been
detained for more than a year. Whether or not Mr. Sanjar believed the
propaganda he uttered, it reinforced the fact that he represented the
government—one that held Americans hostage, lied about it, and celebrated
American deaths. What were we doing in Iran, traveling on questionable
visas with an agent of an enemy government? To make matters worse, with
Mr. Sanjar in earshot, I couldn't even communicate my anxiety to Craig,
who sat poker-faced next to me. All the while, my brain rushed to make
contingency plans, should our visas be expired and should we not be able
to renew them. We'd have to leave Iran, of course. We would have to buy
plane tickets, but to where? Istanbul, perhaps, or maybe Dubai. Anywhere
out of the country would be just fine.

At ten-thirty, we arrived at the visa office and hurried in. It was part of
a police station, and an officer greeted Mr. Sanjar with a handshake, a hug,
and a kiss on the cheek. "If there are any problems with your visa, my
friend will help you out," our guide said. Everyone he introduced us to was
a "friend." He and the officer exchanged a few words in Farsi before he
pulled out our passports.

The police officer examined them and cleared his throat. "These visas
are fine, don't worry," he said in fluent English, repeating what the border
officer had said: we had thirty days to stay in Iran once we entered. He
pointed to a stamp on one of the visas.

We were suspicious. The stamp had only Farsi on it. And why were Mr.
Sanjar and the visa officer so chummy? And finally, why had Mr. Sanjar
been so concerned yesterday?

Mr. Sanjar said that he'd noticed a strange stamp in our passports. But
after scrutinizing it again, he realized what it was: a notation that we'd collected tickets for the meal at the Imam Reza shrine.

But still, we argued, nothing in our visas that we could read indicated that they would *not* expire today. So would it be possible for the police officer to give us an extension anyway, so we'd feel a little safer? After all, we pointed out, we wanted to make sure we didn't violate any Iranian laws.

He couldn't give us an extension, he explained, because we could only apply for one just before our visas were to expire, and as he'd already explained, our visas were good for another few weeks.

Okay, in that case, we said, our voices growing smaller by the minute, would he be able to give us something in writing we could show the authorities if we ran into trouble?

"I'm sorry, there's nothing I can give you in writing," he said, firmly. We would simply have to trust him.

We left the police station defeated—there was nothing we could do. We couldn't even flee. According to Mr. Sanjar, once we'd confirmed "the program" with the travel agency, we couldn't change it. We were trapped in an Iranian vacation. The vagueness of our status was just another thing we'd have to accept, along with the *hejab* and our annoying guide. We would have to put our faith in a system we inherently didn't trust.

After our visit to the visa office, we managed to relax a little. The officer had said everything was fine, we kept telling ourselves. At any rate, there was nothing else we could do; if we were overstaying our visas, it would only be a problem when we tried to leave, in a couple of weeks. So in the meantime, we idled in the desert oasis of Yazd, known for its labyrinth of alleys and for being a center of Zoroastrianism. The mystical religion, which the government still tolerates, preceded Islam by a couple thousand years and is the source of traditions like the celebration of the Persian New Year on the spring equinox.

Fortunately, in Yazd Mr. Sanjar passed off his translating duties to a young man who worked at our hotel. Koshan's job seemed to cover the responsibilities of bellhop, masseuse, waiter, and guide. Though he was only in his early twenties and had a baby face, his balding head and his constantly furrowed eyebrows seemed to indicate he'd had a lifetime of worries.

As every Iranian had, Koshan welcomed me even more graciously when he found out I was American. But even though most Iranians liked Americans, we should be careful, he added as he escorted me to my first cooking class one afternoon. As we walked through an alley that connected the hotel's two buildings, he peered around the corner to make sure we were alone.

"Has anyone given you a pen?" he asked quietly, in an accent that sounded vaguely British.

"A pen?" I asked, confused. "No."

"Oh good," he said with a sigh of relief. "You're probably not bugged."

Koshan accompanied me as I took cooking lessons from a rotation of female chefs, they and I in our *hejab*s. It didn't seem wise to stand so close to a flame when swathed in so much fabric, but that was the protocol. We cooked in a basement in the middle of the afternoon, when all the hotel guests had gone out for the day. We focused on *khoresht*s, thick stews of contrasting sweet and sour flavors.

One woman showed me how to make *khoresht kheme*, a beef-and-tomato stew with chickpeas (or yellow split peas), onions, ginger, turmeric, and cinnamon. More unusual was a camel stew, in which the meat was sautéed with onions, tomatoes, and potatoes along with turmeric and dried lime powder, the flavors melding with a meat that tasted like lean beef.

As the chefs cooked, I wanted to learn about them: How did they become cooks? What did they think of the *hejab*? What about the status of women in Iran? But I didn't get very far. One morning, after I asked one chef her age and she replied that she was forty-four, she turned the question on me, asking how many children I had to boot. "Thirty-three and no children?" she said, her head scarf pulled tight against her face. "I was almost a grandmother at your age!"

Meanwhile, Koshan chatted nonstop, so much so that I was starting to get impatient until he mentioned something unusual: he didn't like beef. As a matter of fact, he added, "I don't like any meat. Do you know how many sheep they assassinate in Mecca every year?"

Most Iranians liked meat, he allowed, but he was different, he said, because he was Afghan. "We eat more vegetables," he said. Or so he'd heard. He'd never set foot in the country of his heritage. His parents had fled Afghanistan in the early 1980s, part of an exodus of more than a million refugees who'd left after the Soviet invasion and before the Taliban's rise. Koshan was born after his parents crossed into Iran, and he'd grown up on the fringes of Iranian society in a refugee community. The Islamic Republic also discriminated against Afghans because they were Sunni Muslims, not Shia like most of Iran. In recent years, with the American invasion of Afghanistan, more refugees had fled to Iran, only to find a hostile reception— they were refused citizenship and remained stateless. Not only that, but the government had recently begun to deport Afghans back to their homeland, even as the American-led war raged on.

In addition to living in constant fear of being deported, Koshan had fewer opportunities. He wanted to study traditional medicine, but Iranian universities refused him admission because he was stateless. That also made it impossible to get a passport to study abroad. Employers passed him over for jobs, as it was officially illegal for him to work. He'd landed a job at the hotel only because he'd agreed to a low wage kept off the books, and he worked harder than everyone else. He'd thrived in the job. In a few short years, he'd become fluent enough in English to sound almost like a native speaker.

Discrimination was rife in Iran, he said. He elaborated on the persecution of Jews and Baha'is, which I'd heard about from Fariborz in Beijing. "And they say there are no gays in Iran!" Koshan laughed and added: "Ha! I think there are more gay men in Iran than anywhere else." His tone made me wonder if he was homosexual himself.

Ordinarily I might have asked. But Mr. Sanjar's warnings stopped me, and Koshan himself pulled back; neither of us felt at home here. He seemed to realize he'd let on more than he should. "If the police found me here working and talking to a foreigner, I could get in a lot of trouble," he said nervously. That comment lingered in the air as he prepared tea to go with the stew. When he struck a match under the samovar there was a loud thud, followed by a collective gasp from the three of us. Koshan rushed to shut off the gas main as he wiped beads of sweat from his forehead.

"Maybe that's a sign we shouldn't be talking about such things," I said semi-jokingly.

Just then, a group of Turkish tourists arrived in the hotel's courtyard and asked to see the rooms. Koshan went to greet them. Several of the women lit cigarettes and begun puffing away. "What exactly will happen if I don't wear my head scarf?" one woman asked tauntingly, to nobody in particular. Smelling the tobacco and hearing the defiant feminine tone, I wanted to teleport myself to Turkey immediately.

On his return, Koshan referred disparagingly to the Turkish tourists as "Mongols!" Iranians had harbored a dislike of Mongolians since the invasion of Genghis Khan, seven hundred years before. "The Turks came in here demanding this, demanding that, as if they'd conquered the place."

Our hotel was cozy, and eating meals in a large courtyard dining room with long rows of tables, we met adventurous travelers from around the world. Three young Chinese women were backpacking through the Middle East. A twenty-something Dutchman was "couch surfing" the world using a website that connected him with locals who hosted him at no charge. A young Romanian couple, traveling with their infant daughter and five-year-old son, were blogging about their adventures driving from Europe to Asia in an ambulance converted into an RV. "The good thing about driving an ambulance is that no one wants to hit you," said the wife one afternoon as her husband drove us around town, swerving at an intersection to narrowly avoid a collision. All in all, the hotel company was excellent, and the stews I learned were delicious; it was the first place I'd happened upon that felt something close to what I imagined a caravanserai might have felt like hundreds of years ago, with travelers passing through for a day or for weeks and swapping their wares—these days, stories rather than goods.

The hotel also had a fair share of Iranians, and the atmosphere made it an easy place to befriend them. One evening, while Mr. Sanjar went to chat up a pretty female guest, an elegant middle-aged woman joined us for dinner. Zari, originally from Tehran, had spent most of her life in Britain but, after a divorce, she'd returned to her homeland. I asked Zari if she found it difficult to adjust to life in Iran.

"It's annoying to wear the head scarf," she said. "I would say the majority of women don't want to wear it, but it's just a fact of life." Before the Iranian Revolution, she told me, only a small percentage of women wore veils. In the 1970s, Iranian society, flush with cash from oil exports, developed strong ties to the West and followed many Western traditions. Since the revolution, the severity of the country's laws had ebbed and flowed, depending on the mood of the government and clerics. Sometimes draping one's scarf loosely over the head and showing a little hair was perfectly acceptable; other times, it could get you hauled off to the police. It was all part of the game, a method of exercising control. Nobody knew exactly when they might cross the line.

"But everyone has a way of getting around the rules," Zari said. "For example, take liquor. In Tehran, my son talks about the parties kids throw, with DJs and drinks and girls showing up wearing next to nothing. They're just as wild as they are in London."

How did people get away with it? I asked.

She rubbed her thumb and fingers together. "Money. As long as you give some to the police, you're fine. Actually," she added, lowering her voice to a low mumble, "it's all supported by the regime."

And just like that, we'd crossed another invisible line beyond what was permissible. Zari cleared her throat and changed the subject, asking about our travels. "Does your guide have to be with you all the time?" she asked. Yes, we replied, it was a regulation that only Americans had to follow. "That sucks!" she said. Just before Mr. Sanjar came back to join us, she warned, "You should be careful around your guide. Don't ask him too many questions."

A few nights later, we decided to test that invisible line yet again. We climbed to the rooftop of the hotel to smoke a mint-and-tobacco hookah with Zari and Koshan. Nahid, the pretty woman Mr. Sanjar had been hitting on, also joined us, but thankfully she'd rejected his advances and brought a long-haired musician with her instead. As soon as she sat down, she whipped off her head scarf, and perfectly coiffed locks fell around her shoulders. Our time in Iran had done something: seeing her exposed hair was almost as shocking as if she'd joined us naked in a Jacuzzi.

"Why should I have to hide such beautiful hair under a scarf?" Nahid purred, playing with her tresses.

"Iranian women care a lot about their hair," Zari said. I'd wondered about where women cut their hair. Just like elsewhere, in salons, she told me, but ones that were hidden from public view, in basements or second floors, or in private homes. "Iranian women spend more time in salons than anyone else I know," she added.

Nahid inhaled deeply from the hookah, an activity that was also deemed illegal in this conservative town. In other cities, men openly enjoyed the tall pipes in teahouses and at sidewalk cafés; in Mashhad we'd seen two women in the basement teahouse trading puffs. It seemed that many rules in Iran were unclear. But even cautious Koshan seemed to think that smoking a hookah, a minor breach of the law, was acceptable. It was past midnight and the hotel doors were locked. The night was barely illuminated by a sliver of a moon. And it had been very many long days since we'd had a drink.

Taking a quick glance around, Zari decided it was also safe to take off her scarf, and I followed her lead. But when someone else appeared on the roof, Koshan urged us to cover our heads again. On the scarves went, then off again as soon as the man left. After smoking for a while, we went down to Nahid's room and listened to Persian music and snacked on pomegranates. We kept the conversation light; we didn't need to push any more boundaries.

The next morning in the hotel lobby, our new friends wished us well on our journey, the women's scarves securely fastened to their heads.

8.

After Yazd, Mr. Sanjar resumed his job as translator during cooking classes, lazy as he was. In Shiraz, I persevered and learned how to make several tasty pilafs that redeemed the bad name miserable Central Asian *plov* had given the dish. In Esfahan, I tolerated Mr. Sanjar at my side and shaped ground lamb and beef into kebabs. But when I got to Tehran, he had worn me down entirely. His constant mantra was a disingenuous "I'm at your disposal," and after several weeks, I truly wished I could dispose of him.

One afternoon not long after we arrived in the capital, I reluctantly climbed into his car for the umpteenth lesson and, after battling horrendous traffic, we eventually arrived in a nice residential neighborhood. I was intrigued when Mr. Sanjar pulled up at a gated residence and told me to get out and ring the bell.

A middle-aged woman poked her head out the gate, exposing her floppy mop of reddish-brown hair while her black head scarf dangled around her neck. She and Mr. Sanjar exchanged a few words in Farsi, then he called to me from the idling car. "Jennifer, since the school is for ladies only, I won't be able to go in with you." I tried to look disappointed as I waved good-bye, and he happily sped away, relieved of his duties.

Come, come, the woman gestured, leading me into a compound that had a familiar suburban American feel. A shiny hatchback sat in the driveway, and fancy patio furniture and a barbecue decorated a pretty garden. She pointed me up a set of stairs and through an entrance to the house on the second floor. In the foyer, I removed my shoes and hung my head scarf on a coatrack. In the kitchen, the woman resumed making *pots de crème* and assembling a trifle, sans wine or spirits. A half-dozen women sitting at a long table paused in their note-taking to greet me warmly. Some of them wore chadors or dark head scarves while one had gone to the opposite extreme—my eyes settled on the women's outfit: a blue-and-white polka-dotted tank top that revealed a black bra. A pointy green feather decorated her dyed blond hair. When she stood up, I couldn't help noticing the black thong sticking out of her jeans.

With the help of her daughter, Yasmin, the woman who'd greeted me at the gate introduced herself as Mrs. Soltani, the head of the cooking school. A short woman with a beak-like nose, Mrs. Soltani had started this home business more than twenty years before, after quitting her job as a school-teacher. She'd begun with Persian baking lessons, added *khoresht*s and *polow*s (rice dishes), and later threw in some international dishes. By the time I visited, she'd taught thousands of women, and some had gone on to successful cooking careers.

Yasmin, the office manager, translated for me during class. In the confines of her home, she looked like she belonged on the streets of Manhattan. She wore tight jeans, heels, and a stylish top. She decorated her ears with multiple studs and brushed her honey complexion with foundation and blush. Though her English wasn't as good as Mr. Sanjar's, her boundless patience made up for it.

I settled into the class as Mrs. Soltani spread a layer of cream over sponge cake before decorating it with canned fruit and gelatin. She put the trifle in the fridge to set it. As in the Central Asian cooking classes, the Western food she taught was rather lackluster, but the Persian dishes dazzled me. Next on the agenda was *tah-cheen*, a rice dish I'd tried earlier on the trip; Mrs. Soltani's was infinitely better. Like the trifle, it involved layers. Tender chunks of chicken sprinkled with sugar, cinnamon, and barberries sat between layers of parboiled rice and a mixture of yogurt, saffron, and beaten eggs. The *tah-cheen* was baked in a round Pyrex dish. After it cooked, Mrs. Soltani inverted the caked rice, revealing a golden crust that had formed around the sides and bottom of the dish. She cut the cake into wedges and the crust crackled as I sank my teeth into it.

During a tea break, the women gossiped about recent weddings and Korean soap operas. They shared pictures of their families on their mobile phones. Among the students were an architect, a beautician, and an entrepreneur. The woman with the black thong didn't work; she told me proudly that her husband was a successful entrepreneur and soon they were moving to Canada. "I can't have any fun in Iran," she complained.

Yasmin invited me to stay after class to learn another dish—the all-important kebab. Though I'd seen plenty of kebabs before reaching the Soltanis, I was impressed with the passion Mrs. Soltani displayed in making them. She mixed ground lamb with saffron, turmeric, minced onions, and the sour red spice called sumac, and kneaded it as ferociously as a lion attacking prey. She scooped up the meat with bare hands, shaped it into a ball, and slammed it against the bowl several times with the force of a baseball pitcher. *"Umph!"* she exclaimed, before explaining that the motion bound the mixture together, avoiding the expedient of adding a beaten egg. She massaged the meat with well-oiled hands and sculpted it onto wide skewers. Just as my mouth watered in anticipation, though, Mrs. Soltani put them aside and said she was reserving them for her husband, who was returning from work soon. We would be going out for dinner.

We donned our head scarves and headed out the door, climbing into Yasmin's new hatchback. Craig had arrived in time to join us, and we sat in the backseat while Mrs. Soltani sat in front with Yasmin. As Yasmin drove, she spoke about some of Iran's limitations. While she could drive, unlike her female counterparts in Saudi Arabia, for example, she chafed at the dress restrictions and the ban on alcohol.

They took us to a beautiful teahouse at one of the city's fanciest hotels. This was the teahouse Mr. Sanjar had mentioned earlier, the one that was "acceptable" for ladies. And indeed, it was a feminine domain: groups of women and children, clustered on sofas in the high-ceilinged room, were attended to by men. A couple of women said hello to Mrs. Soltani, and she hugged them warmly. They were former students of hers, she explained, who'd gone on to become restaurateurs. Yasmin ordered a round of black tea and offered us lollipops of crystallized sugar to put into the drink to aid our digestion.

As we sipped tea, Yasmin asked the questions we'd come to expect: How long had we been married? Did we plan to have children soon? Yasmin herself was single, and like many young Iranian women we met, she was in no hurry to get married, wanting to focus on her career. She added that she didn't like to cook, preferring to leave that to her mother while she focused on the business aspects of the school. After graduating from college, she'd worked as a software engineer, but her company had laid her off two years before, a casualty of Iran's dismal economy, which was growing increasingly stagnant under bad domestic policies and Western sanctions.

While we were at the teahouse, Yasmin's mobile phone rang. It was her brother, Shaheen, who wanted to say hello. Craig took the phone, and Shaheen apologized profusely for not being able to accompany us to the teahouse. We accepted his invitation for dinner another evening. After the call, I asked Yasmin why her family, and Iranians in general, were so friendly and hospitable, when the government had been telling her since the day she was born that America was the enemy.

Yasmin paused before answering. "We have satellite television, we read the Internet. We know the truth," she said. Managing to circumvent the government's controls, they took the onslaught of propaganda with a grain of salt. Although they had mixed opinions on America's foreign policy, they understood that much of the shouting between the countries was politics. It was ironic: despite the censorship, Iranians were better informed about us than we were about them.

.   .   .

At the teahouse, Yasmin and her mother ordered two large bowls of noodles for us. I hadn't yet had a notable noodle dish in Iran, and I was eager. But after I tried a few bites of the *ash-e-reshteh*, long, thin strands of noodle served in a slightly sour broth with chickpeas and greens, I gave up, thankful that I had the excuse that I was full from sampling Mrs. Soltani's cooking all afternoon. But the truth was, they weren't very appetizing. The mushy wheat vermicelli floated limply in the soup, the texture of the noodles a marked contrast to how Iranians liked their rice. Chickpeas, lentils, spinach, and dill vied for attention in the bowl and made for an overly busy mixture. The sour taste I'd noted—most likely *kashkt*, or dried yogurt, the Soltanis told me—had been alien to me. I'd enjoyed noodles salty, spicy, even slightly sweet, but sour was somehow beyond me.

I had noodles on only a few other occasions in Iran. At the teahouse on our first night in Mashhad, tagliatelle-like strands were tossed with butter and flecks of basil, a minor side dish among many. In the friendly desert oasis of Yazd, Craig and I had tried a Persian version of spaghetti Bolognese, a lackluster dish made of minced lamb, tomato paste, and boiled dry noodles. And toward the end of my week with the Soltanis, after the mother had enthusiastically showed me a multitude of stews and rice dishes, she reluctantly agreed to have her assistant show me a vermicelli dish. Into a pressure cooker the assistant threw sliced carrots, lentils, a large hunk of chicken, a knob of butter, and a spoonful of tomato paste. She added a quart of water and sealed the lid. After the soup had cooked for forty-five minutes, she added salt, pepper, a squeeze of lemon, and a package of vermicelli, and closed the lid to cook for another fifteen minutes. The result was only slightly more appetizing than the teahouse's *ash-e-reshteh.*

Some experts claimed Persians had invented noodles and they'd dispersed in either direction, but I was disinclined to believe this after I'd spent time in Iran and researched it further. While some Iranians like Mr. Sanjar held fast to the claim, others like the Soltanis believed the conventional wisdom that noodles had been invented in China.

There is evidence, though, that noodles have long been an important part of Persian cuisine. The Iranian-American author Najmieh Batmanglij writes in her cookbook *Food of Life*, "It is customary to eat noodles before embarking on something new." The food symbolizes "the path among the many that life spreads out before us" and "can bring good fortune and make new endeavors fruitful." Iranians often eat noodles on Nowruz, the Persian New Year, and just before or after loved ones leave on journeys. Rather than a dish of greeting, like *plov*, it seemed noodles were a way of saying good-bye and good luck.

Ash, a word that refers to soup or noodles, began appearing in Persian poems as early as the ninth century, but it was unclear which the poets were referring to. One of the first concrete mentions of noodles appeared during the Ghaznavid Dynasty, an empire that covered much of modern-day Iran, Central Asia, and northern India and lasted from the tenth to the twelfth centuries. *The Chronicle of Beihaghi* records an instance of the sultan Mahmud of Ghazni ordering royal cooks to make *ash-e-lakhshak* (old Persian for *ash-e-reshteh*) for the poor. *Ash*, not coincidentally, is also a word for noodles in Central Asia—witness the two-noodle *ashlyanfu* I'd encountered in Kyrgyzstan. (So important was *ash* that the word for "cook" throughout Central Asia and Iran was *ashpez* or *oshpez*.)

But it seems that noodles diminished in importance as rice began gaining prominence, sometime in the fourteenth century. A century later, the Persian poet Boshaq al-Atameh described in a lengthy work how saffron rice battled noodles and won. And somewhere in my travels between Central Asia and Iran, the Central Asian noodle dishes that reminded me of Chinese ones— dishes like *laghman* (hand-pulled noodles) and *manpar* (noodle squares) had disappeared. Iranians told me that Azeris, an ethnic Turkic group in Iran, ate dumplings, but outside of that community, nary a dumpling did I see throughout my visit. Some older Iranians remembered their families making and eating noodles at home in their childhood; Shirin, our tour guide at the Imam Reza shrine, had told me that her grandmother hired a noodle crafts-man to come to her village. But all that was left in Iran when I arrived were a few lackluster dishes that employed factory-produced vermicelli.

Fortunately, the delicious rice dishes I ate at the Soltanis and elsewhere in Iran made up for the dearth of noodles. Aside from *tah-cheen*, the crusty cake of rice, chicken, and barberries, Mrs. Soltani taught me *bagholi polow*, a pilaf of fresh dill and fava beans. As the chefs before her had done, she carefully rinsed, soaked, and parboiled a batch of rice. She placed a layer of potato slices in a stockpot slicked lightly with oil and added the parboiled rice. She added fresh dill and fava beans, dousing the mixture liberally with butter before adding a splash of saffron water. She steamed the *polow* for forty-five minutes. Once it was done, she inverted the pot onto a heavy plate, gave the pot a hard whack, and a crusty mound of pilaf tumbled out. The *polow* had the perfect *tah-dig*, the golden crust that formed around the bottom of the pot.

Tah-dig was the measure by which Iranian cooks were judged. The key was to begin with a generous layer of oil in the pot before placing a layer of potatoes, *lavash,* or rice mixed with yogurt and eggs (as with *tah-cheen*). Mrs. Soltani packed the rice down firmly, before adding a bit of water and heating the pot over a very low fire until most of the moisture had slowly evaporated. When the *tah-dig* was done, it was deep golden, never dark or scorched, and it made a gratifying crunch when you bit into it.

Along with this delicious *polow*, I tasted a vast array of pilafs across the country; chefs imbued them with candied orange peel, pistachios, and almond slivers; sour cherry jam and chicken; yellow split peas, lime powder, and lamb. After the monotony of Central Asian *plov*, tasting the variety of *polow*s in Iran was like going from black and white to Technicolor. And while rice was central to Persian meals, the *khoresht*s, or braises, that accompanied them were also important. Achieving the right balance of sweet and sour in the *khoresht*s was key. Many stews were flavored with a spice mix that included ground turmeric, ginger, cinnamon, and cumin. The Soltanis and other chefs used an array of souring agents that included powdered dried limes, *kashkt* (dried yogurt), lemon, and sumac. The sweetness was provided by dried fruits, sugar, grape molasses (which I'd also seen in Xinjiang), or pomegranates (an ingredient I'd encounter again farther west).

Despite the dominance of meat, vegetables were more varied and interesting in Iran than I'd encountered elsewhere on my journey. In addition to the fresh herbs that came with the bread and cheese at the beginning of meals and the slices of tomato and cucumber that often accompanied kebabs, Iranians had a special fondness for eggplant. In *kashkt badenjum*, it was simmered and flavored with ground lamb, onions, and dried yogurt. Occasionally I came across dolmas, the stuffed vegetables or grape leaves that spanned from Central Asia to the Mediterranean, and *kuku*s, omelet-like dishes imbued with leafy greens or fava beans. But in general, vegetarians like Koshan had a difficult time in Iran.

Mrs. Soltani also taught me the importance of saffron, which she used liberally, despite the cost—she went through about a hundred dollars of the spice every month. She ground the red threads in a mortar, transferred the powder to a small glass, and added a thimble of hot water, keeping the saffron close at hand during classes. One afternoon, after making the delicious dill-and-fava-bean rice pilaf, Mrs. Soltani took out a few chicken breasts. Salivating, I asked Yasmin what was next.

She paused, searching for the right name. "Do you know KFC?" she asked.

"Fried chicken?" I replied. She nodded and smiled. It proved to be fried chicken, indeed, but the Colonel never put saffron in his secret recipe, I guarantee.

While I was in cooking classes at the Soltanis', Craig was often on his own. Sometimes he stayed in the hotel and read, but as Mr. Sanjar left him to his own devices, apparently having ascertained that we were not national security threats, Craig began taking long walks and visiting teahouses. In the evenings, he joined me, and I was grateful that the Soltanis included him in our after-class plans.

On the evening the Soltanis' son, Shaheen, had suggested for dinner, I finished my cooking lessons for the day and awaited Craig's arrival. Mrs. Soltani, Yasmin, and two cooking assistants sat in front of a large flat-screen television that beamed soap operas, talk shows, and music videos from around the world—but not, I noticed, the BBC or CNN. While the others chatted and watched a Latin American soap opera, Mrs. Soltani crossed her legs on a chair pointed toward Mecca and wrapped a flowery white chador over her head. With her hands grasping the cloth under her chin, she began her *namaz*, or prayers. She mouthed long verses from the Koran and occasionally touched her forehead to a special prayer tile in her lap. While devout Shias prayed three times a day, fewer than the five times that Sunnis prayed, Mrs. Soltani pared down her sessions to once a day.

I asked Yasmin about the family's beliefs. They were divided, she said. While she and her mother were mildly religious, her father and brother were outright atheists. Like her mother, Yasmin prayed every day, though her beliefs weren't as strong since she'd graduated from college. "Praying for me is more of a ritual, a way of giving appreciation to my family," she said.

After Mrs. Soltani finished her prayers, she and Yasmin closed up the cooking school. Yasmin donned a black head scarf and trench coat and left for French class, which she attended several evenings each week. I followed Mrs. Soltani downstairs, to the family's comfortable home. The living room was filled with a fancy sofa and a European dining set, the brand-new chairs still covered in plastic. Mr. Soltani was watching the news. He rose to greet me, and Shaheen got up from a bar stool in the kitchen, where he'd been sitting elbow to elbow with Craig. A haze of cigarette smoke engulfed them. Sporting fancy athletic wear and a gelled hairdo, Shaheen looked just as Westernized and trendy as his sister. He'd told Craig that we were the first Americans he'd ever met in the flesh and that he'd planned for this evening since he'd heard we were coming. His enthusiasm was a little unnerving and awkward, making us feel like celebrities before an adoring fan.

"What would you *lack* to drink?" he asked me with an unmistakable Southern twang, which he explained he'd picked up from a local English teacher, an Iranian who'd spent time in Georgia.

Craig was drinking Heineken, which Shaheen had purchased illegally for seven dollars a can. But I was more curious about another drink he offered—arrack, a clear liquor that ethnic Armenians bootlegged in their homes and sold in water bottles, for twenty dollars each. I'm practically a teetotaler because I have a low tolerance and enjoy only the taste of wine. In Xinjiang, I'd avoided the beer, and in Central Asia I'd dodged the *koumiss* and vodka. In the southern Iranian town of Shiraz, where the grape of the same name originated, Mr. Sanjar had offered to procure wine, but we declined, thinking it best not to buy from him. He'd noted that Persians drank liquor for centuries before the fundamentalists came to power in 1979. (That information, along with the admission that he'd consumed pork and wine in Italy, were the only times he broke with official dogma.) In his travelogue, Marco Polo noted how Persians of his own time had evaded the Islamic ban on liquor: "They quiet their consciences on this point by persuading themselves that if they take the precaution of boiling it over the fire . . . they may drink it without infringing the commandment."

Somehow, though, the ban on alcohol made the prospect of a drink at the Soltanis' more appealing. Shaheen bounded to the fridge, dispensed ice cubes into a glass with the same comforting crushing sound I'd heard in my own home, and poured in the clear arrack. With its distinct anise aroma reminiscent of Greek ouzo, this was a drink I would see in various incarnations farther west.

Mrs. Soltani wrinkled her nose as she strolled into the kitchen, coughing and waving her hand to disperse the smoke. We asked Shaheen if it was okay to drink in the house—as if there was anywhere else we could do it.

"It's *fahne*, it's *fahne*!" Shaheen said, pointing to a glass of arrack and 7UP his father had just poured for himself. "Y'see? Ma father, very soon, will drink from this *cu-up*."

Meanwhile, an image of President Ahmadinejad flashed on the news, prompting Shaheen to launch into a tirade.

"We have no freedom in this coun*tray*," he said, working through his third glass of arrack. With the Southern accent, he was beginning to sound like none other than our former president George W. Bush. "No freedom of thought, no freedom of action. We can't do *anythang* in this *countray*!" I almost expected him to declare his homeland part of the "Axis of Evil."

Because of the restrictions, Shaheen said he wanted to leave Iran, maybe go to Australia. It was the first time we'd heard complaints about the government so candidly spouted, though we later learned that, for many Iranians, these sentiments hovered just below the surface. To be sure, the president had support—his redistribution of wealth, adherence to strict Islamic values, and nationalistic rhetoric appealed to some. But that was not Shaheen nor the rest of his family, he explained. He was getting more worked up by the minute, denouncing the president and railing against the ayatollahs and the mullahs, the religious clerics who enforced *sharia*, religious law. "I *hate* mullahs!" he proclaimed. He dashed into his bedroom to retrieve a document and proceeded to read it aloud in his wobbly, Southern-tinged English, elongating his vowels with wild abandon. The paper sounded like it had come from some anti-Muslim lobby outside of Iran.

"Where did you find this?" I asked.

On a forbidden website, he said, adding that he easily circumvented Iran's firewall through a proxy server.

If Shaheen was any indication, the Iranian government was in serious trouble. His voice contained an almost uncontrollable rage. Listening to him reminded me of the deadly protests that had broken out in Tehran the previous year. They would erupt again, not long after we departed Iran, riding an "Arab Spring" of revolts in nearby countries.

But for the moment, the pressing question was: where would we *lack* to eat? Shaheen wanted to get in his car and head out for the night.

We'd just eaten upstairs in the cooking school, I protested, and there were so many snacks sitting before us—the kitchen counter was littered with pomegranates, grapes, sunflower seeds, and peanuts.

"But this isn't dinner," Shaheen said. "We must have dinner."

Craig and I looked at each other, both of us thinking the same thing. If it was illegal to drink, wouldn't it be doubly illegal to drink and drive?

"Don't be silly," Shaheen said. "I must, must take you out for dinner!"

But what about his parents? Wouldn't they worry about us?

Shaheen crossed his arms and said he was simply not going to take no for an answer. He'd been planning this since he'd heard we were coming!

We looked over at Mr. Soltani. He nodded passively and told us to have a good time. Mrs. Soltani had disappeared back upstairs to watch her soap operas. We hesitantly got into Shaheen's spacious new Hyundai sedan and he drove us to a pizzeria, which was fortunately just a few blocks away. It reminded me of the fake Pizza Hut in Central Asia, and the bland pies and uninspired salad bar paled in comparison to the food his mother cooked. Instead of beer or arrack, we drank cherry *sharbat*, a drink that was usually made from stewed fresh fruit but at the pizzeria came out of a fountain dispenser. Women, adjusting their head scarves occasionally, sat stiffly with their children and husbands. We stuck to safe conversation. Shaheen professed a love for Iranian poetry, promising Craig a volume by Hafez, his favorite poet, whose tomb we'd visited earlier in our trip. He also talked about soccer and his job as an engineer, constantly fidgeting and getting up for more *sharbat*. We argued over the bill. Shaheen prevailed, then announced that he would drive us back to our hotel.

But we could take a taxi, I protested as we got up to leave.

Shaheen stopped in his tracks and looked at me incredulously. "It is *mah duty* to drive you home!" he exclaimed.

As we drove through the dark streets, he turned up the stereo full-blast and sang along off-key to Gloria Gaynor's "I Will Survive." Approaching a narrow alley near the hotel, we asked him to stop by the side of the road—we could walk the rest of the way. But he wouldn't hear of it. "It's not too narrow! Don't tell me such a *thang*!" He slowly coasted down the tight street and deposited us at the front door of our hotel. We breathed a sigh of relief when we got to our room.

Along the Silk Road, we'd seen how deeply Western fast food had penetrated far-flung cultures. But Iran's obsession with hamburgers and pizza surpassed its neighbors' and possibly even America's. The pizza joint that Shaheen had taken us to was one of hundreds in Iran, places as common as kebab shops and bakeries. With no international chains allowed to operate in Iran, small-time entrepreneurs made a lucrative business out of fast food. In Shiraz, we'd ventured into a restaurant called Pizza Hamburger 101 to see what the fuss was about. We sat down to a spongy pie topped with limp, tasteless cheese and fake ham. The tomato sauce was simply ketchup, which diners squeezed from plastic packets onto the finished product.

In Esfahan, after a long stretch of enjoying kebabs and *khoresht*s, Craig had gotten a hamburger craving. "I hear they have good burgers," he said of a nearby hotel restaurant, though he couldn't remember who'd told him. I agreed, a little grudgingly, but figured I'd order a Persian meal while he took care of his craving. But when we sat down and unfolded the menus, I balked—the restaurant served only Western food.

If we had to eat Western, I insisted we find something local. Craig was hungry and didn't want to spend time wandering around looking for food. It could, after all, take hours when I was involved. And he'd been eating stews and rice for weeks, he added. Why not go for a little variety? But I was writing a book about food, I argued back, and I wasn't going to write about a dismal hotel meal.

Craig acquiesced reluctantly, and we returned to the streets. There were plenty of pizza and hamburger joints, of course, but I couldn't bring myself to enter one. Finally, we found a place selling kebab sandwiches that seemed sufficiently Iranian. Craig grumbled as we ate chicken kebab sandwiches slathered with Thousand Island dressing. He was right to complain. The meal was disgusting.

Later when we met up with Mr. Sanjar, he asked us what we'd had for lunch. Craig mentioned that he'd wanted to go to the fancy hotel. "Oh, you mean the Abbasi?" our guide asked. "They have the best hamburger in Iran!"

Hamburgers and pizza aside, shops sold illegally imported Western goods like Nutella, Coco Pops, and Hershey's Chocolate Syrup, which sometimes sat in revolving storefront-window display cases. The all-powerful beverage companies Coca-Cola and Pepsi had managed to skirt the embargo and had turned Iranian youth into soda drinkers. On the streets, I'd even found a pirated copy of a Jamie Oliver DVD selling for just over a dollar. At the cooking school, too, I'd seen the enthrallment with the West.

Mrs. Soltani's saffron-imbued fried chicken aside, her curriculum included roast beef sandwiches and European-style loaves of bread.

Iran's love of Western food was not a recent phenomenon. Under the shah, Western goods had flowed freely from Europe and America. In fact, to celebrate the twenty-five-hundredth anniversary of the Persian monarchy in 1971, the shah flew in chefs from Paris to prepare a banquet. Craig and I learned of the lavish event while touring Persepolis, the ancient city of the Achaemenid Empire. Pointing to a set of abandoned tents in the distance, Mr. Sanjar told us that that was where the feast had been held.

The menu included quails' eggs stuffed with caviar, crayfish mousse, roast lamb with truffles, and roasted peacocks. Not a single Persian dish was served, unless you counted the caviar from the Caspian Sea and the peacocks, Iran's national symbol. Wines, including a 1945 Château Lafite Rothschild, flowed throughout. The dinner made the *Guinness Book of World Records* as the longest and most lavish banquet in history. Dozens of world leaders and dignitaries, including U.S. vice president Spiro Agnew, dined for almost six hours at a cost of more than one hundred million dollars. Eight years later, fierce and bloody demonstrations over the shah's incompetence and corruption finally loosened his grip over the country and he fled, fearing for his life.

Iran seemed to have a love-hate relationship with the West, an unsurprising result of constant meddling by British, Russians, and Americans, who scuffled over geopolitical dominance and oil. It was easy to get the impression from spending time with Shaheen that Iran was in trouble, yet the current anti-Western regime had managed to stay in power for almost forty years. And not everyone I met dissented, not even the more Westernized and affluent. At a party in a private home in Tehran, as Craig and I snacked on salami and sipped whiskey, both smuggled from Europe, an Iranian woman told me, "We were so European growing up, we didn't know who we were as a people. We didn't know our culture, our history. Things are now moving in a good direction. I feel positive about the future."

. . .

The day after Shaheen took us out, I returned to the cooking school for another lesson. In the back kitchen, Yasmin taught me how to bake Iranian cookies called *berenji*, while a group out front learned how to make European bread. The cookies had begun as a snack for the students, but became so popular that the school had opened a side business selling them to a distributor. Like Central Asians and Europeans, Iranians had a long history of baking and sweet-making. Confectionery shops were as plentiful as pizza and hamburger places, many of them family businesses passed down for generations. They sold many types of baked goods, from a dense version of baklava, heavy with pistachios, walnuts, and syrup, to cookies made with not just wheat flour but also ground chickpeas and rice.

So important was rice that Iranians even added it to their cookies. Yasmin pulled open a large Tupperware container of rice flour. I was familiar with the ingredient from China, but this flour had a distinctly earthy, sweet fragrance. We measured out the flour on a digital scale and mixed it with vegetable shortening, sunflower oil, and eggs. Yasmin poured in rosewater and a teaspoon of crushed cardamom. We shaped the biscuits with tiny, thumb-sized cookie cutters, decorated them with poppy seeds and pistachio slivers, and glazed them with saffron water and egg yolk.

As the cookies went into the oven, Yasmin asked how the evening had gone with her brother. I told her we'd felt bad about drinking in front of her parents and concerned about getting into the car with him after the drinks. Mrs. Soltani, who'd just given the class a short break, wandered in and overheard us.

"Shaheen bad!" she said, shaking her head and wrinkling her nose.

"We're all worried about him," Yasmin said. As a child, he'd been the smartest student in his classes, but as he grew older, his intelligence often got him into trouble, she explained. He questioned authority, challenged everyone around him, and was unwilling to compromise. His temperament made him particularly frustrated with Iran's current state of affairs.

"My parents warned him not to drink and drive several times last night but he did it anyway," Yasmin said. Shaheen was headstrong, and once he had an idea in his head, he didn't let go. Her parents acquiesced the night before only because they didn't want to fight in front of us, honored guests from afar.

I asked her how she felt about his desire to leave Iran. She wanted to leave, too, she replied. She hoped to immigrate to Canada, which was why she'd gone to French class the evening before. Every year, Quebec admitted a certain number of skilled immigrants who met certain requirements, including French proficiency. She'd already submitted paperwork for the two-year process. If she studied diligently and passed the language test, she had a good chance of making the cut. Canada had already granted one relative and the relative's husband visas, and several college friends lived there. America was her first choice, but it was nearly impossible to immigrate there without family already in the country.

I asked Yasmin why she wanted to leave. Like her brother, she, too, launched into a tirade, albeit a saner one. Her complaints went beyond the *hejab* and not being able to drink. The morality police had unbridled power to arrest whomever they wanted, she said. Unmarried couples weren't allowed to walk in public together. Police broke up parties in private homes, hauling young people to jail for fraternizing and dancing. I discovered that we could have even gotten arrested for turning up the music in Shaheen's car and singing along to Gloria Gaynor. Granted, his singing was horrendous, but making it a crime seemed a little extreme.

"Women aren't even supposed to ride bicycles," Yasmin said.

"Bicycles? What's wrong with bicycles?" I asked.

"I don't know," Yasmin said wearily. But the police had recently stopped the daughter of one of the school's assistants for doing just that and warned her not to do it again.

Shaheen had been arrested a handful of times, Yasmin added. She'd gotten in trouble as well. Just before graduating from college, she'd been camping with her boyfriend and several friends in the desert. The authorities tracked them down and sent them to a detention center. When the police called her parents, they said that she and her boyfriend were engaged, hoping to buy amnesty. After a court appearance and strikes on their dossiers, they'd been freed. But if she had gotten in trouble again, she would have been expelled from college.

The authorities who monitored social norms were called the morality police. But they weren't the police we'd come in contact with over our visas; they were part of the *basij*, or revolutionary guards who worked under the religious order. So far, they'd been invisible to Craig and me. I asked Yasmin what the morality police looked like. They essentially could be anyone on the streets, she said. That was part of what made them so effective. Some wore black chadors pulled tightly around their faces—that described about half the women on the streets; the men often were plainclothed. Others worked directly for the military. They lurked in certain public areas, keeping watch on young people. It was a game of cat and mouse, as much defined by luck as it was by skill or how careful people were. I shivered. We'd taken a big risk the night before.

Things had relaxed under the previous president, Yasmin said, and the morality police had been mostly concerned that women were properly covered up. But the social restrictions had tightened since Ahmadinejad had taken office, and now the government had made life so untenable that she, like many other young, well-educated Iranians, felt she had to leave. She added that she planned to take her parents with her.

"But what about the cooking school?" I asked.

"My mother's been cooking for a long time. She's tired. And soon, my father will want to retire, too," she said.

It was a shame to think that the vibrant women's-only private space might vanish. But it was worse to think of the family languishing under the tight rule of a government that micromanaged every aspect of their lives. The government even restricted how the Soltanis ran the school—classes had to conform to a set curriculum and the family couldn't change menus without permission.

Mrs. Soltani came back into the kitchen, complaining about her arm, which had been bothering her so much she'd recently signed up for physical therapy. She poked her head into the fridge and, with slumped shoulders, picked at some leftover roast beef with her fingers. She dunked the beef into some cold soup: Not bad, her expression seemed to say. At the end of a hard day in Iran, the food was always there to comfort you.

Craig had liked Iran more than he'd expected, and I'd enjoyed having him with me to experience the delicious Persian dishes and the Soltanis' hospitality. While he never got used to the tea (my husband was addicted to coffee), he could always find packets of Nescafé, and while I was at my cooking classes, he could go off and find an occasional hamburger in peace. He especially admired the country's long history of poetry and hearing locals recite verses spontaneously. Had Craig not come with me, I doubted that my experience would have been as rich. I would not, for example, have heard Shaheen rant about politics, an evening that, odd as it was, would go down as one of the trip's most memorable.

Also, had I been without Craig, the travels with Mr. Sanjar would have been awkward, given the social norms. Thankfully, the tension with our guide had ebbed again, and one morning, I made a truce with him over *kalleh pacheh*, a stew of lamb's head and feet. I'd heard of the dish in Turkmenistan, when we'd visited Michael's village for the sheep slaughter. Throughout Iran, our guide had spoken about the dish, calling it his favorite. Toward the end of our trip, he asked us if we were up to the challenge of trying it. One eatery in Tehran was known for the best *kalleh pacheh*.

"What's in it?" Craig asked.

"Well, you get the feet, of course. And then parts of the head, like the brain, the tongue, and the eyes. I don't like the eyes," Mr. Sanjar said, making a face. "But everything else is delicious!" Our guide added that we'd have to leave early in the morning. It was breakfast, and we'd have to beat the rush.

"I've had enough interesting food experiences," Craig said, declining the invitation.

So Mr. Sanjar and I set off the next morning at six-thirty. On our way to the eatery, the sun began to rise across the city, which was just coming alive with a few bicyclists and vehicles.

"When I was in high school, I used to get up this early and go jogging with my friends," Mr. Sanjar said, as we rounded a corner. "And then we would go eat *kalleh pacheh.*"

As soon as Mr. Sanjar parked the car, my nose detected the smell of lamb's innards wafting down the street. It wasn't the most pleasant fragrance, but the store was already packed. A dozen diners crowded the eatery, standing around a large mustachioed man with a protruding belly who presided over two vats that sat on a stove low to the ground and rose to his waist. One contained a soup made of lamb's stomach, an innard that resembled a squishy sheet of honeycomb, while the other contained the main attraction: sheep's heads and feet. He ladled out the soup, tinged yellow with turmeric. He fished out a sheep's head and shook out the brain, which landed on a plate with a small thud. It resembled dirty cottage cheese. He carved some tongue and cheek onto the same plate and placed it all in front of us.

The shopkeeper had worked in the store for twenty-five years, taking it over a few years before the death of his father, whose framed photo hung on the wall. Each afternoon around five o'clock, he prepared a fresh batch of the soup. First he cleaned dozens of sheep's heads by burning off the remaining hair and removing the noses, then split them in half. A hairy gland was taken off each of the hoofs. He boiled the sheep parts slowly over a low fire, adding salt, pepper, turmeric, and cinnamon, periodically adjusting the seasonings. He left the vats simmering overnight and returned to the store at five in the morning to taste the soup and adjust the seasonings once more. His regulars began to arrive after dawn prayers.

"The eyes are good for your eyes, the brain is good for your brain, and the feet are good if you've broken a bone," he said. It reminded me of what Central Asians and Chinese said about eating various animal parts. "We have a story about *kalleh pacheh.* Two men have been given life sentences"—

highly plausible, given we were in Iran—"and they're told they can eat only one thing at mealtimes, over and over again. One prisoner dies shortly thereafter, because he's chosen kebabs. The other prisoner ends up living for years and years and even gets stronger. His secret? *Kalleh pacheh.*"

Did he eat the soup every day? I asked.

He patted his round stomach. "Not anymore."

I ate the tongue and cheek without a problem—the tongue was a bit more fibrous and slippery than beef tongue, but the cheek was succulent and tender. I hesitated when I got to the brain. Mr. Sanjar had already sprinkled some into his soup, along with torn-up pieces of *lavash.* In between slurps, he assumed his most soothing, parental voice: "Don't worry, I'm here. It's Iranian traditional food. Just close your eyes and enjoy it!" I mustered the courage and inserted the spoon into my mouth. The brain had the same taste as liver, but with a gelatinous, gummy texture. One bite was plenty. In this instance, my husband was right: I'd had enough interesting food experiences.

As we ate, I noticed I was the only woman in the shop. "Women don't like the soup because it's heavy and fatty," Mr. Sanjar said. But strangely, the guide didn't seem to have a problem bringing me here, unlike the teahouses. The diners didn't seem to mind my presence either—they smiled and greeted me as I sipped the soup. As in other parts of the Silk Road, hospitality toward foreigners seemed to override prejudice. And they were busy in the social space, swapping news about their lives and talking about the day's headlines.

After we finished eating, a middle-aged mechanic wearing a jumpsuit invited me to his table. He poured me a cup of tea and offered me sugary saffron wafers to help me digest the soup. Every day, the dish gave him the energy he needed for his job, he said.

As we got back into the car and drove off, Mr. Sanjar looked content. He wasn't so bad after all, I supposed. Evidently he hadn't planned to detain or torture us, and in a sense he'd kept us safe. A few days later, we would pass through immigration and board our flight back to Beijing without a hitch.

"If only young people ate more of this and less pizza, they'd be much better off," our guide said, adjusting his seat belt. "My brain feels light. Oh, we should walk a lot today."

On one of our last evenings in Iran, we went to the Soltanis' for a final meal. I'd offered to make Chinese pan-fried dumplings with lamb-and-carrot filling. It wasn't going as well as I'd hoped. I had the ingredients I needed, which had come from the Soltanis' well-stocked fridges and pantry, but the dumpling skins were drier than usual and kept tearing. And I was nervous, because when I'd stir-fried *kungpao* chicken another day, the smoke from the chilies had made everyone cough. Everyone dug in with makeshift chopsticks fashioned out of wooden kebab sticks. "Good!" Mrs. Soltani proclaimed while everyone else choked on the spice. Afterward, they lit incense and opened the windows to disperse the scent of chili-infused oil. Iranians, like Central Asians, were not fans of spicy.

In the cooking school kitchen, I struggled with the dumpling skins in the face of all kinds of distractions. Mrs. Soltani, in a motherly sort of way, kept shoving sections of an orange directly in my mouth. Another relative was trying to show me a cooking magazine she edited. Craig was trying to make the dumplings as big as he could to get the process over quickly. "Personally, the kind of cooking I like to do is fast," he told Yasmin, who took down the recipe for her mother.

Yasmin had spent the week cooking with me, and for that I was very grateful, especially since she didn't like to cook. As the last pan-fried dumplings came off the stove, we dashed downstairs to the Soltanis' home. I asked if the week had changed her opinion on cooking. "No, not really." She shrugged. She still thought of cooking as a chore. To be honest, she said, she'd rather be cleaning her room.

It was around ten in the evening when we started eating. Instead of sitting at the formal European dining table, as I'd expected, everyone sprawled out across the room, eating on sofas, sitting at bar stools, or standing in the kitchen. I finally got to taste the Soltanis' kebabs, the dish I'd learned my first day with the family but hadn't sampled. Mr. Soltani grilled up dozens of skewers and wrapped them in a blanket of *lavash* to keep them warm. He served them with a simple salad of lettuce, tomatoes, and cucumber with a homemade yogurt dressing. Even though I thought I'd hit my limit with kebabs in Iran, the Soltanis' version, toothsome hunks of tender lamb sprinkled, of course, with saffron, was more delicious than most.

Passing over the chili oil I'd made and the soy sauce, everyone was dunking my dumplings into ketchup. I was horrified, but with Mr. Soltani's encouragement, I tried it: Iranian ketchup, imbued with spices, was actually quite tasty, a cross between Heinz and tangy barbecue sauce. (And ketchup, as it turned out, had Chinese roots—it had begun as a condiment called *kecap* before going to Britain, where tomatoes were incorporated.) I had to admit that the condiment enlivened my dry dumplings.

"Pretty good, eh?" Mr. Soltani said. "But I think they could be improved with something sour." He first thought of lemon, then thought better of it. "I know what will work." He reached into a cabinet and pulled out a bottle of sumac. Shaking the red powder over the dumplings, he took a bite and smiled. Things were always better a little sweet and a little sour.

After dinner, one of the Soltanis' relatives offered to drive us to the hotel. Rather than donning a head scarf, I covered my head with the hood of my jacket and walked out of the cooking school for the final time. We got into a Smartcar parked in the alley, and Yasmin and her parents waved good-bye. Just as we were pulling away, Yasmin knocked on my window, noticing that my hood had accidentally slipped off.

"Jennifer, please put on your hood. It's always better that way," she said. Because even though it was dark and very late, you never knew who was watching.

CHELOW (PERSIAN RICE)

Serves 6

4 cups long-grain rice, Thai jasmine or Indian basmati
2 quarts plus ½ cup water, plus more for washing the rice
1 tablespoon salt
1 cup sunflower or canola oil
1 teaspoon ground saffron, diluted in ¼ cup hot water
2 tablespoons yogurt

Wash the rice in warm water, stirring the grains with your hands to loosen the starch, and changing the water several times. When the water is fairly clear, soak the rice for 4 to 12 hours.

In a large stockpot, bring 2 quarts of water to a boil. Add the salt. Drain the rice and add it to the pot. Boil for 6 to 8 minutes (depending on how long you cooked the rice), stirring occasionally. Test a grain by holding it between your teeth—it should have a bit of give but still be fairly firm, like al dente pasta. Drain the rice and rinse it with cold water.

In a medium bowl, mix together ½ cup oil, ½ cup water, a few drops of saffron water, yogurt, and 2 cups of the soaked rice. Wash and dry the stockpot and spread the mixture over the bottom of the pot, packing it down firmly with your hands.

Place the rest of the rice in the pot, mounding it. Cover the pot and cook the rice for 10 minutes over medium-high heat to form the golden crust.

Mix ½ cup oil and ½ cup hot water. Pour over the rice. Drizzle the rest of the saffron water over the top. Wrap the lid with a clean dish towel and cover firmly. Cook for 1 hour over medium-low heat, or until the rice is fluffy. Remove from heat and allow it to sit, covered, for 5 minutes. Uncover and invert the pot over a dish. Use a spatula to gently loosen the rice from the pot. Serve immediately with either Gormeh Sabzi (p. 236) or Fesenjun (p. 238).

GORMEH SABZI (LAMB AND KIDNEY BEAN KHORESHT WITH FRESH HERBS)

Adapted from Najmieh Batmanglij's Food of Life

Serves 6

6 tablespoons oil

2 large onions, peeled and thinly sliced

2 pounds lamb shank, bone in

2 teaspoons salt

1 teaspoon freshly ground black pepper

1 teaspoon turmeric

4½ cups water

½ cup dried kidney beans, soaked in warm water for 30 minutes

4 whole dried Persian limes, pierced

4 cups finely chopped fresh parsley

1 cup finely chopped fresh scallions or chives

1 cup finely chopped fresh cilantro

*3 tablespoons dried fenugreek leaves, or 1 cup fresh fenugreek
    leaves*

¼ cup freshly squeezed lime juice

1 teaspoon ground cardamom

½ teaspoon ground saffron, dissolved in 2 tablespoons hot water

In a heavy pot or Dutch oven, heat 3 tablespoons oil over medium heat and brown the onions and meat. Add salt, pepper, and turmeric. Sauté for 1 minute.

Pour in 4½ cups water. Add the drained kidney beans and dried limes. Bring to a boil, cover, and simmer for 30 minutes over low heat, stirring occasionally.

Meanwhile, in a wide skillet, heat 3 tablespoons oil over medium heat and sauté parsley, scallions (or chives), cilantro, and fenugreek for about 20 minutes, stirring constantly, until the herbs are very fragrant and aromatic. Do not burn the herbs.

Add the sautéed herbs, lime juice, cardamom, and saffron water to the pot. Cover and simmer for another 2½ hours over low heat, stirring occasionally.

Adjust the seasonings, adding more salt or lime juice if necessary. Remove from heat, discard the dried limes, and serve with Chelow (Persian rice) (p. 234).

FESENJUN (CHICKEN IN WALNUT-AND-POMEGRANATE SAUCE)

Serves 6

2 cups finely ground walnuts (a food processor works well for this)
¼ cup canola oil
1 medium onion, diced
½ teaspoon turmeric
2 pounds chicken or duck thighs and drumsticks
½ cup pomegranate molasses
2 tablespoons sugar
½ teaspoon ground cinnamon
½ teaspoon ground allspice
¼ teaspoon ground saffron, dissolved in 1 tablespoon boiling water
Salt and freshly ground black pepper to taste

Place a skillet over medium heat and add the ground walnuts. Toast them, stirring frequently, for 6 to 8 minutes, until they are browned and fragrant.

Heat the canola oil in a Dutch oven or other heavy-bottomed pot. Add the onions and turmeric and sauté for 3 to 4 minutes, until the onions are soft. Add the poultry and sauté for 5 minutes more, turning to brown the poultry on all sides. Add the walnuts, pomegranate molasses, sugar, cinnamon, allspice, saffron water, salt, and black pepper and simmer over medium-low heat for 1 hour, partially covered, stirring occasionally. Adjust the seasonings, remove from the heat, and serve with Chelow (Persian rice) (p. 234).

TAH-CHEEN (BAKED SAFFRON RICE WITH CHICKEN AND BARBERRIES)

Serves 4

2 cups long-grain rice, Thai jasmine or Indian basmati
½ pound boneless chicken breasts, sliced into 1-inch strips
1 onion, halved and sliced thinly
1 teaspoon turmeric
1 teaspoon salt
1 teaspoon freshly ground black pepper
1 cup water, plus 2 teaspoons water
3 eggs
1 cup plain yogurt
½ teaspoon ground saffron, diluted in 1 tablespoon boiling water
½ cup dried barberries (available from Middle Eastern grocers or
    online)
2 tablespoons sugar
2 teaspoons sunflower or canola oil, plus more for coating the
    baking dish
1 tablespoon ground cinnamon
8 tablespoons (1 stick) butter

Wash, rinse, and soak the rice. Cook it for 8 minutes, drain it, and rinse it, as in the recipe for Chelow (Persian rice) (p. 234).

In a medium saucepan, combine the chicken, onions, turmeric, and ½ teaspoon each of the salt and black pepper. Add 1 cup water, bring to a boil, and simmer over medium heat until the chicken is cooked through, about 8 minutes. Remove from the heat and strain off the liquid. Shred the chicken and place it and the onions in a bowl; set aside.

Beat the eggs in a medium bowl and add the remaining ½ teaspoon salt and ½ teaspoon black pepper, along with the yogurt. Add half the saffron water and mix thoroughly. Pour this mixture over the chicken and onions and place in the refrigerator to marinate for at least 30 minutes.

Preheat the oven to 300 degrees Fahrenheit.

Put the barberries, sugar, remaining 2 teaspoons water, and 2 teaspoons of the sunflower or canola oil in a saucepan and place over medium heat. Cook for 8 minutes, stirring occasionally. Remove from the heat and set aside.

Coat a medium-sized round Pyrex or other baking dish liberally with oil. Strain the marinade and fold it into the rice. Spread half the rice mixture in the baking dish and sprinkle with the cinnamon. Spread the sweetened barberries in a uniform layer over the rice, followed by the chicken and onions. Dot the chicken with half the butter. Cover the mixture with plastic wrap and firmly and evenly press it down. Remove the plastic and place the rest of the rice over the chicken. Melt the rest of the butter and drizzle it over the edges of the baking dish, along with the rest of the saffron water.

Cover tightly with foil and bake for 1 hour. Remove from the oven and let cool for 10 minutes. Then loosen the sides with a knife and invert the rice onto a large serving plate. Cut into pie-shaped wedges and serve immediately.

BAGHOLI POLOW
(DILL AND FAVA BEAN PILAF)

Serves 4

1½ cups long-grain rice, Thai jasmine or Indian basmati
2 cups fresh fava beans or 4 cups frozen fava beans
    (or edamame), shelled
1 teaspoon salt
Sunflower or canola oil
2 small potatoes, sliced thinly
4 tablespoons (½ stick) butter
½ teaspoon ground saffron, diluted in 2 tablespoons boiling water
1 teaspoon ground cumin
2 teaspoons fresh dill, or 1 teaspoon dried

Wash and rinse the rice and soak it as in the recipe for Chelow (p. 234). Drain the rice. Bring a large pot of water to a boil and add the rice. Boil for 5 minutes, then add the fava beans or edamame and boil for another 3 minutes. Remove from heat and drain the rice and beans through a colander. Rinse with cold water and drain again. Season with 1 teaspoon salt.

Slick a Dutch oven or other large, heavy pot with a thin layer of sunflower or canola oil. Spread just enough potato slices in the bottom to cover the surface. Melt the butter and drizzle a third of it over the potatoes, along with a third of the saffron water. Spoon half the rice over the potatoes in an even layer, then sprinkle on half the cumin, half the dill, and another third of the butter and the saffron water.

Add the rest of the rice, along with the rest of the cumin, dill, butter, and saffron water. Press the rice down firmly, cover the pot with a dish towel or other cloth and a lid, and simmer over low heat for 1 hour. Remove from heat and let the pot stand for 10 minutes. Then uncover it and invert the pilaf onto a large plate. Serve immediately, making sure each serving has some rice crust (*tah-dig*).

SAFFRON FRIED CHICKEN

Serves 4

4 chicken quarters (thighs and drumsticks or breasts)
½ teaspoon salt
½ teaspoon freshly ground black pepper
½ medium onion, cut into 8 wedges
½ teaspoon ground saffron, diluted in ¼ cup hot water
Vegetable oil for frying
2 egg whites
2 cups panko or other unseasoned bread crumbs

Mix the chicken in a bowl with the salt, black pepper, onion wedges, and saffron water. Place in the refrigerator and marinate for 1 hour.

Fill a deep fryer or other large pot halfway with vegetable oil and heat to 350 degrees Fahrenheit.

Place the egg whites in a bowl and beat just until foamy. Coat each piece of chicken with egg white, then dredge it in the bread crumbs. When the oil is hot, carefully add the chicken and fry for 8 to 10 minutes for breasts and 13 to 15 minutes for the legs, until fully cooked through. Drain on paper towels and serve immediately.

turkey

turkey and greece

© 2013 Jeffrey L. Ward

9.

t seemed odd that one of my first objectives in Istanbul was to track down a good hunk of pork. Through western China, Central Asia, and Iran, I'd been deprived of my favorite meat, and Turkey, I expected, would be no different—it was 98 percent Muslim. I wasn't particularly craving the meat, either, as I'd arrived from China just a couple of days before. But the Turkish foodies for whom I was cooking a Chinese dinner made it clear: they wanted to eat pig.

"Are you sure?" I asked Selin, my new Turkish friend, again on the morning of the meal. She would be the only non-Muslim at the dinner, but as a Jew, she was, in theory at least, subject to the same restrictions. There was still time to change the menu.

Don't be silly, read the look on Selin's face. "Jews and Muslims have a special fondness for pork!" she half-joked. And she knew just where to source it. We got into a taxi, coasted down the hills of Nişantaşı, the upscale neighborhood where she lived, and pulled up at a Shell station. Just beyond the pumps was a small, unmarked shop. I believe it was my first time entering a speakeasy for pork.

Behind a glass counter sat everything I'd craved through Central Asia and Iran: vacuum-sealed packages of bacon and prosciutto; oversize tubes of salami and mortadella; light pink cuts of pork loin and chops. One of two brothers who owned the shop ran the mortadella through a deli slicer and offered me a thin piece. I gobbled it quickly, hoping that no one refilling their gas tanks would catch me in the act.

Kozma had olive skin, a long nose, and a nest of gray hair. He made the sign of the cross to show he was Greek Orthodox. He was one of the few Greeks left in Turkey after the Great Exchange, a period in the early twentieth century when Christians in Turkey and Muslims in Greece were uprooted and moved to the opposite countries.

Kozma took us to a warehouse behind his shop where several pork carcasses were resting on wide stone counters. The pork bellies were so fresh that indentations still marked where the ribs had been. Here it was an all-or-nothing proposition—if you wanted pork belly, you bought the entire thing, not just a few pounds, the way I normally purchased it. I pointed to the most marbled one. Kozma picked it up, tucked it under his arm as if it were a humongous textbook, and walked over to a scale, where he dropped it with a thud. The needle registered four kilograms, almost nine pounds. We gave Kozma seventy-five dollars—a reasonable figure, especially since he was the only player in town.

Kozma's butchery was, in fact, one of the few places in all of Turkey where the public could buy pork. How did it feel to be one of the few pork butchers in Turkey? I asked him. "Maybe people talk behind my back, but then, I wouldn't know," he said with a shrug. "We used to have a long line out the door every Easter, but after the financial crisis, things haven't been as good." A small flow of customers, mostly European expatriates and restaurateurs who served European, Chinese, and Thai food, frequented his shop.

I would later see bacon on the menus of several international restaurants in the fancy parts of Istanbul, but, in general, pork was a rarity—and becoming more so. Though eating it wasn't actually illegal, it was beginning to feel like a crime. A decade before, there had been ninety official pork farms in the country; Kozma said there were now only three. Turkey had been experiencing a creeping Islamization since Prime Minister Recep Tayyip Erdoğan was elected in 2003, with officials cracking down on non-

Muslim practices. But it was Turkey's conflicting desire to be accepted by the West that kept Kozma's business open.

"The government wants to be part of the European Union," Selin explained. "They can tell the EU, 'See? We allow pork.'"

After a winter hiatus, I'd restarted my trip in Istanbul in the early spring of 2011. From Istanbul, I would fly to Turkey's eastern border with Iran, for continuity's sake, and make my way west until I reached the Mediterranean. From the coast, I would take a boat through Greece to Italy, where, after exploring pasta in the south and north, I would end in Rome.

I restarted the trip reluctantly. I was alone, as Craig was busy with his own book project, which required him to travel as well. He promised to join me somewhere, though when and where were left up in the air. I hadn't realized how much the journey took out of me, mentally and physically. Even though I was an experienced traveler, my longest previous trip had been a summer of backpacking through Europe, and I'd called it quits after ten weeks, weary of hostels, tourist sites, and Internet cafés. As much as I loved exploring, I couldn't quite relate to the hardcore vagabonds I'd met on the Silk Road, like the family traveling in the ambulance we'd met in Iran or a man we'd encountered who'd started his adventures with his wife four years before and divorced while on the road. I wasn't a wanderer by nature, even though I traveled plenty for work and had lived abroad for so many years. By the time Craig and I had reached Tehran, I'd been relieved not only to exit Iran but to return back to Beijing, the closest thing we had to a home.

Back in our tiny apartment in the *hutong*, I reveled in mundane pleasures. I stuffed my washing machine with dirty garments and detergent, overjoyed at the prospect of clean clothes with the twist of a knob, rather than endless scrubbing and wringing in hotel sinks. I appreciated the steady stream of Q-tips. I slept soundly, rather than occasionally waking in the middle of the night, having forgotten what city or country I was in. In the mornings, I rose in anticipation of fresh drip coffee, rather than dehydrated coffee particles. Best of all, Craig and I enjoyed settling back into our routines: walking through the narrow alleys and chatting with neighbors, socializing with our expatriate friends, and eating at our regular hole-in-the-wall restaurants and snack stands. I ate a lot of pork and we made the rounds of the favorite international restaurants, still trying to exorcise those monotonous meals of *plov*.

The cooking school was also keeping me busy. It was growing quickly. Despite its success and a wonderful staff whom I trusted without reservation, I also had to put in time to allow the chefs themselves to travel. A restaurateur in Bali recruited Chairman Wang to teach her home-style Beijing dishes and dumplings, while the celebrity chef José Andrés invited Chef Zhang to Las Vegas for a guest stint. For my chefs, it was their first time traveling overseas. Chairman Wang enjoyed the tropics, collecting samples of various exotic fruits and smuggling them back to China, where her husband attempted to grow them in his garden. Despite Chef Zhang's lack of English, he'd made friends with everyone who crossed his path in America, from the doorman in the luxury apartment building where he'd stayed to Andrés himself to various customers, including one who left him a hundred-dollar tip. I asked him what he thought of America. "Las Vegas is small. Why are there so few tall buildings?" he sniffed. He was even more nonplussed by Washington, DC. "I didn't like it. All the buildings are old."

Along with my reluctance to leave Beijing, the revolutions in the Middle East, dubbed the Arab Spring, were giving me pause. While Turkey remained stable, some speculated that the revolutions could galvanize certain ethnic Kurds in eastern Turkey to rise up, as they had in the past.

But when I reflected on the first half of the trip, I realized that nothing could replace my experiences on the road. When I returned to my Persian friend's restaurant in Beijing and sat down for a meal of stews and kebabs, it just wasn't the same as dining with the Soltanis in Iran. The greens didn't include tarragon, which couldn't be found in China, and the bread, little round, pita-like pockets, was a distant approximation of the deliciously chewy *sangek*. Plus, I was curious to find out how the food would change as I moved west, and where noodles would reemerge.

And I was no longer traveling through repressive dictatorships, but through a string of honeymoon-like destinations: Turkey, Greece, Italy. Craig noted his envy, as he watched me browse books and websites.

"I went to Iran with you, and now I'm skipping the five-star part of your trip?" he said as I packed. In addition to my green backpack, I filled a small suitcase with knives, rolling pins, a wok, and a bunch of Chinese ingredients that my Turkish contacts requested: noodle-like mung bean vermicelli, Sichuan peppercorns, and squishy jellyfish in water, sealed in a bag.

"You can always change your mind," I said as Craig accompanied me in a taxi to the airport. Sometime during the first half of the trip, I'd abandoned my reservations about traveling with my husband. Sure, we'd had our issues, and I'd had to endure the occasional hamburger. But none of my worries materialized: everyone expected me to have my husband in tow, his presence hadn't infringed on my autonomy, and he had tolerated the meals just fine. But while I had gotten used to the idea of more togetherness, Craig seemed to have become accustomed to time apart. He hummed to himself as we rode to the airport, and all his comments about my journey were upbeat. A new concern popped into my head: Was he going to miss me at all?

On our way to the airport, I hid my doubts. Craig lugged my baggage to the check-in counter, and we hugged and kissed good-bye. Then I boarded a flight that in nine hours swept me over a route that had taken me almost four months to traverse by land.

Still bleary-eyed when I landed at daybreak in the chilly early morning, and with smelly luggage (the jellyfish, predictably, had leaked), I wasn't prepared for the beauty of Istanbul. Stepping out of the airport, I heard the call to prayer. On the ride into the city, the Sea of Marmara stretched out like an ocean on one side, while the crowded alleys and wooden Ottoman homes of the Old City sat behind an ancient wall. As the highway curved along the sea's edge, the city opened before me, a hilly metropolis of historic buildings with European neoclassical flourishes. I thought I'd spied the Blue Mosque, with its limestone walls, skinny minarets, and pale blue domes, until I gazed over the hills and saw a landscape dotted with similarly picturesque mosques. The tranquil waters where the sea, the Bosporus River, and the Golden Horn met were lined with boats resting at the docks. What a contrast to the deserts of Iran and Central Asia, and what a sign that this half of the trip would be quite different.

The plans for the party in Istanbul had come together over the previous weeks, as I was making preparations in Beijing. I'd heard that connections were important in Turkey, just as they were in China and, not knowing a single Turk, I did some research and came across a website advertising food tours and cooking classes in Istanbul. I e-mailed the proprietor, Selin, explaining that I was a food writer and, like her, the owner of a cooking school, and that I was coming to Turkey. She responded right away. Over Skype I learned that more than twenty years separated us ("You are young enough to be my daughter!" she remarked), she had a noisy Jack Russell terrier named Yo-Yo, and she liked blue-and-white textiles (I'd asked what sort of gift I should bring her). "Dress like a cabbage—it is very cold," she advised me before inviting me to her market tours and cooking classes and offering to introduce me to her extensive group of friends, who included the country's top restaurateurs, chefs, and food writers. The least I could do, I told her, was cook a Chinese meal for her and her friends, an offer she enthusiastically accepted.

Selin lived in an imposing building in Nişantaşı, the equivalent of Manhattan's Upper East Side. But after entering the grand foyer and riding the steel-cage elevator, I was immediately set at ease when her apartment door opened and a zaftig woman with wavy brown hair and eyeglasses warmly greeted me with a hug. "Would you like something to drink?" she asked, as I settled into her kitchen, which had a large island counter cluttered with cutting boards. She brought me a cup of Nescafé, a drink that was more popular than the coffee that outsiders associated the country with. But still, the most popular drink was black tea, ubiquitous all over Turkey the way it had been in Iran.

Selin hadn't been kidding when she'd told me she liked blue-and-white things—an entire wall of her living room was filled with Oriental porcelain vases and dishes in various hues of blue that she'd inherited from her mother. The apartment, too, was an inheritance. Until a few decades before, her family had owned the entire building, and her mother had raised her on the ground floor. But as she got older and relatives died, the building had been parceled off into smaller units, some retained by the family (like Selin's apartment) while others were sold; the rooms where she'd been raised had been converted into a bank.

Over the next few days, I learned more about Selin's background, which illustrated Turkey's multicultural legacy. Her ancestors had been expelled from Spain during the Inquisition and had traveled across the Mediterranean to Istanbul after hearing that the sultan welcomed Jews. Though as many as 200,000 Jews lived in Istanbul during the Ottoman era, by the early twenty-first century their number had dwindled to less than twenty thousand—and it was continuing to shrink as Turkey grew more conservative. Though Selin had spent some time in Israel, she remained committed to Istanbul. And while she wasn't observant, on holidays she did prepare traditional Sephardic dishes like phyllo dough stuffed with smoked eggplant and zucchini flan with dill.

Selin was the only child of a woman who came of age during the era when Ataturk, the founder of the Turkish Republic, increased women's rights. The mother was a successful businesswoman who'd imported European fashions and had divorced Selin's father after she'd discovered his philandering. Burned by the experience, she raised Selin to be self-sufficient. But Selin's independence had been undermined in college, after she was involved in a bad car accident while on a date. Only after multiple surgeries and years of bed rest did she recover and finish college. To the day I met her, Selin still walked with a limp and had a scar that ran around the outer edge of her eye. Even so, she managed to follow her mother's independent footsteps, and she'd never had children or married.

Selin introduced me to Can (pronounced *Jan*), her live-in boyfriend of five years. Though many Turkish Jews dated within the community, Selin did not. Like all her previous boyfriends, Can was Muslim. He was a middle-aged man who'd developed a ruddy complexion as an avid sailor on the Bosporus. She'd called Can her husband when we'd spoken via Skype, explaining when we met that it was usually easier to avail herself of the societal convention. With the cooking school thriving, she was the breadwinner in the relationship and had bought him a boat so he could run a sailing business. She wasn't the least bit interested in marriage.

"I don't need the blessing of the government to approve my relationships," Selin told me. "When you're married, it becomes, 'I am your possession, you are my possession.' It's more romantic not to be married."

Selin had gotten the idea to open a cooking school about a decade before, when she was working as a travel agent. She and her mother, while vacationing in New Orleans, had attended a Creole cooking class. Why didn't they have anything like that in Istanbul? she'd wondered.

When she returned to the travel agency, she shared the idea with her boss, who wasn't receptive. Since 9/11, tourism had fallen, and sure enough, the agency soon folded. That gave Selin the push she needed to set up Turkish Flavours.

As I'd done in Beijing a few years earlier, Selin had used her dinner parties as a model for her cooking classes. Growing up, she and her mother had invited friends over for international meals. "One night we would do Balinese, another night we would do Chinese," she said. While she'd worked as a travel agent, Selin had made a side business of inviting acquaintances to her home and teaching them foreign dishes. A group of female plastic surgeons became her regulars. "I wrote out menus and had all the ingredients prepared. The women did the cooking. It was a cooking club," she said. After the agency closed, she decided to revise her classes to attract foreign tourists, who began returning to Turkey. She remodeled her kitchen, knocking down a wall to open it to the dining room, and advertised her classes on the Internet. She guided guests through preparing a typical Turkish meal, which they then sat down to eat in her spacious dining room. To demystify the ingredients, she also developed culinary walking tours. In a few short years that dovetailed with the rise of the Internet and the world-wide boom in culinary tourism, Selin's business became a success. She hosted hundreds of visitors per year, and an ever-increasing ranking on TripAdvisor.com meant she even occasionally beat out iconic Istanbul sites like the Blue Mosque and Ayasofya.

"But I don't want to rejoice too much because that brings bad luck," Selin said on our first afternoon together. She fumbled with a bracelet that was adorned with the icon of a blue evil eye—the same talisman I'd seen across Central Asia and Iran. Changing the subject, she asked me about the menu for the Chinese meal I planned to cook. We went over my shopping list. "Are you sure you only want one kilo of chicken, one kilo of lamb?" she asked. "I must warn you, Turks eat a lot."

I assured her that the number of dishes would mean plenty of food for the twenty guests. While I didn't know much about the Turkish appetite, I'd estimated for the biggest eaters at my cooking school—the Australians, Germans, and Americans.

"I think I'll buy double these quantities," Selin told me. "Just in case."

When we returned from the pork butcher, I discovered she'd tripled—and in some cases quadrupled—the quantities I'd asked for. The shelves and drawers of her refrigerator were jammed with produce and meats, and more spilled onto a nearby counter.

After cubing the pork belly, I parboiled the squares. Selin's housekeeper grimaced. A middle-aged woman who wore a head scarf, she would be the only devout Muslim among the company that evening. "Don't mind her," Selin said breezily.

Early in the afternoon, several of Selin's female friends arrived. They, too, fretted over the quantities. As we prepped, the women kept asking if I'd bought enough food. Were two packages of vermicelli enough for the glass noodle salad? What about the chicken? That couldn't possibly be enough for twenty people!

They watched as I made a monstrous portion of fried rice that reminded me in size (but not taste) of the giant vats of *plov* in Central Asia. The wok that Selin had procured for the event had the diameter of a truck tire. Overflowing with rice, ground pork, shrimp, carrots, shiitake mushrooms, and eggs, it was so heavy I couldn't lift it. "Is that enough?" somebody asked skeptically.

"Are you sure there's enough garlic in there?" another woman added, scrutinizing a different dish. "Turkish people like a lot of garlic!"

"This dish needs more salt!" declared another of Selin's friends, a food writer. In between dishes, she cornered me to invite—or rather, command— me to her home. "I'm going to have to lecture you on Turkish food. You see, no one else is going to tell you that you don't know anything about Turkish food, but I have to set the record straight. And no one knows more about Turkish food than I."

I showed them how to make dumplings, patiently explaining as I kneaded and rolled out the dough for the skins and folded the dumplings. "Looks like our *manti*," someone commented. That was intriguing, I thought. But before I could inquire further, one woman asked, "Don't you think we should start cooking them now?" And then the food writer was at my side again, looking at me askance and pointing to the pot crammed with red-braised pork. "Will that be all the pork you're serving?" she said.

I forced a smile and told the food writer I appreciated her unexpected enthusiasm for pork but, yes, that was all I was making. "And the dumplings," I added, turning to the second woman, "can wait!"

That seemed to mellow everyone out. As we prepped, I learned that Chinese food had the good fortune of being haute cuisine in Turkey. Because the country had been closed to the rest of the world from the fall of the Ottoman Empire until the 1980s, it had received very few immigrants of any kind, and cheap takeout had never made an incursion here. Chinese food was still a rare luxury. "The three best cuisines in the world are French, Chinese, and Turkish," one woman told me, a refrain I would hear throughout the country. Most Istanbullus associated Chinese cuisine with a fancy restaurant called Dragon that had thrived at a five-star hotel since the 1990s and had closed only recently.

I also learned about the women, which went a long way to explaining how opinionated they were. The food writer was one of Turkey's most successful. Another guest was Selin's former boss, who was worldly, having grown up partly in London and having journeyed to the Far East. A mother-daughter duo owned a restaurant in the Old City that served the cuisine of their native Crete. Ayse, the mother, was divorced. "Everyone is divorced these days," she said with a laugh. "It's the fashionable thing to do."

With everyone helping, the cooking proceeded at a clip. At seven-thirty, when nearly all of the guests had arrived, my hardworking cooking assistants helped me line up the entire spread so that the feast could begin without delay.

My own work done, I helped myself to a glass of red wine and chatted with Selin's friends. A young woman named Didem had recently returned from New York City, where she'd attended the French Culinary Institute and interned at the upscale Eleven Madison Park. She'd recently opened a restaurant that reflected the ethos of Alice Waters, founder of Berkeley's Chez Panisse and a pioneer of the organic food movement. Another woman, Semsa, ran a restaurant that catered to the neighborhood's "ladies who lunch" crowd. Semsa had also been the name of the mute wife of our Turkmen host who'd slaughtered a sheep in our honor, but that was all the two women shared. The Turkish Semsa was a large-framed redhead, with arms that had been firmed by years of pastry making. When I asked her if she'd ever felt discriminated against as a woman in a male-dominated industry, she said, "Who would dare?" with a menace that instantly made me regret I'd asked.

Much as these independent-minded women jibed with the outside perception of Turkey as a modern state, I also gleaned from them that the country wasn't as progressive as the media and the government made it out to be. Since arriving, I'd already learned that pork was becoming more difficult to procure and Jews were leaving at an increased rate. Caught between East and West, Turkey was a precarious place, said Maisie, Selin's former boss. The conservatives in the government, including the prime minister, wanted to enact measures to reduce drinking and force women to cover up. "If they get their way, we could go the way of Iran," she said. "But we won't put up with that!" Another woman pointed out that this group was fortunate in a country where a woman's status depended greatly on her wealth, education, and locale. "This is a country where honor killings still happen," she said.

I was impressed with the serious yet lively conversations I could enjoy with these women, so different from the stilted interactions I'd had with other women on the road. And I was grateful to have their help in getting everything done on time. "You see, Turkish people are very impatient," someone commented. The other thing about Turkish people, said another, was that they were very honest. So when I asked for their comments on the meal, I braced myself. After everyone deliberated, the verdict came back: though one or two of the dishes had been too spicy, everything else seemed to pass muster. And when I asked them what their favorite dish was, the response was unanimous: "We loved the pork belly!" they declared.

After the Chinese dinner party, I turned my attention to Turkish food. In her kitchen, Selin taught me homestyle dishes that were often stuffed: phyllo-dough pastries called *borek* were filled with cheese, vegetables, and meats and rolled into the shape of cigars, triangles, and coils before being baked or deep-fried. Split-belly eggplant, known as *karniyarik*, called for the long, sweet Asian version of the vegetable to be stuffed with ground beef and red pepper paste, the smooth, mild condiment that is one of the defining flavors of Turkish cuisine. After classes, though, Selin was tired. It was not so much cooking that energized her, I learned. It was being out and about on the streets of Istanbul.

So one morning, I joined an American couple on one of Selin's culinary walking tours. Over six hours, she overwhelmed us with samples of street food and alluring ingredients from vendors she'd befriended over her years living in Istanbul. We began on the Europe side, at the Spice Bazaar, and ended in Asia at an acclaimed restaurant. I quickly realized the key to Selin's success: she had a natural product. Istanbul was blessed with a bounty that made it one of the world's most interesting food destinations.

I'd always been a fan of street food. It appealed to my inner child, my younger self who'd hated sitting down to grown-up dinners. I still felt there was no better way to learn about a city, and I was mildly suspicious of any culture that didn't have street food. Plus, the exercise involved in hunting it down helped mitigate the calories I consumed, something that was especially true that day with Selin.

I'd heard that snacking and small dishes called *meze* were a big part of Turkish cuisine, but I hadn't expected the diversity. Bites of seafood ranged from fried mussels bathed in a sauce of lemon, bread crumbs, and ground walnuts to pickled herring stuffed with olives and bell peppers. The intense sweets included fried balls of dough basted in thick honey to chewy squares of Turkish delight dusted with powdered sugar and infused with different fruits or exotic flavorings, such as mastic, a tree sap that tasted like earthy spearmint. And there were heavenly slices of flaky baklava crammed with pistachios and drenched in syrup, in a shop that smelled of warm butter.

In my first few days ambling about Istanbul on my own, I'd haphazardly run into culinary reminders of the places through which I'd passed. Endless five-pound tubs of plain yogurt piled atop one another in the refrigerator section of a supermarket reminded me of Central Asian pastures and Iranian storefronts. Down a small side street, I'd eaten breakfast at a restaurant whose disk-shaped flatbreads reminded me of those to the east. I even found an item that reminded me of Beijing—in the confectioneries, wispy noodle-like strands of sugar wrapped into mounds called "*helva* floss" were a carbon copy of an imperial Chinese dessert known as "dragon thread pastries." Did the Mongolian Yuan Dynasty, which stretched from Beijing to Asia Minor and beyond, have anything to do with it? Or was the culinary echo simply a product of the friendly relations and exchanges between the Ottoman Empire and the later Ming Dynasty?

My research didn't turn up any definite connection, though I learned that Turks traced it as far east as Iran, which had a similar sweet called *peshmek*. And the foods Selin introduced raised more questions. At a little eatery selling baked goods, she pointed to a dish of large, flat sheets of pasta layered over a fluffy, light cheese filling that reminded me of ricotta. "I call this Turkish lasagna," Selin said, as we tasted the small savory squares. This *su borek* was the first noodle dish I'd seen since the limp noodle soups in Iran, and while I learned in the coming weeks that noodles weren't central to the Turkish diet, certain pasta dishes would reappear in alluring forms that hinted at ties to China and Italy.

At the Spice Bazaar, we stopped at a stall brimming with blocks and wheels of cheese. I'd associated cheese almost exclusively with Europe and the West, though, of course, that assumption had been challenged already with "imperial cheese" in China and *paneer* in Iran. Like the Iranians, Turks loved feta-like cheese, called *beyaz peynir*, which came in white blocks labeled with their salt and fat content, and, like wine, their ages and the names of the villages from which they hailed. Some varieties were herbed and braided; others reminded me of Greek *halloumi* and Swiss Gruyère. Selin pointed out a popular fatty sheep's cheese that was harder and milder than the fetas and tasted like provolone; its name, *kaşar,* sounded like "kosher," suggesting that it had originated within the Jewish community. Also on offer was a veined blue cheese from central Turkey that reminded me of French Roquefort.

Along with the cheese came bread, another harbinger of what awaited me to the west. Delivery boys hung European-looking baguettes in plastic bags on the doorknobs of residences near the bazaar. But Turkish bread also recalled the East. In front of the docks where we took a ferry to the Asian side, vendors pushed wooden carts stacked with bagel-like *simit* that reminded me once again of the bread we'd eaten in Xinjiang.

Once on the Asian side, we wove our way through the back alleys to a famous restaurant called Çiya. Over the years, it had become an institution, renowned in international food circles for the specialties from far-flung villages across Turkey that its founder, Musa, had brought back to Istanbul. The meal gave me a preview of what I'd encounter across the country. Bakers brushed long tongue-shaped *pide,* a flatbread, with *ayran*, the watery yogurt drink that was equally popular in Central Asia and Turkey. The bakers slid the pieces of bread into the oven, where they puffed like balloons. The *pide* slowly deflated at our table, where it was served with several *meze,* including the spicy red pepper dip called *muhamara*, a dish popular throughout the Middle East; yogurt with diced eggplant; and cold wild greens seasoned simply with lemon and olive oil. We weren't prepared to sit down to a meal after our prodigious snacking, but that was what Selin intended, to stuff us until we were as fat as Kozma's pigs.

The dishes continued in rapid succession. After the *meze* came a creamy white soup with garlic scapes (an ingredient I used in China) and threads of saffron. Next, *kofte*, crisp and savory lamb meatballs coated with bulgur; succulent lamb intestines stuffed with more ground lamb; and sautéed okra from a village in central Turkey. And before we could protest, dessert was placed in front of us, sweet balls of something we couldn't identify even after tasting them. Selin divulged the secret ingredients: eggplants, tomatoes, and pumpkin that were dried before they were candied, topped with the clotted cream *kaymak*, which was as delicious as the dairy from the wilds of Kyrgyzstan.

Before I left Istanbul, I returned to Çiya one afternoon to meet Musa. As we snacked on flatbread and tarragon tea, he inquired about China, saying he was a fan of Communism, a comment I heard from a number of Turks and later Italians. I mentioned I was more American than Chinese, and anyway, China wasn't so Communist anymore. He told me he'd recently started a magazine dedicated to tracing linkages between food and geography. Turkey's vast number of small villages each had distinctive food traditions thanks to variations in climate and terrain, Musa said. While geography was important, what about history? I asked him. Hadn't the movement of people also influenced diets? Sure, he said, before repeating the myth that I'd heard many times before: "Marco Polo definitely brought noodles from China to Italy! There is no question about that." I smiled and took another sip of tarragon tea.

Another guest at the Chinese dinner was Batur, a friendly Turkish man in his late thirties who invited me to his restaurant kitchen. Asitane was near the Old Quarter next to Chora Church, which dated to the Byzantine era, when Istanbul and Rome were capitals of the Holy Roman Empire. The restaurant served Ottoman cuisine, catering to wealthy Turks and international jet-setters. Batur boasted that Dan Brown, author of *The Da Vinci Code*, had recently visited, as had the celebrity chef Anthony Bourdain. His head chef was a young woman who'd trained in France and recently returned to Turkey.

The spacious restaurant was an oasis of opulence—a contrast to many of the eateries on the Silk Road. Attendants shined the wooden floors and straightened the framed Arabic calligraphy hanging on the walls. The white tablecloths were crisp and anchored with vases that held delicate fuchsias. Green and purple velvet covered the plush armchairs. Handsome waiters, dressed simply in white button-down shirts and black slacks, made sure wine and water glasses were punctiliously refilled. Batur often padded through during the lunch and dinner rush to review the reservation list and chat with guests. In the evenings, a group of classical musicians played traditional stringed instruments.

In Istanbul, I met a number of female chefs, but none was quite like Batur's head chef, Bengi (pronounced with a hard *g*). A tiny woman with delicate features who wore her hair in a ponytail, she made up in personality what she lacked in stature. Outside the kitchen, she often wore a leather jacket, and her voice was husky from chain-smoking. She was in the midst of getting an elaborate tattoo, one that covered her arm with an elongated vegetable garden, the colors of which were slowly being filled in. She channeled the personality of Gordon Ramsay, and when I checked her Facebook page not long after my journey I saw that she'd quoted the notorious British chef on her wall: "Cooking is the most massive rush. It's like having the most amazing hard-on with Viagra sprinkled on top of it, and it's still there twelve hours later."

Bengi didn't have the typical background of a Turkish chef. Many hailed from families in which cooking was an inherited profession. Most restaurants in Istanbul specialized in either kebabs or seafood. Since the Ottoman Empire, kebab chefs often came from the town of Bolu, 150 miles east of Istanbul. The seafood restaurants were generally staffed by Kurds from southeastern Turkey. Bengi, by contrast, was from Ankara, the country's capital, and had grown up in an upper-middle-class household. Her mother was a doctor and her father was a politician, and they'd divorced when she was little. As an only child of parents with busy careers, Bengi had often prepared meals for herself.

"I always wanted to create stuff when I was young," she told me. "But I wasn't a good visual artist. So cooking was the way I could express myself." She thought of cooking as a hobby, though, until her senior year of college. After countless hours writing her sociology thesis, she decided she didn't want to spend her life at a desk. So after graduating, she opted for cooking school. Her mother was supportive, but her father was less than enthused. She'd graduated third in her class; it seemed a waste, he'd said as they lunched one afternoon at an *esnaf lokantası* a cafeteria-style eatery that catered to tradesmen. He pointed to the cook behind the counter, who was slapping ladles of stew onto trays. "You want to be that guy?" he said.

Because there were few established cooking schools in Turkey, Bengi went to Europe. Rather than enrolling in the Cordon Bleu or its ilk like most foreigners, though, Bengi attended a vocational school in Paris called École Grégoire-Ferrandi. Kitchen discipline was drilled into her—"it was the kind of place where the chefs screamed at you if you were late," she said—and she interned at a one-star Michelin restaurant. Shortly thereafter, she returned to Turkey.

Just as Bengi arrived, Batur became the general manager at Asitane, which his father, a successful businessman, had opened almost two decades before. The restaurant had been a vanity project and had lost money for years. Other family members wanted to close it, but Batur hoped to turn it around. After assuming the position, though, he realized the job was more difficult than he'd thought. He'd never worked in a kitchen and the chefs, many of whom had cooked there for years, were resentful of their new boss. "I was dealing with chefs who would turn off their stoves in the middle of making a dish if their shift happened to be over. They acted like security guards at a bank, coming in at nine o'clock and leaving at six," Batur said.

By happenstance, Batur and Bengi met through friends and he immediately hired her. She had the passion for cooking that Batur was looking for. Plus her upper-middle-class background and vocational training allowed her to relate to both the chefs and her boss, and she became a crucial link between them. Batur hired her as a line cook but, more important, as a "mole" who would help him figure out exactly what was going on.

The chefs, all men, were baffled by Bengi's arrival, but they treated her well and with respect. Batur and Bengi found out later that this was because they suspected that Bengi was Batur's girlfriend. "There was a cocky-man-ego thing going on in there. But I was already used to that kind of sexism," Bengi told me, rolling her eyes. "Think about it: the sultans were always men."

As Bengi reported back to Batur on who was doing his job and who wasn't, the kitchen staff was plotting, too. Within a few months of Bengi's arrival, a mutiny broke out: three chefs abruptly quit and left for another Ottoman restaurant across town—in the middle of Ramadan, the busiest time of year for dinner. With the remaining chefs and the dishwashers, who assumed cooking responsibilities, the kitchen just barely managed to eke through the holiday month. Not long after, Bengi was promoted to head chef. In the two years since she'd joined, the kitchen staff had stabilized, the restaurant had stopped losing money, and the international fame of Asitane had grown.

With its emphasis on Ottoman cuisine, Asitane had an allure that the fish and kebab restaurants didn't have. When Batur's father had first thought about opening a restaurant, Ottoman cuisine wasn't on his mind. Sure, from the fifteenth to the twentieth centuries the Ottomans had ruled Turkey and the surrounding areas, including Greece, the Balkans, and parts of the Middle East and North Africa, and they had left a lasting influence on Turkey's ethnic composition. Many Turks could trace their ancestors to those surrounding areas; I met descendants of Greeks, Bulgarians, Egyptians, Afghans, and Syrians. But the last century of Ottoman rule, as the empire dissolved, was mired in corruption and ineffectual rule, and Turks weren't particularly proud of the past. Ataturk had swept Ottoman history under the rug and focused on the country's ties to Central Asia; he trumpeted the fact that the first settlers in the Asia Minor peninsula had been Turkic nomads who came from the east. Ataturk also looked toward the West for inspiration: he promoted women's rights, abandoned Arabic script in favor of the Roman alphabet, and had people take on surnames (Turks, like Persians and other nomadic groups in the region, traditionally went by first names only).

A friend of Batur's father, an amateur historian, had always been interested in the Ottoman era and persuaded Batur's father that the concept could work. After all, cooking was important to the Ottoman court—the kitchens, still on display to the public, took up ten domes in Topkapı Palace in Istanbul, where the Ottoman sultans lived. The Ottomans employed hundreds of chefs, each with his own area of specialty—soups, pilafs, kebabs, vegetables, fish, breads, pastries, *helva* (a Turkish sweet), syrups and jams, and beverages. The royal kitchens fed as many as ten thousand people a day and delivered meals around Istanbul to the well-connected. Cooking also had symbolic value. The ranks of Janissaries, the Ottoman military elite selected from various regions of the empire, made reference to the kitchen: commanders were known as "soupmen," and other high-ranking officers were called "chief cook," "baker," and "pancake maker." "Overturning the cauldron" is an expression still used to indicate a rebellion in the ranks.

There was one major obstacle to creating an Ottoman restaurant, though: there were few, if any, recipes. Chefs had guarded their dishes as secrets. Batur's father's friend began to piece together recipes by researching history books, Ottoman ledgers that recorded purchases, and the journals of visiting foreigners. Asitane's menu included dates that indicated when the dish had been served in the palace.

Like most Turkish meals, dining at Asitane began with soups and *meze*. Next came a main course of meat or seafood, often accompanied by salad or savory pastries called *borek*. And finally, there were desserts, an extensive category that itself could contain many courses. Because some dishes dated as far back as the fifteenth century, few ingredients from the Americas were used—the absence of tomatoes and potatoes was conspicuous.

And I noticed that nuts, pomegranates, dried fruits, and meats were used in greater quantities than in an average Turkish meal. Interestingly, the focus on these Old World ingredients made the food more similar to what I'd tasted in Iran and Central Asia, showing how influential commerce along the Silk Road had been to the food of earlier times. Along with kebabs, some of the restaurant's most popular dishes had elements common to Persian food. The *mutancana*, braised leg of lamb stewed with apricots, raisins, and almonds, reminded me of the meat-and-dried-fruit *khoresht*s, while the roasted sea bass was flavored with a dressing of two Iranian cornerstones, rosewater and saffron. *Pekmezli ayva dolmasi*, quince stuffed with lamb, beef, and rice pilaf, was flavored with grape molasses, an ingredient I'd first seen at Nur's home in Xinjiang, all the way back in China. One ingredient the kitchen had adjusted from Ottoman times was the cooking oil. Eschewing sheep's tail fat, the chefs sautéed with olive oil and butter, to make the dishes more healthful and palatable. "We're cooking for seventy-year-old Japanese tourists," Batur said. "If you gave them sheep's tail fat, they would have a heart attack."

Over the last couple of years, Bengi had gone through the two-hundred-plus recipes on file. She'd experimented with different techniques to make meats more tender and succulent, sauces more playful (she'd created a pink béchamel sauce for one of the meat dishes, for example), and presentation more creative. "To be honest, I thought the food was shit when I arrived," Bengi told me in her usual no-nonsense way. She hired younger, more passionate chefs, including two other women. Burcak (which means "wheat") was a former artist with a lip piercing who'd recently graduated from a new culinary institute in Istanbul, while Esra was a recent high school graduate with a pale complexion who floated through the kitchen like a fairy, gracefully carrying heavy pots filled with stews. Also in the kitchen was another foreigner, a South African intern in his mid-twenties named Mark. A few of Asitane's old-school chefs had managed to adjust to the new management, including one everyone called Uncle because of his seniority.

The ambience of the kitchen contrasted sharply with the sedate dining room. Safely separated by two sets of swinging doors, the kitchen was a cacophony of sound that competed with the raucous music blasting through the speakers. The sizzle of searing meat and sautéeing pilafs and the whirring hand blenders whipping up cold dips were punctuated by Talking Heads, Metallica, and early Michael Jackson, a sound track that got even Uncle dancing every so often.

Despite the emphasis on royal Ottoman cuisine, my favorite dishes were those that had stood the test of time. From Mark, the South African, I learned a basic rice pilaf preparation that was as delicious as the pilafs in Iran. After soaking the short-grain rice in water for several hours, he drained it and sautéed it in olive oil, salt, and a small sprinkle of sugar. He tossed in diced celeriac and a generous hunk of butter. ("Buttah's the secret of restaurant cuisine," he said with a wink.) He submerged the rice in chicken stock and allowed it to simmer until the water evaporated. As in Iran stewed meat or kebabs accompanied the rice. Mark and other chefs made variations on the basic pilaf that were just as delicious and nearly as diverse as Persian ones, incorporating nuts, eggplant, tomatoes, lentils, chicken livers, and dried fruit; my favorite combination was currants and pine nuts. Sometimes chefs added thin wheat noodles (as in Iran), ground bulgur, or orzo to thicken the pilaf's texture.

"It's amazing, I tell you," Mark said. "All we do with rice in South Africa is boil it."

From one of the grandmotherly dishwashers, I learned how to make *borek* of the highest refinement. Rather than buying the dough, as many households and restaurants did, the staff at Asitane kneaded and rolled out their own enormous circles of phyllo, known as *yufka* in Turkey. They were even more adept with the pin than Andrea and Chef Zhang, rocking and rolling the baton over the dough until it was super-thin, wispy, and translucent. Dividing a sheet into quarters, the dishwasher spread cheese-and-leek mixture atop each and rolled the pastries into long ropes, enclosing the filling. After sealing the edges with egg white, she coiled them into the round, flower-like shapes that gave the pastry its name, rose *borek*. After it was deep-fried, the pastry was served with honey. The sweet-and-savory flavors and the crispness of the *yufka* remained permanently emblazoned in my memory.

From Uncle, I learned how to make *kofte*, the meat patties common across Turkey. The everyday dish was too lowly to be on the menu, but it was served for staff meals. The particular version I learned was called *kadinbudu kofte*, or "lady's thigh *kofte*." Uncle mixed minced beef with black pepper, parsley, and mint. He added a combination of cooked and uncooked rice, which gave the *kofte* the right texture, he told me; as in China, mouth feel was paramount. He shaped the mixture into patties and dipped them into flour and egg, then fried them in hot oil. It was like a succulent fried meatloaf and, thankfully, it didn't remind me of my thighs.

One morning when I was talking with Batur and Bengi in a second-floor office, an assistant called Batur to say that another visitor had arrived. Puzzled, they went down to meet the woman, who introduced herself as a graduate student at a university in Denmark who was researching the kebab. She was hoping he could answer a few questions.

The kebab was to Turks what fish and chips was to Brits, and I sensed that Turks resented the dish because it was one of the few things the world knew of their cuisine. The kebab had spread across the world in the form of the *doner*, a revolving spit of pressed lamb or chicken that was often served at street-side stands.

In truth, I hadn't given the kebab much thought before the trip. To me, it was just meat on a stick, delicious but lacking in finesse. I'd never been a fan of the *doner*, though I'd had it in places as far and wide as New York, Berlin, and Beijing. I always wondered exactly what parts of the animal were in it and how long it had languished on the rotisserie. I hesitated over the mystery sauce that varied from stall to stall, and I didn't like the limp lettuce and bland tomatoes that generally came with it.

But kebabs had been a part of my journey from the very beginning, and I had gained greater appreciation for them as I'd traveled. In China,

Muslim street-side vendors strung skinny pieces of mutton on thin wooden sticks and roasted them over coals, sprinkling them with chili pepper and cumin. It was the perfect late-night snack and usually went for less than a quarter a stick. As I traveled west, the meat was a constant companion, even as noodles became rarer. The meat got chunkier and the sticks larger and wider. *Shashlyk*, as it was called in Central Asia, was often served with *plov* and downed with plenty of tea, occasionally beer. In Iran, I'd watched Mrs. Soltani shape minced beef and lamb onto wide metal skewers, and accompany the meat with saffron-tinged rice, a generous pat of butter, and a roasted tomato. In Turkey, I learned that kebabs were more varied and delicious than I'd imagined.

At Asitane, Batur explained to the Danish student some of the basics. "Well, let me first explain, we don't serve kebabs here. Or at least, not what *you* think of as a kebab. *Doner* kebabs are street food in our culture. We don't eat them in fancy restaurants or at home." He went on to explain that many of the *doner* kebab stands in Europe were run not by Turks but by Arabs or Iranians.

The Dane seemed baffled, and I was perplexed, too, especially the more I learned about kebabs. One of Asitane's most touted, called the "Fatty Apron" kebab, blended minced lamb and beef with mint, pine nuts, coriander seeds, and cumin, all of it wrapped in the thin, fatty membrane of a sheep's intestine. A chef, usually Mark, grilled the meat until it plumped into a juicy burger before topping it with demi-glace. Even more alluring was the *kaz kebab*, rice pilaf flavored with succulent slices of slow-roasted goose and pine nuts, all of which was wrapped in phyllo dough and baked into something resembling a savory pie. But, as delicious as it was, where was the stick? Where was the spit? After several days in the kitchen, I couldn't help but pull Batur aside to ask, just as the graduate student had, what exactly was a kebab?

"Oh, back to square one," Batur said with a sigh. But despite trying for several minutes, even he couldn't produce a succinct definition, and only after referring to a pile of cookbooks and food encyclopedias did he conclude that it depended on where you were. In western Turkey and the Black

Sea region, a kebab was "any sort of meat grilled over a fire." On the Mediterranean Coast near Syria, a kebab was "anything—meat, vegetables, or fruit—cooked over a fire." Batur finally produced his own definition. "It's any sort of meat—fish, chicken, beef, or lamb—that is grilled, baked, or roasted without added water"—in contrast to stews or braises. "It is always served with an accompaniment," such as pilaf or bread. To Batur, these were the defining attributes: "Something grilled on a stick isn't necessarily a kebab. It's cooked over a fire of some kind, and has to be served with something else." Like other dishes I'd learned about, including noodles, names and definitions varied, depending on where you were, how you viewed the dish, and what was important to a particular place.

One evening, after I'd spent the day cooking at Asitane, Selin suggested that we go out for kebabs. A shop around the corner from her home served some of Istanbul's best, she said. Behind the counter at the unassuming eatery was a long, revolving spit and a burly owner with crossed arms who refused to divulge much about his product. He commanded us upstairs to the dining area, where just moments after we were seated, plates of thinly sliced lamb arrived, basted in its own fat. The meat met Batur's definition—it was served with an accompaniment: the glistening lamb slices rested on cubes of toasted flatbread, smothered in a tomato sauce, thick yogurt, and butter. I dug in with a fork and knife, following Turkish protocol, as there was no polite way to eat the dish with one's hands. I finished every last bite, reveling in the tender meat and the smooth, tangy sauce. I soaked up the last smudges of gravy with the bread, wiping the plate clean. The kebab was called the Iskender, which in Turkish means Alexander, as in Alexander the Great, for reasons Selin could not explain. Still, it seemed an appropriate name for the greatest kebab I'd ever tasted.

I enjoyed my time at Asitane, but I grew increasingly aware that the emphasis on antiquated dishes was a huge source of frustration for Bengi. One afternoon, between the lunch and dinner rush, we tested a recipe for an

Ottoman cabbage soup. Bengi had me chop up some heads of cabbage, then sauté them with leeks and lemon juice. We poured in several quarts of stock and, after it had simmered, she beat several egg yolks with *beyaz pey-nir*, the feta-like cheese, and tempered it into the soup. Bengi handed me a spoon and helped herself to some as well, dipping in the ladle and picking out a piece of cabbage with her bare hand.

"Do you eat with your hands?" she asked. Occasionally, sure, I told her. "That's good," she said, nodding approvingly. "Not touching your food . . . that's like cybersex!"

Bengi shook in some salt and pepper, added more lemon juice, and again sampled some cabbage with her hands. She picked up a spoon, tasted the broth, and frowned. "What do you think?" she asked.

It was bland, I told her.

She nodded. "That's what's so annoying about these recipes," she grumbled. Another day she railed about adhering to the restaurant's strict Ottoman regime. "It makes my life boring. Sometimes I just want to bang my head against the wall! I can't use strawberries because they didn't eat them. They thought that anything red was poisonous. I've played with the chemistry, I've modified the techniques. I'm at the point where they are the best version that they're ever going to be. It's not going any further."

One afternoon, Batur rushed from the dining room to the kitchen and pulled a bag of saffron from a drawer. An international CEO out in the dining room had been interested in seeing the product they used, he explained.

"He told me he bought some saffron from the Spice Bazaar yesterday, but it can't be as good as ours," he told us. "His probably came from Iran in a truck driver's socks."

Batur held out his saffron for me to sniff, and my nose was filled with an intoxicating, subtly sweet, earthy fragrance. It was, in fact, more potent than Persian saffron, the most reputed in the world. "It's from Kashmir, from a friend who sends it through a diplomatic pouch," Batur said, with a mischievous grin. He told Bengi to vacuum pack a bunch of threads in a small bag for the CEO.

"That's not enough," he said when she handed him the bag. He uttered a Turkish adage that embodied a mentality I knew well from the Chinese: "You can't take without giving first!"

Batur returned to the kitchen with a piece of paper that he folded up and tucked into his shirt pocket. "I got his information," he said with a smile, patting his pocket. "That's more valuable than all the money this restaurant makes. You never know when those contacts will come in handy."

Bengi wasn't interested in networking. She kept her head down and concentrated on the food. After the rush one day, she showed me how she liked to cook. She butchered a couple of ducks that a supplier had brought as samples, blood dripping from her hands onto the white tiles of the kitchen floor. "I'm bleeding! I'm having my period!" she joked unabashedly, as she rushed for paper towels. After cleaning up, she returned her attention to the ducks. She reached under the skin to rub the meat with salt, pepper, and Sichuan peppercorns I'd brought from China. (She'd become obsessed with them, occasionally popping them into her mouth like mints.) Ladling goose fat into a pan, she expertly pan-fried the duck meat until the skin had crisped. For another dish, she used some extra whitefish that she had on hard. She went to the office and proudly showed me her knife case, pulling out various models: a super-light, Japanese slicing knife, a German one used for filleting with an extra-flexible blade, and a small paring tool. She expertly boned the fish in several minutes flat, then took half the fillets and pan-fried them with butter, sumac, and parsley before finishing them in the oven. She sliced the rest of the fish into pieces thinner than sashimi and sprinkled them with orange and lemon juice, parsley, and minced red onion, and served it raw.

I asked Bengi what kind of restaurant she'd like to run. "A place without classification," she said without hesitating. I wasn't surprised when she told me a couple of months later that she'd put in her notice at Asitane. She hadn't decided what she would do next. Maybe she would go east to learn about Asian cuisines, or maybe she would work with a few partners to open a French *boulangerie*. Or maybe she would create something that blended East and West.

But before I finished my time at Asitane and before Bengi quit, we went out one afternoon with Batur and Mark. Although they were proponents of fine dining, they, like many chefs, felt that it was in the back alleys of the city, in the small eateries and stalls that dotted the streets and lined the riverfront, where the food was most authentic and at its best.

At the Spice Bazaar, Batur led us through a labyrinth of lanes to his favorite stand for *kokorec*, grilled lamb's intestines. I'd seen the dish all over town but hadn't had the nerve to try it. Though some Turks didn't think of it as a kebab, it met Batur's definition: the offal, which looked like thick rubber bands, was strung on a spit and slowly rotated over a fire; the vendor sliced thin pieces of intestine, seasoned them with salt, pepper, and chili flakes, and stuffed them into an accompaniment, a long bun. It was like a crispy, chewy, spicy hot dog, and after going without chili peppers through Central Asia and Iran, I appreciated the kick. I could even enjoy the *ayran*, which helped the spice go down. Afterward, we strolled to Batur's favorite candy shop. The line of customers had once stretched out the door, he told us, before "Nestlé arrived and people forgot what good candy tasted like." (I liked that in Turkey even adults were passionate about candy and had their favorite stores.) I bought a box of delicately powdered Turkish delight, and then we wandered into a dessert parlor. Batur ordered a round of *muhallebi*, a sweet pudding made with chicken.

"Chicken?" Mark said dubiously.

Indeed, the dessert contained poultry—super-thin shreds of it, the blandest of meats adding texture, not taste, to the thick, cinnamon-flavored rice pudding that was the very definition of comfort food. As we left, satiated, I thought about the array of foods I'd sampled. In a country that bridged East and West, many things remained entirely Turkish.

10.

Craig and I were separated for much less time than I thought we'd be. It took only a few phone calls in which I described the food and the people to convince him to fly to Istanbul. Perhaps he had missed me, I thought happily. My new network of friends helped me set up the perfect vacation, just in time for his arrival. Through Selin's friends, a beautiful studio in the Old Quarter was arranged. Bengi, Batur, and Selin treated us to delicious meals, during which we guzzled rakı and ate *meze* doused in olive oil and lemon. We toured the Topkapı Palace with its sprawling kitchens, shopped for spices in the bazaars, and tossed *simit* to the seagulls on the ferry across the Bosporus. It was all a welcome antidote to the stress of Central Asia and Iran, and the food, the gorgeous sites, and, most important, the friends made it my favorite stop on the Silk Road so far.

So it was with reluctance that we left Istanbul. But it was important to explore the rest of the country; the city was as representative of Turkey as New York City was of America. Very early one morning, we left the quiet Old Quarter just as the call to prayer began. At the airport, we boarded a flight filled with men in cheap suits and a smattering of women, all in head scarves and long coats. We were scheduled to arrive in Van, on Turkey's eastern fringe, in time for breakfast.

Eastern Turkey wasn't much of a tourist destination. Most travelers stuck to the west, venturing no farther than the stone chimneys of Cappadocia. "There's nothing in Van!" my Istanbul friends told me with bemusement. Well, nothing except for Kurdish separatists, whom they warned me to avoid.

With a population of thirty million (half of whom lived in Turkey, the rest in surrounding countries), the Kurds were the world's largest ethnic group without nationhood. Though it was difficult to differentiate Kurds by their physical appearance, they spoke their own language, Kurdish, and largely kept to themselves in tight-knit rural communities. Relations between Kurds and Turks were tense. Turks tended to look down on Kurds, who were usually poorer, less educated, and more devoutly Muslim. ("A good Kurd is a dead Kurd," said one Turk I'd met, who until that moment had seemed pleasant and mild-mannered.) Discriminatory practices like banning Kurdish-language media and instruction in schools had spurred a separatist movement, sparking acts of terrorism across Turkey and turning the southeastern part of the country into a war zone in the 1980s and 1990s. In the early 2000s, the Turkish government signed a peace treaty with the separatists, and calm was largely restored. But around the time I arrived, the Arab Spring had galvanized the ethnic minority. Protests so far had been mostly peaceful, but many predicted it was only a matter of time before they turned violent, and the government had tightened security in the east.

Nevertheless, I wanted to go. Van, on the border of Iran, was famous for its breakfast. The surrounding villages each produced their own honey, cheese, and breads, which they brought to sell in Van. Back in the 1930s, one enterprising Kurd had decided to showcase the foods, and the first breakfast joint was born. Others followed, and by the time we visited, one alley containing a bunch of restaurants had been dubbed Breakfast Street. They were largely the domain of men, who stopped in for hearty meals and copious cups of tea before work.

Never mind that I had a theory about breakfast: I was pretty certain that any culture that emphasized breakfast did not traditionally have a good cuisine. One only had to look at the Germans and the English. By contrast, the world's best cuisines had boring breakfasts. The Chinese ate leftovers and congee. Italians, I would soon discover, consumed dry crackers. Even in France, breakfast was a simple croissant—delicious, yes, but simple—a far cry from their elaborate lunches and dinners.

But we'd come to Van for breakfast, and once I'd stubbornly insisted to my Istanbul friends that I was going, they'd sighed and out came a flood of recommendations. So we knew to push past the hired touts and make a beeline for a place called Sütçü Kenan.

As we entered the echoey hall, a waiter pointed us to the second floor. But since we had our baggage, we opted for a table just short of the stairs. The waiter shrugged helplessly, unable to communicate. Later in the trip, after we were invariably escorted to second or third floors of restaurants across eastern Turkey, I noticed the absence of women on the first floor of eateries. They were invariably tucked away upstairs in the "family" section, almost always wearing head scarves or the black chadors that reminded me of Iran.

Unaware of our faux pas, we made ourselves comfortable and ordered up a large meal. I'd fasted all morning, chiding Craig for eating the airplane meal, and I was beyond famished. The waiter laid down flatbread, tomatoes, cucumbers, and feta, a spread that reminded me of our perfunctory breakfasts in Iran. But then came plates of soft herbed cheeses, olives, tangy honey, clotted cream sprinkled with crushed walnuts, and a paste called *kavut*, made of cracked wheat toasted in oil over a low fire. It looked and smelled like the paste that had nursed me back to health in Uzbekistan. I spread honey, *kaymak*, and *kavut* over the flatbread, a combination that was tangy, creamy, sweet, and instantly worth the four-thirty wake-up call. The waiters also brought a small cast-iron plate of *menemen*, Turkish omelet with tomato paste and diced vegetables. With numerous refills of strong black tea, my hunger was satiated.

Craig, always the journalist, got out of his seat and attempted to make conversation with the waiters, more with hand gestures than with words. A waiter pulled out his cell phone and dialed a number. Within a few minutes, a man who spoke fluent English arrived and introduced himself. His name was Harun and he was a tour guide. (This was a repeating pattern as well, and it played out across the region: waiters and bellhops, for a tip, speed-dialed enterprising guides whenever clueless people like us blew into town.)

We invited Harun to sit down, and a waiter, unprompted, brought him a glass of hot milk. Harun, like most of the town, was Kurdish. Kurds were not so different from Turks, he told us. "We look the same, we eat the same," he said. The chief difference, he said, was language. Some Kurds were still disgruntled with the government and wanted their own homeland, he allowed. But things were getting better. "The government treats us more equal now. We have Kurdish radio and television. And they give a lot of welfare money to the poor."

Harun offered to take us to a nearby village for lunch. He seemed amiable enough, and we had no itinerary beyond breakfast, so we agreed. Walking through town to his car, we passed by signs that reminded us of the East: the bakers made bread that was round and *nang*-like, and the butchers seemed to sell mutton and lamb exclusively, rather than a range of meats as in Istanbul.

"I eat sheep ten times, beef one time," Harun said. "Cow does not have a good taste. If I don't eat sheep, I'm not happy."

We climbed into his shabby minivan and drove around beautiful Lake Van. A haunting Christian church that Armenians had built a thousand years before sat on a lone, rocky island, reminding me of the troubled history between that ethnicity and Turks; toward the end of the Ottoman era, the military had forced more than a million Armenians out of eastern Turkey, and many had died, in an event that Armenians labeled genocide and the Turkish government had yet to address.

We passed a sign with an arrow that pointed to Iran. After making a turn onto a narrow, muddy road, we drove for another few miles past cement-block homes before we arrived at a small village nestled in rolling hills covered with snow. It was early April, but winter still.

This was Kayala, Harun told us, and it brought to mind what my Istanbul friends had said of Van: "But there's nothing there!" We followed a dirt footpath to a ramshackle dwelling in which a woman boiled a pot of milk on a stove in a bare room, while watching two children. The walls and floor of the room were made of dirt.

Harun poked around the village, looking for friends. One had gone to Istanbul, the villagers told him, while another had gone to Van for the day. As we trudged up the muddy path, we ran into someone Harun recognized—the village imam, a lanky man named Nezmettin. He didn't look like imams I'd seen elsewhere; instead of a long, flowing robe and long beard, he was dressed in sweatpants, a worn sweater, and a wool cap. He was also a beekeeper, he said. He jotted down the name of his website, and asked if I would be kind enough to promote his product.

"Maybe you would like to sell my honey in China?" he said.

I asked for a sample. Unfortunately, he said, he'd run out and wouldn't have more until summer. He pointed to a shed by his home where we could hear bees buzzing. In twenty days, after the snows had melted, he'd open the shed and the bees would pollinate the blooming wildflowers and return to make the sticky fluid that Nezmettin would appropriate and sell to the world.

"Honey is good, especially for us men," Harun told Craig with a nudge. The imam listed the benefits: honey prevented arthritis, kept one's weight in check, and boosted virility. He ate a spoonful every morning and night, he said.

Nezmettin was apologetic about the village. Early summer was really the best time to visit, he said. Not only was honey plentiful, but the sheep produced their sweetest-smelling milk then, after grazing in the spring grasses. In June, the villagers made cheese, and each household bought as much as four hundred pounds and buried it in their yards, taking out a chunk at a time to savor it slowly throughout the year. "It's like wine. It gets better with age," Harun said. But since we were at the very tail end of the cycle, there was little left to enjoy.

Just as we'd concluded we'd come at the worst time possible, Nezmettin asked if we wanted to stay for lunch. But wouldn't we be an imposition, given the lack of food? "No, no, it's fine," the imam said, waving us into his home.

We removed our shoes at the door and stepped into a humble yet comfortable living area that contained a television with a satellite feed, a modern-looking stove for heating, and a small sofa. Nezmettin invited us to sit at the round, low table on which Central Asians and Turks traditionally ate meals, although the custom had largely disappeared in Istanbul.

In the kitchen, the imam's wife and sister, unfazed by the unexpected company, began to prepare lunch. They invited me to watch as they cooked a version of *menemen*, the Turkish omelet we'd eaten that morning, this one made with tomato paste, onions, and wild greens that grew beneath a walnut tree in the yard. They used sunflower oil, a contrast from coastal Turkey, where olive oil was the staple. They remained in the kitchen during our visit, only coming out to the living room to serve the food: heaping dishes of tomato-and-cucumber salad, stewed chicken in tomato sauce with French fries, and plain, creamy yogurt. The ubiquitous flatbread was propped up like old LPs on the table. Like the bread we'd seen in Central Asia and Xinjiang, it was baked in underground tandoor ovens, Harun said, going on to describe breads that reminded me of the East. *Lavash,* he added, was stockpiled just like cheese. The thin bread, which I'd first encountered in Iran, was dipped into water or tea before eating. "That makes it very good for war times," Harun said solemnly.

Also gracing the table was the imam's precious honey. He kept a reserve for his family, and I could see why. Still embedded in the comb, the dark, viscous liquid had bits of pollen suspended in it. The comb crumbled like good pastry and the honey was tangier and sweeter than any I'd ever tried. The taste lingering in my mouth, I began thinking about ways I could peddle it, as Nezmettin had requested.

I asked what accounted for the honey's intensity. The imam replied that he didn't adulterate it. "Some beekeepers give their bees sugar to make the honey sweeter." And the flowers helped, the imam said. It was a shame we wouldn't see the rainbow of flora that would soon blossom—the greater the range, the more complex the honey. It turned out that the secret to good honey was also the key to many distinctive dishes across the Silk Road: the more cross-pollination, the better.

After we'd finished everything, the women reemerged with *helva*, a common nougat-like sweet, and cake made with honey and walnuts. We lingered over cups of black tea. As the imam laid out a carpet for Harun to pray on—he'd missed one of his prayer sessions while driving—I wanted to give praise to Allah, too, for the bounty of food we'd enjoyed in this impoverished village, even at the tail end of winter.

All along the Silk Road, locals had showered us with amazing hospitality. In Xinjiang, I'd been treated like part of Nur's family; in Central Asia, strangers had invited us to weddings and mere acquaintances had slaughtered a sheep for us; Iranians saw beyond politics and had been eager to make friends.

Even so, the Turks outdid everyone. Selin and several of her friends had put me up in their homes and hotels without asking for a penny, and they'd treated me to dozens of meals in Istanbul. But city folk had the means to afford such generosity. It was a surprise to show up unexpectedly in one of Turkey's poorest places and receive the kind of welcome and sustenance we'd experienced in Kayala.

It seemed that Turks were always ready for guests. I grew to understand that the massive volume of Chinese food that Selin and her friends had wanted me to cook was not a sign of gluttony; it was a sign of charity. My stingy quantities hadn't allowed for the possibility that a guest might bring more friends, or that neighbors might come knocking.

My Turkish friends explained that the hospitality was related to their country's unique history and its position on the Silk Road. For centuries, outsiders and their exotic goods had passed through Anatolia en route to Asia and Europe. Turkey had once been part of the Holy Roman Empire, and Istanbul (then known as Constantinople) its eastern capital. Turks, according to the mythology, were also guests in their own land, since they'd originated in Central Asia and migrated to Anatolia more than a thousand years before. As far back as the thirteenth century, Turks had set up a system of *wakifs*, religious charitable organizations dedicated to feeding travelers across the country. At these soup kitchens, visitors could receive a meat dish, rice and wheat soup, vegetables like spinach and turnips, and *helva* for dessert. A spread of butter, cheese, and flatbread awaited those who arrived late in the evening.

The *wakifs* were an outgrowth of Sufism. I learned more about this mystical offshoot of Islam in the Anatolian town of Konya where I visited the tombs of Mevlana, a poet who founded Sufism, and Ates Baz Veli, his chef. The graves were the most important shrines in Turkey, and the only places in the country where I felt the need to wear a head scarf. That it was mid-April but snowing the day I visited only added to their mystical quality.

At Mevlana's shrine, a peaceful compound where the poet had lived and was buried, I visited the kitchen, one of the more important rooms. Sufism is probably best known to outsiders for its whirling dervishes, who wore fezzes and gowns and spun in circles to reach spiritual enlightenment, but here I learned that they had another, equally important duty: cooking. During Mevlana's time, a dervish's education began in the kitchen. Initiates prayed and fasted for several days in the kitchen foyer before taking on duties that included grocery shopping, washing dishes, and cooking. Once a disciple graduated from the kitchen, he was permitted to eat in the dining room with more senior members. Cooking provided a pathway for living: you started out "raw" and ended up "ripe" or "well-cooked."

Not far from Mevlana's shrine, in the suburbs of Konya, was an unassuming tomb to his chef, Ates Baz. I traveled there by taxi, with a driver named Abdullah, and I thought he was lost when he turned down a side street lined with modest houses that petered out into an empty field. But there it was, a narrow brick two-story shrine with a pointy roof. The humble building was one of the country's most popular attractions. Ates Baz, my driver explained, wasn't just any chef. One day, Mevlana had instructed him to make a particular dish, but midway through cooking, Ates Baz ran out of wood. As a sign of devotion, he stuck his leg in the fire to feed it. Fortunately, Mevlana intervened before the cook self-immolated and promptly elevated him to his second-in-command.

Not long after we arrived at the tomb, a bus pulled up, and dozens of women from Istanbul disembarked, each carrying a small plastic bag of salt. They placed the bags in a basket near the shrine, exchanging them for sacks left by other pilgrims. The salt was regarded as holy. "It cures depression," said the gatekeeper, an elderly woman whose family had looked over the shrine for more than two centuries. "Maybe it's psychological," Abdullah said with a shrug. On the way back to town, though, I noticed my driver was counting beads. I asked what he thought of Sufism. "It is very hard to say," he said. "How do you define a Sufi?" Ataturk had stamped out the dervishes, and Sufism had become more of a philosophy than a religion. But the idea that cooking and hospitality were sacred had endured.

Craig and I discovered that traveling across Turkey by bus was incredibly comfortable, in accordance with Turkish hospitality. Bus stations had ample seating and plenty of tea, served by mobile vendors. (Tea, always sipped from small tulip-shaped glasses, even on the go, was so common that the country often seemed to be one giant teahouse.) Buses were punctual, and the attendants were more attentive than the average American flight steward. In their button-down shirts and ties, they served a range of complimentary drinks and snacks, and they passed around bottles of lemon cologne to freshen travelers' faces and hands. The food at rest stops was made with care and included a range of delicious stews, the Turkish pizza called *lahmacun*, and kebabs. I would take a Turkish rest stop over the ones that line I-95 any day.

Traveling in the Kurdish-dominated east had its moments of tension, though. At one bus station, a friendly tea vendor asked us how we liked "Kurdistan." Every so often, police pulled over a bus, examined everyone's identification, and threw open the luggage compartment to inspect bags at random. On one bus ride, it happened three times. They were looking for separatist-minded Kurds, some of whom they suspected were terrorists.

But compared to our paranoid experiences in Turkmenistan and Iran, eastern Turkey was relatively relaxed, and we got through the Kurdish area without incident.

Even so, a new sort of tension was building between Craig and me. With my Silk Road journey more than half complete, both of us had started thinking about the next step. We knew the immediate future: after the Silk Road, we would fly back to Beijing for ten days and then go on to Washington, DC, where a think tank had awarded Craig a fellowship. But beyond that, we had no plans. Bouncing across the Pacific and roaming the world was starting to wear on me, and I suspected on Craig as well. But what alternatives did we have? Did we want to move back to China? Or did we want to settle down somewhere in the United States? Surely, we had to figure that out before we thought about children.

On the long bus rides across Turkey, we started talking about possibilities. I was still ambivalent about the cooking school; sometimes I thought about giving it up entirely, while other times I imagined throwing myself into it full-steam, building it into something bigger. Freelancing left a lot of freedom. "We could live in Hawaii," Craig said. "Or the coast of Maine." But writing seemed unstable, only more so since the rise of the Internet and the decline of traditional publications. So if that wasn't a good option, maybe something else was, Craig said, bringing up a completely different idea: joining the Foreign Service and becoming a diplomat. Not only had he given the idea some thought, but he'd even brought test materials for the Foreign Service exam and begun studying on the long rides.

The prospect of Craig joining the Foreign Service was intriguing. It meant that he'd be posted at various American embassies around the world, for several years at a time. It seemed like a natural fit. As a foreign correspondent, he'd written extensively about international issues. He was fluent in Mandarin, a language that had become increasingly valuable. And a career like that, with its stability and benefits, would mean a significant step up from our current lifestyle. We would have comfortable, American-style housing and comprehensive health insurance, both of which we'd lived without in China. If we had children, they would be able to attend good international schools. And it would be an ideal circumstance for me to continue writing. Moving every few years would mean that I'd always have something new to write about.

But I couldn't help feeling resistant. If Craig joined the Foreign Service, I would become the classic trailing spouse. I'd never moved anywhere for anyone. Would I have control over where we lived? How would I fit in with the other spouses, whom I imagined as tennis-playing, tailor-visiting ladies who lunch? Would I take up bridge and mahjong and start drinking after lunch out of boredom? I shared my fears, caricatured as they were, with Craig.

"Well, how about we think about other options," he said, as we settled into another long-distance ride. One alternative he proposed was that we could work together at the cooking school. "We could build it up and maybe open another one in the United States and split our time between the two."

Surely he was joking, I said. He was not, he replied. But he'd never been interested in cooking before! I said. And how would that work anyway? Would he want to work for me? Or I for him?

It wasn't about me working for him or him working for me, he said. We would work *together*. The same way we worked together in our relationship.

But what if there were disagreements? Who would prevail? I asked him. Sure, we'd been colleagues, at *Newsweek*, when we first met. But we hadn't been a couple then, and we'd never worked in the same office. And the cooking school was different—I felt possessive of it and wasn't ready to share it. It was, after all, *my* cooking school. Working on it together was a concept I couldn't wrap my head around.

In the central Turkish town of Gaziantep, I met a pair of Sufi sisters who embodied the spirit of Mevlana and his chef. Near the border of Syria, Gaziantep was known for its hearty cooking, which had remained unchanged for centuries. Unlike Mediterranean Turkey, where olive oil, vegetables, and

seafood were a large part of the diet, traditional Anatolian cuisine consisted
of sheep, butter, grains, and lentils. My guide in Gaziantep was a food
writer named Filiz, who promptly took me to her sister's house for lunch.
The sisters, both in their fifties, were very close, and for years they'd lived
downtown in the same apartment building, along with their mother. But a
few months ago their mother had died, and Ferda and her husband, who
together ran a successful plastic-wrap business, had moved to a wealthy
suburb. The house, a sparkling American-style McMansion, was the grandest I'd visited on the Silk Road. A large green lawn surrounded the property, and the walkway to the front door was paved with marble. There was
more marble on the counters of the eat-in kitchen, which also contained a
huge stainless-steel refrigerator and all the other appliances you'd expect
in a fancy Western kitchen, plus a Sony flat-screen television mounted on
one wall.

And yet the home was also traditional. Beautiful woven rugs covered the
kitchen floor, and above the doorway to every room hung framed Arabic
calligraphy. A round glass evil eye sat in a marble bowl. "That blocks bad
spirits," Filiz said, echoing what I'd heard all along the Silk Road. A white
head scarf embroidered with colorful threads that had belonged to the
sisters' grandmother hung on a wall of the living room. I asked the sisters
why they didn't wear head scarves themselves, as many women did in this
region.

"We are Sufi," Filiz said. "For us, religion is very private and personal.
There are two kinds of Muslim believers. There are those who say you must
cover up, you must wear a head scarf, and pray five times a day. But we
believe that devotion comes from within. We don't abide by particular
rules. We are against that."

After the sisters showed me around the house, we sat in Ferda's comfortable patio, drinking tea. Like many Turkish women, Ferda had met her
husband through family. Together, they'd built their business. I was particularly interested in her experience after Craig had brought up the idea
of working together. Ferda said it was frustrating when the occasional

new business associate dismissed her as "the wife." "Some people don't take me seriously as an equal partner, though my husband insists otherwise." Women in central Turkey were more traditional than their counterparts in Istanbul, she added. "In Istanbul, if women want freedom, they just divorce. But the problem is everywhere, and the problem is here," she said, pointing to her head. "Most marriages don't run smoothly all the time. Do you think I never have conflicts in my marriage? The aim is to balance things out."

"In places like Gaziantep, where people choose to stay close to their families, the bonds are stronger," Filiz added. "Finding someone to marry isn't like buying a shirt that fits well. It takes a long time for marriage to fit. It takes patience and love."

After several cups of tea, we returned to the kitchen, where Ferda cooked a meal of *mercimekli kofte*, red lentil and bulgur patties, and *yuvalama*, yogurt soup with tiny balls made from ground lamb and rice. Complementing the two dishes was a rice pilaf and a simple salad of lettuce, tomatoes, and carrots. The *kofte*, flavored with butter, garlic scapes, and Aleppo chilies, hinted at our proximity to the Middle East. I'd had a number of yogurt soups across Turkey, but Ferda's was the most delicious—the lamb and rice gave the soup a chewy, tapioca-like texture, and the mint-infused oil she drizzled on top of it added a dazzling scent. Then Ferda poured glasses of *ayran*, the yogurt drink that reminded me of Central Asian *koumiss*. *Ayran* was a little better and I'd become lukewarm about it. This one, though, was particularly fresh and pungent, having come directly from Ferda's housekeeper's village. I reverted to my initial reaction to fermented mare's milk in Kyrgyzstan and almost gagged.

I was impressed that the sister had put together a rather complicated meal so quickly, especially since I'd only gotten in touch with Filiz the day before to confirm I was coming. Ferda didn't have to do any shopping, my guide explained, because she was used to having guests. "Some of the guests I invite, others invite themselves," she said. She showed me the contents of her freezer. She pulled out some chicken, which she could use for soup or stew. A Costco-sized bag of frozen pistachios could be used for a dessert. Rifling through the freezer, she found disks of *lahmacun*, the Turkish pizza I'd encountered at rest stops. "This is what I use if I run out of everything else. Do you want to try it?" she asked, popping some in the oven.

"Look at how thin the crust is," Ferda said, holding up the *lahmacun* after it had warmed. Her favorite baker had made the dish. Indeed, it was delicious, a crisp savory flatbread topped with tomato paste and minced lamb, parsley, and red peppers.

"It's kismet," Filiz said, using a word that I later discovered had Turkish roots. "You see, the food is here before the guest. Everyone brings their own fortune when they go to someone's house. There is often no time to shop when guests announce themselves. So it depends on your luck."

After the home-cooked meal and hospitality, Filiz took me out to show me how *lahmacun* was made. It wasn't baked in homes, nor was it store-bought; the flatbread required the participation of a neighborhood. First, you procured the vegetables—parsley, red pepper, and tomatoes—at a greengrocer or a supermarket. Then you took the produce to a nearby butcher. He—it was always a he—would pick out a good hunk of lamb, mince it with the vegetables, and puree your tomatoes through a mill. Then you took your minced meat and vegetables and tomato sauce to a nearby baker. The baker would knead a ball of dough, flatten it, spread the produce and meat over it, and slide it into a deep, wide oven.

The butcher and the baker were particularly important to communities and benefited from symbiosis, Filiz said. Aside from making *lahmacun* filling, butchers often prepped kebabs and other meat dishes, which were baked in commercial ovens, invariably just a few steps away. While everyone had an oven at home, most locals thought that food baked better in the hands of a professional baker. On Sunday afternoons, the bakeries were crowded with people waiting for their items to bake. The importance of the butcher and the baker seemed to reflect something about central Turkish cuisine that I'd heard all the way back in Kyrgyzstan from my friend Gulzat: "It's basically meat and dough." In Gaziantep, dough in particular was prepared with a refinement that flabbergasted me.

The most important use of dough was for baklava. Greeks and Turks argued over the provenance of the sweet, each claiming it as their own. But, in fact, the dessert may have had deep Silk Road ties. Filiz suspected that the idea of a layered pastry actually originated farther east, in Central Asia, with its tradition of layered breads. (Though I'd only seen a crude version of baklava in Uzbekistan, I had come across old recipes for layered breads in my research.) In fact, the word *baklava* might be derived from a Mongolian word, *bayla*, which means "to tie up." Even more interesting, a recipe similar to baklava, for a dish called *gullac*, is found in a Chinese cookbook written during Mongolian rule. Others theorized that the pastry came out of the Ottoman kitchen.

But wherever the dessert had originated, it was unquestionable that Gaziantep had the most baklava shops of any city in the world: more than five hundred, Filiz said. The luggage compartments under the buses at the main station were stuffed full of baklava boxes distributed across the country. And while baklava was as common to Gaziantep as *plov* was to Central Asia, it was much more appetizing. At Gulluoglu, one of the town's most celebrated baklava shops, we sat down for squares of the famous pastry, made with pistachios and sugar syrup rather than the walnuts and honey that flavored Greek baklava. To feel all the layers in my mouth, Filiz suggested eating the dessert upside down. The layers of phyllo crushed together as I bit into them, making a crunch as gratifying as stepping on a pile of autumn leaves. My tongue was immersed in flaky, buttery sweetness.

The next day, Filiz took me to Gulluoglu's kitchen. I was as excited as a kid visiting Willy Wonka's chocolate factory. We met Bayram, the sixty-one-year-old head pastry chef with a round stomach whose story was just as myth-like as that of Willy Wonka. He'd worked at the factory ever since he was a child. His father had been a gardener for the previous head chef, and one day, his father brought young Bayram to the chef's home. The chef noticed that the child had a way of playing with mud that reminded him of the proper way to knead pastry dough. The chef promptly commanded Bayram to work in the factory, and Bayram's family, seeing the apprenticeship as a way out of poverty, readily agreed. Because the sweet was such an important dish in Gaziantep, those who made it carried a certain esteem, and the role could be passed down for generations.

After we'd donned lab coats, shower caps, and shoe protectors, Bayram showed us the exacting steps it took to create the pastry. The key was flattening the phyllo to the point of absolute translucency. In the old days, this was done by hand, a process Bayram demonstrated for my sake: he rocked a long rolling pin over the dough until beads of sweat dripped from his forehead and narrowly avoided landing on the pastry sheet. But nowadays the factory had a machine. A chef fed a piece of dough into the conveyor belt of the "RONDO Dough-how & More" and out came a long sheet less than half a millimeter thick. Another chef held a Turkish flag behind a sheet; the brilliant red of the flag shined through. The machine, speedy and precise, had doubled the output of the baklava factory. But that aside, Bayram made the dessert exactly as his mentor had taught him, and when he passed down the recipe to new chefs, he warned them, "If any part of the process is messed up, the bones of our ancestors will feel the pain."

Bayram's underlings assembled the baklava. One chef carefully placed a single layer of *yufka*, the Turkish phyllo, into a large square tray while another chef dipped a straw brush into a vat of clarified butter heated to 104 degrees Fahrenheit and flicked a uniform coating of it onto the dough. The two chefs worked together, alternating *yufka* and butter, stopping every ten layers to add a coating of milk and a dusting of semolina flour. A layer of finely crushed pistachios went over that, and then a layer of more coarsely chopped pistachios. Another five layers of *yufka* were placed over the pistachios, then another ten layers of *yufka* with clarified butter. The chefs cut the baklava into exact diamonds—Bayram took the knife from one underling to correct the angle at which he sliced. Another chef slid the tray into an oven set to 320 degrees Fahrenheit. After fifty minutes, the pastry was doused in sugar syrup heated to 223 degrees Fahrenheit. All the precision made my head spin and gave me a new respect for the dessert.

Filiz took me to watch another pastry chef, who spun sheets of dough even thinner and by hand, something I thought impossible until I witnessed it. He rolled out the dough for a pastry called *katmer*, thumping the pin back and forth with a hurried rhythm. Then, after the pin was no longer useful, he took the transparent sheet and began twirling it with rapid force to make it even thinner. The spinning was similar to how I imagined a Neapolitan pizza maker would work dough, but this sheet was so light that when the chef paused for a breath, it floated down to the counter like a slow-moving UFO. The chef spread crushed pistachios, sugar, and *kaymak*—that amazing clotted cream again—over the dough, folded it into a square, and baked it until it was crisp. It instantly supplanted baklava as my favorite Turkish pastry, one that the Turks had selfishly not shared with the rest of the world.

But for all the craft I saw with dough in Gaziantep, it produced a question: where were the noodles?

11.

From Gaziantep, Craig and I took a bus to the Mediterranean coast. On the highway, we passed by the first Western fast-food chain stores we'd seen in thousands of miles: a McDonald's, and later a Popeye's and a Sbarro. We drove over valleys and emerald green mountains that looked like Switzerland, but with mosques. On the coast, we idled in Antalya, a tourist town filled with establishments serving espresso, gelato, and bland international buffets. We walked for a few days along the Lycian Way, an old pilgrim's trail that connected coastal villages. We didn't need a guide this time, as the path was clearly marked, nor did we need a cook, as we passed through towns with plenty of restaurants. The harshest weather we faced was clouds and drizzle. To my surprise, I found myself feeling nostalgic for the challenges of our Kyrgyz hike.

Our final long-distance bus took us to Bodrum, a town on the Aegean coast. Its harbor was filled with wooden yachts called *gulet*s. On the main drag, unveiled, cosmopolitan women walked fluffy dogs. At night, downtown pulsed with music from nightclubs where wealthy Turks mingled with vacationing Europeans. All the buildings were painted white, from the McDonald's to the mosques to the luxury hotels lining the shore. We transferred from the bus to a private car and wound to the town's outskirts. We

drove up a steep incline. At the top of the hill was a resort with a pano-
ramic view of the Aegean Sea. Several small Greek islands glimmered in
the distance.

Craig stayed with me at the resort for a few days before leaving for
America, to do some reporting for his book. We suspended our discussion
of the future until our next reunion; we both had a lot to think about.
Where that would be, though, we were unsure. Though I knew he wasn't
excited about Italy and the requisite four-hour meals, Craig said he'd aim to
meet me in Rome, at the very latest. I watched him leave with regret.

I was even more sorry because Bodrum, like Istanbul, was a place in
which I could imagine us idling, perhaps even settling down. A friend of
Selin's named Asli, a woman with shoulder-length brown hair and sor-
rowful eyes, had invited me to stay at Yarbasan resort. She managed the
property and owned Erenler Sofrasi, the on-site restaurant. We'd set up a
deal. For Turkish cooking lessons, plus free room and board, I would cook
Chinese meals and teach dishes to her guests. With a beautiful villa, a
swimming pool, and a beach at my disposal, I couldn't help feeling like I'd
gotten the better end of the bargain.

Days started with delicious breads and dips, which continued to throw
a wrench into my global theory about breakfast as a reverse indicator of
great cuisine. With the bagel-like *simit* rolls, Asli served a tomato and olive
salsa with cumin and garlic and *beyaz peynir* (the white, feta-like cheese)
whipped with dill, olive oil, and creamy *kaymak*. Pork salami, which she
brought back from the Greek islands, occasionally graced the table, too.
The eggs, served sunny-side up, were the most delicious I'd eaten—the
whites had a sweet meatiness that tasted almost like lobster. It helped that
my new restaurateur friend cooked them in a pool of butter.

Mediterranean cold *meze*, which had disappeared in the Turkish hinterlands, returned to the dining table. Asli sautéed greens like Swiss chard,
purslane, and nettles before dousing them in olive oil and lemon juice. She
used sunflower oil sparingly. A trifecta of parsley, dill, and mint flavored
many dishes. Young lamb, rather than mutton, was often served as a main
course, or beef or fish. Other meals were vegetarian, something unheard of

anywhere else I'd been. "The land is very fertile and the weather is temperate," Asli said. "You can eat fresh vegetables all year long."

More so here than anywhere else in Turkey, the food seemed Greek, reflecting the two countries' shared heritage. One afternoon, Asli taught me how to make dolmas, which I'd always thought of as Greek, though I'd found them as far east as Central Asia. She sauteed rice with black currants and pine nuts, before adding an array of seasonings: scallions, parsley, dill, cinnamon, cloves, and allspice. "The spices are a legacy of the Ottomans," she said. We wrapped the rice into grape leaves and steamed the rolls in a large pot, in between slices of onion and lemon.

Asli's grandparents were born in Greece and had been moved to Turkey during the Great Exchange. Though the Greek and Turkish governments were constantly at odds, I met many Turks who, like Asli, felt connected to Greece. "They are like our brothers," she said. But that didn't mean there was much contact: though it was easy for Westerners to hop from Turkey to Greece, Turks went through an arduous visa process for entry into the European Union and were often denied.

Between meals, we shopped at a nearby farmer's market. Unlike at the American equivalents, the produce was cheap enough for average Turks. Asli went twice a week, not trusting her staff with the duty. She was picky. Because it was still too cold to grow eggplants outside of greenhouses, she opted for dried ones that had ripened naturally the summer before. The eggplants, along with other dried vegetables like red bell peppers, hung in garlands above the stands, like Christmas ornaments. Asli pointed out the woman who sold eggs, explaining that I'd liked my sunny-side-up egg because the vendor allowed her hens to peck freely at wild greens. Other stands were piled high with leafy spinach that tapered into bright pink roots and green bell peppers so crisp that one made a snapping sound when Asli bit into it. Small, dark strawberries perfumed the air. The restaurateur noted that most farmers refrained from using pesticides, in part because they were expensive, but mostly because they were unnecessary here. "Healthy eating is economical," she said. "Olive oil is practically free at the markets because everyone grows their own olives."

I omitted pork from my Chinese dinner menu this time, knowing that the meat was difficult to procure outside of Istanbul and uncertain whether the guests would eat it. But I found most of the vegetables and meats I needed at the market, and even a few unexpected ones, like Chinese chives. I bought long, skinny Asian eggplants, dried mushrooms, scallions, fresh ginger, and garlic. I'd brought condiments from China, and Asli had sourced tofu. At the market, I also found traces of the East in the hardened rolls of bread and chunks of dried yogurt that seemed to speak to the Turks' nomadic past.

Somehow, though, the meal in Bodrum didn't go as smoothly as the Chinese dinner in Istanbul. I blamed the idyllic setting. As I chopped my ingredients, the waiter, a dark-haired man named Metin, asked if I wanted a Turkish coffee. "Sure," I said. "How many sugars?" he asked, pointing to a container. "One? Two?" I said. Neither seemed to be the right answer. "Three is good," he said, dropping them into the espresso-sized cup. As I sipped the sugary shot, I paused to admire the gorgeous view. Maybe Craig and I could live like this, I thought, daydreaming about us opening a seaside bed-and-breakfast while I leisurely continued prepping.

When seven o'clock crept up on me, I was far behind. And this time I didn't have a crew of bossy Turkish women to help. As the first guests arrived, including the owner of the resort, I nervously waved from behind the stove and managed to knock over a pot of chicken stock I'd been simmering all afternoon.

"Oh my god, oh my god!" Metin exclaimed, scrambling for dish towels. It was one of his few English phrases, and he repeated it with unnerving frequency through the night in response to everything I did, good or bad: "Oh my god, oh my god!"

To stave off the guests' hunger as I hurried, Asli brought out bread and cheese, a good entrée to a Turkish meal but a distinctly un-Chinese one. After I sent out chili oil with plates of pan-fried dumplings, I got a report: "They're saying it's too spicy, too spicy." I changed the sauce for a spicy tofu dish to a sweet-and-sour one and sent that out along with several other dishes, including fish-fragrant eggplant. "They want yogurt with the eggplant," Anna, another waitress, reported, explaining that eggplant dishes always came with yogurt in Turkey.

Halfway through the meal, I went to check on the guests and was relieved to discover that all the food had been eaten, but my relief quickly gave way to panic: had I not made enough? "They're not complaining, that's the most important thing," Anna said. By the time the last dish had been sent out, I was so exhausted that I could barely stand. I felt better when I heard the feedback on dessert, a Chinese imperial dish of candied apples. "They give it five stars!" Asli said approvingly.

Save for *su borek*, the Turkish lasagna that Selin had pointed out at an Istanbul bazaar, fresh noodles had proved elusive in Turkey, even though I'd heard that the dried variety was common. I'd been told that certain villages near the Black Sea and Cappadocia specialized in making pasta by hand, but after passing through many small towns and two major culinary destinations—Istanbul and Gaziantep—I'd yet to find a noodle maker in action. Professional women no longer had time to do that kind of labor, Selin and her friends had told me. The restaurants I visited in Istanbul offered very few noodle dishes, and at the Ottoman restaurant Asitane, not a single noodle dish graced the menu. Batur said that the fall menu usually featured triangles of *pirouhi* (a cousin of Eastern and Central Europe's pierogi), a dish that appeared sparingly in imperial records and was thought to have come from the Caucasus with women who'd ended up in Ottoman harems.

In both Istanbul and Gaziantep, I'd found chefs who were amazingly adept with dough. The granny dishwashers at Asitane rolled out sheets of *yufka* to a thinness that was only surpassed by Bayram and his baklava chefs and the maker of that amazing gossamer *katmer* in Gaziantep. But for all their artistry with phyllo, they weren't making noodles. I felt like I was getting warmer when I visited a friend of Filiz, who added small triangles of baked dough to her soup. She'd even planned to make homemade vermicelli, she said, but her cooking docket was too full. I'd eaten bits of wheat vermicelli folded into rice pilaf a couple of times throughout Turkey, a treatment I'd heard was also common to Iran. But a dish where pasta played second fiddle to rice could hardly be considered a noodle dish. No one had served me even the dried pasta, called *eriste*, that I'd seen in supermarkets from the Uighur region of China to Turkey. I'd been told it was only filler food, served as a side with a slap of butter like a baked potato. As in Iran, it was not considered fitting for guests. So, while noodles did exist, it seemed clear from my time in Iran and Turkey that neither country made them a priority.

Yet certain food historians and writers have argued that Turkey might have been among the first places where noodles were made, because some of the earliest evidence of wheat has been found in southwestern Turkey, as well as the Fertile Crescent and the Nile Delta. In any case, there was one pasta dish I knew Turks still made by hand, and I was determined to learn it: *manti*, tiny meat dumplings. Everyone knew of them and told me how common the dish was, but strangely, as with noodles, I rarely saw it on menus. Perhaps it was Turkey's macaroni and cheese and had yet to hit its restaurant revival? It was difficult even finding someone willing to teach me the dish. "I don't have the patience to fold those little things," Selin said, pinching her fingers together to demonstrate. She said that when the guests asked to learn *manti*, she outsourced the lesson to someone else.

Finally, in Bodrum, I'd found Asli, who thankfully knew how to make *manti* and was willing to teach me. The morning after the Chinese dinner, we set to work. We used the dough left over from the Chinese dumplings I'd made the previous day. The dough was just the right consistency. Like other skilled pasta makers I'd met, Asli had a three-foot-long rolling pin. She played with the shorter rolling pin I'd brought from China, and, marveling at how much easier it was to use, began rolling out a sheet of dough with it. She flattened the dough to about the same thinness I'd use for dumpling wrappers and cut it into squares just shy of an inch. She placed a tiny dollop of meat filling, made simply of ground lamb, minced onions, salt, and pepper, in the center of each square, then folded it into a triangle and clasped together the two opposite edges.

As we worked, she told me that perhaps the reason I hadn't seen *manti* on my journey was that it was mostly cooked in villages. *Manti* was a bonding activity among women; usually it was a whole-day affair, and when they were served, they were served in abundance. Sometimes they were boiled in broth while other times they were served in sauce, as Asli would do today. After we pressed together several hundred minuscule dumplings, each no bigger than my pinkie nail, Asli boiled them quickly and drained them. She topped them with a sauce made of yogurt, crushed garlic, mint, and ground chili peppers and served them in shallow bowls like the ones for Italian pasta.

Of all the dumplings on my trip, it was *manti* that most reminded me of *chuchura*, the Uighur dumplings I'd learned to make at the religious woman Hayal's home in Kashgar—which in turn reminded me of Chinese wontons. And the name—*manti*—sounded most like *manta*, the larger steamed dumplings I'd also learned to prepare in Kashgar, a name that, in turn, reminded me of a Chinese word for steamed buns, *mantou*. And while I'd yet to reach Italy, the *manti* seemed to bear resemblance to tortellini as well. Had *manti* migrated with Silk Road travelers all the way from China?

Some food historians think so. As Alan Davidson writes in *The Oxford Companion to Food*, "Filled pasta has proved less vulnerable to encroachment by pilaf than ordinary noodles." Perhaps *manti* had become widespread across the Silk Road because "the combination of a meat or similar filling and a cereal envelope was convenient for nomadic cultures and more generally for people with very simple cooking facilities. One cooking pot would do, and the filling could be varied according to what was available." I was also inclined to think that the Mongolian conquerors who'd swept across the Silk Road had something to do with the transmission of the dumplings, as they were integral to cuisines all the way to Central Europe, the western edge of Genghis Khan's empire. Similar dumplings had even reached the eastern fringes of the empire, in the form of *mandu*, a beef dumpling in Korea, and *manju*, a steamed bread in Japan. Still, the roots of the name—*mantou*—are vague. In Mandarin, it sounds like "barbarian head." Could that be a reference to the Mongolians themselves?

In any case, there on the Aegean coast, thousands of miles from where my journey began, the delicious little dumplings certainly reminded me of dishes that spanned back to China. And a comment of Asli's echoed as well: "Tradition says that forty should fit on a spoon. Mothers-in-law judge their daughters-in-law accordingly."

Asli was no one's idea of a servile daughter-in-law. She'd been raised in a family that had believed in Ataturk's reforms and that respected women as much as men. Her mother-in-law was not much a part of her life; she and her husband, Haluk, had left his family behind in Istanbul to build the restaurant in Bodrum.

Much as it stoked my nascent fantasy of working with Craig, I was mindful of how such an arrangement had played out in Asli's case. Though the couple co-owned the restaurant, she was the boss and her husband played a supporting role. Asli also did the bulk of the work. Cooking aside, she took care of the accounting and marketing and responded to e-mails and phone inquiries. When their son returned from school, she looked after him. When Haluk wasn't off painting or reading, he often sat at the bar with a glass of wine, munching on finger-length cucumbers. I asked Asli if she wanted him to be in the kitchen more, the way I wanted Craig in the kitchen with me.

"No, never!" she responded. "I was married to someone before who liked to cook, and that didn't work out very well. One cook is enough for a household."

Perhaps that was where I'd been mistaken—maybe Asli was right. But did it mean that a woman's greater autonomy in a relationship invariably meant that she carried the heavier burden?

Early one evening, when Asli and I were cooking, two women stopped by for wine. They were both from Istanbul and lived part-time at villas they owned at the resort. They looked on as Asli and I made a bulgur pilaf. Patsy Cline sang "[You Are] Always on My Mind" over the stereo, followed by an album of Frank Sinatra tunes. Asli directed me as I sautéed the bulgur in sunflower oil rather than olive oil, in deference to the provenance of the dish, before adding minced green peppers, onions, and to-matoes. She added water and chopped, peeled tomatoes and brought the mixture to a simmer before covering the pot and allowing the bulgur to steam.

"If you want to add cumin, that's optional," she said.

"I add cumin," said one of the women, as she smoked a cigarette. She spoke with a British accent and had deep blue eyes passed down from her Russian Caucasus ancestors.

"I *never* add cumin," said the other.

I was used to the opinionated nature of Turkish women by then, and in Bodrum they were even more so. Bodrum was known as "Ladies' Paradise" and had a reputation for offering women an escape from the constraints of Islam. These two women, like many others, had moved to the seaside town after divorcing. Asli, still married, was an anomaly. "Not long after I moved here, I ran into a friend, and she said, 'Welcome! Have you gotten a divorce, too?'" she recalled.

"Divorce rates are an indication that women aren't putting up with men anymore," said the British-accented woman. "Turkish women are ten years ahead of the men. We're more open-minded. Men are traditional."

Her friend agreed but argued that this was a shift. "In the olden days, we used to worship our husbands."

"I never got that far!" Asli said.

The friend added, "I used to cut my ex-husband's toenails. I used to take the pits out of grapes for him!"

I mentioned that I'd seen a huge range in female autonomy across Turkey, from the women on the coast who ran their own businesses and didn't put up with much to those in the east, who weren't allowed to socialize freely in restaurants or even in their own homes. Asli and our visitors said it came down to a woman's social class and education. "If you're not educated, there's a much bigger gap. Men in Turkey respect women who are educated, or at least they can't be easily taken advantage of," Asli said.

Her cell phone rang. It was Haluk, who wanted to know what time she was coming home and what was for dinner. Asli told him that if he wanted to eat, it was best that he come to the restaurant, because we were still cooking.

"You see, Turkish men want their wives at home," Asli said. "But he knows he doesn't have a chance with me. I'm lucky to have him as my husband."

As the bulgur finished steaming, the women left and Haluk showed up, in search of dinner. As he looked on, Asli showed me how to make *sac kavurma*, strips of beef stir-fried with red bell peppers and onions. *Sac* referred to a pot that resembled a wok, and Asli suspected that the dish itself had originated in China. It was still commonly served at rest stops that lined the highway. "In any case, it's a very ancient way of cooking meat," she said.

"It has a nomadic taste," Haluk added. "And nomadic Chinese . . . are Turks!"

Asli laughed. Despite her gruff demeanor and a certain moroseness that she and Haluk shared, they had a nice relationship, particularly in a land littered with divorces. Yes, Asli seemed to shoulder a greater share of the burden, but their arrangement seemed to work for them. Every so often, I caught a glimpse of one reaching for the other's hand or a shared tender glance.

As we ate, I asked Haluk about his views on Turkey. "After World War II, Turkey started becoming a country of the Western world," he said. "But we've never been truly respected by the West. Instead, we are a manipulated state, in the middle, even with our strong historical relations with the world. Turkey is a bridge, the slogan goes. But we're more than just a bridge. We're a nation."

"We'll never get into the EU," Asli said. "It's a Christian club! They won't take us in."

"If they let in the Czechs, the Romanians, the Bulgarians, we should be let in as well," Haluk argued.

The conversation was rendered somewhat moot several months later, as the European Union collapsed into chaos and Greece and Italy found themselves in dire financial straits. Perhaps it was better that they weren't part of the EU, Turks began to believe.

Even in the moment, Asli had moved on from thinking about politics to serving dessert, hunks of roast candied pumpkin with dollops of creamy *kaymak*.

"Do you like my pumpkin?" she asked Haluk. "That's what's most important."

From the resort, the three glimmering Greek islands in the Aegean beckoned like sirens in *The Odyssey*. The islands were my passage west to Italy. For two hundred dollars, I could have boarded a plane and arrived in Italy two hours later. But flying didn't seem right after my overland travel; I wanted to journey the way the old adventurers had before planes. So I opted for more costly arrangements that involved a speedboat, an overnight ferry, a dash across mainland Greece by bus, and yet another overnight ferry.

My goal was to arrive in Italy by Easter, just three days away when I set out. Early in the morning, I boarded a speedboat at the Bodrum harbor. The thirteen-mile journey to Greece took less time than the lengthy border formalities on either side; passports were scrutinized carefully before passengers were allowed through the official gates of Europe.

I stepped onto the tiny Greek island of Kos and ambled about town as I waited for my overnight ferry to Athens. The blue-and-white striped Greek flag replaced the red-and-white Turkish flag. The Greek alphabet appeared in place of Roman script. While there were two mosques on the island, there were many more churches, their steeples graced with the Greek Orthodox cross. Signs of Greece's economic meltdown the year before were everywhere—virtually every other store was shuttered or empty.

I asked around for a restaurant serving good local fare and ended up at Mummy's Cooking, a family-run tavern on a quiet street. Mummy, a stout, grandmotherly lady, showed me around the kitchen, opening the lids of various pots that contained vegetable stews, which in this Lenten season were more plentiful than usual. But I was starved for pork, my appetite piqued by the salamis and ham hocks hanging in the delis, filling the air with their sweet, smoky essence, and the abundant signs for pork souvlaki, pork gyros, and bacon sandwiches.

Mummy's son seated me and promptly brought a plate with a huge braised pork chop smothered in cheese, tomatoes, and onions. I asked him what the dish was called. "This is Mama's pork! No name for the dish!" he said, kissing the tips of his fingers and spreading them with a flourish. The rice-and-vermicelli pilaf and stuffed grape leaves that accompanied the pork reminded me of Turkey. And after lunch, as I walked around town, I saw all kinds of familiar treats. At a café, the little unfiltered cups of strong coffee were called Greek coffee. At confectionery shops, the powdered-sugar-dusted jellies were Greek delights. Spinach-stuffed phyllo triangles were not *borek* but spanakopita. At the bars, men guzzled shots of ouzo that smelled suspiciously like rakı. The Turkish candy *helva* was rechristened *haitoglou*. Meats roasted on vertical spits went by souvlaki and gyro rather than kebab. I also came across plenty of yogurt on menus, and after ordering it at one café, I devoured the enormous dessert glass of creamy dairy that arrived, topped with honey and whipped cream. The yogurt had been so good all along the Silk Road, in fact, that I had a hard time enjoying it elsewhere and especially in America, where exorbitant "Greek" yogurts began invading supermarkets.

Waiting for the ferry, I fell into conversation with a friendly Greek woman. Greeks and Turks, she told me, were essentially the same. She was certainly as friendly and hospitable as the Turks, insistently offering me an entire box of chocolate cookies she'd brought when she learned how far I was traveling. "When I went to Turkey," she told me, "it didn't feel like I was in a foreign country at all. Everything was so familiar."

"What about the religion?" I asked.

"Sure, that's what makes us different. But I don't understand. Why can't people of different religions live together?" she said. In the reverse of many stories I'd heard in Turkey, she told me that her grandfather had been born in Turkey but had been forced to move to Greece because he was Christian.

The ferry, an eight-story behemoth with restaurants, a casino, and private cabins, was fully packed with passengers trying to make it home for the holidays. It seemed to be particularly popular with Greek truckers, who brought their vehicles on board, and pet owners, who carried their dogs and cats in crates. I'd been lucky to get a cabin. I fell asleep easily, lulled by the gentle rocking of the ocean, but awoke past midnight as the waves grew rough. I walked around the ship, swaying to and fro like a drunkard, grasping the rails to steady my balance. The passengers and attendants were all still asleep in the common areas, as if a spell had been cast over the entire boat. I cursed my decision to take the ferry but returned to my cabin and eventually fell asleep, too.

The ferry docked near Athens just as dawn broke, casting a honey-orange hue over the industrial edge of the ancient city. With the morning to spare, I took the train into town and headed to the Acropolis. But it was closed that morning for Good Friday, and aimlessly wandering around, I stumbled into a huge market nearby. It was filled with shoppers, who made it plain that sheep were as important to Greeks on Easter as they were to Muslims on Eid. I was whacked in the face more than once by the limbs of a lamb carcass carried on the back of a barrel-chested shopper. Housewares stalls did a brisk business selling large rotisserie grills. The meat aside, the market featured beautiful olives that ranged from deep purple to pale green, along with generous hunks of cheese and jars of honey. After buying samples of each, I caught a taxi to the bus station, and not a moment too soon. The bus pulled out of the station just after I boarded, and as I sank into my seat I was hit with a brutal migraine. My reflexive skill of dozing off on uncomfortable modes of transit came to the rescue.

My migraine continued as I boarded my second overnight ferry, and I heard American voices all around me. I'd encountered few Americans along the Silk Road, but once I arrived in Greece, they were everywhere—foreign exchange students on spring break, families with whiny children, older couples on day jaunts from cruise ships. I overheard conversations about Bulgaria and McDonald's, pickpockets and California. Listening to Americans jabber around me, I felt a sudden pang of loneliness and alienation. But I didn't envy the backpackers, with their endless itineraries and complaints about the road, and I felt a certain smugness that my trip had a purpose theirs lacked. But, then again, did it? What exactly was I pursuing? Was I still trying to discover where noodles came from, or was I just asserting my independence? And how was I—were we—going to live after my journey was over?

I didn't have to ponder these existential questions for long. Once the boat docked in Puglia, the Americans hightailed it for the usual circuit of Rome, Florence, and Venice, and I had the heel of Italy's boot to myself.

SU BOREK (TURKISH LASAGNA)

Serves 6 to 9

FOR THE DOUGH:

4 cups all-purpose flour

1 teaspoon salt

4 extra-large eggs

12 sheets phyllo dough

FOR THE FILLING:

½ cup crumbled feta cheese

1 cup finely grated kaşar *(or substitute another mild white cheese such as mozzarella or provolone)*

1 egg

½ cup finely chopped parsley

8 tablespoons (1 stick) butter, melted

Make the dough: Combine the flour and salt, and using eggs, prepare the dough as for Chef Zhang's Hand-Rolled Noodles/Andrea's Pasta (p. 96). Divide the dough in half and, working on a large, floured surface, roll each half into a long rope. Divide each rope into 6 pieces. Roll each piece into a ball and flatten it into a disk with your hand. Sprinkle the work surface and the surface of the dough occasionally with a little flour to prevent sticking. Roll each disk into a circle slightly larger than a 9-inch pie pan to the thickness of 2 millimeters. Trim to the exact circumference of the pie pan. Do the same with the phyllo dough.

Make the filling: Mix together the feta cheese, *kaşar* (or other cheese), egg, and parsley.

Preheat the oven to 350 degrees Fahrenheit. Bring 2 quarts of water to boil in a large stockpot. When the water boils, place a sheet of dough into it. Boil for 1 to 2 minutes, remove the sheet, and plunge it into a large pot of cold water. Then drain the dough carefully in a colander, making sure not to tear it. Repeat until all the dough is boiled and drained.

Brush a little melted butter in the pie pan and layer 6 sheets of the phyllo dough into it, stopping every 2 or 3 layers to brush it with butter. Place a sheet of boiled dough over the phyllo and brush with a little butter; repeat with two more layers of boiled dough. Spread a third of the *borek* filling over the third layer of boiled dough. Repeat the layering sequence with the rest of the dough and filling. After the last sheets of boiled dough have been layered atop the last third of the filling, place 6 sheets of phyllo over the boiled dough, again brushing every 2 or 3 layers with butter. Brush the top layer with butter.

Bake for about 30 minutes, or until golden. Cool for 30 minutes and cut into 9 pieces, tic-tac-toe style (rather than wedges) to serve.

KARNIYARIK (SPLIT-BELLY EGGPLANT)

Serves 4

½ cup sunflower oil

4 long Japanese eggplants, stemmed and peeled in alternating stripes

1 medium onion, grated

½ pound ground beef (30 percent fat)

2 tablespoons tomato paste diluted in ½ cup cold water

2 tablespoons mild Turkish red pepper paste (available at Middle
     Eastern grocery stores)

½ cup chopped parsley

1 teaspoon ground paprika

½ teaspoon sugar

½ teaspoon salt

½ teaspoon freshly ground black pepper

4 cloves garlic, minced

4 slices tomato

2 small green bell peppers, halved and cored

1 tablespoon olive oil

¾ cup hot water

Preheat the oven to 350 degrees Fahrenheit.

Heat half the sunflower oil in a large frying pan on high heat for 2
minutes and add the eggplants. Allow them to cook, turning occasionally, for about 8 to 10 minutes, until the flesh is golden brown all
over. Remove from the heat, cool slightly, and make a lengthwise slit
in each eggplant, being careful not to cut all the way through and

stopping short of both ends. Place them in a single layer, slit side up, in a baking dish.

Clean the frying pan and add the rest of the sunflower oil. Place over medium-high heat, add the onions, and sauté for about 6 to 8 minutes, until the onions are golden. Add the ground beef and sauté for 10 minutes, then cover and cook over low heat for another 5 minutes. Add half the diluted tomato paste and half the Turkish red pepper paste. Then add the parsley, paprika, sugar, and half the salt and black pepper. Stir for 1 minute and remove the pan from the heat.

Stuff the eggplants with the meat mixture and sprinkle with garlic. Place a tomato slice and bell pepper half atop each eggplant. In a small bowl, whisk the rest of the tomato paste, the rest of the Turkish red pepper paste, the olive oil, the rest of the salt and black pepper, and the hot water. Pour into the baking dish.

Bake in the preheated oven for 15 to 20 minutes. Serve immediately.

ROSE BOREK (PHYLLO DOUGH STUFFED WITH LEEKS, CHEESE, AND HONEY)

Makes 8 boreks

½ cup thinly sliced leeks, white parts only, separated into rings

2 tablespoons sunflower or canola oil

6 ounces feta cheese, crumbled (or ricotta or cottage cheese)

1 egg

½ teaspoon salt, or less if the feta cheese is salty

8 sheets phyllo dough

1 egg white

2 tablespoons toasted sesame or nigella seeds

IF FRYING:
Sunflower or canola oil

IF BAKING:
1 egg yolk, beaten
4 tablespoons (½ stick) butter

½ cup honey

Place a small frying pan over medium heat, add the leeks and sun-flower or canola oil, and sauté for 8 to 10 minutes, until they are very tender. Remove from the heat and place in a medium bowl. Add the feta or other cheese, egg, and salt and mix well.

Place a sheet of phyllo dough on a flat, dry surface. Using about an eighth of the leek-feta filling, make a line of filling about ½ inch from the near edge of the phyllo dough. Wrap the dough around the fill-ing, rolling the stuffed phyllo into a long, skinny tube, dabbing a little egg white along the inside edge of the phyllo dough to make it seal. Starting from one end of the tube, roll it into a tight coil. Repeat the wrapping and rolling with the rest of the phyllo. Sprinkle with toasted sesame or nigella seeds.

If frying: Fill a deep frying pan, Dutch oven, or other wide, heavy pot with 1½ inches of sunflower or canola oil and place over high heat for 5 to 6 minutes. Add the pastries, fitting them in snugly but not allowing them to touch; fry them in batches if necessary. Fry for 3 to 4 minutes, until crisp and golden, then turn and fry for 3 to 4 minutes more. Remove from the heat and drain on paper towels.

If baking: Preheat the oven to 350 degrees Fahrenheit. Brush the tops of the pastries with beaten egg yolk and dot with butter. Bake for 18 to 20 minutes, until golden.

Serve immediately, with honey.

KADINBUDU KOFTE (LADY'S THIGH KOFTE)

Serves 4

½ cup short-grain rice
2 tablespoons sunflower oil
1 medium onion, minced
1 pound ground beef, 30 percent fat
3 eggs
½ teaspoon salt
½ teaspoon freshly ground black pepper
¼ cup minced parsley
2 tablespoons minced fresh mint
½ cup flour
Vegetable oil, for frying

Bring a quart of water to boil in a medium pot. Add the rice and cook for 8 to 10 minutes, until al dente. Remove the pot from the heat and drain the rice. Place the rice in a large bowl.

Place the sunflower oil in a large frying pan over high heat and add the onions. Sauté for 4 to 5 minutes, until browned. Add half the beef and sauté for 4 to 5 minutes, breaking the beef into bits with a spatula, until it is fully cooked. Remove from the heat and add to the rice. Add to the meat-rice mixture the uncooked beef and 1 egg, along with the salt, black pepper, parsley, and mint. Knead with your hands (as for dough) for 2 to 3 minutes.

In a medium bowl, beat 2 of the remaining eggs. Place the flour in another bowl.

Place a large frying pan over high heat and add vegetable oil to a depth of 1 inch. Heat for 6 to 8 minutes, or until a grain of rice added to the pan sizzles immediately.

While the oil is heating, shape the rice and beef mixture into palm-sized oval patties. One at a time, dip the patties into the beaten eggs, then dredge them in the flour. Fry the patties in batches, being careful not to crowd the pan, for 4 to 5 minutes on each side, until they are crisp and brown on the outside. Drain on paper towels and serve immediately.

DOLMA (STUFFED GRAPE LEAVES)

Makes 12 to 15 dolmas

1 cup short-grain rice

½ cup olive oil

2 medium onions

2 tablespoons black currants or raisins

2 tablespoons pine nuts

3 to 4 scallions, white parts only, chopped

1 tablespoon minced fresh parsley

1 tablespoon minced fresh dill

1 teaspoon ground cinnamon

1 teaspoon ground cloves

1 teaspoon ground allspice

1 tablespoon tomato paste

½ teaspoon salt

½ teaspoon freshly ground black pepper

½ teaspoon sugar

12 to 15 young grape leaves, fresh or bottled (or substitute fresh
    cabbage or Swiss chard leaves)

1 to 2 lemons, thinly sliced

Place the rice and olive oil in a large frying pan and sauté over medium heat for 3 to 4 minutes. Mince half of 1 onion and add it to the pan; sauté 3 to 4 minutes longer, until the onions are soft. Add the currants or raisins, pine nuts, scallions, parsley, and dill and cook for 3 to 4 minutes longer. Add the cinnamon, cloves, and allspice and stir for another minute or two, then add the tomato paste; if the mixture seems dry, add a couple of tablespoons water. Add the salt, black pepper, and sugar, stir for another minute or two, and remove from the heat. (The rice should still be fairly hard.)

Blanch the grape leaves for 2 to 3 minutes in a pot of boiling water. (If using prepared grape leaves, skip this step.) Remove from heat and drain well.

Working with one leaf at a time, place a heaping spoonful of filling near one end of the leaf, fold the sides over the filling, and roll into a log-shaped parcel, so that the filling is enclosed on all sides. Repeat with each leaf.

Thickly slice the remaining 1½ onions and place a layer of the slices in a large stockpot. Add a layer of dolmas and top with a layer of sliced lemons. Continue to layer the onions, dolmas, and lemons until all the dolmas have been placed in the pot. Cover the dolmas with a heavy heatproof dish that fits inside the stockpot. Add water to cover the dolmas, then cover the pot. Bring to a boil and cook over medium heat until all of the water has been absorbed and the filling is tender. Remove from heat and let cool. Dolmas are usually served chilled and can be made a day or two ahead.

MANTI (TURKISH DUMPLINGS)

Serves 4 to 6

FOR THE DOUGH:

4 cups all-purpose flour

2 cups water

FOR THE FILLING:

1 pound ground lamb or beef

½ cup minced onions

1 teaspoon salt

1 teaspoon freshly ground black pepper

FOR THE SAUCE:

1 cup yogurt

3 to 4 cloves garlic, minced

1 tablespoon minced fresh mint

1 teaspoon ground dried chilies

FOR COOKING THE DUMPLINGS:

1 bunch scallions, white parts only, thinly sliced into rings

8 tablespoons (1 stick) butter

¼ teaspoon salt

1 tablespoon paprika

¼ cup chopped walnuts

Make the dough: Using the flour and water, follow the instructions for kneading and rolling out the dough in Chef Zhang's Hand-Rolled Noodles/Andrea's Pasta (p. 96).

Make the filling: In a medium bowl, mix together the ground lamb or beef with the onions, salt, and black pepper.

Make the sauce: Mix together the yogurt, garlic, mint, and ground chili; store in the refrigerator until serving time.

Unroll each portion of dough in one long sheet and cut it into 1-inch squares. Place a dot of filling in the center of the wrapper. Bring the opposite corners of the square together and seal the edges, forming a triangle. Bring the opposite edges of the triangle together and pinch them together to form a circle. Repeat with the rest of the dumplings.

Cook the dumplings: Bring 2 quarts of water to boil in a large stockpot. Add half the scallion rings. Boil the dumplings in batches, about a quarter at a time, for 4 to 5 minutes. Drain and repeat until all the *manti* are cooked.

While the *manti* are boiling, melt half the butter in a large frying pan, and add half the salt, half the paprika and half the walnuts. Add half the dumplings, toss, and divide among several pasta bowls. Repeat with the rest of the dumplings.

Serve immediately, garnishing each plate with some of the remaining scallions and the yogurt sauce.

italy

12.

had no idea eating could be so exhausting.

I was no stranger to big meals, thanks to the hospitality I'd experienced along the Silk Road. But Italy managed to outdo them all.

I'd arrived in Puglia, the heel of Italy's boot, known for its ancient connections to Greece and its ear-shaped *cavatelli* and orecchiette, which intrigued me for their similarity to Chef Zhang's noodles. My guide was Daniela, an energetic woman in her mid-twenties who sported a short, angular bob and a leather jacket. I'd been lucky to find her. Because of the south's dismal economy, many people had gone north for jobs, leaving few English speakers behind. But Daniela, a graduate student in foreign literature, had returned home the year before to finish her thesis. I'd found her through a network of distant colleagues and friends, and she'd graciously invited me to dine and cook with her friends and family for the week.

Just a few hours after my ferry docked in Bari, I drove to the nearby town of Monopoli and sat down to Saturday lunch with Daniela, her fiancé, Sandro (whom she'd known since childhood), and Sandro's family. Daniela's future mother-in-law, Maria Antoinette (I wondered if she was as fierce as her name suggested), whipped up a typical family lunch as her adult children, all of whom lived at home, looked on. The meal began with *burrata*, a heavenly improvement on fresh mozzarella—its center filled with gooey, rich ricotta—and *pizza ai carciofi*. The pizza was unlike others I'd had: Maria Antoinette baked sautéed artichokes, prosciutto, and pecorino and mozzarella cheese in between two layers of crust. The crust was flaky, feathery, and fragrant with white wine. (Wine was a cooking ingredient I hadn't seen since China.) Those ear-shaped *cavatelli* followed, tossed with a quick sauce of cherry tomatoes, garlic, clams, mussels, and *quanto basta*—a lot of—olive oil. Raw fennel bulbs and carrots cleansed our palates before dessert, a lamb-shaped cake filled with marzipan.

As soon as lunch was over, Daniela and I set off for dinner, a few blocks away at her grandmother's home. When we arrived at Nonna's, she'd just finished pulsing a batch of pasta dough through a food processor. She kneaded the pasta on a *madia*, a large wooden tray, before shaping it into *cavatelli*. The method was strikingly similar to how cat's ear noodles were made in China: she pressed pieces of dough the size of pencil erasers with her thumbs to stretch them quickly into tight curls. But her preferred shape was orecchiette, which took a little more craft. She pressed slightly larger bits of dough between a butter knife and the *madia*, carving them into looser curls, like thin pats of butter. She turned them inside out, and stretched them over her thumb to create an indentation. She let the orecchiette dry for a couple of hours to retain their shape, then boiled them quickly. She tossed them into a heavenly sauté of anchovies, onions, toasted bread crumbs, and turnip tops with a nice bitter bite, like broccoli rabe. Each rounded piece of pasta was the perfect vehicle for the heavenly sauce. Just as with the pasta I'd had at lunch, this dish, called *orecchiette con le cime di rapa*, was a revelation: pasta and sauce were not separate entities but a whole, fused together in a pan with a splash of the pasta water.

To accompany the pasta, Nonna baked potato focaccia and fried a dozen artichokes in a batter of eggs, freshly grated Parmigiano-Reggiano, and white wine. She rolled up thin slices of veal, secured them with toothpicks, and braised them in tomato sauce. Nonna's *zucchini alla poverella*, despite the name, was anything but poor: she fried thin slices of sun-dried zucchini before drizzling them with garlic, red wine vinegar, and mint. After we'd devoured everything, out of the oven came *pizza di ricotta* (I learned that pizza meant any pie-like dish, savory or sweet). At first I resisted the dessert, so full was I from the day's culinary abundance. But then my dining companions urged me on and I succumbed to the seductions of ricotta, lemon, cinnamon, and shaved chocolate.

The next day, Easter Sunday, Charlotte and Mayling, two old American friends who happened to be traveling through Italy, joined me on my food fest. Thoughtful Mayling presented me with an ample supply of lactose pills to help me digest Italy's dairy-laden meals. The gift arrived not a moment too soon, just as cappuccinos were placed before us at the breakfast table of our guesthouse, along with the limp Italian croissants known as *cornetti*. What Italians ate in the morning lent fresh support for my theory about how the world's best cuisines neglected breakfast, Turkey notwithstanding. And later in the day, I'd come to regret the morning's wasted calories.

For lunch, we joined Daniela and her family at a cozy trattoria called San Domenico next to the town's main square. I'd envisioned a home-cooked meal on Easter, but most Italians went out for the big holidays, including Christmas, to give the home cook—usually the matron—a break. The town buzzed with activity before lunch, but as soon as one o'clock rolled around, the main square completely emptied out as everyone headed inside to eat. Daniela's relatives were dressed in clothes fit for church, though they hadn't gone to services that morning; they preferred to commemorate Easter by eating rather than praying.

In a space just large enough for four extended families, we sat down for a marathon meal. Everyone filled their glasses with Chardonnay or a local red wine called Negroamaro, and we toasted the occasion. The waiters brought a procession of antipasti: shrimp tossed with raw grated artichoke and shaved Parmigiano-Reggiano; pan-seared cod with tomato-and-parsley salsa; fried octopus with yellow pepper puree; raw salmon, called *crudo*, finely minced and seasoned with extra-virgin olive oil and a squeeze of lemon; baked mussels stuffed with bread crumbs; and—a dish that spoke of rustic origins—sheep's head stewed in a clay pot called a *pignatta*.

When the plates were cleared, Daniela's brother, a dark-haired, well-groomed young man named Francesco, announced, "Now lunch will begin." A trio of pasta courses arrived, each better than the next: orecchiette with salted pork and tomatoes; a light asparagus risotto; and last, my favorite—long strips of pasta dressed with thick tomato sauce and tossed with fresh seafood. The dish was called *maltagliata alla pescatore*—"the fisherman's badly cut pasta"—like "zucchini for the poor," a humble name for a sublime dish. I wiped the last smudges of sauce from my plate with bread, called *scarpetta* or "little shoes," when used for this purpose. Bread, I was discovering, was as important to the Italians as it was to everyone else on the Silk Road.

The waiters brought more: *secondi* of giant prawns, grilled and seasoned simply with coarse salt, lemon, and parsley. As at Maria Antoinette's table the day before, sharp anise-flavored fennel bulbs cleansed our palates, after which the waiters returned with dessert glasses of lemon gelato. Each sweet-and-sour bite danced lightly on my tongue. I figured we were done when shots of espresso arrived. But then the waiters poured a round of the lemon liqueur called *limoncello*, which aided our digestion and allowed us to linger further. The waiters returned a final time, bringing the check, which came to a mere thirty euros (less than forty dollars) per person.

"Is that too expensive?" Daniela asked, noticing the look of shock on my friends' faces, and mine.

My girlfriends and I thanked Daniela and her family and left to attend yet another meal: a friend of a friend had invited us to dinner. But that evening, my taste receptors were overwhelmed, and my head was spinning from the wine. I had no more than a few bites and hardly remembered the meal. This must be why no outsider had written good literature about Italy, I thought: they were so intoxicated by the food and wine that they went to bed each night in a haze of pleasure. The only dish I recalled faintly was something with horsemeat—was it shaped into meatballs or patties? Was it flavored with Parmigiano-Reggiano or pecorino? And had I eaten that meat way back in Kyrgyzstan? But that evening, my travels on the Silk Road seemed a distant memory, washed away by the antipasti, the pastas and the novel pizzas I'd ingested in the last thirty-six hours.

. . .

I'd finally made it to Italy, but I still had plenty to explore. After Puglia, I would go on to Naples and Emilia-Romagna, gastronomic centers of Italy's south and north, respectively. In Naples, I would learn the simple truth behind delicious southern Italian food; in Emilia-Romagna, I'd make pasta with *sfogline*, female chefs devoted to a slowly fading craft. Only after these pilgrimages would I end in Rome, where the idea for the trip had first struck me.

Except for China, Italy was ostensibly more familiar than any other place I'd traveled. But on earlier trips there, I'd learned that having frequented Olive Garden in my childhood and waitressed at a "Sicilian" restaurant in college did little to prepare me for real Italian food. Italians didn't eat shrimp scampi or fettuccine alfredo, nor did the dish called spaghetti Bolognese exist across the Atlantic. Most Italian chefs used garlic sparingly, onions and shallots generously. Parsley was sprinkled atop pastas as often as basil, and the latter was never, never cooked. Many pasta sauces didn't bubble on stoves for hours on end, but were cooked as quickly as the pasta itself. Italians used balsamic vinegar rarely, reserving the expensive flavoring for special occasions; the kind that appeared in supermarkets and restaurants outside of Italy was a cheap bastardization no Italian would deign to touch.

And even though I had some knowledge of Italy and its cuisine, Puglia was a whole new territory. It wasn't high on most tourists' itineraries, lacking the glorified history and culture associated with Tuscany, Venice, or Rome—but that was precisely why I'd chosen it. Having already hit the usual places, I wanted something more authentic. In Puglia, orchards of gnarled olive trees thrived under a bright, harsh sun, very different from the warm glow of Tuscany. I woke to azure skies and looked out at an equally blue and tranquil sea. And I'd heard about the region's delicious cuisine, which was Mediterranean but carried hints of the East. Fresh pastas resembled Chinese ones, a popular cheese called *caciocavallo* reminded me of Turkish *kaşar*, and Apulians, like most Italians and cultures to the east, had an obsession with bread.

At meals, Italians required some form of bread (even more than pasta), and Apulians had a strong affection for dried bread that reminded me of the East. They ate little packets of dry toast for breakfast and bags of crostini lined supermarket aisles. In Puglia, dried rolls called *friselle* were dunked in water and sprinkled with olive oil, tomatoes, and oregano; sweet biscotti were served with espresso. Some version of this tradition extended all the way back to the western border of China. Had nomadic tendencies run from China all the way to the Mediterranean? Dry bread was the perfect food for travel—light, portable, and unlikely to spoil. Christopher Columbus had allegedly taken a version of biscotti when he sailed to the West in search of the Far East and instead discovered America.

As much as there were culinary linkages, each region of Italy also retained its specialties. In Puglia, I was struck anew by distinct traditions. I tasted dishes there that I'd rarely encountered in my travels farther north in Italy, much less overseas: pureed fava beans served with wild chicory and toasted bread; fresh sea urchins, split open and served like sashimi, or tossed in a pan with olive oil, garlic, and pasta; eggplants mashed with mint and pecorino cheese and fried into light, savory balls.

Puglia had been settled by the Greeks as early as the eighth century BC and retained its own identity, a reminder that before Italy was unified in the mid-nineteenth century, the peninsula had consisted of feuding city-states. The Apulians identified more with the Greeks—whom they called their "brothers"—than with their fellow Italians. Some villagers still spoke a dialect of Greek called Griko. Daniela's town was called Monopoli, which means "only city" in Greek. The Apulians' rugged, independent spirit set them apart from their more refined, effete countrymen to the north.

So little did Apulians identify with other Italians that they displayed little pride in or knowledge about some of Italy's best-known heroes, including Marco Polo. At a dinner party one evening, a friend of Daniela's named Giuseppe told me that most Apulians only vaguely knew of the explorer.

"Really?" I asked skeptically.

To make his point, Giuseppe gathered his friends. What, he asked, was Marco Polo famous for? A lot of head scratching ensued. "Did he invent the telescope?" "Did he discover America?" No one associated Marco Polo with his travels to the East, much less with pasta. One guest shrugged. "We have too many explorers to remember them all. Plus, he's a Venetian. We don't know anything about Venetians."

But Apulians, like other Italians, did display the same stereotypical machismo. Upon meeting my two American girlfriends, Giuseppe swaggered and flirted aggressively, as if upholding a sworn duty of Italian men. "I would really like to continue our conversation after dinner," he said suggestively, to both. "Perhaps we can go for a walk on the beach?"

Giuseppe, though, knew not to start with me, as he was aware that I was married. But he did question me about my husband. Where was he? Why wasn't he traveling with me? Where did we consider home? All good questions.

In our comfortable platonic rapport, Giuseppe explained the psyche of the Italian male. "We are all mama's boys. Everything is related to our relationship with our mothers. . . . We're macho and sensitive." He was a lawyer who'd worked in Milan until recently, when he'd decided to open his own firm in his hometown. Milan was a rat race, he said. "It's like America. Everything is all about work, work, work." In Puglia, he could take long lunches and have a life.

In southern Italy, a leisurely lunch was practically a mandate. One afternoon Daniela and I rushed to make a lunch reservation. When we pulled up at the restaurant, my guide looked at her watch and hesitated. "Maybe we should go somewhere else," she said. We had an appointment at a winery afterward.

"But why?" I asked, pointing out that we had an hour and a half.

"Well, I've . . . I've never eaten lunch in less than two hours. At home, yes, but not at a restaurant!" she said.

"Let's try," I said.

After we ordered, an embarrassed Daniela asked the waiter to speed up the meal. He grimaced, as if our request was a huge imposition, and disappeared into the kitchen. We finished the meal in just over an hour, skipping the usual espresso and *digestivo*. But the experience taught me the importance of the two-hour lunch. I belched my way through the winery and felt bloated from inhaling my pasta. Deprived of my shot of caffeine, I also had difficulty concentrating.

It was easy to get the impression that Italian eating was an all-out glutton fest. But glancing up from my second gelato while sitting in a busy town square one day, I noticed that few Italians were overweight. (The one exception in view was a stereotypically stout *nonna*, but grandmothers could get away with anything, including probably murder, in Italy.) Younger women were particularly svelte and fashionable. I wondered how they could pull it off, given how much food there was, everywhere I went.

It was very simple, my new Italian friends told me. There were rules to eating. It started with breakfast, which was no more than a stale *cornetto* or packet of dried toast. That was washed down with an espresso or a cappuccino. A cappuccino was heavy enough that many Italians considered it a meal in itself. Committing the atrocity of ordering one after lunch brought a look of flushed what-will-the-waiter-think-of-us embarrassment to my companions' faces and an admonishment: "We don't drink cappuccinos after eleven o'clock in the morning!"

Italians didn't snack. To my alarmed surprise, even big urban centers like Rome were devoid of streetside food vendors. "If we need a snack, we have a cigarette," a Roman friend told me later. Eating was done strictly at the table, at set mealtimes. Not only was it a faux pas to eat while standing or walking, it was disgraceful to eat while in transit. In contrast to the incessant snacking on Chinese trains, Italian passengers refrained from eating on board, even around the lunch and dinner hours. The same rules applied to cars: one afternoon, rushing to make a meeting, I searched in vain for a drive-through restaurant, then parked illegally in front of a pizzeria. As I pulled away with a slice of pie in my lap, I felt like I'd committed more than one traffic violation.

I also wondered how most Italians could stomach three courses—menus were divided into antipasti, *primi* (the pasta or risotto course), and *secondi*—until I realized that only outsiders like me felt pressured to consume all three. Most Italians ate an antipasto and either a *primo* or a *secondo*, only ordering three courses on special occasions. Whether at home or in restaurants, pasta was generally served in set portions of one hundred grams. Plated, a pasta dish took up no more space than a compact disk. Many women ate pasta only once a day. Italians drank water, wine, or espresso, rather than calorie-laden soda, juice, or beer. Dessert usually consisted of no more than a kiddie-sized scoop of gelato or a fruit salad, enlivened with a dash of sugar and lemon.

Most important, I learned in Puglia that cooking was an act of love, bestowed on those closest to you. That was what made it healthful and nourishing.

Dinners with Daniela and her friends and family started around nine o'clock. I remembered the late meals from the last time I'd visited Italy with Craig—sometimes we'd walked into empty restaurants around seven-thirty and practically begged the staff to serve us. And here in Puglia, ten o'clock on a weekday was not too late for Daniela to assemble a dozen friends and family for a casual meal of *panzerotti*, fried pockets of soft dough stuffed with mozzarella and tomato sauce. No one stood on ceremony. Instead of awkwardly waiting for others to take the first bite, everyone simply filled their cups with wine and dug in. In addition to the *panzerotti*, Daniela served chunks of fresh mozzarella and grilled eggplant slices drizzled with olive oil. For dessert, we nibbled on fruit, chocolate, and *zeppole*, Sicilian cream puffs. When one guest fell over in his chair, everyone clapped and laughed.

This was the night Giuseppe quizzed his friends about Marco Polo. After they drew a blank, I asked everyone what their favorite dish was. They objected at first, one saying, "That's like making us choose our favorite family member!" But then the names of now-familiar dishes—including that delectable orecchiette with turnip tops and the pasta with sea urchins—came tumbling out of their mouths.

"What is *your* favorite food?" someone asked me.

"No, no, we want to know, what is your favorite *American* food?" another insisted.

I thought for a moment. What counted as American food, after all? Pizza or lasagna? Those, they would argue, were Italian. I tried to think of something unique to Southern California, but all that came to mind was Mexican food. "Guacamole," I blurted out.

That resonated. "I've always seen guacamole in the movies but I've never eaten it!" Daniela exclaimed. She was so intrigued that I promised to make it for her the next day.

Avocados, a fruit from the Americas, had only recently arrived in Italy. In Beijing, markets aimed at foreigners occasionally carried them, and in Istanbul they'd appeared as part of a novel *meze*, but mostly they'd been absent along the Silk Road. Daniela and I arrived at Nonna's the next day with a bagful from the supermarket, along with tortilla chips. Nonna greeted us with several kisses on either cheek. "Did you eat well today?" she asked Daniela, and, reminding me of how Chinese greeted loved ones, she added, "What did you eat? You are too skinny!" She peered into our bag for a look at the mysterious fruits. Because her granddaughter had described them as "mushy," she'd expected something banana-like, she told us.

We settled into Nonna's kitchen. It was a room that was lived in, like so many others I'd seen across the Silk Road. The usual amenities aside, it was furnished with a sofa, a flat-screen television, and a large dining table. The formal dining room down the hall went unused. Outside on a balcony was a second oven and a stove, for baking during the hotter months and deep-frying year-round.

At the dining table, I mashed the avocados in a bowl with onions, parsley (the stand-in for cilantro), lime, tomatoes, ground chili peppers, salt, and black pepper. After tasting it, Nonna decided it would make a decent antipasto. Daniela practically did a little dance as she dipped chip after chip into the spicy green puree, my favorite comfort food. I'd unknowingly picked a dish that she thought was as American as apple pie. "You know, in Italy, at least here in the south, we still believe in the American Dream. We think everything is so great in your country, we have that idea in our heads," she said. I told her the feelings were mutual, that we romanticized Italy just as much.

And then Nonna began making another epic meal, the centerpiece of which was mussels and rice, that other Silk Road staple, which even had a hold on Italy. She flattened several garlic cloves with the side of a knife and removed the green shoots from the center of each, gritting her teeth. "We're taking out the soul of the devil," she said. In a baking dish, she layered potato slices, shelled mussels, and short-grain arborio rice, and liberally sprinkled the garlic, along with parsley, Parmigiano-Reggiano, and pecorino over the dish. She poured in some chicken broth and placed the dish in the oven.

I thought about the care Nonna put into her dishes. She was a repository of recipes she'd never written down. Cooking was her solace—she didn't get out much these days, but she could still socialize by cooking for loved ones. Barely five feet tall, she prepped at her dining table, and worked with careful precision, her curly golden hair arranged neatly so as not to obstruct her vision. Whatever the task at hand—whether it was slicing strawberries thinly to lay them on a cake or shaping little ears of pasta—she put all of her attention into it, as if it was the only thing that mattered. Her style of cooking was a dying art—in Italy and elsewhere.

Nonna's upbringing resembled those of women in the East. She'd been born in the 1930s, during the Mussolini era, and she hadn't gotten beyond fifth grade. She told me that when she was young, she'd lived in a society similar to the one I'd seen in Iran: single men and women weren't permitted on the streets together; she'd never worked outside the home but considered herself freer than many of her peers. "Some of my girlfriends weren't allowed to go out without their husbands," she said. Even today, religion was the center of her life. She still prayed every day, and, until recently, attended mass weekly. Indeed, one still encountered the occasional woman draped in swaths of black cloth in southern Italy, Catholics as rigidly devout as strict Muslims.

Tradition: that was what had preserved Nonna's dishes, but it had also limited her options. I was beginning to realize that "traditional" was a word I liked when it applied to food but not so much when it was associated with women. And could you have one without the other? Daniela, with her professional aspirations, wasn't interested in cooking. Like many other young women I'd met on my journey, including Nur's sister and Yasmin in Iran, Daniela associated cooking, pasta-making, and baking with being held back, being rooted in old ways.

I couldn't blame them for not wanting to cook. Growing up, I hadn't been interested in it either. My parents had never expected me to learn the skill, seeing it as irrelevant to my future. And for that, I was grateful. I'd come to cooking freely, as a woman in my twenties, and while I'd started to resent the task after marriage, it had been more or less optional. I wouldn't have traded my position for Nonna's. But still, there was something to bemoan if Nonna's way of cooking was lost. I couldn't help wondering, who would know how to make her *orecchiette con cima di rapa* or her rice and mussels after she was gone?

13.

After a week of *la dolce vita* in Puglia, I reluctantly packed my bags. I was hesitant about my next destination, Naples, but my Apulian friends convinced me that I had to go. Naples was home to many of Italy's eating traditions, from pizza to *ragù* to a delicious rum-soaked cake called *babà*. As one of the biggest ports in Italy, it had enjoyed continuous links to the East and a storied past. And—as one friend had gushed—it was beautiful.

Beautiful? That was a word I'd never associated with Naples. Craig and I had planned to visit on our previous Italian vacation. On our drive from Pompeii to the Amalfi coast, we figured we'd spend the night, soak up the atmosphere, and enjoy a slice of its world-famous pizza. But as we got closer, the rows of public housing, the smokestacks, and the decrepit factories seemed too ominous. Rather than turning off the *autostrada*, we pushed on to Amalfi.

My Apulian friends understood. "It's kind of like going to India," Giuseppe joked. "You have to be prepared." The Camorra, a Mafia-like criminal network of powerful family clans, unofficially ruled the city. Aside from controlling the lucrative port, they dictated how many things ran in the city, from essential services like trash collection to daily businesses like bakeries. They settled disputes outside of the law, and Camorra-sponsored gang warfare broke out unpredictably. Robbery and other petty crime—some related to the Camorra, some not—was also common. The stories gave me pause. But after traveling thousands of miles through Central Asia and Iran, I decided I was not going to let a little gang warfare get in the way of eating the world's best pizza.

I deliberated over how I'd get to Naples. In contrast to other countries along the Silk Road, renting a car was easy. Driving it was another story. To begin with, I disliked driving; I'd never owned a car, having spent my adult life in cities with decent public transportation. When Craig and I rented a car, he usually got behind the wheel. It wasn't that he liked driving more; in this case, I didn't mind giving in to the societal convention. Plus, I truly did have a tendency to "misjudge distances" (as he kindly put it)—not just between cities but between the car and other objects on the road. Driving in Italy came with extra challenges—break-ins and carjackings were common, particularly in the south, I was told. I'd also have to reckon with crazy Italian drivers who treated pedestrians as nuisances and took the narrowness of sixteenth-century alleys as an invitation to speed down them faster.

But then I thought about showing up in Naples with only my bags and decided that the risks were probably worth it.

I was still in doubt the morning I left. The weather conspired against me—as I drove through the Campanian countryside, sheets of rain swept my windshield, the wipers swinging frantically back and forth to no avail. I had a headache from the measly amount of wine I'd drunk the night before, and it didn't help that I was sleep-deprived from my intense schedule of eating and cooking. My friends' last piece of advice echoed in my head: "Just don't go anywhere by yourself and you should be fine," they said, forgetting that I was, in fact, traveling alone.

That was the funny thing—everyone seemed to be surprised that I was traveling alone, especially because I was married. Where was my husband? Why wasn't he with me? He was okay with my traversing a good part of the planet by myself? To the Italians and the others before them on my travels, that seemed to suggest that something was off.

And at that moment, I wondered if they were right. What *was* I doing alone on an autostrada in the driving rain? In Puglia, I'd felt more distant from Craig than I had during the rest of the trip. I'd been so busy cooking with Nonna or eating long meals that when he'd called we couldn't talk for long. (Italians frowned at stepping away from the table to speak on the phone—it was a violation of their eating rules.) Late in the evenings when I called him back, I could manage no more than a few sentences before doing a face plant into my pillow. I wasn't even sure where he was at the moment—somewhere on the West Coast of the United States, I thought.

As the rain continued to blanket my windshield, my loneliness turned to anxiety: my heart quickened, and I felt a panic attack coming on. Of all the things I'd done on the trip—which included visiting unstable western China, revolutionary Kyrgyzstan, totalitarian Turkmenistan, and the Islamic Republic of Iran—it was highway driving that gave me the greatest anxiety. Taking a deep breath, I moved to the right lane and slowed to the speed of a senior citizen in Florida. The Italian drivers who whizzed past me must have cackled with laughter. I thought about pulling over and calling Craig, but wherever he was, it would be early in the morning, and the roaming charges would be exorbitant. Better to wait to Skype later.

By early afternoon, I managed to make it to the boutique hotel I'd sprung for, in a neighborhood I'd heard was safe. I collapsed in bed and awoke to my guide, Marina, knocking on my door.

"You drove here by yourself?" Marina said, surprised. "I couldn't do it. I get anxious when I drive on the autostrada."

"It wasn't so bad," I said, shrugging off my earlier anxieties. I didn't mention them to my husband either when we later spoke.

Marina was a pretty woman in her fifties with light brown hair that fell to her shoulders. She'd dressed formally for our meeting, in a blue blazer and slacks. She spoke in lofty sentences peppered with words that sounded as if she'd looked them up in an Italian-English dictionary. ("Naples is a city of integration. We *amalgamate* different cultures.") She was born and raised in Naples, and had only spent a few years away when she was in college. "I'm Neapolitan DOC," she said proudly, referring to a certification standard for fine Italian wine and food products.

Marina called her private tours "No-Stress Itineraries." She wanted tourists to know that Naples could be fun if you ignored the media. Most tourists did exactly what I'd done the year before—bypassed the city on their way to places like Capri and the Amalfi coast. The few who came were often in search of their roots. It was a shame, because tourists missed out by skipping Naples, Marina said. For starters, they missed the Neapolitans themselves, who were loud and boisterous and more "Italian" than other Italians.

"We talk more with our hands," she said. She curled her fingers so they resembled bristles on a broom and flicked them. "That means *go away.*" She tapped her mid-section. "*I'm hungry.*" She put a palm up in the air and bobbed it up and down as if she were weighing a heavy rock. "*What are you doing?*"

As we hopped on a bus that took us to the historic district, Marina gave me a brief introduction to Naples. Greeks had ruled the area, and much of southern Italy, early on. The Romans then took over, making the nearby countryside a cavorting ground for their emperors. Naples enjoyed a period of independence after Rome fell, but starting in the twelfth century, a string of small European monarchies colonized the area: first the Normans ruled, followed by the German Swabians, the French Anjous, the Spanish Aragons, and finally the Spanish Bourbons.

"As a result of all the conquering, we are very tolerant," Marina said. In contrast to Puglia, I noticed more ethnic diversity in Naples—Africans, Chinese, and Orthodox Jews walked the streets. On the bus, Marina pointed out a few Sri Lankans, immigrants who'd begun arriving two generations before.

But with the mixing came tension. When a group of Neapolitan teenagers quietly harassed an elderly woman at the back of the bus, she shouted, "You boys are worse than the black people!"—a reference to the Sri Lankans. Marina mentioned that the recent revolution in Libya had brought an unwelcome wave of Arab immigrants. "They come here and take advantage of the system," she said. "Italy has always been a paradise for them." Though many likened Italy's shape to a boot, Marina described it as a plank—an easy entryway to Europe.

Just as my Apulian friend had said, Naples *was* beautiful. Sure, the outskirts were dilapidated. Graffiti covered many buildings and the bases of statues. And yes, enormous piles of rubbish overflowed onto downtown sidewalks, a sign of an ongoing dispute between officials and the Camorra that had ground trash collection to a halt. But if anything, the grit heightened the beauty that managed to persist around it. Naples was full of striking modern towers and ornate historic buildings, legacies of its French and Spanish past. The city sat along dramatic cliffsides and atop steep hills. All afternoon, the rain poured, casting a Gotham-like darkness across the city's narrow gridded streets: if there were ever a city made for Batman, Naples would be it. I instantly liked the place more than Venice or Florence, which had felt to me like giant museums clogged with tourists. Naples by contrast was full of ordinary people going about their usual business.

Marina guided me through the city's thirteenth-century Duomo and the baroque Chapel of the Treasure of San Gennaro, the city's patron saint whose name graces Italian-American festivals. In between, we stopped at a *limoncello* factory, where I learned that the best lemons came from the nearby Amalfi coast and that the secret to the digestive was to use just the very yellow part of the zest, which soaked for ten days in pure liquor made from sugarcane. At one of the best bakeries, I sampled the famous *babà* cake infused with rum-flavored syrup, as intensely sweet as the desserts I'd tasted farther east. The numerous butchers reflected a cuisine that had grown more meat-heavy since Puglia, though the two places were less than two hundred miles apart. Pork was popular and veal even more so, for its tenderness and because it was considered safer than beef—diseases like mad cow usually developed in older livestock.

Like many Italians, Marina only bought meat raised in Italy. "We respect the rules in raising animals. It's not like other parts of Europe," she said disdainfully. "That's why the cow went mad."

Our last stop was a pizzeria called Sorbillo, where we were invited into the kitchen. The owner's son, Gino, gamely fielded my questions while making pizzas for the dinner rush. He didn't spin the dough as I'd imagined, but stretched, slapped, and banged it against the counter in a rhythmic fashion before he sprinkled it with olive oil, buffalo mozzarella, fresh basil, and a light sauce made of San Marzano tomatoes—the classic Margherita. He graced other pies with various toppings: sun-dried tomatoes, black olives, and prosciutto, either the cooked variety called *cotto* or the cured version, *crudo*. Another chef, using a long wooden spatula, pushed the pizzas into a deep wood-fired oven, similar to the ones for *lagmacun* in Turkey. The pies baked for no more than a few minutes, just long enough for the crust to crisp but for the pizza's center to remain chewy. As with the hand-pulled noodles in China and the bagel-like buns of Kashgar, the pizza's secret ingredient was the local water, Marina told me.

I was practically drooling, but Marina said our time was up; her husband was waiting for her to make dinner. I tried to insist that I could stay for the pizza and return to the guesthouse alone, but there was no way Marina was going to leave me unaccompanied, especially at night. (Naples, she admitted, did have its dangers.) Her husband, Maurizio, a gruff man with limited English, awaited us in his hatchback, and just in time, as the relentless rain was turning the gutters into fast-moving rivers.

Marina and her husband dropped me off at a pizzeria near my hotel—"This place is pretty good," she said—and then sped off. I sat down at a table, bemoaning my missed opportunity. I suspiciously examined the pizza that appeared before me. It was oblong like a tongue, rather than round, and only a sprinkling of tomatoes and mozzarella graced the crust. It hadn't been cut or even thoroughly baked—the dough in the center still seemed raw.

But to my amazement, it turned out to be the most delicious pizza I'd ever tasted. Just like the best pastas, the best pizzas were made quickly, with the least adornment, I learned. The crust melted in my mouth, and the plum tomatoes were so fresh and sweet that they sent pleasure signals to my brain, amplified by the gooeyness of the fresh cheese. No pizza I tasted after that, anywhere else, came close.

Before dropping me off with apologies, Marina had invited me to her house for a traditional Sunday lunch the next day. She met me on the street, dressed in jeans and an oversize plaid shirt. With her hair in an unkempt bun and her large hoop earrings, she looked more like a homebody than the urbane fashionista of the day before. She greeted me with the usual Italian kisses on alternating cheeks and led me to her spacious second-floor apartment, where she introduced me to her two sons, Gianluca and Riccardo. Though their physiques made them intimidating—they were both muscular and more than six feet tall—they said hello shyly, peeking out of their shared bedroom. They were both students at a nearby university but honored the Italian tradition of living at home, sleeping in the same twin beds they'd had since childhood.

Marina told me she'd named Riccardo after her favorite movie star, Richard Gere. "Riccardo is my boyfriend, my lover. More than Gianluca. I don't know why," she said with a light shrug. "Gianluca is instinctive, a bit of an artist, temperamental. Riccardo is rational." She worried when they went out with their friends on the weekends ("What if some woman takes advantage of them?"), and she waited up for them, only sleeping after they were safely tucked in their beds.

Her relationship with Maurizio seemed more distant. He occasionally padded into the kitchen, plunked himself down on the sofa to watch television, delivered a baffling sequence of Neapolitan hand gestures to his wife, and went elsewhere in the apartment before returning to repeat. Marina mostly ignored him as we cooked in the roomy, bright kitchen made colorful by a small turquoise refrigerator and green wooden chairs around a rickety old table.

My guide started on the *ragù*, the most important component of the Sunday meal. *Ragù*, which simply means "sauce," refers to a mixture of gently stewed meat and tomatoes. While most Italians approved of dried pasta, they abhorred premade sauces. And "red" and "white" sauces only appeared on the same table in American restaurants. Indeed, southern Italians didn't eat cream-based sauces; those existed only in northern Italy and, to the southerners, seemed suspiciously French.

Sunday dinner carried its own traditions. "Some people immortalize the day with fish. But most people make *ragù*," Marina said, adding that in the old days, meat was expensive, so often Sunday was the only day of the week families ate it. "My mother still prepares *ragù* every Sunday, even though she lives by herself. If you go to any apartment building in Naples on a Sunday, you'll smell this sauce from the hallways." The meal was typically eaten after mass, in the afternoon. But while not very many people went to church anymore—Marina did, occasionally, but the men in the family did not—the tradition of the Sunday meal remained.

Marina guided me through the cooking as deftly as she'd led me through the streets of Naples. She laid out on a cutting board two pork ribs, a slab of pork thigh, and a flank steak of Tuscan veal. Meat was the base of the *ragù*. She donned a pair of yellow-framed eyeglasses and cubed the pork thigh. She seasoned the steak with salt and pepper and placed two layers of thinly sliced prosciutto, one cooked, one salt-cured, over the steak. She grated Parmigiano-Reggiano over the meat and sprinkled it with a few bits of the cheese's darkened crust. She rolled the meat and cheese together tightly and fastened it with toothpicks. The wooden sticks were called *stuzzicadente*, she noted, "teeth toys."

She held up a bottle of olive oil to the kitchen windows. "Look at the color," she said. It was translucent green. "It must be pure. Clean. Every year has a different taste, depending on the climate and the sun." She doused the bottom of a shallow pot with the liquid. Olive oil was healthy, she noted—it had vitamin A and no cholesterol. Maurizio used to drive to the nearby region of Basilicata every year to fill a tin drum with olive oil from a friend's farm, but nowadays they bought their olive oil from Carrefour, the French supermarket chain that was changing how people shopped from Italy to China.

"It's a good supermarket," Marina said. "You have sanitary controls. You are safe when you go there. It's less expensive than the local shops."

"Is there any resistance to it because it's French?" I asked.

She paused. "Well. As I told you, Neapolitans are tolerant of all cultures."

After the oil was hot, she added the meat and a couple knobs of butter, an ingredient I'd see more of in the north. She used the Danish brand Lurpak. "That's one thing Italy doesn't do very well," she admitted.

As Marina turned the meat with a spatula, the scent of sizzling veal, pork, and olive oil wafted through the kitchen. She added a cup of red wine, two chopped onions, and more olive oil. She spun two large cans of whole tomatoes through a food mill set over the pot. "It doesn't *amalgamate* well when you don't strain the tomatoes first," she said, using one of her favorite English words.

She plucked several fresh plum tomatoes from the vine and held one to my nose so that I could catch its sharp scent. She diced and added them into the pot as well. "Those are from Mount Vesuvius," she said. Because of the volcanic ash, the soil below the mountain was among the most fertile in Italy. "That's why the Greeks and Romans settled here—to take advantage of the good land," she said. "The sulfur purifies." Though the volcano that had devastated Pompeii two millennia before could one day erupt again without warning, the land's curse was also its blessing.

Marina placed another tomato on a slice of thick bread, then cut it into slivers. She flicked salt over the tomatoes and bread, drizzled them with olive oil, and handed it to me. I took a bite and seized up momentarily; I was unprepared for the tomato's juiciness, the bread's chewiness, and the lively oil. It was as incredible as the pizza I'd eaten the night before. But this wasn't a proper dish—it couldn't even be called *bruschetta* without the toasted bread and the garlic. I also knew that when I tried to re-create it elsewhere, it wouldn't be the same. The pizza and that simple snack revealed the key to Italian food: it was about the ingredients, grown in the right terrain, with proper care.

All that was left was to allow the sauce to concentrate in the simmering pot for a few hours—*ragù* was one of the pasta sauces that needed time. "The sauce should gather into a thick cream," said Marina. "The density should be intense. It should make little explosions like Vesuvius."

She decided that we'd go out while the sauce simmered. "Gianluca!" she hollered. "Come and stir the sauce occasionally." He nodded obediently. "Keep well," she said tenderly to the *ragù* as we left.

We climbed into the hatchback and drove through two imposing high-security gates. Liberated from the kitchen, Marina seemed happier. Like many other women I'd met on my journey, she didn't have a particular passion for food, she told me. Cooking was just a duty she'd had since she was an adolescent. As the eldest child in her family, she cooked for her younger sister and brother, a role that prepared her for the obligations of marriage.

We pulled up at a bakery, one of the few businesses that was open on Sundays. It was bustling, too, with locals buying bread and pastries. Marina told me she was careful about which bakeries she patronized because the Camorra controlled certain ones. "Occasionally, they'll hire street kids to bake bread in ovens heated by toxic material, like old car tires," she said. She yelled her order to the baker behind the counter and he handed her a dessert box.

As we drove around Naples, Marina pointed out the Phlegraean Fields, a wide, partly submerged caldera that was the mythical home of the Roman god Vulcan. Before the fields loomed Mount Vesuvius. "Pliny, one of the earliest journalists in the world, documented the volcanic eruptions that covered Pompeii. He wrote about the columns of gas and smoke," she said, slipping into tour guide mode.

As natural a tour guide as she was, Marina told me she'd started her business only recently. She'd been a stay-at-home mother for most of her adult life—not that she hadn't had career ambitions, particularly when she was young. Her father had been a jeweler, and as a child, she helped out in his store, greeting customers and explaining the attributes of various gems. "I was always taking care of his public relations," she said proudly. She graduated from the best high school in Naples, received degrees in foreign literature and gemology, and apprenticed at her father's shop. She also worked briefly for the United Nations, and thought about becoming an interpreter or a flight attendant. Then she met Maurizio.

"I resisted marriage for many years," Marina said. "I wanted my independence." She noted it wasn't her suitor as much as her mother who pressured her into marriage. "She wanted me to have the white dress and the Catholic wedding." After nine years, Marina caved in and tied the knot. She got pregnant right away, on her honeymoon in North Africa. As good Catholics, she and Maurizio had waited until they married to consummate their relationship, and they hadn't used birth control.

The pregnancy caused Marina much anxiety. She worried that the antimalaria pills she'd taken on her honeymoon would affect the fetus. She had an amniocentesis, which she believed almost caused her to miscarry. She was put on bed rest later in her pregnancy. During her labor and delivery, the umbilical cord had gotten tangled around the baby's neck, and she had to undergo an emergency Caesarian. The pregnancy left her with some lasting side effects, including a dulled sense of taste.

As scarring as the pregnancy was, Marina fell into the role of full-time mother and soon gave birth to a second son. Her sons became the center of her life. "They grow so fast and you only have a certain number of years to spend with them," she said. In any case, her previous aspirations now gave her anxiety. Not only did she no longer want to become a flight attendant; she no longer wanted to fly anywhere. And her husband, a traditional man, expected her to stay at home anyway.

"You didn't think about working after your sons were born?" I asked.

Marina thought for a moment. She'd been too absorbed in being a full-time mother. She hadn't had a moment to think about what she wanted for herself. "So my advice to you: if there is anything you want to do, you should fight for it now. You should declare your independence early. Otherwise, it will be too late."

I'd done that, all right. But had I taken it too far? What was the right balance? I realized that for many women, even those with very different stories, it was a struggle.

Marina parked the car by the shore, and we walked around the waterfront. "I love the movement of the water," she said. "It helps me, soothes me. When I go anywhere else, I feel the lack of water. In Rome, I have to go to the fountains."

Stray cats lazed on the seawall. In the distance was Capri—it looked like a magical rock, poking out of the calm sea. But while the water was tranquil, the morning sun had given way to clouds.

Marina had found meaning in raising her sons, but "now everything is done," she said. "My sons are grown. I want to find new meaning in life. Women my age, they are concerned with their sexuality. They are interested in money. They want to look better. They don't want to accept their old age." They wanted face-lifts; they wanted Botox. They were chasing youth. "But all of that is empty."

When we arrived back at Marina's, the scent of *ragù* hit our noses as soon as we opened the front door. As promised, the concentrated sauce had begun to emit little lava-like plops. She had me adjust the salt, since she had a dulled sense of taste. I added a pinch, not wanting to overseason her hard work. Marina boiled a brand of dried pasta called Libera Terra—"Free Land"—that had been produced on land the government had recently reclaimed from the Camorra. The oversize ridged tubes were called *paccheri*, derived from *paccarià*—Neapolitan for "slaps." The pasta was so large, it supposedly slapped you in the face when you ate it. After they were boiled, the tubes became floppy, ideal for soaking up the *ragù*; half a dozen were enough to make a meal. Marina spooned *ragù* and a healthy dollop of ricotta over the *paccheri*. She left the meat in the pot; it had given its all to the sauce. But she set out veal meatballs she'd made, to be eaten on the side, along with grilled zucchini doused with olive oil. Everyone poured themselves glasses of wine and water. Marina groaned when her family kept their eyes glued to the soccer game as they ate, in violation of the etiquette I'd learned. "I only have peace in the summer, when football season is over," she said.

Marina scrutinized her food. "How do you like it?" she asked, frowning.

"It's good," I said, though in truth the meal didn't compare to the pizza the night before, or even the tomatoes on bread she'd served me earlier. The simple stuff had been better.

"It's not very good," she said, looking at me skeptically. She hadn't been expecting false praise; Italians were brutally honest with each other, but my American sensibilities had held me back. And anyway, I had a nagging feeling that it was my fault: I'd undersalted the dish.

We finished the pasta and moved on to dessert, fruit tarts from the bakery. Afterward, Marina said, "Come with me. Let me show you something."

She took me to the end of the hall and opened an iron door. Beyond was an enormous sunny balcony, filled with lemon trees and jasmine flowers. Marina's dog, an aging beagle with a floppy chin, dozed in a corner. The balcony offered a view of the Phlegraean Fields and the street below, where a busker stood in the middle of traffic, playing a classical tune on a violin against the backdrop of the Mediterranean Sea. It was the beauty of Naples, and the sense of home she had there, not cooking, that gave Marina pleasure.

14.

There was something about the mist that drifted through the Po River Valley and the breeze that blew through the undulating hills of the Apennines in Emilia-Romagna that created the right conditions for Italy's best food products. That's what Valerie, a *sfoglina*—a female pasta maker—told me as I toured the most divine factory I'd ever visited. This emporium in the small, mountainous village of Castel d'Aiano produced the mother of all Italian cheeses: Parmigiano-Reggiano. Across Italy, I'd learned a lot about the cheese, known to Americans as Parmesan. It was sprinkled onto nearly everything, "aside from our espressos," one *sfoglina* joked. Marina in Naples mentioned that because the cheese could be stored for years, some Italians invested in wheels of it, like certificates of deposit. It was regarded as health food, a source of calcium, vitamins, and protein, which made it especially good for children and pregnant women. (The ten to fifteen grams usually grated over a serving of pasta had more protein than a serving of chicken.) Parmigiano-Reggiano, however, had to be produced within a certain geographical limit of Emilia-Romagna, from the milk of a special breed of cow fed a strict diet of hay and barley. It was not to be confused with *grana padano*, another cheese made nearby with milk from cows fed a looser regimen of corn and other grains. "Why is *grana padano* not as good?" I asked Valerie. I'd had a tough time differentiating the two cheeses in the past. The *sfoglina* clucked. "Sometimes *grana padano* goes like this—" she said, making the sound of a bomb exploding— "*Psh!*"—and throwing her hands up in the air. During its production, the lesser cheese was prone to burst.

I would never mistake any other cheese for Parmigiano-Reggiano after visiting the factory. A man everyone called Il Maestro explained the early steps of the process: He and his workers heated fresh milk with rennet until it curdled. They drained the curds, shaped them into large wheels, and placed them in vats of brine. Then he opened a large door to the warehouse where the cheese was aged, and a distinct, unforgettable fragrance hit my nose. The scent was a heavenly mix of grassy (from the pastures where the cows had grazed), nutty (from the aging process), and subtly sweet (from the milk itself). The drafty, cavernous room reminded me of a vault where rare books or precious works of art might be stored. The warehouse didn't need heating or cooling—the temperature was naturally between 55 and 68 degrees Fahrenheit throughout the year, the right range for the cheese to ripen naturally, which took eighteen to thirty-six months. Round, yellow wheels resembling oversize snare drums, each resting on its own platform, stretched from floor to ceiling in neat rows. The Maestro pulled out a small hammer and thumped the sides of several wheels, where the name of the cheese was etched. Banging a well-aged cheese yielded not an echo but a resounding thud, an indication that the proteins had reached the proper density.

One of the by-products of Parmigiano-Reggiano, whey, was fed to pigs for another Emilia-Romagna specialty: *prosciutto di Parma*, the salt-cured, tissue-thin pork that Italians, from north to south, often served as antipasto with cheese and bread. But in this region, I was introduced to a whole range of charcuterie that Italians had managed to conceal from most of the world. The buttery pink mortadella at one bed-and-breakfast was nothing like its Spam-like American offspring, baloney. It seemed blasphemous to even link the two. At a pig *fattoria*, or farm—the Italian word inspiring pleasant images of animals happily fattening away—I reached for slice after slice of *lardo*, razor-thin, nearly transparent wisps of pork fat that melted on my tongue. At a dinner party in the town of Parma, the host, the sister of an Italian-American friend, went into her kitchen and turned on an industrial-looking deli slicer, a fixture of many Emilia-Romagna households. She loaded a football-sized hunk of meat and shaved off a plate's worth. Literally the "little butt" of pork, the sheets of velvety *culatello* were cured in a method similar to prosciutto, but the precious cut yielded a richer, sweeter flavor and sold for twice the price.

Then from the town of Modena, I found balsamic vinegar that was a stark contrast to the abominations that American supermarkets stocked. A husband and wife showed me around their warehouse filled with giant barrels of the authentic product. Their balsamic was made from grapes alone. "All you need is a vineyard and a lot of time," said the wife. A true balsamic bore either an IGP or DOP appellation, which verified its provenance and meant that it was aged for at least five or twelve years, respectively. Some vinegars were stored even longer, for up to twenty-five years, and with age, the product became richer, darker, and more viscous. The wife asked me to hold out my hand, palm down, and poured a drop of the twenty-five-year-old vinegar into the crevice just below my thumb. It was so thick it didn't run. I asked what they thought the best use was for the aged product. They huddled for a minute, then sent their adult son out to the nearest *gelateria* for a generous tub of vanilla gelato. They scooped the ice cream into little paper cups and drizzled vinegar over it. The vinegar cut the creamy sweetness of the gelato with a subtle acidity that tasted a little like lemon but had a depth that lingered on my tongue. It was divine.

I'd come to Emilia-Romagna to learn pasta, though; the cheese, meat, and vinegar were mere bonuses. (It was like that scene in *Jerry Maguire* when Renée Zellweger says to Tom Cruise, "You had me at hello." Emilia-Romagna had me at pasta.) But Paolo, the ponytailed, thirty-something director of the local tourism board, went out of his way to ensure that I tasted everything the region had to offer. Emilia-Romagna suffered from an inferiority complex, despite being blessed with delicious food, beautiful mountains, and historic cities like Ravenna and Bologna. The region was like the pretty but ignored middle sibling in a brood of attractive sisters. As with Naples, tourists often bypassed the region, opting for Tuscany. So why was Emilia-Romagna better than Tuscany? I asked Paolo one afternoon.

"Well . . . It's not better than Tuscany. Tuscany *is* beautiful," he said, going into the typical swoon. I waited in vain for a little hustle. Come on, Paolo, I thought. Wasn't he taking the Italian tendency toward candor too far?

One thing was certain: there was no better place to learn fresh pasta—even if, nowadays, most Italians used dried pasta. The latter was more convenient, certainly, and some chefs argued that the dried version retained its shape better after boiling and was better suited for heavier sauces. But still, nothing was more amazing than the freshly made lasagna, ravioli, and tortellini of Emilia-Romagna. In big cities like Rome, I'd been surprised to discover that even restaurants known for their fresh pasta often didn't make them in-house. Most young Italians had little, if any, experience making pasta from scratch. In Emilia-Romagna, though, I found a handful of entrepreneurial *sfogline* who kept the craft alive at their *agriturismos*—farmhouse bed-and-breakfasts—in the Apennines.

I started by learning how to make the region's signature *ragù*, known to the outside world as Bolognese. The stern *sfoglina* named Nadia emphasized that spaghetti was never served with the *ragù*: *"Spaghetti Bolognese NO exist-oh!"* she said in horror, the mere idea an offense to her ears. She explained that the thick, meat-based sauce simply slipped off thin spaghetti—the sauce required a flatter, wider noodle like tagliatelle or even better, lasagna, which we were making that day.

The Bolognese sauce—I couldn't help calling it that—was similar in principle to the *ragù* I'd learned from Marina: you took meat and tomatoes and simmered the essence out of them until they *amalgamated* into a thick pool of goodness. "The simpler the beef *ragù*, the better," Nadia said. She began with a *soffritto*, the holy trinity of sautéed finely diced carrots, onions, and celery that perfumed kitchens across Italy and was the base of many sauces. Her *soffritto* was cooked in sunflower oil rather than olive oil, a sign we'd departed from the Mediterranean. She added three pounds of minced beef, using a fatty cut for more flavor. (The cuisine of Emilia-Romagna was often referred to as *la grassa*—the fat one—with good reason.) She added a considerable amount of tomato paste, a smaller quantity of tomato sauce, and a generous quantity of rock salt that confirmed my suspicion that I'd undersalted Marina's *ragù*. While the sauce simmered, she turned her attention to the lasagna noodles.

Unlike the ear-shaped pastas of Puglia, which consisted simply of flour (mostly semolina, thicker than durum wheat) and water, the pastas of Emilia-Romagna invariably contained eggs, giving them a thicker body and richer flavor. Locals raised a certain type of hen whose eggs had especially yellow yolks that nicely tinted and flavored the pasta. The flour was also important—the *sfogline* used "doppio zero" flour, a super-refined white variety with no equivalent elsewhere. One afternoon later in the trip, when I made Chinese dumplings for an Italian family, I was stunned by the light, feathery texture this silky flour gave the wrappers—and they crisped to perfection when I pan-fried them. (*"Delizioso!"* the husband said. "What do I call these if I want to order them in a Chinese restaurant? *Ravioli fritti*?")

Nadia combined half a dozen eggs, six hundred grams of flour, and pureed boiled spinach for color and extra flavor. She kneaded the dough on a *tagliere*, a flat wooden board that was as sacred as a wok was to a Chinese chef. "We never use soap to wash it. Only water," she said. "The wood is a living thing. You will dry it out if you use soap." Italy was the only place I'd visited where people described kitchen implements as having souls of their own.

After the dough sat for half an hour, Nadia began rolling it out by hand with a fat rolling pin, preferring it over a pasta machine. "Rolling by hand is better because the pasta will be able to breathe," Nadia explained. "If you use a machine, the air in the pasta is squeezed out." She held up the sheet of dough. On close inspection, it had ridged little bumps formed by the tiny imperfections of the rolling pin and the *tagliere*. For comparison, she showed me what happened when the pasta went through the machine, an appliance as heavy as a typewriter. After feeding a gob of dough through it several times, she held up the sheet. It was slick and slippery, a little too perfect. "This pasta won't hold the sauce as well. The sauce will just slip off," she said.

Nadia made a béchamel of butter, flour, and milk and began assembling the lasagna: she spread a small amount of the béchamel in the baking dish, then topped it with alternating layers of pasta, *ragù*, and grated Parmigiano-Reggiano. She placed the dish in the oven, where it baked and bubbled, before she took it out and cut the lasagna into hearty squares. Though the sauce was rich and dense, the delicate spinach noodles kept the texture light. When I made lasagna at home, it was invariably a half-day affair, even with the aid of packaged lasagna noodles. Under Nadia's skillful hands, it had taken a mere ninety minutes from scratch.

From Valeria—the *sfoglina* who'd taken me to the Parmigiano-Reggiano factory—I learned that restraint was important. I sampled her pasta at her tiny bed-and-breakfast nestled high in the mountains overlooking a particularly breathtaking valley. The stone guesthouse, which dated back to the 1700s, had only three rooms and a dining room for ten. She'd made the tortellini the day before, stuffing them with ricotta, Parmigiano-Reggiano, and parsley. I watched her make the simplest of sauces to go with the filled pasta: she melted butter in a pan and added sage leaves. The herb infused the butter with a sweet, earthy fragrance. She added the tortellini to the pan, tossed them in the glistening sauce, and served them piping hot. A heavy sauce was overkill for filled pasta; after all, sauce was already wrapped in the pasta. And indeed, the sage butter worked its magic, letting the tortellini reach its full, mouthwatering potential. I demolished my portion, had a second helping, and fought the impulse to slip some into my pocket for the road. (Takeaway boxes were rare in Italy.)

Luisa, a third *sfoglina*, taught me how to fold tortellini. She ran a bed-and-breakfast that featured a stuffed panther her husband had shot in Africa and a sprawling yard where pigs, ducks, and chickens roamed. She rolled out pasta dough made of eggs and flour and cut it into small squares of less than an inch—the same as the size of *manti* wrappers in Turkey. As with *manti*, she dotted each square with a dab of meat filling, this one made of a mince of cooked pork loin, prosciutto, mortadella, eggs, and Parmi-giano-Reggiano. She grated in fresh nutmeg—a touch of the distant Orient. She and her assistants wrapped each small square, sealed it into a triangle, then clasped together its opposite corners, almost the same method as for *chuchura* in western China and *manti* in Turkey. As with the *manti*, tortel-lini making was very much a communal activity done among women.

"We call this shape of pasta the 'Venus belly button,'" Luisa said. And then, sending a chill up my spine, she spoke almost the exact words that Asli had said of *manti*: "A good tortellini maker can wrap them small enough to fit a dozen on a spoon. In the old days, daughters-in-law were judged by how well they could wrap tortellini."

Luisa boiled the tortellini in a simple chicken broth and served the two together. Asli had mentioned that Turks had a tradition of serving *manti* in broth. As I dipped my spoon into the soup, I wondered if tortellini and *manti* were actually one, a legacy of the Silk Road that had brought them, in various shapes and forms, all the way from China.

When Craig arrived in Emilia-Romagna, I was in the middle of making pasta with a *sfoglina*. When we'd parted ways in Turkey, he wasn't sure if he would make it to Italy. I was so thrilled to see him that I covered his face in flour as we embraced. But when I pulled back, he had a look on his face that seemed to say, *When will my wife be done with all the cooking?*

Craig and Italy were a little like oil and water. It wasn't just the super-long meals that tried his patience. It was also the coffee. Elsewhere on the Silk Road, my caffeine-addicted husband had happily downed cup after cup of Nescafé. But instant coffee disappeared the moment you stepped into Italy, replaced by the ubiquitous cafés where baristas brewed coffee at expensive machines that forced steam through finely ground beans. Italians stood at the bar while they downed shots of espresso, and then, having had their morning dose of caffeine, left in a hurry to go about their day. This was antithetical to how Craig liked to drink coffee. Nescafé aside, he loved the American drip-style variety. When we weren't traveling, every morning he brewed a giant pot of it and drank it leisurely at the breakfast table while reading. He liked it black—additions like steamed milk were too froufrou for him. He carried a tall commuter mug of black coffee wherever he went.

On our previous visit to Italy, Craig had been ecstatic to find a McDonald's in Rome, only to discover that the restaurant, just like the rest of Italy, didn't have his drink. En route to Amalfi, he pulled over at a gas station mini-mart, hopeful that here at last he would find a dose bigger than a shot. My six-foot-tall husband returned holding a tiny disposable cup by its even smaller paper-wing handles.

Tuscany did little to change Craig's perspective on Italy. And I couldn't help agreeing with him this time. We were bored in Florence, exhausted by the lines to see the Michelangelos and the overpriced, touristy restaurants. Admittedly, we enjoyed some good wine and stayed in a nice farmhouse in the countryside near Siena. But the rolling green fields reminded me of a gigantic golf course, Craig yearned for mountains, and after the great food I'd eaten elsewhere in Italy, the much-touted Florentine beefsteak was boring. I would have taken a hunk of Parmigiano Reggiano with a splash of balsamic vinegar in Bologna's romantic—and quiet—town square over Tuscany any day.

And even as the journey's end loomed, we still had no plans beyond our summer in Washington, DC. One evening in Tuscany, at a pizzeria—decent enough, but not up to Naples' standards—we resumed our discussion of what we might do. The idea of working together on the cooking school came up again.

I'd given the idea some thought, particularly as I'd seen quite a few husband-and-wife businesses on our travels, especially in Italy. Even the pizzeria where we were eating was such a partnership. The bald husband worked the cash register and checked on the pizzas while his attractive, pregnant wife, who looked at least a decade younger, waited tables. But so far, seeing couples who mixed their personal and professional lives hadn't convinced me.

"Oh hon, I don't know if it would work," I said. I could be a pain to work with. I was demanding. I was bossy.

Craig knew all of this, of course—and he wasn't even sure about the idea himself, he said. But he saw my unwillingness to consider the idea further as just another indication of my obstinacy. At least we should weigh all our options, he said.

I looked over at the waitress. "Let's ask her what *she* thinks about working with her husband," I said.

After I summoned her over, she took a breath before she answered. I waited smugly, certain she was about to launch into a tirade, a long list of complaints. Instead, she sighed. "It's fabulous! Twenty-four hours a day we can be together." Her husband joined her. "With love, you can do anything!" he proclaimed, touching her rounded belly.

I was incredulous. *Gimme a break. These guys must be joking!* I grumbled. But then I caught the look on Craig's face. He was incredulous at my incredulity, I realized. Was I so obstinate that I couldn't accept that this couple enjoyed working together?

That was the beginning of my regret.

We pushed on to Rome, where I'd taken that fateful pasta class a year and a half before, setting in motion my great Silk Road adventure. But as we sat in morning traffic just outside the Eternal City, our arrival felt anticlimactic. We were both exhausted and out of sorts, and I had a busy Roman agenda. I planned to visit more restaurants and cook with another woman or two. I still had to do some culinary sleuthing, though I knew by now that there was no simple answer as to how Italian pasta and Chinese noodles were linked.

I was determined, though, to celebrate the end of the journey with Craig, and I'd booked a table at a Michelin three-star restaurant called La Pergola.

"Didn't you tell me that Italians are suspicious of it because it's run by a German?" Craig reminded me.

Yes, I admitted, some Italians didn't like the restaurant because an outsider was at the helm.

"And how much would the meal cost?" my husband wondered. He had a theory: the more expensive meals were often less tasty. Sometimes it was true, I had to admit.

"Oh, around a hundred and fifty euros per person," I said nonchalantly.

"You mean four hundred dollars?" he asked, incredulous.

My estimate didn't include wine, I added.

Craig sighed. "It's a good thing we don't have kids. With meals like that, we wouldn't be able to put them through college."

Yes, it was expensive, and some Italians harbored suspicions about it. But Michelin had given the place its top rating, I pointed out, and after a trip of no-star meals I thought it might be nice to end with a blowout.

"What are the specialities?" Craig asked skeptically. "Cock's comb? Pig's snout?"

I couldn't help laughing. Evidently, in our time apart, my husband had been keeping up with the latest trend of "snout-to-tail" eating. That was a surprise.

Our moods lifted considerably after we arrived in Rome at last. After dropping off our rental car, we boarded a local train at busy Stazione Termini and went through the center of town. On our last trip, Craig and I had spent Christmas Eve shopping at the markets and cooking together in an apartment we'd rented near Vatican City. We'd laid out thin slices of prosciutto, boiled fresh pasta (I didn't have the courage to make my own back then) and tossed it with butter, pan-fried steaks, and opened a bottle of red wine. After dinner, we'd walked to St. Peter's Square for the Pope's midnight mass, chatted with enthralled pilgrims from afar, and admired the nativity scenes. It had been only our second Christmas since we'd married and we had yet to form our own traditions, though one had stuck since then: Craig and I cooked together on the holiday.

On our arrival to Rome this time, we went directly to a neighborhood called Trastevere, which means "across the Tiber." The river snaked along one side of the district, which didn't have many important monuments but was full of narrow, twisting alleys, with an intimacy that reminded me of our Beijing neighborhood. After we checked into a cozy bed-and-breakfast, Craig stayed in to write while I headed to the city's north to meet Oretta Zanini De Vita, a food writer whose *Encyclopedia of Pasta* detailed the Italian staple's hundreds of shapes and sizes.

The picture of elegance, Oretta invited me into her home. She was a well-dressed, middle-aged woman who'd worked for the government before she began writing full-time. She poured us glasses of Prosecco, toasting my arrival in Rome with the sparkling wine. She showed me around her home, her kitchen cabinets filled with artisanal pastas and the walls of her study lined with cookbooks. She shared memories of growing up in Emilia-Romagna, where she ate *tortellini in brodo*—in broth, the traditional way of eating it, as I'd experienced with a *sfoglina*.

Best of all, she and I could commiserate about the Marco Polo myth. "Oh, it is so *stupid*!" Oretta said. "Did you know in Europe they've even written it into some children's textbooks?" I told her how I'd met food professionals across the Silk Road who believed the story. Even on my last day in Rome, an executive at Gambero Rosso, Italy's version of the Food Network, was adamant about Polo's supposed contribution.

As I learned from Oretta and other food experts, while it was certain that Italians ate pasta before Marco Polo, exactly how far back the tradition went was still a matter of debate. Some Italian experts claimed that Etruscan reliefs from tombs dating to the fourth century BC depicted rolling pins and boards and were evidence of indigenous pasta, though no pasta was depicted in the drawings. Others pointed to mentions of a Greco-Roman dish called *laganum* by the Roman poet Horace in the first century BC and by the Greek writer Athenaeus in the second century AD. Although historians saw it as a possible precursor to lasagna, the dish—sheets of dough made from wheat flour, crushed lettuce juice, and spices, which was then deep-fried—bears only the faintest resemblance to today's pasta.

I was more inclined to believe food historians who looked beyond Italy's borders. The development of pasta in the country seemed to be the result of cross-pollination with other cultures, unlike in China, where evidence suggested that noodles were homegrown. But in Italy's case, exactly which cultures were responsible remained in dispute.

What many experts agree upon is that ethnic groups along the Mediterranean had something to do with it. One of the earliest mentions of a boiled type of dough—called *itrium*—in the West has been traced to the Jerusalem Talmud dating back to the fifth century AD. A document, written by a Syrian physician several centuries later, described *itrium* in further detail— string-like pasta made of semolina and dried before cooking. (Though the practice of boiling pieces of dough came to China earlier than to the Middle East, the Chinese didn't shape dough into noodle-like strings until later.) Furthering the idea that itinerant groups played a role (something that had struck me earlier in my research, when I'd read about Turkic nomads and Mongols preparing noodle dishes), Jews who'd moved to northern France boiled kneaded dough as early as the eleventh century AD, calling it *vermishelsh*—a word that sounded similar to *vermicelli*—according to documents that debated whether Jews should be allowed to boil dough on certain holidays.

Meanwhile, by the twelfth century AD, Sicily had become a center of trade in dried pasta, as evidenced by royal Sicilian maps published around 1150 that charted the locations of water sources and flour mills in a territory called Trabia. From Trabia, merchants distributed long strands of pasta across Calabria, the toe of Italy's boot, and nearby Muslim and Christian lands, according to the twelfth-century Arab geographer Idrisi. Oretta speculated that Sicilians had learned pasta from Arabs in North Africa, who'd eaten small bits of it called couscous for centuries. "Perhaps the Sicilians saw the Muslims making couscous, and it inspired them to do something new," she told me. Other food historians added that Arab traders went on to play a decisive role as middlemen and popularizers of pasta, spreading it to Spain.

By the Middle Ages, Italy had developed a full-fledged pasta repertoire. As Silvano Serventi and Françoise Sabban write in their book *Pasta: The Story of a Universal Food*, "While Italians may not have invented pasta, they invented the art of shaping and cooking it . . . in a very different way than the Chinese." Dried pasta became an important commodity not just in Sicily but also in Sardinia. Traders sent it to Genoa's port, from where they dispersed it through Europe. In the Apennines, twelfth-century Catholic monks wrote of fresh pastas like lasagna and *tortelli,* a larger tortellini. In Naples, a fourteenth-century writer gave instructions on something similar to lasagna: after boiling sheets of noodles, season them, layer by layer, with grated cheese and spices. A Renaissance cookbook author named Maestro Martino described how to make vermicelli: "Moisten the dough . . . and spread it out into a thin sheet," he wrote. "Using your hands, break it into little pieces that look more or less like worms, and place these in the sun to dry." The maestro's recipe for macaroni called for fine-quality flour, egg whites, and a touch of the Silk Road: rosewater.

But throughout the Renaissance, pastas were cooked for up to two hours, creating a mush-like gruel that sounded like Iranian noodles. And many of the preparations were sweet. An early Renaissance recipe called for cooks to submerge vermicelli in almond milk and douse it with plenty of sugar and saffron (which sounded vaguely like what Iranians did with rice); other cooks sprinkled it with sugar and cinnamon. Doctors recommended sweetening pasta to make it easier to digest (an idea that reminded me of the Uighur doctor who'd prescribed a no-noodle diet and Iranians who ingested sugar cubes and wafers with tea after meals). But there were more appetizing pasta dishes from the era: Genoans ate pasta with capons and eggs while Neapolitans ate macaroni with poultry, albeit boiled. During the Renaissance, Italians began sprinkling Parmigiano-Reggiano and other cheeses over pasta, along with spices like nutmeg and cinnamon (both still used in Emilia-Romagna). But it was not until the end of the eighteenth century, after tomatoes arrived from the New World and Italians adopted them into the cuisine, that *ragùs* began to appear. And the idea of serving pasta "al dente" didn't come into fashion until the twentieth century.

Though I'd established a fairly solid link between Chinese, Central Asian, and Turkish dumplings, I didn't find any material that linked Italian pasta with traditions of the countries through which I'd passed. But still, the echoes nagged at me—the uncanny likeness between tortellini and *manti*, the strikingly similar words Luisa and Asli had uttered about them. Maybe noodles and filled pasta had taken a roundabout tour of the Middle East and North Africa on their journey to Italy. Or perhap during the Byzantine Empire, culinary exchanges had taken place between the Italian peninsula and Asia Minor. Or perhaps it was a coincidence? After seven thousand miles, the connection was still a mystery.

Long after I left Oretta's and long after my journey had ended, I came across an article about noodles that, after all my travels and research, struck a chord. The piece, by the food historian Charles Perry, had appeared in a 1981 issue of a rare magazine called *Petit Propos Culinaires*, and although I'd seen it quoted in many other pieces, it had taken me a while to track it down. Researchers had cited the article when attributing noodles to either the Romans (with their *laganum*) or to the peoples of the Middle East (based on the string-like boiled noodles mentioned in the Jerusalem Talmud). But those researchers had missed the point of the article, which was titled "The Oldest Mediterranean Noodle: A Cautionary Tale."

"It is our romantic habit to believe the popular foods of a culture are eternal," Perry writes. "As a corollary, we believe a food was probably invented by people whose descendants eat it today." After entertaining various theories, Perry does not try to determine where noodles began and instead ends the article with three morals for food historians:

1. If a people eat much of a dish, this does not mean that they have eaten it forever.
2. If a people eat little of a dish . . . it does not follow that they never ate much of it.
3. Time and chance and fashion rule cookery as they do the rest of our social behavior.

Putting the pasta puzzle aside in my last days in Rome, I explored and enjoyed the city's food. I met a tomato vendor who sold more than fifty types of the fruit and interviewed him in feeble Italian, bastardized with three years of high school Spanish. (Me: *"Quanti . . . tipo . . . pomodori?"* Tomato vendor: *"Cinquanta."* Me: *"Quanti tipo pomodori . . . en el mundo?"* Tomato vendor: *"Centinai,"* which meant hundreds and was followed by a lot of Italian I didn't understand.) I visited the Jewish quarter and, at a sidewalk table, ate *carciofi alla giudia,* deep-fried artichokes. I cooked in the Roman countryside with a woman named Giovanna who topped her gnocchi, made of just potatoes and flour, with a spectacularly simple sauce: halved cherry tomatoes sautéed with shallots, and a shower of hand-ripped basil at the very end. An American friend named Kathy, who lived in Italy and accompanied me to Giovanna's, commented, "In America, we'd be throwing in all kinds of things."

Late one morning, a Roman friend named Federica took me to a market near the train station, where Bangladeshis, Chinese, and Egyptians sold produce and meats. Around the market was one of the few pockets of Rome with international restaurants. Like many people I'd met on my journey, Italians didn't eat much foreign food, but here the smell of butter chicken collided with the scent of chilies and ginger in stir-fries. Federica mentioned that Giovanni Fassi, one of the city's best *gelaterias*, was nearby. "Let's go there," I said. She looked at her watch and frowned. "But it's not even noon!" Italian eating rules notwithstanding, I talked her into it, and we arrived to find many customers waiting in the marble-walled institution. But before I could feel vindicated, Federica said, "They're all tourists." Still, she pushed her way to the front of the line and treated me to a very generous cup of raspberry and strawberry gelato—"in season," she said—and a dollop of whipped cream. She even deigned to take a taste. Then she took me around the corner to a most unusual restaurant.

La Sorgentine had the aesthetics of a Chinese restaurant. The interior looked like it had been hastily finished. The tables were round and the chairs had white covers and floppy bows on their backs. Kenny G–like Muzak played over the speakers. A friendly, stocky Chinese man with a distinctly Italian accent introduced himself as the restaurant's owner. Michele had left China for Italy two decades before, he explained, and worked his way up in the Chinese restaurant industry. La Sorgentine, which he'd opened six months earlier, had a unique business model: his Chinese chefs cooked Italian food. He catered to Chinese guests, especially the increasing tide of mainland tourists, who found traditional Italian restaurants too intimidating. An Italian maestro had taught his chefs the dishes. But Michele tweaked them to make them more appealing to his clientele, using Parmigiano-Reggiano only sparingly, focusing on seafood, and boiling the noodles slightly longer. (Chinese noodles were generally served soft, though not to a medieval degree.) The *spaghetti ai frutti di mare* was particularly popular, as were the risottos, with their congee-like consistency.

But after La Sorgentine opened, Italians came in and, seeing the Chinese wait staff and decor, asked for Chinese food. So Michele added Asian dishes to the menu, and thus one of the world's very few Chinese-Italian restaurants was born. But the schizophrenic menu caused some problems, he admitted. "Sometimes at the same table, one person will order Chinese while the other person orders Italian. Everything is fine when the meal begins: the appetizers come out together. But when you get to the *primi*, you start having problems. Chinese food is always cooked faster. So we'll bring out the Chinese *primo* first, the Italian *primo* second. And ditto with the *secondi*. So the Chinese eater finishes and the Italian eater is only halfway through his meal!"

To avoid the timing problem, Federica and I shared everything: it was the way I liked to eat anyway. I left the ordering to my friend. A waiter appeared with a salad of octopus and calamari and a plate of bruschetta. Pieces of imitation crab and shrimp came sizzling over rice on an iron plate. Another waiter brought Michele's touted spaghetti with seafood. I ate with a fork while Federica used chopsticks. We drank Tsingtao beer out of wineglasses. We ended with fried gelato, a dessert as Chinese as fried ice cream was Mexican. The fried gelato reminded me of what Charles Perry had written: *Time and chance and fashion rule cookery as they do the rest of our social behavior.* If you were to extrapolate from a visit to La Sorgentine you'd end up with many a confused notion of both Chinese and Italian food.

As we finished our meal, Michele came and sat down at our table. I couldn't resist taking one last stab: Where did he think noodles had originated? Perhaps his twenty years in Italy had given him some insight.

Michele paused before answering. "I like to study history," he said. "China developed early, that is true. In the past, everything in China was good. But then it began to lag behind the West. Now the Italians are lagging, becoming stagnant. They say, 'We have two thousand years of history. We used to be the best in the world.' But where does that get you? It gets in the way. You can't say spaghetti is one culture's or another's. You'll never discover your answer."

But still, I was disappointed. After all these miles, I hadn't gotten any further with an explanation not just for how noodles originated, but for how they ended up in Italy. Why was I so bothered? Perhaps it was because my noodle quest had paralleled my own identity struggle: were they—and was I—Eastern or Western? Could I, too, seamlessly blend into both East and West? And wherever I happened to be, was it possible to maintain a dual identity?

But then I reflected on my journey. Somewhere along the way, I had, in fact, stopped worrying so much about straddling two cultures. I'd felt welcome everywhere (except in Turkmenistan), and I'd met others who struggled with their identities, too. There had been the extreme cases, like Isabel on the Tibetan Plateau, who was a fan of Mao Zedong but loved red wine and tennis. Or Shaheen in Iran, who'd railed against mullahs and Ahmadinejad and took us out for pizza, but was steadfast in his love for Persian poets. And I'd met whole ethnic groups (like the Uighurs) and entire countries (like Turkey) that for centuries had struggled to find a balance between East and West.

As I traveled from East to West, my gender had become more important. Being female had given me access to women in all kinds of situations. I'd been glad to see the journey through a woman's eyes. It had made me incensed to see how women were treated in certain situations in Central Asia, though I realized it might not be fair to judge a region based on only a few experiences. But spending time with women in distant cultures had made me more appreciative of my own situation, and at the same time made me realize that I needed to take a harder look at gender relations in the United States and China, places I'd lived for years.

And what had also helped me alleviate my identity issues was my discovery that East and West weren't so different, after all. Across the Silk Road, I'd discovered palpable connections among cultures. I'd seen how food crossed geographical, religious, and political borders and blurred the divide. I'd seen how family traditions and hospitality had tied together the Silk Road cultures and made them as similar to each other as places we lumped together as "the West." It occurred to me that the idea of the West was as much of a construct as the concept of the Silk Road, and it was only a lingering Orientalism that kept our ideas of Asia and Europe so divided in our heads.

Moreover, I'd learned that the process that brought us the dishes we know and love is mostly an organic one that has unfolded over years and generations. Dishes are living things, little documented, that are passed down from parent to child (or, as I saw on the road, from mother to daughter-in-law). Methods are altered, names evolve, and individuals claim the dishes as their own. I'd enjoyed "Chef Zhang's" noodles, savored "Asli's" manti, indulged in "Nadia's" lasagna. And when I returned from the trip, I would think of the dishes I learned as "mine," even though they'd been created by the collective minds and hands of many generations.

That was another reason why it was difficult to determine where noodles had begun. Like a guest from a distant land, they had been welcomed into far-flung homes and assimilated into kitchens, melding with different flavors, from East to West.

In Rome, I had one last person to see: Andrea Consoli, the Italian chef who'd inadvertently inspired my journey. His restaurant, Le Fate, which was down the street from our guesthouse in Trastevere, had been built out of a six-hundred-year-old horse stable. The Christmas tinsel I recognized from our previous visit was still strung around the cozy dining room, even though it was May. Andrea was finishing his daily cooking class, and a group of Americans and Australians were at a long table, polishing off the last smudges of chocolate soufflé on their plates. Andrea's father was at the cash register behind the bar and his brother was lugging boxes through the front door. His mother and his fiancée, a pretty American Midwesterner named Erica, were tidying the room.

After hugging and saying good-bye to the last guests, Andrea and Erica invited me to a table and uncorked a bottle of wine. I learned that things had changed over the last year, for the busier. "Jen, I'm done," Andrea moaned. "I'm way over my limit. I have too many requests, too many people asking me for classes." He looked slightly gaunter than he had the year before, though it didn't dim his classic Italian features. Everything had been going steadily, he told me, and then—he gestured toward his fiancée accusingly—"this American created an explosion in the business!"

"I have no idea what you're talking about!" Erica said, her blue eyes widening.

Leave it to Italians to think that too much success was a bad thing. Le Fate had opened six years before and started with a small flow of customers. Then Andrea had met Erica, who was studying abroad, and she'd suggested that he teach tourists how to cook. In the beginning, he charged just twenty euros (less than thirty dollars) per guest. "I never cared about the money," Andrea had told me the year before. "In my little universe, in my little world, it makes me happy. It gives me satisfaction if I can help tourists understand what *real* Italian food is like." Even now at fifty euros (around sixty dollars), the classes were a bargain.

Andrea looked tortured. He'd become so busy that his brother had taken over the dinner service, and he told me he was looking for a new space.

"So you can expand?" I asked.

"No, not to *expand*," he said forcefully, as if I'd suggested something criminal. "The idea is not to become *McDonald's*. It's so I can devote more time to my students. Plus, you know, Americans can be quite . . . big . . . and they have this thing about 'space.'"

When I mentioned that I planned to eat at La Pergola, Andrea made a face. "It's not worth it," he said. "It's like buying a pair of brand-name Diesel jeans. The food is important, not the place, the name, or the brand." He rattled off a list of places I should visit. "Divide up the money you'd spend at La Pergola and go to four restaurants." He pulled from a shelf a respected Italian restaurant guide and translated snippets from La Pergola's review: "'Bottles of wine from forty to two thousand euros . . . there is nothing wrong with the kitchen, but there is something wrong with the service . . . zero kilometer products . . . innovative dishes that include octopus, avocado, and peaches.'" Before I could say anything, Andrea slapped the book shut. "We don't eat avocados in Roman cooking. It's not our cuisine. What's the point of trying avocados here when you can get them at home? You are here to taste *our* food. With food, you cannot make innovation anymore, not these days. Everything has been done." I heard this repeatedly from Italians. Italy was a place where trends like tail-to-snout cuisine and molecular gastronomy were destined to fail. Tradition reigned on the peninsula. It wasn't exactly true that cooks couldn't innovate, but rarely did food change in leaps and bounds overnight. Marco Polo had not suddenly brought noodles from China to Italy. Andrea was getting at something that was at the heart of my journey: treasured dishes like tortellini, *manti*, or hand-pulled noodles, the ones that defined a cuisine, were created over the centuries, the methods evolving slowly—not quite as lumbering as human evolution, but something like it, incremental changes stacking up over the years.

I asked Andrea if he cooked at home, explaining that I'd found few men in the tradition-bound cultures I'd visited who cooked for their families. He looked surprised. "I always cook at home. I am the one who goes shopping. Erica buys milk, and maybe cereal." But Andrea added that he was an anomaly; not just because he was a man, but also because his peers mostly eschewed cooking. "The grandmothers—they all know how to make pasta. Then my parents' generation began forgetting. Now nobody knows how to make pasta, or even how to clean an artichoke." Those were the two lessons with which his classes generally began.

It occurred to me that Andrea was the missing link: if we were to preserve the making of fresh pasta and other traditional dishes, we needed men to be more involved. I vowed that if I ever had a son, I would initiate him into the work of the kitchen. A daughter might get off a little more easily, but not by much. As for my husband, well, he, I supposed, was a lost cause. In the end, he'd made most of the trip with me, and he'd spent just as little time in kitchens as he did at home. But he'd accompanied me half-way around the world, and he'd given me plenty of autonomy. To preserve marital happiness, I would have to let the cooking slide. And, perhaps, as Asli in Turkey had said, one cook was enough for a household.

Sitting down with Andrea, I was reminded of what I'd learned across the Silk Road. I'd gone through a string of places where hospitality was more important than making money. Where people made good, honest food without having to market it or spin it into something bigger. Where people had invited me into their homes so warmly and treated me to so much without asking for anything in return. Where you could sit down for a two-hour lunch in the middle of a workday and feel good about it. That was what the trip was about—the importance of friends and family, of slowing down enough to enjoy life. Searching for the origin of noodles had allowed me to come to those realizations.

The day before Craig and I left Rome, I stopped by Andrea's a final time to say good-bye. The daily class had just begun, and he was going over the menu with a dozen guests from the United States and London. When he mentioned gnocchi with tomato sauce, several of the students let out audible gasps of excitement. The main course, *straccetti alla romana*, was greeted with silence—nobody had heard of the thin slices of beef with tomato and arugula. "And then for dessert: tiramisu." One student's jaw dropped so far that it looked like he would need a clamp to shut it. "We lucked out!" another shrieked, as if she were a winning contestant on a game show.

Andrea interrupted the guests' reverie to divide up the potatoes. "Now turn *on*—not off!—your brain and pay very close attention!"

The students donned their aprons, and as I slipped out of Le Fate, my cell phone rang. It was Candice, the manager of my own cooking school, calling to give me an update. The chefs said hello and told me they were fully booked for the night. I told them I would be back soon enough. For now, in Rome, I had something more important to attend to: my husband.

On our last night in Rome, Craig surprised me with a tour of the city's best gelato shops. Forget that the first time the dessert ever came up, early in our relationship, he'd shuddered. "*Gelato*? That sounds gross. You want to eat something with *gel* in it?" he joked.

Craig knew how obsessed I was with Italian ice cream. Backpacking through Europe in my mid-twenties, I'd subsisted on a diet of gelato, often eating four or five cups of it every day. But on our last night in Rome the year before, an unfortunate thing happened. At a *gelateria* in Trastevere, I ordered a scoop that turned out to be the worst I'd ever tasted, and I desperately needed another ice cream to undo the taste that lingered in my mouth. But it was late, and all the gelato shops we came across were closed. There would be no time for the dessert the next day, either—we were leaving in the morning, very early. My levelheaded husband tried to put it in perspective—"It's just a scoop of ice cream, we'll get you one somewhere else, promise . . . maybe there will be a gelato shop at the airport"—to which I responded with hysterics and accusations that he didn't understand me and the seriousness with which I approached food, my livelihood. I reluctantly got into a taxi with him to return to our bed-and-breakfast. En route, I saw a glimmer of hope: a gelato shop with the lights still on. We had the taxi stop then and there, only to be greeted by an employee who said they were closing. I begged him to let me in for one last, redeeming scoop. He relented, and our trip ended with a delicious cup of frosty hazelnut creaminess. My husband breathed a sigh of relief. Crisis averted.

On this trip, I'd indulged in the occasional cup of gelato, but there was so much else to enjoy that it had become a side note. Plus, when I learned how the dessert was made, it lost some of its allure. It had become perhaps the most mechanized dish in Italian cuisine—gelato makers bought expensive machines and poured in custard, premade in some shops, made from scratch in others. The machine decided how long to churn the ice cream for the right consistency. Even so, gelato was infinitely better than most ice creams in the world, thanks to the inclusion of egg yolks in its smooth, cream-based varieties and fresh seasonal fruit in others. The standard flavors, pistachio and hazelnut, were more appealing than vanilla and chocolate. And this was one aspect of Italian cuisine that had bucked tradition: recent innovations included chocolate and chili; ricotta, fig, and caramel; and amaretto and pine nut.

Craig had asked me to reserve a few hours on our last afternoon for him, and we began our tour at the Pantheon, the most beautiful building in all of Rome, which had endured for two millennia. After we admired it and Raphael's tomb inside, my husband led me down a string of narrow alleys to an institution called Giolitti, where Pope John Paul II used to send his driver when an ice cream craving struck. Inside, swarms of locals and tourists piled around a long counter, in a line that had no apparent beginning or end, shouting their orders to gruff attendants. When we finally emerged from the ruckus, with a huge cone in my hand like a victory torch, I understood what the commotion was about: the creamy scoops of hazelnut and pine nut were as smooth as cake frosting, and a nut allergy sufferer might have wanted to think twice about even getting close to the ice cream, so bold were the flavors. We paused at a classic Roman café called Tazza d'Oro for shots of espresso. My American-coffee-loving husband even downed one. We then strolled on to another shop called San Crispino for a scoop of their trademark honey gelato, which we ate on the steps of the Trevi Fountain. There were more shops on the list, but my time in Italy had taught me to stop before I regretted it—restraint was indeed necessary, given that we had a dinner reservation.

I'd canceled our booking at La Pergola. I'd come to realize that my husband and Andrea were right. The more I thought about it, it seemed wrong to end our trip at a three-star Michelin restaurant, however nice it would be. And we hadn't packed the right shoes anyway. Instead, with the help of local friends, I'd chosen a little trattoria in southern Rome called Il Ristoro degli Angeli, which served traditional Italian dishes with twists thought up by its chef, a fifty-something-year-old woman with dyed green hair named Elisabetta who, coincidentally, had been a journalist before starting the restaurant.

Craig and I sat outside, at a table fashioned out of a wooden barrel, and uncorked a bottle of Sangiovese from Tuscany. We started out with delicious focaccia topped with thin wisps of *lardo* that spoke to Italy's love of pork fat, an obsession the country shared with China. A decadent plate of Italian cheeses came with honey and preserves that reminded me of distant Central Asia and Turkey. We had the classic Roman pasta preparation of *cacio e pepe*, spaghetti with pecorino cheese and black pepper. After Craig dug in, though, he frowned. "There's too much pepper in this," he said.

I had another taste—he was right. "Hey, your taste buds are better than mine!"

"That's the first time you've said *that*," he replied.

I asked Craig if the trip had changed his perspective on food: was he more interested in it than when we'd begun? He shrugged. "I'm not sure. You know me, I'm not a foodie."

"But wait a second . . . before this trip, you would never have thought you'd enjoy slices of pure pork fat. Or passed up an Americano for an espresso. Or gone out for gelato," I said. It occurred to me that he hadn't complained even once about the length of a meal. And to my utter delight, after the journey, my husband began cooking for me on occasion, making spectactular blowout meals that I'd never expected. When he cooked, he put his all into it, reducing honey-orange glaze on the stove for roast duck, stuffing pork chops with ricotta before grilling and topping them with a delicious marinara sauce, a recipe I had to steal.

"I'm not a foodie," Craig repeated. "But I like food. Who doesn't like food? Now, if I could get you to spend as much time hiking as we spend eating, that would be progress."

But the real question was: How had I changed? Had the journey altered my views on marriage? And, just like my husband, I didn't know. But I knew I wanted to stop moving, and I didn't want to take another seven-thousand-mile journey anytime soon. And I was okay with the word "wife." The many versions of them I'd encountered on the journey had broadened my notion of what the label meant. Each of these wives, in circumstances different from my own, had had to find her own balance, and different from me as they were, I could relate to them all. The word "wife" bonded me not just to my husband but also to a network of women from China to Italy—and beyond. I was grateful that my husband had accompanied me for so much of my adventure. We'd managed to maintain a good degree of togetherness after all these months, in large part because of him. And we weren't so different as I once thought—that, I realized, was simply a matter of perspective. Despite our contrasting interests and opinions, we had plenty of commonalities, like East and West, that made us more similar than we were different.

Funny enough, though it was the end of our journey, we didn't feel the need to talk about the future that evening, or in the days that followed. That night, Craig and I just wanted to enjoy a meal, the way that Romans did every night. The travel had settled us. And, as it turned out, things would become clear in a matter of weeks. I would discover, rather unexpectedly, that I was pregnant and soon after, Craig would pass the Foreign Service exam, which began a new chapter in our lives.

But at that moment, lingering over dinner in a casual restaurant in southern Rome, we were okay with the uncertainties. And the possibilities. Just as we finished eating, the owner, Elisabetta, came out to say hello and introduced her husband, who ran the restaurant with her. While the couple chatted about the ins and outs of operating their trattoria, I thought, maybe that *could* be us someday. That could be our dream and ambition, if—just as I'd done with the noodle mystery—we just let it be.

ORECCHIETTE

Serves 6

2 cups semolina flour
1 cup all-purpose flour
1⅓ cups water

In a medium bowl, combine the semolina flour and the all-purpose flour. Follow the directions for mixing and kneading the dough in the recipe for Chef Zhang's Hand-Rolled Noodles (p. 96), although this dough will be slightly firmer. Cover the dough with a damp cloth or wrap in plastic and set aside for 30 minutes.

Transfer the dough to a clean, lightly floured surface and knead for 3 to 5 minutes, then cover it with a damp cloth or wrap it in plastic and let sit for at least 30 minutes.

Dust the work surface with flour. Break off a quarter of the dough to work with, leaving the rest under the damp cloth. Knead the dough for a couple of minutes and shape it into a long rope about ¼ inch thick, then cut the rope into ¼-inch pieces. Working with a butter knife and one bit of dough at a time, run the butter knife over the dough, pushing the blunt, curved part of the blade into the center of the dough and pulling the dough against the work surface so that the dough curls around the knife into a concave round. (For a demonstration of this process, see http://www.youtube.com/watch?v=nEy 4DiN6lL4.) Repeat with the rest of the dough, inverting the orecchiette so that they are bowl-side up and sprinkling them lightly with flour. Allow the orecchiette to dry for 2 hours before cooking.

ORECCHIETTE CON LE CIME DI RAPA
(ORECCHIETTE WITH TURNIP TOPS)

Serves 6

1 pound turnip tops (or substitute broccoli rabe or Chinese broccoli),
  washed, trimmed, and cut into bite-sized pieces
1 recipe Orecchiette (p. 369) or 1 pound packaged dried orecchiette
½ cup coarse bread crumbs
½ cup olive oil
2 cloves garlic, minced
½ onion, minced
6 flat anchovies, minced
Salt and freshly ground black pepper

Bring a large pot of water to a boil. Add the turnip tops (or broccoli rabe or Chinese broccoli) and the fresh orecchiette and cook for 3 to 4 minutes. (If using dry pasta, boil until nearly done before adding the greens.) Reserve 1 or 2 cups of the cooking liquid, then drain the pasta and vegetables in a colander.

In a small frying pan, toast the bread crumbs in 2 tablespoons of the olive oil over medium-low heat for 3 to 4 minutes, until golden. Remove from the heat and set aside.

Place the garlic, the onion, and the rest of the olive oil in a large frying pan and sauté over medium heat for about 4 to 5 minutes, until the garlic and onion are just beginning to color. Add the anchovies and stir for a minute or two. Add the drained greens and pasta and toss, adding a little bit of pasta water. Season to taste with salt and black pepper and serve immediately, topped with the bread crumbs.

RAGÙ (BOLOGNESE PASTA SAUCE)

Makes enough for 2 pounds pasta, or 8 servings

¼ cup sunflower oil

1 large carrot, finely diced

1 medium onion, minced

3 ribs celery, leaves discarded, finely diced

3 pounds ground beef (30 percent fat)

¾ cup tomato paste

½ cup tomato sauce

1 tablespoon salt

1 cup water

Make the soffritto: Heat the sunflower oil in a large, heavy pot over medium heat. Add the carrots, onions, and celery and sauté for 10 to 12 minutes, until the vegetables soften.

Add the beef and sauté over medium heat for 10 to 15 minutes. Reduce the heat to medium-low and cook for 20 minutes, allowing the flavors to meld. Add the tomato paste. Reduce the heat to low and simmer for 20 minutes more, stirring occasionally. Add the tomato sauce and salt and simmer an additional 5 minutes, stirring occasionally. Add the water, stir, and let the sauce simmer for an hour before serving.

LASAGNA BOLOGNESE

Serves 8

FOR THE DOUGH:
8 cups flour
6 extra-large eggs
*1 cup (about 7 ounces) spinach, boiled until tender and chopped,
    then squeezed in a colander to remove all excess moisture*

FOR THE BÉCHAMEL SAUCE:
1 cup (2 sticks) butter
1 quart milk
1½ cups flour

1 recipe Ragù (p. 371)
1 cup grated Parmigiano-Reggiano

Make the dough: Heap the flour on a large, clean, sturdy, dry surface and make a well in the center. Break the eggs into the center of
the well. Add the spinach. Beat the eggs and spinach into the flour
with a fork, then continue mixing with your hands until all the flour
has been incorporated. Transfer the dough to a clean, lightly floured
surface and knead with your hands or a stand mixer for 3 to 5 minutes, until the dough is soft, pliable, and smooth. If it feels a little
dry, knead in a few drops of water. Cover the dough with a damp
cloth or wrap it in plastic and let it sit for at least 30 minutes.

Make the béchamel sauce: Melt the butter in a medium saucepan.
Add the milk and bring just to the point of boiling. Reduce the heat

to low and slowly whisk in the flour, stirring constantly, until the sauce is thick and pasty. Remove from the heat and use immediately.

Follow the instructions for rolling out the dough in Chef Zhang's Hand-Rolled Noodles/Andrea's Pasta (p. 96), cutting the dough into 3-inch strips and then cutting the strips to fit the width of the pan in which you'll be baking the lasagna.

Bring a large pot of water to a boil and add the noodles. Boil for 1 minute, then drain the noodles and plunge them into a basin or pot of cold water for a minute to arrest the cooking process. Drain thoroughly.

Preheat the oven to 350 degrees Fahrenheit.

Spread a thin layer of béchamel sauce in the baking pan. Add a layer of lasagna noodles, then a layer of *ragù*, then a layer of béchamel, then a layer of the grated Parmigiano-Reggiano. Repeat the layering, starting with the lasagna noodles and ending with the Parmigiano-Reggiano.

Bake the lasagna for 30 minutes, until it is bubbling. Allow it to cool for a few minutes before cutting it into squares and serving.

CHEESE TORTELLINI
WITH SAGE-BUTTER SAUCE

Serves 4

FOR THE DOUGH:
2½ cups all-purpose flour
3 eggs

FOR THE FILLING:
½ pound ricotta cheese
½ cup grated Parmigiano-Reggiano
1 tablespoon minced fresh parsley
2 cloves garlic, minced
1 egg

FOR THE SAUCE:
¼ cup water
12 fresh sage leaves
4 tablespoons (½ stick) butter

½ cup grated Parmigiano-Reggiano for serving

Follow the directions for kneading and rolling out the dough in Chef Zhang's Hand-Rolled Noodles/Andrea's Pasta (p. 96). Cut the sheets of dough into 1-inch squares.

Make the filling: Mix the cheeses together with the parsley, garlic, and egg.

Follow the instructions for wrapping dumplings as in the recipe for Manti (p. 176).

Make the sauce: Place the water and sage leaves, torn into pieces, in a large frying pan and place over medium heat. Reduce to low heat and simmer the leaves for 3 to 4 minutes, then add the butter and allow it to melt. Keep warm.

Bring a large pot of water to a boil. Add the tortellini and boil for 3 to 4 minutes, then drain well and toss with the sage-butter sauce. Garnish with the cheese and serve immediately.

Variation: Tortellini in Brodo (Meat Tortellini in Broth)

Instead of the cheese filling, stuff the tortellini with a mixture of ½ pound cooked minced pork, 3 eggs, 1 cup grated Parmigiano-Reggiano, 2 tablespoons minced prosciutto *crudo*, 2 tablespoons minced mortadella, and ¼ teaspoon freshly grated nutmeg. Boil the tortellini for 3 to 4 minutes in good, homemade chicken stock and serve in soup bowls, with the stock and accompanied with additional grated Parmigiano-Reggiano.

acknowledgments

One of the unexpected surprises, and an idea that's at the heart of this book, was the incredible support and assistance I received from friends and strangers far and wide.

In China, I'd like to thank Bai Jianbo; Isabel and her Tibetan friends; Nur, Malika, and their family; and Mahmood. Across the border in Kyrgyzstan, I am indebted to Gulzat Baialieva and her family for inviting me into their home and for Gulzat's painstaking research. In Uzbekistan, I received warm hospitality from Marina Tsoy, the Mashhura School, Fara, Murad and Shaista. Aziza and Kutbiya of the Antica B&B nursed me back to health. Lola and Anastasia translated for me. Russell Zanca furthered my understanding of Central Asian noodles. Kennon Lee connected me with valuable friends in Turkmenistan.

In Iran, Ingo and Almut Koll and Fairy Behnam were gracious hosts. I'd like to thank Tina in Mashhad and the many friends I met in Yazd, Ishfahan, and Tehran. I also benefited from the help of Iranians abroad, including Fariborz, Hamid and Missy Yazdahpanah, Babak Behnam, Najmieh Batmanglij, and Abdi Sami. I was saddened to learn of Abdi's recent passing.

I cannot thank Selin Rozanes of Turkish Flavours enough for all the time and effort she has put into my project. Also in Istanbul, Batur Durmay, his staff at Asitane, Bengi Kayhan, and Ayse and Ipek of Giritli gave me a sense of home. Filiz Hosukoglu thoroughly guided me through Gaziantep. Asli Mutlu and Betül-Arif Obdan at Yarbasan Holiday Homes near Bodrum generously hosted me. Aylin

Öney Tan, Tangör Tan, Afyer Tuczu Unsal, and Nevin Halıcı always responded promptly and eloquently to my many questions about Turkish cuisine. A thank-you goes out to Ayse Adanali and Levent Ulucer for initial ideas and translation.

In the southern heel of Italy, Daniela Mandriota, her fiancé, Sandro Gentile, and their families—especially Nonna—provided me with endless meals and laughs. San Domenico restaurant in Monopoli allowed me into their kitchen. I'd also like to thank Martina Milelli and Daniel Alberman in Salento. Marina De Martino of No-Stress Itineraries guided me through the streets of Naples and her kitchen. In Emilia-Romagna, the list of people to thank is long: Paolo Canto, Siriana Tanfoglio, and Margherita Benvenuti of the Tourism Board; the *sfogline* Nadia Pelliconi, Luisa Seppi, and Valeria Vitali; and elswhere in Emilia-Romagna, Roberta Tedeschi, Fabrizio Zivieri, Patrizia Vecchi, Maria Luisa Soncini, Giovanni Tedeschi, and Roberto Farina. In Rome, I am indebted to Federica Bianchi, Stephan Faris, Kathy Beamis, Giuseppe Cerroni, Giovanna De Mattia and Adolfo Bigini, and the family of Alessandro Campitelli. Sarah Ting-Ting Hou, Cara McAvoy, Paolo Longo, Allesandro Spiga, and Alessia Pirolo helped with contacts across Italy. And most important, in Italy, Andrea Consoli gave me inspiration for the journey.

Elsewhere, David Wilson and Yasemin Uyghurmen of the Ritz-Carlton arranged a respite on the road. In the United States, Karl Squitier, Ed Cornelia, Corky White, Gus Rancatore of Toscanini's, and Ana Sortun of Oleana helped with initial thinking about the project. Joan and Mario Soncini helped with introductions and research.

Friends East and West provided support before, during, and after the long journey. I'd like to thank Adrienne Mong, Yun-Yi Goh, Leslie Chang, Peter Hessler, Jenny Chio, Michelle Garnaut, Evan Osnos, Sarabeth Berman, Tom and Peggy Simons, Ed Gargan, Tang Di, Barbara Demick, and Mayling Birney.

In Chengdu, I'd like to thank the U.S. consulate community, in particular Kerryn Sullivan and Dusadee Haymond, and Kim Dallas.

Editor Becky Saletan deserves enormous praise—again. From the initial book proposal to the final product, Becky focused the material, gave me ample space, tweaked and edited with care, and encouraged me throughout. Becky, you're a true editor and friend. Also at Riverhead, I'd like to thank Glory Plata and Jynne Martin. And I appreciate the ear and enthusiasm of my agent, Flip Brophy. Chris Calhoun helped sell the book.

I am indebted to my colleagues at Black Sesame Kitchen. Wang Guizhen and

Zhang Aifeng accompanied me on my travels before resuming their work at the kitchen. Candice Lee kept it running in my absence and has enthusiastically supported my endeavors. Michelle Tang, who took over operations, also deserves enormous praise for her hard work and for juggling a multitude of tasks with grace. I'd also like to thank Cai Yuejin and Chef Wang for their efforts and contributions, and Larissa Zhou for her work in Beijing and beyond.

Finally, I'd like to thank my family: Caroline and David for traveling with us and for allowing me to write about them with humor; and Mom, Dad, and James for their love and care all these years. Thank you, Sierra, for blessing us with your existence and exuberance. And last, I give my deepest gratitude to Craig, who inspired this journey with his gift of a pasta class and his willingness to support me in even the most challenging of endeavors. Husband aside, he is also my best friend, trusted editor, favorite travel companion, and co-conspirator in the adventures described in this book. May we have many more journeys in our future.

Chengdu, China
March 2013

index of recipes

Narrowing down my list of recipes for inclusion in this book was painful. I encountered so many delightful and unique dishes in my travels that the process reminded me of what the Italians said when I asked them to name their favorite dish. "That's like making us choose our favorite family member!" they said.

All the recipes have been adapted to an American kitchen. As much as possible, I have retained ingredients and methods that keep them rooted in their place of origin but, as I've learned on my travels, recipes—whether they be noodles, pilafs, or *meze*—evolve in different settings, adapting to new climates, geography, and culture.

Noodles are at the heart of many of the recipes. Making noodles is not difficult; if you know how to make pie crust, you can master noodles. But because noodle making is unfamiliar to many Americans, I have uploaded videos demonstrating the process to my website, www.jenlinliu.com, where additional recipes gathered on my journey can also be found.

Most of the noodle and pasta recipes can be made with all-purpose flour—I recommend King Arthur brand. Special blends of "pasta flour" that include semolina and/or durum wheat flour can be substituted, although they will yield a stiffer dough.

The only special equipment you'll need for making noodles is a rolling pin and a large, sturdy surface that is clean and dry. I came across three kinds of rolling pins in my travels. The first was the simple, handle-less Chinese rolling pin, about one inch in diameter and about a foot long. The second, which I saw in Central Asia and Italy, was more similar to a typical American rolling pin with handles, about two inches in diameter and a foot long, not counting the handles. The third, found all across the Silk Road from China to Italy, was a baton about one inch in diameter and three feet long, used by true pasta experts. My personal preference is a Chinese rolling pin, which is easier for most amateur cooks to manage and can be found in most Asian supermarkets and on websites like Amazon.com.

Buon appetito!

CHINA

CENTRAL ASIA

IRAN

bibliography

A few sources were particularly helpful in piecing together the culinary history of pasta and noodles. *Pasta: The Story of a Universal Food* by Silvano Serventi and Françoise Sabban, translated by Antony Shugaar (New York: Columbia University Press, 2002), provided a wealth of information about China and Italy. The "pasta," "noodles," and "reshteh" entries of Alan Davidson's *Oxford Companion to Food* (Oxford: Oxford University Press, 2006) gave a broad perspective on the staple from East to West. Another valuable source was Paul D. Buell and Eugene Anderson's *A Soup for the Qan: Chinese Dietary Medicine of the Mongol Era as Seen in Hu Szu-Hui's Yin-Shan Cheng-Yao: Introduction, Translation, Commentary and Chinese Text* (London; New York: Kegan Paul International, 2000). Bai Jianbo, Russell Zanca, Aylin Öney Tan, and Najmieh Batmanglij also provided information on the noodle traditions across the Silk Road through phone and e-mail interviews. The Marco Polo quotations come from Everyman's Library's *The Travels of Marco Polo*, translated by W. Marsden (New York: Alfred A. Knopf, 2008), the most readable version of his diaries.

I received assistance on the recipes from Selin Rozanes, Najmieh Batmanglij, Gulzat Baialieva, Nevin Halıcı, and www.ottomancuisine.com.

I also drew on the following sources:

Akyol, Elif. "Su Boregi." www.ottomancuisine.com. *Ottoman Cuisine.* Accessed March 2013.

Algar, Ayla. *Classical Turkish Cooking: Traditional Turkish Food for the American Kitchen.* New York: HarperCollins, 1991.

Arsel, Semahat, Ersu Pekin, and Ayşe Sümer. *Timeless Tastes: Turkish Culinary Culture.* 2nd ed. Istanbul: Vehbi Koç Vakfı, 1996.

Asfendiyarova, S.D. and P.A. Kunte. *Kazakhstan's Past in Sources and Materials Collection I (5 B.C.–18 A.D.).* In Russian. Almaty, Kazahkstan: 1997.

Bainbridge, James, et al. *Turkey.* Footscray, Victoria: Lonely Planet, 2009.

Batmanglij, Najmieh. *Food of Life: Ancient Persian and Modern Iranian Cooking and Ceremonies.* Washington, DC: Mage Publishers, 2011.

"Beijing Halal." www.chinaheritagequarterly.org. *China Heritage Quarterly*, March 2006. Accessed June 2, 2010.

Bergreen, Laurence. *Marco Polo: From Venice to Xanadu.* New York: Alfred A. Knopf, 2007.

Bertuzzi, Barbara. *Bolognese Cooking Heritage.* Bologna: Pendragon, 2006.

Bilgin, Arif, and Özge Samancı. *Turkish Cuisine.* Ankara: Republic of Turkey Ministry of Culture and Tourism, 2008.

Bill, James A. *The Eagle and the Lion: The Tragedy of American-Iranian Relations.* New Haven, CT: Yale University Press, 1988.

Buell, Paul D. "Mongol Empire and Turkicization: The Evidence of Food and Foodways." In Rueven Amitai-Preiss and David O. Morgan, eds., *The Mongol Empire & Its Legacy,* pp. 200–221. Leiden: Humanities PR, 2001.

Burke, Andrew, and Mark Elliot. *Iran.* Footscray, Victoria: Lonely Planet, 2008.

Capatti, Alberto, and Massimo Montanari. *Italian Cuisine: A Cultural History.* New York: Columbia University Press, 2003.

Chang, Te-Tzu. "Rice." www.cambridge.org. *Cambridge World History of Food.* Accessed March 2013.

Dickie, John. *Delizia!: The Epic History of the Italians and Their Food.* New York: Free Press, 2008.

Fragner, Bert. "From the Caucus to the Roof of the World." In Sami Zubaida and Richard Tapper, eds., *A Taste of Thyme: Culinary Cultures of the Middle East,* pp. 49–62. New York: I. B. Tauris, 1994.

Garnaut, Anthony, et al. "The Islamic Heritage in China." www.chinaheritage quarterly.org. *China Heritage Newsletter*, March 2006.

Gürsoy, Deniz. *Turkish Cuisine in Historical Perspective.* Istanbul: Oğlak Yayıncılık, 2006.

Halıcı, Nevin. *Nevin Halici's Turkish Cookbook.* London: Dorling Kindersley, 1989.

———. *Sufi Cuisine.* London: Saqi, 2005.

Harper, Damian, et al. *China.* Footscray, Victoria: Lonely Planet, 2009.

Hazan, Marcella. *Essentials of Classic Italian Cooking.* New York: Alfred A. Knopf, 1992.

Hekmat, Forough-es-Saltaneh. *The Art of Persian Cooking.* Garden City, NY: Double-day, 1961.

Hou, Jinglun, et al. *Medicated Diet of Traditional Chinese Medicine.* Beijing: Beijing Science & Technology Press, 1994.

Köçümkulkïzï, Elmira, and Daniel C. Waugh. "Traditional Culture: Food." depts .washington.edu/silkroad. *Silk Road Seattle.* Accessed June 2010.

Loveday, Helen, et al. *Iran: Persia: Ancient and Modern.* Hong Kong: Odyssey Books & Guides, 2005.

Lu, Houyuan. "Millet Noodles in Late Neolithic China." www.nature.com. *Nature.* Published online October 12, 2005. Accessed June 2010.

Mack, Glenn R., and Asele Surina. *Food Culture in Russia and Central Asia.* Westport, CT: Greenwood Press, 2005.

MacLeod, Calum, and Bradley Mayhew. *Uzbekistan: The Golden Road to Samarkand.* Hong Kong: Odyssey Books & Guides, 2008.

Mayhew, Bradley, Greg Bloom, John Noble, and Dean Starnes. *Central Asia.* Foot-scray, Victoria: Lonely Planet, 2007.

McWhirter, William A. "The Shah's Princely Party." *Life*, October 29, 1971, pp. 22–30.

Noodle Road Documentary. KBS America, 2009.

Noodle. www.wikipedia.org. Accessed June 2, 2010, and April 3, 2011.

Oldest Noodle Unearthed in China. www.bbc.co.uk. BBC News. Updated October 12, 2005; accessed June 2010.

Omrani, Bijan, and Jeremy Tredinnick. *Asia Overland: Tales of Travel on the Trans-Siberian & Silk Road.* Hong Kong: Odyssey Books & Guides, 2010.

Perry, Charles. "The Oldest Mediterranean Noodle: A Cationary Tale." In *Petits Propos Culinaires*, issue 9, pp. 42–44.

Perry, Charles. "The Taste for Layered Bread Among the Nomadic Turks and the Central Asian Origins of Baklava." In Sami Zubaida and Richard Tapper, eds., *A Taste of Thyme: Culinary Cultures of the Middle East*, pp. 87–92. New York: I. B. Tauris, 1994.

Riley, Gillian. *The Oxford Companion to Italian Food.* Oxford: Oxford University Press, 2009.

Rudelson, Justin Jon. *Central Asia Phrasebook.* Footscray, Victoria: Lonely Planet, 2008.

Shaida, Margaret. *The Legendary Cuisine of Persia.* New York: Interlink Books, 2002.

Simonis, Damien. *Italy.* Footscray, Victoria: Lonely Planet, 2008.

"Sister Cuisines." www.turkish-cuisine.org. Turkish Cultural Foundation. Accessed June 2010.

Steward, Rowan, and Susie Weldon. *Kyrgyz Republic.* Hong Kong: Odyssey Books &
    Guides, 2004.

Visson, Lynn. *The Art of Uzbek Cooking.* New York: Hippocrene Books, 1999.

Wood, Frances. *The Silk Road: Two Thousand Years in the Heart of Asia.* Berkeley:
    University of California Press, 2002.

Yerasimos, Marianna. *500 Years of Ottoman Cuisine.* Translated by Sally Bradbrook.
    Istanbul: Boyut Publishing Group, 2007.

Zanca, Russell. "Central Asian Food." In Andrew F. Smith, ed., *The Oxford Encyclo-
    pedia of Food and Drink in America*, pp. 198–99. Oxford; New York: Oxford Univer-
    sity Press, 2004.

Zanini De Vita, Oretta. *Encyclopedia of Pasta.* Translated by Maureen B. Fant. Berke-
    ley: University of California Press, 2009.